THE INQUIRY

THE INQUIRY

AMERICAN PREPARATIONS
FOR PEACE, 1917-1919

BY LAWRENCE E. GELFAND

GREENWOOD PRESS, PUBLISHERS
WESTPORT, CONNECTICUT

Library of Congress Cataloging in Publication Data

Gelfand, Lawrence Emerson, 1926-
    The Inquiry : American preparations for peace,
1917-1919.

    Reprint of the ed. published by Yale University
Press, New Haven.
    Bibliography: p.
    Includes index.
    1. European War, 1914-1918--Peace. 2. Paris.
Peace Conference, 1919-   U.S. Territorial
Section. I. Title.
[D644.G4 1976]   940.3'12   75-31364
ISBN 0-8371-8526-2

Originally published in 1963 by Yale University Press,
New Haven

Reprinted with the permission of Yale University Press

Reprinted in 1976 by Greenwood Press,
a division of Williamhouse-Regency Inc.

Library of Congress Catalog Card Number 75-31364

ISBN 0-8371-8526-2

Printed in the United States of Amrica

FOR MIRIAM

and

JULIA, DANIEL, RONALD

CONTENTS

INTRODUCTION

WAR AND PEACE are continuously weaving their distinctive patterns into the unfolding tapestry of human affairs. Each only occasionally constitutes an exclusive phase of social existence. More frequently, war and peace entwine to the extent that men living in peace often prepare for war, while nations and peoples at war often turn their attention to the problems of future peace. It is commonplace for general staffs in time of peace to anticipate the problems of strategy, improvements in weapons, and the training of personnel for the eventuality of war even though the possibility of conflict may appear remote. Governments, often operating through their departments of foreign affairs, have usually made plans in time of war which affect the ultimate peace settlement. The American pattern for peace in 1919, for example, was conceived, designed, and studied for more than a year prior to the termination of hostilities, while the United States was still involved as an active belligerent in the Great War.

Forty years have now passed since the American people moved decisively from neutrality to belligerency in World War I. When perceived through the distance of time, more was involved in this official action than merely the sending of military and naval contingents into the front lines of battle. President Wilson and the Congress were actually signaling a fundamental transformation in American foreign policy. From its role as a relatively minor supporting observer and occasional mediator, the United States emerged during the years of war and peace, 1917–19, as a stellar performer in the continuous drama of *Weltpolitik*.

Viewing the momentous events of World War I and the en-

ix

suing Paris Peace Conference through the perspective of forty years offers certain marked advantages for the student which were not afforded to earlier writers. Vast manuscript collections containing personal correspondence and official records, hitherto closed to scholarly perusal, now permit the student to penetrate the stratum and attack the bedrock in seeking answers to his questions. Details seemingly important to an earlier generation of writers concerned with World War I can now be fitted into their rightful, subordinate notches. At the same time, the distance of forty years offers an opportunity for the student to discuss the questions at hand with many of the former participants still surviving who, even considering memories dimmed by time and intervening events, can often communicate something of the local color and charged emotional state which are usually lacking in the preserved documents.

In the past forty years scholars have brought forth a highly useful literature dealing with World War I and the Paris Peace Conference. Numerous monographs have attempted microscopic examination of particular facets of the peace settlement. Publication of the Minutes of the Council of Ten and the Council of Four has encouraged studies of the Peace Conference at the highest level. Nevertheless, there has not thus far appeared a single study describing the policies and operations of the American Commission to Negotiate Peace, the American delegation to the peace conference. Nor has there been any study of the American preparatory commission, called "the Inquiry," which functioned under the direction of Colonel House for some fourteen months prior to the armistice.

Organized at the behest of President Wilson in early September 1917, a few months after the United States declared war on Germany, the Inquiry was composed largely of academicians—political and social scientists for the most part—and its purpose was to prepare the United States government's program for peace in advance of the termination of military hostilities. Throughout its existence, the Inquiry's staff, numbering about 150 scholars, produced and collected nearly 2,000 separate reports and documents plus at least 1,200 maps. At the end of the war, certain members of the Inquiry accompanied President Wilson to Paris where they served as advisers to the American plenipotentiaries and, in some cases, as negotiators on international commissions.

The Inquiry undertook studies of virtually every region of the globe. Even Latin America was not ignored. Formal recommendations made by the Inquiry were used by President Wilson in drafting the territorial propositions in the Fourteen Points of January 1918. Later, a substantial number of the Inquiry's recommendations for Western Europe, Poland, the Balkans, the Middle East, the Pacific Islands, and a mandate system were incorporated in the peace treaties. Prominent among the members of the Inquiry were Colonel House, Sidney E. Mezes, Isaiah Bowman, David Hunter Miller, Walter Lippmann, and James T. Shotwell.

This investigation of the Inquiry attempts to probe behind the surface of the peace settlement. It presumes that the story of the Paris Peace Conference cannot be understood strictly in terms of the Big Three, the Big Four, or the Big Ten. It takes the view instead that the conference at Paris was the culmination of many months of active preparation. If the Inquiry is observed as a microcosm within the larger sphere of government planning in international affairs, then the study of its operations takes on fundamental implications not only for an understanding of 1917–19 but also for the present and the future. Social planning, so enthusiastically espoused by Progressives like Herbert Croly during the Wilson era, was only in its infancy at the time the Inquiry was inaugurated. Since 1919, the practice of utilizing the talents of academia in government service has become well established. The Inquiry provided the earliest precedent of use by the United States government of numerous scholars whose special talents were directed toward the shaping of American foreign policy.

Although a better understanding of American foreign policy during and immediately following the First World War provides sufficient justification for this study, other important values may be derived as well. From the perspective of the Inquiry, the objectives, methods, and achievements of Woodrow Wilson and his construction of a foundation for world peace emerge with less of the moralistic fiber than is customary. Indeed, the Wilson who inaugurated the Inquiry was a sturdy nationalist attuned to the realities of international politics. By suggesting a reappraisal of Woodrow Wilson and Colonel House from the vantage point of the Inquiry, this study seeks to make more comprehensible the means and ends of Wilsonian foreign policy.

As James T. Shotwell once wrote:

> This strange experiment in the mobilization of the political and social sciences to help in shaping the outlines of the new world structure which had to be built out of the ruins of the war will offer a subject with unique possibilities.[1]

The chronological limits of this study are April 1917, when the United States intervened in the war, and January 1919, when the Inquiry as an administrative entity ceased to exist. Occasionally it has been necessary to move beyond these chronological boundaries but only for the purpose of clarifying some relationship or idea concerning American preparations for peace. With the formal termination of the Inquiry, some of its members served the American Commission to Negotiate Peace at Paris as expert advisers and negotiators in the Division of Territorial Economic and Political Intelligence, which was, to some extent, the successor organization of the Inquiry. A sequel volume is planned which will consider the administration, policies, and operations of the American Commission to Negotiate Peace at the Paris Peace Conference. It will then be possible to carry forward the story of the expert adviser through implementation and modification of the Inquiry's program during the peace negotiations.

Over the past eight years during which I have pursued the "tracks" of the Inquiry, it has occurred to me time and time again how terribly difficult, even hazardous, the task of historical scholarship would be were it not for the legion of librarians, archivists, and colleagues whose unstinting helpfulness and technical assistance proved invaluable to me. I want to acknowledge the many services and acts of kindness tendered by librarians and archivists at the following institutions: Foreign Affairs Section in the Legislative, Judicial, and Diplomatic Records Branch of the National Archives and Records Service; Manuscripts Division, Library of

1. James T. Shotwell, *At the Paris Peace Conference* (New York, 1937), p. 11.

Congress; the American Geographical Society; Special Collections Division, Columbia University Library; Manuscripts Division, Sterling Library, Yale University; Manuscripts Division, Houghton Library, Harvard University; Hoover Library, Stanford University; Huntington Library, San Marino, California; University of Hawaii Library; University of Washington Library; and the University of Wyoming Library. One of the gratifying features of the research was the correspondence which I maintained with several surviving alumni of the Inquiry. Their most candid letters describing their experiences with the government during World War I proved to be very valuable source materials. Most particularly, I want to express appreciation to the following persons who offered me personal interviews: Professor Frank Maloy Anderson; the late Professor Robert J. Kerner; Mr. David Hunter Miller; and Professor James T. Shotwell. I have also reaped numerous benefits from my teachers at graduate school and later from my colleagues at several universities: To the members of the Advanced History Seminar at the University of Washington who criticized several early drafts of chapters; to my colleagues in the Department of History, the University of Hawaii and at the University of Wyoming, I am most appreciative. At various crucial stages of the work, Professor Robert E. Burke, Professor Thomas J. Pressly, and Dean Solomon Katz, all of the University of Washington, were very helpful. Professor Marion C. Siney of Western Reserve University, in whose graduate seminar I was introduced to the intricacies of the Paris Peace Conference, painstakingly read and criticized the final draft of the manuscript, giving me the benefit of her rich knowledge of European diplomacy during World War I. To Professor W. Stull Holt of the University of Washington I owe my most heartfelt appreciation. It was he who first brought to my attention the possibilities for a study of the Inquiry, and he has been a source of encouragement as well as of trenchant criticism throughout all stages of the project's development. The Department of History, University of Washington, and the Graduate Research Committee, University of Wyoming, provided grants which financed the purchase of microfilm and the typing of the final draft, respectively. Mrs. Shirley Sostrom and Mrs. Mary Mosier, both of Laramie, Wyoming, performed the yeoman chores of typing the manuscript. Mrs. Marian Neal Ash of the Yale University Press offered numerous suggestions and criticisms of immense value. All of these persons will recognize their special contributions to the study; I only trust that they will not be grossly disappointed with what they find. Obviously, responsibility for whatever deficiencies may exist rests with the author.

LAWRENCE E. GELFAND

Iowa City, Iowa

Chapter 1

THE BEGINNING OF PREPARATIONS
FOR PEACE IN AMERICA

WOODROW WILSON brought to the Presidency in 1913 the scholarly temperament of a man long immersed in the study of politics, law, and governmental administration. Like so many scholars and politicians of his generation, Wilson had received little formal training in international affairs, nor had he previously manifested any very serious involvement in questions of foreign policy A personal and intellectual attachment to British institutions had been acquired through close study of the parliamentary system and constitution as well as through the writings of British political scientists. A mild concern with the peace movement had led the future President to affiliate with the American Peace Society, one of the oldest, most respectable of the pacifist societies, in 1908.[1] Yet, despite his obviously limited background in international affairs, Woodrow Wilson as President was compelled to devote a proportionately larger part of his official life to questions of foreign policy than were any of his immediate predecessors.

For almost two years following the outbreak of the European war in August 1914, Woodrow Wilson explored various avenues for bringing the conflict to an end. His frequent public addresses drew incessant attention to the eventual settlement of the war. These early pronouncements reflected the President's lively con-

1. Harley Notter, *Origins of the Foreign Policy of Woodrow Wilson* (Baltimore, 1937), pp. 77, 83, 90, 277, 433.

1

cern, but at this time the concern was expressed only in general terms. All the stock solutions popularized by the peace movement in the prewar years—judicial arbitration, disarmament, a greater reliance on the alleged disposition of mass public opinion toward peace—found a place in these Wilsonian invocations. On May 27, 1916, however, a notable departure from the well-worn phrases of the peace societies became evident. Henceforth, instead of the vague appeals to men's conscience, President Wilson's utterances started appealing for a world organization capable of maintaining the long-sought international peace.[2] This new note was first sounded in an address before the recently organized League to Enforce Peace.

One year earlier, in June 1915, this novel institution had come to life in Independence Hall, Philadelphia. Founded by a committee of prominent Americans headed by former President William Howard Taft and Hamilton Holt, editor of the *Independent*, the League to Enforce Peace had been gaining a steady stream of adherents throughout the United States. Within its first year, chapters had been formed in forty-six states, while the League's operating budget already approximated $250,000.[3] Clearly, this was a highly dynamic organization whose definite program held considerable appeal for many Americans. Based upon an ancient concept, the program called for the establishment of an international organization with sufficient authority to settle disputes among nations without resorting to war. The League to Enforce Peace did, however, offer a new departure. Its member states would, in practice, constitute an alliance to oppose with military force if necessary any aggressor state which threatened the peace. Especially auspicious, therefore, was the choice of the League to Enforce Peace rally in Washington as the platform for Woodrow Wilson's first forthright pronouncement dealing with the postwar settlement.

2. Wilson's discussion of peace in his public addresses during 1916 were: Speech at Aeolian Hall, New York, Jan. 27, 1916; Speech at Arlington, Virginia on May 30, 1916; Speech at Detroit, Michigan, July 10, 1916; Speech at Shadow Lawn, New Jersey on Sept. 2, 1916. Published in Ray S. Baker and William E. Dodd, eds., *Public Papers of Woodrow Wilson, The New Democracy 1913–1917* (New York, 1926), 2, 1, 7, 194, 231, 287.

3. Ruhl J. Bartlett, *The League to Enforce Peace* (Chapel Hill, 1944), pp. 61 ff.

In this address of May 27, 1916, President Wilson virtually embraced the League's entire program. He committed himself publicly to an association of nations with strength adequate to prevent future international conflagrations. At the same time, Wilson observed that the European war had developed out of powerful alliances and understandings negotiated for the most part in secret without the consent of the very peoples who had to bear the military burdens they imposed. To correct this malignancy which he recognized in the body politic, he proceeded to prescribe three principles of therapy: (1) the right of every people to choose its sovereign affiliation, a concept later expressed popularly as "self-determination"; (2) equal respect to be accorded the sovereign rights of weak and strong nations; (3) the right of every people "to be free from every disturbance to its peace having its origin in aggression or in disregard of the rights of peoples and nations." Though still a neutral, the United States government was displaying an intense interest in the European conflict and in the eventual settlement of that conflict. Here, in bold, clear language Woodrow Wilson asserted what might rightly be termed an American obligation to participate in the ultimate peace conference. His words rang with an idealism blunted with a sober sense of reality:

> And when it [the war] does come to an end we shall be as much concerned as the nations at war to see peace assume an aspect of permanence, give promise of days for which the anxiety of uncertainty shall be lifted, bring some assurance that peace and war shall always hereafter be reckoned part of the common interest of mankind. We are participants, whether we would or not, in the life of the world. The interests of all nations are our own also. We are partners with the rest. What affects mankind is inevitably our affair as well as the affair of the nations of Europe and of Asia.[4]

A more intelligible rationale for justifying American participation in the peace settlement could hardly be conceived; even though the suit of neutrality were never exchanged for the uniform of belligerency, the United States would assert its influence at the peace table.

Through the next eleven months the various themes with variations were fortified and expanded in numerous public addresses.

4. Baker and Dodd, *Public Papers*, 2, 185–87.

At Omaha, on October 5, Woodrow Wilson warned the world of America's willingness to cooperate "without stint" in the preservation of peace.[5] Later that same month, at Cincinnati, he announced the right of neutral nations to share in the making and preservation of the peace.[6] Again, in a memorable address before the United States Senate on January 22, 1917, Wilson went even further. Before an actual settlement, he counseled, "this Government should frankly formulate the conditions upon which it would feel justified in asking our people to approve its formal and solemn adherence to a League for Peace." There followed a reiteration of previously expressed provisos—the desirability of an independent Polish state; "the inviolable security of life, of worship, and of industrial and social development . . . to all peoples"; the right of all peoples "wherever practicable" to have direct access to the seas; military disarmament; and the "freedom of the seas."[7] A final pronouncement for peace prior to American intervention in the war was made by the President in his Second Inaugural Address on March 5. Again, the familiar liberal conditions for peace were cited.[8] Throughout these public statements during the period of American neutrality, Woodrow Wilson was directing public attention to the vast stake held by the United States in any settlement of the war. The President gave advance notice that the United States fully intended to cooperate with other nations in making the peace secure.

Despite his lack of knowledge and experience in handling foreign relations, Woodrow Wilson from the outset of his first administration exercised a dominant, personal control over the operations of American foreign policy. Latin American and Far Eastern relations had undergone a continuous Presidential scrutiny almost to the extent of depriving the Department of State of any but the most routine responsibilities. As Wilson's first Secretary of State, William Jennings Bryan had accepted this subordinate status with few vocal objections, possibly because Bryan

5. Ibid., 346–48.
6. Ibid., 376–82.
7. Ibid., 407–14.
8. Baker and Dodd, *Public Papers, War and Peace 1917–1924* (New York, 1927), *1*, 1–5.

had not been vitally interested in foreign relations. When later the strain of frequent discord with the President proved unbearable, after the Lusitania disaster, Bryan resigned. His successor, Robert Lansing, the Counselor of the State Department and a man far more familiar with the configurations of foreign policy than had been his predecessor, apparently accepted Wilson's well-nigh complete dominance over his department's activities stoically, or at least without noticeable protest. One member of the Cabinet at this time, Secretary of the Treasury William G. McAdoo, later recalled a conversation with the President held shortly following Lansing's appointment. The President, in McAdoo's words, effectively announced his intention to be his own Secretary of State, leaving to Lansing the slight responsibilities "to put diplomatic notes in proper form and to act as an adviser on points of international law." [9] For his part, added McAdoo, Lansing accepted the appointment knowing full well and beforehand that all negotiations of consequence with foreign governments would be transacted from the White House. Whether or not the relationship was actually achieved on as formal a basis as McAdoo implies, Robert Lansing did not criticize the arrangement until later when he started writing his memoirs after the Peace Conference.

Rather than depend upon the State Department to deal with important matters of foreign policy, President Wilson early in his first administration had favored the practice of sending executive agents to foreign governments.[10] These agents were personal representatives of the President who functioned outside orthodox State Department channels. John Lind had been sent to Mexico to handle delicate negotiations; William Bayard Hale had gone off to Latin America on another mission. It was, however, with the use of Edward M. House—popularly known as Colonel House—that the Wilsonian scheme of short-circuiting the State Department came to public attention. The President had met House for the first time only in November 1911, but the friendship blossomed

9. William G. McAdoo, *Crowded Years* (Boston, 1931), pp. 338–39.

10. Notter, *Origins*, pp. 248–49. The use of executive agents by President Wilson was nothing unique; the practice extended back to the eighteenth century. See Henry M. Wriston, *Executive Agents in American Foreign Relations* (Baltimore, 1929).

and continued through the trying years of neutrality and war. That it lasted so long was remarkable, for House and Wilson were quite different in temperament. Moreover, their backgrounds were quite dissimilar, and even their values, their ideals, and their methods did not fundamentally coincide.

Earlier than most men, Edward House had made his fortune and then decided to spend his remaining years calling the plays in the political arena. His mastery over the good business virtues of bargaining, negotiation, and general give-and-take would stand him well. Insofar as can be learned from available documents, House did not possess any personal ambition for holding political office; his goal was to be the power behind the nation's Chief Executive. Not long after Wilson moved into the White House in 1913, House made known to the President his deep-seated desire to serve in the realm of foreign affairs. House believed his services would be invaluable if he could travel, meet with important persons, and in short become a roving ambassador without portfolio always ready to render information and advice to the Master of the White House.

For his new role, House's special qualifications were limited. Indeed, he had neither acquired special knowledge of international relations through formal training nor had he traveled extensively in foreign countries where he might have met people who exerted strong influences on foreign policy matters. It is surely an exaggeration to compare Woodrow Wilson with Edward House in the following terms: "For Colonel House, on the other hand, foreign problems were always of the first interest and importance." [11]

Edward House left behind for the scrutiny of posterity a voluminous diary which he fed almost daily by dictating its contents to a private secretary. As with most diaries kept by men ever mindful of the verdict of history, House's diary portrays its author as one who was forever exercising a truly decisive influence upon the national and world political scene. All too often, House etched the President in the guise of a wise but sometimes stubborn leader whose administration could easily have committed numerous blunders had it not been saved at crucial moments by the politi-

11. Charles Seymour, ed., *The Intimate Papers of Colonel House* (Boston, 1926–28), *1*, 176–77. Editorial statement of Charles Seymour.

cally sagacious House. The hero of the Wilson administration emerges as the keeper of the diary who in his quiet unobtrusive fashion masterminded the strategy credited to the President. Since House's diary is by far the most extensive day-by-day record of "high policy" in the Wilson years, there is a constant tendency to witness the drama through this single veil. Surely Edward House exerted an important influence upon both the domestic and foreign policies of the Wilson administration—even his bitterest critics must admit this much—but that his influence was truly decisive on so many momentous occasions is at the very least open to serious question.

House's first mission to Europe as Wilson's representative had begun in April 1913. In May 1914 House was sent abroad again for the avowed purpose of averting a general European war. When the European war exploded, House became a frequent visitor in belligerent capitals. Even during the years of American neutrality, this representative of the President participated in Allied councils at least when questions involving the future peace settlement were discussed. At one such conference, held in early 1915, British Foreign Minister Sir Edward Grey introduced the subject of war aims. In response to Grey's proposal calling for American participation in the general peace conference through some separate convention, House expressed warm sympathy.[12] Later, when specific questions were considered, he demurred at France's announced plans to annex Alsace-Lorraine. Instead of annexation, House preferred the creation of a neutral buffer zone composed of the two provinces. At subsequent discussions with Allied officials, House went so far as to suggest that the true path toward peace could be discovered only when nations ceased manufacturing the instruments of warfare. Thereafter, those remaining armaments would quickly become obsolete, and *ipso facto* wars would become passé. House apparently felt perfectly free to exercise personal discretion at these tête-à-tête or even larger conferences. At least it is not certain how rigidly he was bound by any formal instructions from his friend in the White House.

On April 30, 1915, there appears a most revealing passage in House's diary. He chose this day to explain his ideas with regard

12. Ibid., 368–70; for other discussion, see 387–88, 362–64.

to the future peace conference and its organization. These ideas are described as part of a report of another conversation with British Foreign Minister Grey:

> I told Grey . . . how I planned to organize this convention by getting the material that was to come before it thoroughly prepared and digested, in order that nothing should be left to chance. I would try to get the commissioners from each of the neutral states and from as many of the belligerent states as possible, in accord with us before they came to the convention.
>
> I explained my methods of organization in political conventions in the past; that while they were seemingly spontaneous, as a matter of fact nothing was left to chance.[13]

What should not escape notice here is House's plan for the gathering of materials relevant to the work of the peace conference in advance of the meeting. The concept of planning was already present in House's thinking about the settlement.

All through these discussions with British officials, as decribed in House's diary, runs the unmistakable *leitmotif* of intense sympathy toward British policy and personnel. House sincerely believed that America's national interests were dependent on maintaining close ties with Great Britain. The one basic assumption in foreign policy which House surely possessed in 1913 and which he undoubtedly then shared with the President was his overwhelming conviction that the United States must pursue a course in world politics closely aligned to that of Britain. Whereas during the ensuing years of neutrality President Wilson was to question sharply the parallelism of Anglo-American national interests, House was never to waver. The Colonel's cordial ties with British leaders extended even to the point where cooperation in the writing of dispatches intended for the American government was not beyond his concept of duty.[14] House's utter sincerity as he conducted his activities could never be interpreted as sinister or unpatriotic. He apparently saw no serious divergence in national interests between Britain and America on matters pertaining to

13. Ibid., 427–28.

14. Ibid., 326. For other statements showing intense sympathy for Britain, see *1*, 306; *2*, 320.

the conduct of the war and later the negotiation for a peace settlement. Throughout the years of American neutrality and belligerency, he worked assiduously to bring the President around to his views.

The spring and summer of 1916 brought numerous British restrictions on American neutral commerce. A mounting reaction swelled in the United States against the severe treatment accorded American shippers by the London government. Then, too, American public opinion resented British interference with overseas mails and the so-called blacklisting of American business firms. French and British reluctance to take seriously President Wilson's several attempts at mediation also caused an additional breach in Allied-American cordiality. Cognizant of an impending crisis, Colonel House bent his efforts to prevent a rupture. In September, he confided to his diary:

> The President came to my sitting room in the morning and we spent several hours going over foreign affairs principally our differences with Great Britain. . . . It was my opinion that the real differences with Great Britain now were that the United States had undertaken to build a great navy [the Naval Construction Act of 1916]; that our commerce was expanding beyond all belief; and we were rapidly taking the position Germany occupied before the war. . . . The President replied: "Let us build a navy bigger than hers [Britain] and do what we please." I reminded him that Germany had undertaken to do that and Great Britain had checked her before she could accomplish her purpose, and in the spring of 1914, I had predicted that she would . . .[15]

Woodrow Wilson's apparent resignation to deteriorating Anglo-American relations continued to vex House. Two months later, in November, when House was conversing with Frank Polk, Counselor of the State Department, House recorded the exchange in his diary:

> I urged him [Polk] to have Lansing keep in close touch with me until the skies are clear. We must do team work and keep our wits about us. We not only have foreign countries to deal with, but the President must be guided. . . . His tendency to offend

15. House MSS Diary, Sept. 24, 1916, Yale University Library; Seymour, *Intimate Papers*, 2, 316–17.

the Allies . . . is likely to lead us into trouble with them. Were we to have war, let it be with Germany by all means.[16]

The adroit House continued to think of his function as one of guiding the President away from disastrous policies.

With the passing of neutrality and the assumption of belligerent status by the United States, President Wilson at all times carefully avoided the conclusion of any alliance with members of the coalition at war with the Central Powers. He always made it a point to nurture the phrase, "associate," and to remind his deputies never to employ the term "ally" in government correspondence or publicity. Likewise, the President's reluctance to permit the integration of American military forces into a general Allied command provided another illustration of his desire for the greatest possible independence of action for the United States. Throughout the balance of the war, and also at the peace conference, Wilson's healthy recognition of American national interests resisted any restriction on America's autonomy within the coalition. Professor Seymour, in editing the House papers, has explained the President's growing antagonism toward the Allies by the latter's unresponsive attitude to Wilson's address of May 1916 before the League to Enforce Peace. "From this period dates his suspicion of the Allies' motives in the war, which was not entirely dissipated by co-partnership against Germany after 1917, and was intensified during the Peace Conference." [17] Whatever the first cause, the symptoms of suspicion can readily be perceived. When the Presi-

16. Diary, Nov. 17, 1916, House MSS, Yale; Seymour, *Intimate Papers*, 2, 327. As late as Sept. 16, 1918, House wrote in his diary: "We have been endeavoring to bring about political unity among the allies in order not to be wholly at the mercy of Germany. The President and Lansing both seem determined that it shall be known to the world that this country is acting independently of the allies." House MSS Diary, Sept. 16, 1918, Yale. Cf. notation in the Chandler Anderson MSS Diary, Library of Congress, Feb. 24, 1918: "I told Mr. [Elihu] Root of the statement made to me yesterday afternoon by Henry Taft, to the effect that the President had recently told his brother William that he was anti-British in sympathy and very much opposed to establishing closer relations with Great Britain either during the war or afterwards. Taft was very much excited about this, and said that some action should be taken to force the President to see the necessity for bringing about harmonious action between Great Britain and the United States in dealing with world problems both now and in the future."

17. Seymour, *Intimate Papers*, 2, 304–05.

dent learned of the secret Allied arrangements for the postwar settlement, his attitude was not likely to grow more sympathetic toward the coalition.

The same month in which Congress declared war, April 1917, there took place in Washington the first formal discussion of war aims and peace terms in which the United States government was represented as a full-fledged belligerent. The occasion was the visit to Washington of the Balfour Mission. Arthur Balfour, newly appointed British Foreign Minister, arrived in Washington on April 22, 1917. Handling the visitor with care, House lectured Balfour on the best strategy for presenting the British case to the American President.[18] In these preliminary conversations, Balfour fully oriented House concerning the details of the several Allied secret treaties, and the Texas Colonel indicated to the British Foreign Minister his own favorite device for breaking such information to Wilson. Some time later, when House reported to his diary, he devoted far more space to the information disclosed by Balfour in the preliminary conferences than he did to those conferences in which the President was a participant.[19] Consequently, it is difficult to be sure precisely what information concerning secret Allied commitments was actually divulged to the American Chief Executive.[20] If, as seems likely, Balfour treated the matter of the secret treaties generally or incidentally when talking with Wil-

18. House stated that he had told Balfour on April 22, 1917: "I advised Balfour to be entirely frank in his statement to the President of the difficulties under which the allies are struggling. I suggested that he might exaggerate rather than minimize them which would cause the President to feel that it was necessary for this country to go in up to the hilt rather than in a desultory way. I urged him not to talk peace terms, and to advise the President not to discuss peace terms with any of the other allies. If he did, differences would be certain to arise, and the problem now was to beat Germany and not discuss peace. Balfour agreed to this in full, and said he would not talk to the President about peace terms unless the President himself initiated it." House MSS Diary, April 22, 1917, Yale.

19. Seymour, *Intimate Papers*, 3, 43–46.

20. President Wilson after the war asserted that the United States had no official or unofficial knowledge of postwar peace arrangements prior to the Paris Peace Conference. See 66th Congress, 1st Session, *Senate Document No. 76, Report of Conference Between Members of the Senate Committee on Foreign Relations and the President of the United States, August 19, 1919*, p. 29. For a detailed study of American knowledge of the secret treaties, see Nancy Tozer, "The American Response to the Allied Secret Treaties Negotiated During World War I," (Unpublished M.A. Thesis, University of Wyoming, 1961), Chap. I.

son, there might be a valid suspicion that the President was never made familiar with the complete Allied program. The evidence, however, would suggest that he was fully informed about these treaties at least when the British government supplied the State Department with copies of the principal documents relevant to the treaties. There is, however, one curious feature in House's diary description of the discussions between Balfour and Wilson about the treaties. At no time did the usually careful House record the President's response or comments upon learning the extent to which the Allied commitments ran contrary to his ideals for the eventual peace settlement. House's sole reference to the Balfour revelation, in fact, is contained in just two sentences: "I asked Balfour again about the Allies' treaties with each other and the desirability of his giving copies to the President. He agreed to do so." [21]

After the war and the peace conference, House insisted that knowledge of the treaties had been conveyed to the President at the time of the Balfour Mission and that knowledge of the Italian treaty had arrived at the White House sometime earlier.[22] One letter from Wilson to House, dated July 21, 1917, would seem to imply rather strongly that the President had some information about the Allied plans for the final settlement. Wilson anticipated a conflict with the Allied governments over the formulation of the peace settlement, but, being an optimist, he believed the Allies would in the end yield to American wishes. The President phrased his thoughts as follows:

> [The] Allies must perforce yield to American pressure [economic power] and accept the American peace program: England and France have not the same views with regard to peace that we have by any means. When the war is over we can force them to our way of thinking.[23]

21. House MSS Diary, April 30, 1917, Yale.
22. Seymour, *Intimate Papers*, 3, 40–41.
23. Wilson to House, July 21, 1917, as set forth in Ibid., 51. Copies of published versions of the secret treaties publicized through the columns of the *New York Evening Post* were sent regularly to the White House during the winter of 1918; see Oswald Garrison Villard, *The Fighting Years* (New York, 1939), pp. 469–72.

Whether or not the President had the secret treaties in mind when he wrote this passage is not clear; what is significant is his expressed realization of fundamental differences separating the Allied program for peace from his own. Certainly by this time the State Department was cognizant of the extent of the secret treaties,[24] and it is highly improbable that such information did not come to the President's attention.

Some Allied secret treaties had been negotiated during the first two years of the war, as diplomatic devices for winning over wavering neutral countries like Italy and Rumania.[25] Still other treaties were simply means whereby the Allies agreed beforehand just how they were to divide and deal with conquered territory at the peace conference. When House was next in London, during the fall of 1917, Balfour tried to draw him into a discussion of the expected territorial spoils following the war. In characteristic fashion, House reported the conversation that ensued:

> We then went into the question of war aims. Maps were brought and Mr. Balfour started in with his ideas of territorial division. I did not allow him to go far when I spoke of the futility of such a discussion. I thought what we agreed upon today might be utterly impossible tomorrow, and it seemed worse than useless to discuss territorial aims at this time. They both caught the point and agreed to drop the discussion. [The British Prime Minister was also in attendance.]
>
> What I thought was necessary and pertinent at this time was the announcement of general war aims, and the formation of an international association for the prevention of future wars. I urged that Allied statesmen refrain from saying the things the German government wished them to say.[26]

On this occasion House refused to discuss the postwar settlement with British leaders. He feared possibly that such a discussion

24. *Papers Relating to the Foreign Relations of the United States, The Lansing Papers* (Washington, 1939), *2*, 23. Cf. Secretary Lansing's testimony before the Senate Foreign Relations Committee, 66th Congress, 1st Session, *Senate Document No. 106*, pp. 216–18.

25. A convenient summary of the Allies' secret treaties can be found in H. W. V. Temperley, ed., *A History of the Conference at Paris* (London, 1920–24), *1*, 169–71.

26. House MSS Diary, Nov. 21, 1917, Yale.

could only lead to undesirable confusion and misunderstanding within the coalition. Whatever the motive, the evidence is abundantly clear: it was the United States government which insisted upon the postponement of all discussion with Allied governments concerning the nature of the postwar settlement. House's rationale for postponement was that any discussion concerning postwar arrangements with the Allied governments while the war was still in progress might seriously hinder the war effort. And as already mentioned, the President's optimism rested on the belief that there would be time enough after the fighting ceased for the American government to bring dissident members of the coalition around to its position. Balfour's mission and subsequent conversations with Allied leaders served, however, to clarify the fundamental differences between the American program for peace, as it was developing, and the plans of those governments associated with the United States in the coalition.

It was only a matter of days following the departure from Washington of the Balfour Mission, in May 1917, before Colonel House took it upon himself to begin an informal but systematic program of collecting information intended to benefit an American delegation to the eventual peace conference. The initial impulse for this undertaking had actually been generated in the mind of the veteran American diplomat Henry White. The idea was mentioned in a letter to White's half-brother, the American archaeologist, William H. Buckler, who was serving in 1917 as a special assistant at the American Embassy in London.[27] Henry White knew, trusted, and even respected Colonel House, considering him more detached and impartial than Secretary of State Lansing.[28] Consequently, when White encouraged his half-brother to begin gathering confidential information in England which could then be transmitted to Colonel House and presumably the White House, he was not only avoiding the State Department but was recognizing Colonel House as the dominant adviser to the President. On April 27, while Balfour was still in the

27. Allan Nevins, *Henry White: Thirty Years of American Diplomacy* (New York, 1930), pp. 338–39.
28. Ibid., p. 340.

United States, Buckler broached the whole scheme to Colonel House:

> My regular work having now ceased owing to our breaks with Austria and Turkey, I am thinking of suggesting to Mr. [Walter Hines] Page [American Ambassador to England] . . . that I should "work up" either the Balkan question or the League of Nations proposals with a view ultimately to "devilling" for some Delegate at the Peace Conference (say yourself) who *might* not wish to carry in his own head the multifarious details of these problems. Such knowledge may of course already be possessed by James Brown Scott or by some expert in the Department [of State] who has trained for this particular job. If not, I should like to tackle it.[29]

Having made his point, Buckler proceeded to transmit a thirteen-page draft proposal containing several possible subjects which he felt merited investigation. Included were the following: (1) a league of nations; (2) restoration of Belgian, Serbian, and Rumanian independence; (3) Alsace-Lorraine and a possible plebiscite; (4) Poland; (5) an international commission for Balkan boundaries; (6) internationalization of the Turkish Straits and the status of Armenia; (7) the adoption of a federal constitution for Austria plus Italian claims to Austrian territory; (8) the German colonies in Africa and consideration of a free trade zone in tropical Africa.[30] Of these, Buckler indicated his personal preference to study Balkan problems.

On April 30, Balfour requested permission of Ambassador Page to make use of embassy facilities for the purpose of collecting information about the Balkans. American foreign policy, Buckler observed, had undergone a fundamental transformation as a consequence of American intervention in the war. No longer isolated from world politics, the United States would henceforth bear an active responsibility with other nations in formulating the ultimate peace settlement. The kind of role might depend upon the state of preparedness achieved by American policy-makers prior to the peace conference. Buckler's words rang with the sense of

29. Buckler to House, April 27, 1917, Buckler MSS, Yale.
30. Draft Program of Decisive Settlement Committee, no date or authorship, Buckler MSS, Yale.

15

the new role thrust upon the United States as a member of the world community of powers. He wrote to Ambassador Page:

> We cannot, as at Algeciras in 1906, act as mere conciliators but, in order to frame a "scientific peace" we must necessarily adopt and support at the Congress—probably against much opposition —constructive plans in regard to Bulgaria, Albania, Greece, etc.

However large the American delegation to the peace conference, it would include technical specialists on various subjects, Buckler predicted. By the term "scientific peace," he had in mind a peace settlement which was not predicated on the national power interest of any single government but instead would be a settlement based on the disinterested findings of specialists whose work would reflect those principles acceptable to the nations participating in the peace. Such a peace, being scientific, might presumably hold promise for permanency. A scientific peace, too, would need technicians in its construction. Since Balkan tensions had ignited the explosion in 1914, Buckler reasoned, there would be real need for an American specialist "familiar with the recent history, personalities, frontiers, resources, etc. of the Peninsula." Moreover, he thought, England would provide an advantageous location for the study of modern Balkan problems because through such English leaders as Brailsford, Buxton, and Lord Bryce, with whom Buckler was well acquainted, it would be possible for him to pick up much information and meet with representative people from the countries of southeastern Europe. And, besides study, Buckler was willing to prepare briefs and reports pertaining to the Balkans, Turkey, and the league of nations.[31]

Within a matter of days, Buckler's proposal was referred to the Department of State. There William Phillips, Assistant Secretary of State, took the plan to Colonel House for consideration before discussing it with his superiors.[32] This procedure was somewhat irregular though not entirely unheard of during the war years. While endorsing the proposal, Phillips added that it would indeed be unfortunate if American representatives arrived at the peace conference and found themselves handicapped by a lack of ac-

31. Buckler to Walter Hines Page, April 30, 1917, Buckler MSS, Yale.
32. William Phillips to House, May 19, 1917, House MSS, file 11-57, Yale.

curate information about the Balkans. To his knowledge, there was but one American, Professor Archibald Cary Coolidge of Harvard, who had systematically studied the Near East. Yet a single person, "no matter how good he is should not have the preparation of such an important field of work." Buckler, Phillips suggested, might work with Coolidge as a team, Buckler operating in England and Coolidge "working on the spot." But Phillips added a new dimension:

> In my opinion we should have many experts studying the Near Eastern problems, and perhaps it would be wise to start with these two and increase our sources of information gradually as it may become necessary.[33]

Having received warm encouragement from Phillips, Page,[34] and House, Buckler proceeded in quest of information relevant to the most pressing Near Eastern questions which he expected to arise at the peace conference. For better than a year, Buckler kept feeding information garnered in England to Colonel House. Much of this material was routed to House by way of Buckler's half-brother, Henry White. At length, on July 27, 1918, following Buckler's suggestion, House agreed that the need for his assistance no longer existed. By this time a full-scale investigation into the questions involved in the ultimate peace settlement had already begun in the United States.[35]

The importance of Buckler's efforts does not necessarily rest on the information he furnished Colonel House. For the most part his reports were culled from rumors and quoted statements from ranking members of the British government and a miscellany of Liberal spokesmen. Even heresay gossip, the droppings from dinner conversations, was not below his standard for evidence. Neverthe-

33. Ibid.

34. Walter Hines Page to President Wilson, June 8, 1917, Page MSS, Harvard.

35. Page had earlier withdrawn permission for Buckler to gather material for House in view of the existence of the Inquiry, so on July 27, 1918, House wrote to Henry White: "I quite agree with him [Buckler] that it would be well to discontinue sending data without the knowledge of the Ambassador. As a matter of fact there are now several sources through which I am getting what I desire, not only for my personal information, but for the Peace Inquiry. I want to again thank you and Mr. Buckler for your kindness and trouble." Buckler MSS, Yale.

less, of far greater consequence was the impetus which the Buckler-White proposals gave to preparations for peace in the United States. Buckler's idea of collecting information in advance and for the benefit of American plenipotentiaries struck favorable responses in both Colonel House and the Department of State. Though William Buckler was not to participate personally in the formal organization he had done so much to inspire, the importance of his initial proposals must be recognized.

From April through August 1917, much anxiety concerning American preparations for peace was expressed both in and outside government circles. Peace societies intensified their activities with meetings and active discussions in virtually every city and hamlet across the nation.[36] Newspapers and magazines devoted considerable coverage to this widespread popular interest in the eventual settlement of the war. They not only reported an enormous number of petitions and meetings and opinions, but their editorials attempted to focus public attention on various features recommended for incorporation in the peace treaties. The political parties, which had previously not taken any decided stand on foreign policy, continued their general detachment,[37] but ranking members of both parties displayed an active interest in the establishment of an international organization, usually one corresponding to the general plan of the League to Enforce Peace.

The general absence of Congressional debate over the shape of the ultimate peace should not be particularly astounding. Except

36. Box 263, Series VI, Wilson MSS, Library of Congress, contains a great deal of peace material originally sent to the President by various individuals and peace organizations.

37. Kirk H. Porter, *National Party Platforms* (New York, 1924), pp. 395–96 gives the text of the Republican party platform for 1916. The Democratic party platform can be found on pp. 375–76. The Democratic platform took a far more affirmative stand: "We believe that every people has the right to choose the sovereignty under which it shall live; that the small states of the world have a right to enjoy from other nations the same respect for their sovereignty and for their territorial integrity that great and powerful nations expect and insist upon; and that the world has a right to be free from every disturbance of its peace that has its origin in aggression or disregard of the rights of the people and nations, and we believe that the time has come when it is the duty of the United States to join the other nations of the world in any feasible association that will effectively serve those principles to maintain involate the complete security of the highway of the seas for the common and unhindered use of all nations."

for a tiny nucleus of isolationists, Congressmen were prone to exhibit a united front in this period of national emergency. These early months following American intervention found Congressmen caught under the spell of wartime unity and reluctant to embarrass the administration with vehement criticisms of the nation's foreign policy. By summer, however, when the importance of peace terms was becoming appreciated, a serious interest was kindling on Capitol Hill.

Peace resolutions had been introduced even during the period of American neutrality, in 1915–16. These had most often espoused some kind of international organization, whether judicial, a league of nations, or some variety of world government. Following American intervention, however, the Congressional resolutions began to express more specific solutions. They asked, to cite a single example, the Allied governments to pledge not to negotiate any separate arrangements for peace in the absence of the United States. A just peace, another asserted, should include the restoration of Allied countries disturbed by the war while at the same time Germany should be allowed to repossess its colonies.[38] Throughout the summer months of 1917, Congressional resolutions did not reveal any central theme concerning the peace settlement. The Congress, not unlike public opinion generally, had not become identified with any particular policy for peace.

There were some eighteen Senate resolutions respecting the future peace settlement introduced during the first session of the 65th Congress from April 2 to August 29, 1917. Virtually the entire lot was tabled or died naturally in committee. A few reached the floor; none ever arrived at a vote. When the Senate's decisive action of 1919 is recalled, it might seem ironic that Congressmen showed such reticence to act more forcefully during the months of American belligerency. Actually, until the election of 1918, President Wilson continued to command a Democratic majority in both Houses. A national unity imposed by the war disposed the Democratic Congress to leave the Democratic Chief Executive unfettered in his attempts at reaching a satisfactory peace settlement.

Early in August 1917, certain Senators did manifest their con-

38. *Congressional Record*, 65th Congress, 1st Session, April 17, 1917, p. 743; June 4, 1917, p. 3255.

cern over the conditions of a peace settlement. Four resolutions were introduced in the Senate during that month. Not only did this represent a sharp spurt in such resolutions, but the resolutions succeeded in generating more discussion of the subject on the floor of the Senate than heretofore. It was also during August that the Pope's plea for peace, addressed to all the principal belligerents, was publicized. While the papal note was not inserted in the *Congressional Record* until August 22, its contents were divulged to individual Congressmen presumably right after its earlier arrival at the White House. But what made interest in the peace settlement even more lively at this time was the allegedly authoritative information about the secret treaties which circulated on Capitol Hill.

Senators William E. Borah and Robert M. LaFollette, both critics of the President's wartime policies, opened the debate concerning peace on July 27. Borah proposed that the President indicate in precise fashion what would constitute reasonable terms for settling the war insofar as the United States was concerned. Then, two weeks later, Senator LaFollette drew attention to the "secret treaties," and introduced a resolution (Senate Concurrent Resolution 11) that the United States publicly disavow any intention of continuing the war for the territorial aggrandizement of any belligerent. LaFollette's resolution asked:

> that Congress declares that there should be a public restatement of the allied peace terms based on a disavowal of any advantages, either in the way of indemnities, territorial acquisitions, commercial privileges or economic prerogatives, by means of which one nation shall strengthen its power abroad at the expense of another nation, as wholly incompatible with the establishment of a durable peace.[39]

A somewhat watered-down version was introduced three days later by Senator Lawrence Y. Sherman of Illinois, who added that the peace treaty should include some strong provision banning certain kinds of blockades during future wars.

Meanwhile, rumors of imminent peace circulated on both sides of the Atlantic throughout the summer of 1917. By August, both

39. Ibid., Aug. 11, 1917, pp. 5956–57; Belle and Fola LaFollette, *Robert M. LaFollette* (New York, 1953), 2, 749–58; *New York Times,* July 27, 1917, p. 1.

official and unofficial comments focused upon the dramatic appeal which Pope Benedict addressed to the belligerent governments on August 1. In his note, the Pope defined certain conditions for peace which he hoped would be acceptable to the nations at war and which might provide a basis for the termination of hostilities. These conditions included the following:

> 1. A moral force of right to be substituted for the material force of arms, leading eventually to "simultaneous and reciprocal reduction of armaments" with necessary guarantees provided for adequate preservation of law and order in each country.
> 2. Creation of machinery for obligatory arbitration which would include a system of "penalties" to be imposed on any state failing to submit its disputes to the arbitral court and on any state failing to abide by the decision of said court.
> 3. "Liberty and community" of the seas for the purpose of promoting adequate bases for "prosperity and progress."
> 4. Restoration of Belgium and evacuation of French territory on the basis of the status quo ante.
> 5. Restitution of Germany's colonies on the basis of the status quo ante.
> 6. Disputes involving territorial boundaries should be settled by negotiations in which consideration would be accorded to the aspirations of those populations inhabiting the lands in question as well as to the general welfare of the "great human society." [40]

With the disclosure of the papal note in England, France, and the United States, there commenced a concerted drive to use the Pope's intercession as a German or Austrian vehicle for driving a wedge between America and the western Allies. Colonel House was especially anxious to avoid any rupture within the coalition over the terms of peace. He therefore advised the President to make a plain, noncommittal response which would leave open the possibility for future peace discussions while at the same time placing the onus for continuing the war strictly with the "Prussian militarists." [41] The British, for their part, were not anxious to announce publicly the nature of their peace terms. In fact, Foreign Secretary Balfour wrote to House:

40. *Congressional Record*, Aug. 22, 1917, pp. 6252–53. The text was published almost simultaneously with its arrival in the United States by leading metropolitan newspapers, about August 15.

41. House to Wilson, Aug. 17, 1917, House MSS, file 50-9, Yale.

> For my part, I greatly dread the idea of any joint endeavor of composing an elaborate document dealing with complex problems necessarily looked at from somewhat different angles by each belligerent. Drafting difficulties alone seem to render the task impossible.[42]

The chance remained that Woodrow Wilson, left to his own devices, might choose to repudiate the Allied secret treaties, at least insofar as the United States was concerned, and proceed diplomatically upon a completely independent course. Even the President's closest advisers were rarely sure of the extent of the Chief Executive's commitment to the coalition "team." Might Woodrow Wilson decide that the Allied peace terms were not in keeping with America's objectives? Perhaps he would go so far as to repudiate the secret treaties. The President could very well set forth a fresh series of objectives for the peace settlement. At the time, the fears of his associates over the tenor of the President's reply to Pope Benedict's appeal were hardly academic.

Before the end of August, Wilson had submitted drafts of his reply to the principal Allied governments, thus seeking their approval in advance. Once having received approval, the reply was duly dispatched to the Vatican. In this reply Wilson relied heavily upon a simple contrivance, one he had employed earlier in his Message to Congress of April 2.[43] He drew a sharp distinction between the German people and the German government. The war, he maintained, was being waged against the latter, not the former. Here the President with characteristic polish, painted the conditions in contrasting hues, white and black:

> The object of the war is to deliver the fine peoples of the world from the menace and the actual power of a vast military establishment controlled by an irresponsible government, which having secretly planned to dominate the world, proceeded to carry the plan out without regard either to the sacred obligations of treaty or the long established practices and long cherished principles of international action and honor. . . . This power is not the German people but the masters of the German people.[44]

42. Seymour, *Intimate Papers,* 3, 156.
43. Baker and Dodd, *Public Papers, War and Peace 1917–1924, 1,* 6–16.
44. Ibid., 93–96.

Until such time as the German government was reformed on the "inside," the United States could not consider the feasibility of any settlement to the war.

Both the British and French governments expressed keen satisfaction with the President's words. If German and Austrian militarists had been exploiting the Pope to serve the interests of the Central Powers by calling forth a peace settlement on the basis of the status quo ante,[45] such a settlement was not at all satisfactory to the Allied governments in the summer of 1917. Nothing could have been further from the aspirations of those governments associated with the United States in the war. The very vagueness with which the President responded to the Pope's appeal, so Woodrow Wilson was later to assert, was caused by a conscious "sparing [of] allied feelings: I have not thought it wise to . . . be more specific because it might provoke dissenting voices from France and Italy if I should say . . . for example that their territorial claims did not interest us." [46] Again, the overtone of the secret treaties seems audible. The clash of American and Allied conditions for the peace was not absent from the President's mind when he was writing his reply to the Pope. Undoubtedly the Pope's plea for peace exerted a profound influence in bringing Woodrow Wilson to the point of thinking about the wisdom of beginning in earnest America's preparations for the peace negotiations.

Several weeks earlier, in the middle of July, Felix Frankfurter, then a special assistant to the Secretary of War, was in Paris. Under date of July 19, the Department of State requested Frankfurter to provide information on the existing situation in France. When Frankfurter's report reached the State Department on August 7, it was passed on to the White House. Frankfurter had appended to the document a definite suggestion for a planning organization in the United States to prepare for the eventual peace conference. His idea was stimulated by knowledge acquired in Paris of French efforts in the field of diplomatic planning. In ex-

45. See M. Jusserand (French ambassador to the United States) to House, Aug. 23, 1917, in Seymour, *Intimate Papers*, 3, 160–61. Other related documents are found on pp. 161–67.
46. Ibid., p. 168.

plaining the genesis of the American preparatory effort, Frankfurter's proposals must be credited seriously:

> France is at work, through committees, in the preparation of material for the Peace Conference. We should equip ourselves with like knowledge. Competent persons should be set to work on the various questions that are bound to come up, so that all the material which is pertinent will be at hand for our commissioners. Of course, a good deal of this material we have, but is it in an organized form and directed to the specific objective here suggested? [47]

Upon his return to the United States, Frankfurter continued to press the case for American preparatory studies on several members of the Wilson administration.[48]

On August 4, three days before Frankfurter sent off his report, Third Assistant Secretary of State Breckinridge Long and the Department's Legal Counselor, Lester Woolsey, had presented a draft proposal for such an organization to Secretary Lansing.[49] Long and Woolsey recommended the formation of a board consisting of five officials: (1) a high naval official; (2) the Naval Instructor; [50] (3) the head of the War College; (4) an official of the Department of State; (5) an expert on international law. Working under the supervision of this board would be expert advisers in charge of technical research, presumably compiling reports concerning each region of the world to be considered in the peace settlement. As might be expected from the standpoint

47. Frankfurter to Secretary Lansing, Aug. 7, 1917, in House MSS, Yale.

48. House to Buckler, Aug. 21, 1917, Buckler MSS, Yale. House wrote: "Felix Frankfurter of the War Department is just back from Paris. He tells me that the French Government are getting their experts busy preparing for the peace conference. I am sorry to say, we are doing little or nothing in that direction and I am afraid we will have to depend largely upon outsiders for the information we desire."

49. Breckinridge Long to the Secretary of State, Aug. 4, 1917, *Papers Relating to the Foreign Relations of the United States 1919, The Paris Peace Conference* (Washington, 1942–47), *1*, 9–10.

50. "There was and is not now any official title of Naval Instructor in the United States Navy. The civilian teaching staff at the Naval Academy were designated Instructors and Professors in 1917. . . . The phrase *Naval Instructor* may have been used as an unofficial designation of the type of work performed." Letter from F. Kent Loomis, Assistant Director of Naval History, Department of the Navy, to author, dated Feb. 27, 1956.

of both logic and the vested interests of those who proposed this board, there was the expectation that the preparatory operation would be performed under the supervision of the State Department even though it might have its headquarters apart for purposes of greater security and secrecy.

Secretary Lansing met with his closest associates in the State Department before the end of August to discuss the Long-Woolsey recommendation. At this first meeting, he directed his associates to offer suggestions as to which questions they expected would arise and involve the United States during the peace negotiations. Joseph Grew, one party to this discussion, has recorded a part of the assignment:

> His [Lansing's] instructions were broad, but we held a meeting and decided that the first phase of the subject we would deal with would be "the aims and desires of the present belligerents." This phase of the subject is in itself broad, but I understand that it is not intended to be historical; we are only to trace the development of these aims and desires during the period of the war. . . . My share of this seemingly colossal task includes, Germany, Austria-Hungary, England, France, Belgium, and Portugal. We have been given no time limit, but I gather from insinuations, that we should turn in our work "sometime soon." [51]

In the evolution of the American preparations for peace, Lansing's instructions assume considerable importance. The concerted study of "the aims and desires of the present belligerents" was to provide the focal emphasis of the work.

Apparently, the person Secretary Lansing had in mind to take charge and coordinate the State Department's effort was his close friend, the former Counselor of the State Department (in the Taft administration), Chandler P. Anderson.[52] On September 8, Anderson conferred at some length with Lansing. By this time,

51. Joseph C. Grew, *Turbulent Era: A Diplomatic Record of Forty Years 1904–1945* (Boston, 1952), *1*, 330–31.

52. In 1913, Assistant Secretary of State Huntington Wilson had registered a complaint against Anderson to the effect that Anderson was being a most difficult counselor of the State Department, and that he could not get along with nor did he respect his superiors. It was impossible to discuss anything with him. See Wilson to Secretary Bryan, March 16, 1913, in Wilson MSS, Series VI, Library of Congress.

however, the Secretary had still not thought through the full dimensions of the task. He already had several people in mind to assist with the work, and at this time the names of two eminent scholars in international law, John Bassett Moore and James Brown Scott, were mentioned. They might assist, but Anderson would have the chief responsibility for organizing the "programme," making appropriate suggestions, and choosing the subjects worthy of study.[53] Lansing assured Anderson that there should be no sense of pressure on those participating in this assignment. The war, after all, was not expected to end soon. As for finances with which to carry on the work, Lansing was unwilling to make any promises. The Secretary would not even promise salaries. Up to this moment, Lansing had not sought the President's approval for the plan. When Anderson was first approached, the entire discussion of American preparations for peace was limited to conversations between Lansing and his chief advisers at the State Department. Yet these preliminary discussions are important. They suggest that the Department seriously expected to undertake this new assignment, at least to the extent of exercising a supervisory control over the work. Unfortunately for the Lansing plan, Wilson was already contriving a similar but alternative plan, then unknown to his Secretary of State.

While Lansing's scheme called for placing the machinery of peace directly under the supervision of the Department of State, the President intended to form quite a different kind of organization. Early in September 1917, he was thinking in terms of placing the machinery directly under the supervision of Colonel House. On September 2, House, who had been spending the summer at his summer home, Magnolia, in Massachusetts, received the following communication from his friend at the White House:

> I am beginning to think that we ought to go systematically to work to ascertain as fully and precisely as possible just what the several parties to this war on our side of it will be inclined to insist upon as part of the final peace arrangements, in order that we may formulate our own position either for or against them and begin to gather the influences we can use: in brief, prepare our case with a full knowledge of the position of all the litigants. What would you think of quietly gathering about you a group of men to assist you to do this? I could, of course, pay all the bills out of

53. Chandler P. Anderson MSS Diary, Sept. 8, 1917, Library of Congress.

26

the money now at my command. Under your guidance these assistants could collate all the definite material available and you
would make up the memorandum by which we should be guided.

Have you had a talk with Frankfurter? If you have not, I wish
you would have. He knows what some of the other governments
are doing to get their cases ready and their pipes laid, and he
might be able to give you a lead as to doing what I am here suggesting.[54]

Wilson's intentions are patently clear in this letter. He had become
familiar with Frankfurter's proposals and therefore was cognizant
that other governments associated with the United States in the
war were already busy accumulating information and preparing
their cases for the peace conference. What was even more momentous, House was instructed not only to prepare the American
case, but, and here the President employed careful, precise language, he was instructed to formulate the American program for
peace as it related to the objectives of the "several parties to this
war on our side of it." In order to accomplish this purpose, House
was authorized to gather about him a group of men able to handle
the materials relevant to the peace settlement. Likewise, it seems
manifestly clear, the President fully expected the work to be done
independently of the Department of State, for, Wilson added,
funds would be made available from the special reserve at his
disposal.

The President's letter reached Colonel House on September 4.
That day House reflected in his diary upon how much of an additional burden the new assignment would probably be. He was
pleased with the new responsibilities, though he solemnly confessed: "I do not quite know how I shall do this." [55] Nevertheless,
in spite of this obviously sincere expression of humility, when the
Colonel responded at last to the President he neither suggested
any personal inadequacies for the responsibilities nor did he
credit the President with having suggested anything at all novel.
House wrote:

> In your letter of September 2nd you mention some of the things
> I have had in mind for a long while and about which I intended
> to talk with you upon my first visit to Washington.

54. Ray S. Baker, *Woodrow Wilson, Life and Letters* (Garden City, 1927–39),
7, 254.

55. House MSS Diary, Sept. 4, 1917, Yale.

I have been trying to do in a quiet and not very efficient way what you have suggested as wanting me to do systematically and thoroughly. I shall be delighted to undertake the work and will go about it at once.

Frankfurter has been here, and many others interested in the subject, and there will be no difficulty in bringing together a group that will be able to get the data and information you desire. At my suggestion, Buckler has been informing himself on the Balkan situation but he has been handicapped by working only in London.

What would you think of putting a man on each of the most complicated problems, and, if necessary, sending them to Europe? [56]

Central to the President's proposal was the presumption of an independent course for the United States during the eventual peace negotiations. Nowhere was such an independent course implied in the House-Buckler correspondence; at least it was never so stated as the objective of the preparations for peace. Only Lansing, in his instructions to the staff working at the State Department, approximated the President's intent. Moreover, the Wilsonian objective was never again to be suggested. One looks in vain through the House diary, the correspondence surrounding the preparations for peace—there is no further reference or mention, stated or implied, that the signal purpose was to prepare an independent American program for peace vis-à-vis the Allies.

Why the President chose to bypass the Department of State in granting this assignment to the already overburdened House is a question deserving of some speculation. Just one week after making the decision, Wilson paid one of his infrequent visits to the Colonel at the Magnolia retreat in Massachusetts. There was much conversation both before and after dinner, with the subject seeming to center upon the State Department. According to House, the President had traveled north expressly to seek the Colonel's advice concerning the wisdom of calling for Secretary Lansing's resignation. The two men talked calmly and freely about the Secretary. Many qualities in Lansing distressed the Chief Executive. He raised objections to the manner in which Lansing handled diplomatic notes—making them too conservative for

56. House to Wilson, Sept. 4, 1917, House MSS, file 50-9, Yale.

Wilson's taste—to Lansing's failing health and overwork, even to the character of his friends, who were described as a type "not conducive to a broad outlook as they are mostly society folk and reactionaries." At last the discussion turned to the alternatives, persons who might presumably be more satisfactory to the President. After weighing various candidates, the decision was postponed. What is important if this incident is reported accurately (and there is no reason to doubt it) is that at the critical moment when the idea of forming some preparatory body capable of developing an American program for peace was being considered, insofar as the President was concerned the Secretary of State was barely *persona grata*.[57] House, in direct contrast, was thought to be absolutely loyal; he was a man having numerous and important contacts in both the political and intellectual arenas at home and abroad. Above all, House did have an exalted reputation as an organizer *par excellence*. Moreover, the President's practice of utilizing unofficial, informal agents to perform special assignments in the sphere of foreign relations had already been established. But on this occasion the idea of using academicians rather than the more legalistically inclined diplomats for the project may have turned the President away from the Department of State.

Lansing, however, was not to remain aloof entirely from the preparatory activities. On September 19, Wilson informed House of the Secretary's enthusiasm and willingness to cooperate, as desired, in the new work. Perhaps to allay House's continuing concern that Lansing would resent interference, the President added that Lansing did not resent House's assumption of these responsibilities. Cautiously the President concluded his note, "Of course we shall have to define the studies of our assistants with as much precision as possible or they would all be as thorough and ex-

57. House MSS Diary, Sept. 9, 1917, Yale. Gordon Auchincloss (House's son-in-law then employed in the State Department as Polk's assistant) recorded in his diary on September 10: "The Colonel has been having very serious talks with the President about Lansing, whose statements make him mad. Lansing refused to play with George Creel the publicity man and then unfortunately he makes a statement one day and the next contradicts it. In my opinion it would be disastrous for W.W. to supplant L. at this time. He is an awfully sweet man and he is thoroughly loyal to W.W. . . . W.W. watches the State Department closer than any of the other Depts and consequently is more critical of it." Auchincloss MSS Diary, Yale.

haustive (and therefore as useless) as Frankfurter would be if he went to the depths he proposed." [58]

Meanwhile, Chandler P. Anderson was moving ahead with plans for a preparatory study within the framework of the State Department. On October 2, after the newspapers publicized the existence of House's new duties, Secretary Lansing conferred a second time with Anderson. The latter, quite naturally, wanted to know exactly where he stood. Lansing urged Anderson to work closely with House rather than to steer an independent course. [59] Anderson's special assignment for the State Department was not going to interfere or conflict with the preparatory chores being undertaken by Colonel House. Several weeks later, Anderson was at his club where he ran across an old friend, Hugh Wallace. Wallace was also well acquainted with Colonel House. Before long, the conversation turned to the subject of House's new responsibilities; Anderson later recorded the remarks of his friend:

> He [Wallace] said that he knew only that Colonel House had told him that he wanted to take the work out of the hands of the State Department. I said that I did not see how they could get together the necessary data without the assistance of the State Department. He said that what House wanted was to direct the work himself, and to do it quite independently of the Department. [60]

There is no corroboration of the assertion in this reported conversation that Colonel House was anxious to arrogate responsibilities at the expense of the Department of State. Colonel House, it should be recalled, had made numerous bitter foes, and Anderson's diary bears ample testimony to his deep-seated resentment against the Texan.

In the months that followed, Anderson tried to become involved in the work of Colonel House's organization, but his effort to do so was spurned. [61] American preparations for peace thence-

---

58. Wilson to House, Sept. 19, 1917, in Baker, *Life and Letters*, 7, 275. Gordon Auchincloss MSS Diary, Sept. 13, 1917, Yale.

59. Chandler P. Anderson MSS Diary, Oct. 2, 1917, Library of Congress.

60. Ibid., Oct. 13, 1917, Library of Congress.

61. In November 1917, Anderson was offered a temporary assignment in the international law section, but this connection was soon terminated in February 1918. See Chandler Anderson to House, Nov. 1, 1917, Sidney Mezes MSS, Co-

forth remained the special province of Colonel House. That is not to say, however, that the State Department was entirely indifferent or aloof. With the passage of time and the approach of peace, the prophetic quality of Hugh Wallace's observation became more and more evident. How could the necessary data be collected without the assistance of the State Department? Certainly by the beginning of 1918 the leaders both of House's organization and of the State Department were aware that the latter had to provide an increasing amount of assistance to House's forces, on almost all levels of the preparatory work.

lumbia, infra p. 73, David Hunter Miller to Anderson, Feb. 9, 1918, Inquiry Archives.

Chapter 2

EXPERTS AND "EXPERTS"

WARS SHARE with certain games like chess, wrestling, and bull fighting an unpredictable tendency for abrupt finales, often ending before the various contestants fully realize the decisive turn of events. In the case of wars, this tendency sometimes works to the disadvantage of the victorious belligerents who must ultimately assume responsibility for deciding on what terms the foundation for peace will be constructed. In 1917, the public imagination was already stirring to the elixir of peace slogans. "Make the world safe for democracy" was fast becoming associated with "the war to end wars." Woodrow Wilson's public addresses kept instilling in his listeners the conviction that the next peace settlement would be both just and lasting; men and nations must no longer decide their disputes upon fields of battle. Out of the conflict, a peaceful international order would emerge, prospering without fear of future war. Whether this optimistic promise of lasting peace would in fact blossom into reality could easily depend upon how the victorious nations behaved at the eventual peace conference. American success or failure in the peace negotiations might easily hinge on the very preparations placed by President Wilson in the charge of Colonel House. Surely no one could foresee the end of the war; how much time remained for the preparatory work was a question without an answer. One thing seemed reasonably certain: the preparatory work would be racing the calendar, and, correspondingly, the progress of the war.

32

When Colonel House proceeded with the business of setting up shop in September 1917, the first matter of business was the selection of personnel. The President expressed confidence that the necessary tasks could best be accomplished with a minimal organization "and the information gotten from a few specialists in this country such as historians, professors, etc." [1] For Woodrow Wilson, former university president and political scientist in his own right, the work involved in preparing for peace would properly fall within the province of academic scholarship, making use of men trained in the handling of factual evidence. New government agencies initiated by the New Freedom had already been forming their staffs with the benefit of political and social scientists drawn from several university faculties. By 1917, the United States Tariff Commission, the Interstate Commerce Commission, the Federal Trade Commission, and the Federal Reserve Board were staffed heavily with academic teachers turned public servants.[2] These scholars supposedly could apply their special training and base their judgments solely upon a disinterested review of the factual evidence, because in their case there were not the usual axes to grind, political bosses to serve, and lobbyists to heed. Colonel House would draw the best trained minds capable of developing the American government's plans for the peace conference.

The doctrine of government planning, making use of expert counselors, had emerged as a salient feature of progressive thought just before and during the war years. Editor Herbert Croly of the *New Republic*, a leading spokesman of the progressive reformers, characterized the case for planning with the simple phrase, "The way to realize a purpose is not to leave it to chance." [3] Though the employment of experts as governmental administrators and planners might provoke diehard Jacksonian democrats and laissez faire economists, reformers representing both political parties

1. House to H. C. Wallace, Oct. 14, 1917, Wilson MSS, Series II, Library of Congress.

2. Joshua Bernhardt, *The Tariff Commission: Its History, Activities and Organization*, Institute for Government Research, Service Monographs of the United States Government Number 5 (New York, 1922), p. 19. See also Ralph H. Gabriel, *The Course of American Democratic Thought* (New York, 1940), pp. 335–38.

3. Quoted in ibid., p. 336.

looked to the principle of governmental planning for an efficient avenue to progress. The progressive spirit, of which Wilson's New Freedom formed a national incarnation, was already sanctioning the practice of planning in government.

Historical precedents could moreover be cited for the use of expert-consultant-advisers at international conferences.[4] Nearly every important conference since 1815 had relied to some extent upon the services of consultants.[5] To be sure, advisers had more frequently been drawn from the military services than from university faculties, but the resort to consultants possessing special knowledge was a regular feature of every national delegation's standard operating procedure. At the Congress of Vienna, expert advisers formed a statistical commission authorized to gather population statistics which presumably would be used in the adjustment of international boundaries. Expert advisers were no less conspicuous in the discussions of care of prisoners in wartime at the Geneva conferences of 1864 and 1868. When it came time for the United States to send a delegation to Paris for the peace conference called to terminate the Spanish-American War, the Department of State sent along as adviser to the American plenipotentiaries Columbia University's scholar in international law, John Bassett Moore. Other Americans from the academic community accompanied American delegations to the two Hague peace conferences in 1899 and 1907. By and large, the century's experience had shown that expert advisers were no less susceptible to national passions or less influenced by special interests than were diplomats.

Colonel House's crew would differ in one significant regard from these earlier precedents, however. In 1917, the idea was to start the experts working in advance of the peace conference, plan the program, and gather the relevant information. A war to end wars demanded a peace that would be lasting. International problems, being infinitely more complicated than formerly, would

4. For the American precedents, see Richard Humphrey, "The 'Official' Scholar: A Survey of Certain Research in American Foreign Policy," in *Essays in Honor of Conyers Read,* ed. Norton Downs (Chicago, 1953), pp. 36–37.

5. Norman L. Hill, *The Public International Conference* (Stanford, 1929), pp. 37–43.

require a larger task force intimately acquainted with its materials.

Before the war, American universities had provincially disregarded extensive scholarly consideration of the world beyond the Americas and Europe.[6] Historians, economists, political scientists, and even geographers who possessed facility in Slavic, Asian, or African languages or whose knowledge of Eastern Europe, Asia, or Africa rose above the superficial level were absolute rarities. The study of international relations had been confined to diplomatic history and international law. With the sole exception of the *American Journal of International Law*, established in 1907, there was no specific outlet for scholarly research and criticism pertaining to international relations. Columbia University, whose President Nicholas Murray Butler displayed intense interest in world problems, offered no course with a political-economic orientation dealing exclusively with Russia, East Asia, or Africa. Yale, Cornell, Michigan, and Johns Hopkins each offered courses in international law and diplomatic history. At Harvard, an international polity club "to promote the thoughtful discussion and study of modern international problems" had been launched only in 1912.[7] Otherwise, Harvard offered occasional courses on Northern and Eastern Europe and the Middle East at such times when Archibald Cary Coolidge was available to teach them. America's leading universities were clearly not providing opportunities for the systematic study of world affairs.[8]

History, being the most ancient of the so-called social-political sciences, provides a good case in point. Few American historians had delved beyond the screen of Western civilization. From the

6. Edith E. Ware, ed., *The Study of International Relations in the United States* (New York, 1934), pp. 5–9; Farrell Symons, *Courses on International Affairs in American Colleges 1930–1931* (Boston, 1931), p. x.

7. Samuel E. Morison, *Three Centuries of Harvard 1636–1936* (Cambridge, 1936), p. 437.

8. Ibid., pp. 334, 376, 395; R. Gordon Hoxie, et al., *A History of the Faculty of Political Science, Columbia University* (New York, 1955), pp. 73–75, 135–36, 242–43; Nicholas Murray Butler, *The Rise of a University*, 2, *The University in Action from the Annual Reports 1902–1935* (New York, 1937), pp. 100–01; George W. Pierson, *Yale College: An Educational History 1871–1921* (New Haven, 1952), pp. 293–96; Walter P. Rogers, *Andrew D. White and the Modern University* (Ithaca, 1942), pp. 131–32. See also the particular universities' catalogues for the pre-1918 years.

standpoint of Colonel House's requirements, historical studies were even more severely limited. Research as well as instruction had focused almost exclusively upon the pre-contemporary periods, then defined to mean the years before 1815. That grave disease to which historians are especially susceptible, a reluctance to tread the paths of the immediate past for fear of distortion, was claiming an extraordinary number of patients. Of the nearly 400 articles published in the *American Historical Review* during its first twenty years, down to 1914, hardly a dozen articles pertained to the most recent century.[9] Moreover, of the historians selected for assignments on House's preparatory commission who were listed in the Directory of the American Historical Association for 1918, two were labeled as specialists in the ancient world, three as medievalists, three as students of the Near East, one in European economic history, and only four placed themselves broadly within the boundaries of modern history.

Scholars plowing the furrows of international law suffered from a penchant for preconceptions and even misconceptions. In its first ten years, from 1907–17, the *American Journal of International Law* published numerous articles dealing with the peaceful settlement of international disputes. Judicial arbitration—both voluntary and obligatory—was the most commonly espoused vaccine against the dreaded virus, war. Other writers sought remedies through disarmament, open diplomacy, and progressive democratization.[10] Political scientists frequently called attention to the need for extending democratic institutions, for, according to the prevalent theory, where the peace-loving public controlled the

9. W. Stull Holt, "Historical Scholarship," in *American Scholarship in the Twentieth Century*, ed. Merle Curti (Cambridge, 1953), pp. 102–03; Harold J. Coolidge and Robert H. Lord, *Archibald Cary Coolidge, Life and Letters* (Boston, 1932), pp. 43–46.

10. For some examples of the writings of American scholars in this field, in particular those whose articles concerned the peaceful settlement of international disputes, published between 1907–17, see Floyd R. Clark, "A Permanent Tribunal of International Arbitrations: Its Necessity and Value," *American Journal of International Law* (hereafter cited as *AJIL*), 1 (1907), 342–408; William T. Hull, "Obligatory Arbitration and the Hague Conferences," *AJIL*, 2 (1908), 731–42; Amos J. Peaslee, "The Sanction of International Law," *AJIL*, 10 (1916), 328–36; William L. Penfield, "International Arbitration," *AJIL*, 1 (1907), 330–41; Amos S. Hershey, "Adjustment of International Differences," *AJIL*, 2 (1908), 32–33.

reins of government, the desire for war vanished. Robert Lansing, America's wartime Secretary of State, phrased this concept succinctly in these words:

> Briefly let me recall to you my line of thought which I discussed with you a year and a quarter ago: No people on earth desire war, particularly an aggressive war. If the people can exercise their will, they will remain at peace. If a nation possesses democratic institutions, the popular will will be exercised. Consequently, if the principles of democracy prevail in a nation, it can be counted upon to preserve peace and oppose war.[11]

Judging from published journal articles, scholars in international law did not advocate an association or league of nations as practical deterrents to war. Legal scholars from John Bassett Moore to Elihu Root strongly placed their weight against international organization because of its alleged incompatibility with national sovereignty.[12]

Some generals might have become disturbed, to say the least, by a serious shortage of qualified talent to fill the ranks on the eve of battle. Not so Colonel House. Equipped with the President's authority to build an American organization capable of making the advance arrangements for the peace settlement, he proceeded cautiously but steadily to form his high command. Before the middle of September 1917, recommendations were requested from President A. Lawrence Lowell of Harvard and from Herbert Croly,[13] the former representing the academic community and the latter presumably representing the liberal, progressive

11. Lansing to Colonel House, April 8, 1918, *Papers Relating to the Foreign Relations of the United States, The Lansing Papers, 2,* 118–20. For other statements pertaining to public opinion and its relationship to world peace, see Frederick N. Judson, "The Education of Public Opinion," in *Lake Mohonk Conference Reports, 21* (1911); Oscar S. Straus, "Democracy and Open Diplomacy," *Proceedings of the American Academy of Political Science, 8* (1917–18), 348–50. For Admiral Alfred T. Mahan's views, see William E. Livezey, *Mahan on Sea Power* (Norman, 1947), pp. 28–29.

12. Richard W. Leopold, *Elihu Root and the Conservative Tradition* (Boston, 1954), p. 133; Philip Jessup, *Elihu Root* (New York, 1938), *2,* 376, 382 ff.; John Bassett Moore, "Some Essentials of a League for Peace," *Collected Papers of John Bassett Moore, 5,* 67; Moore, "International Cooperation," *Collected Papers, 4,* 51–58; Moore, "Law and Organization," *Collected Papers, 2,* 226–45.

13. House MSS Diary, Sept. 5, 1917, and Sept. 28, 1917, Yale.

community. It was apparently no very complicated chore for House to choose his first lieutenant, for by the end of the month the decision was made. The man designated to organize and assume actual direction would necessarily be a man whom House could trust implicitly. He would likewise have at least some qualifications in college-university administration. Curiously enough (but perhaps not so unlikely to those acquainted with House's career), the position was offered to a member of House's family, Sidney E. Mezes, then president of the City College of New York. Though Mezes' special qualifications were somewhat remote from international relations—he was a philosopher of religion—his administrative experience as dean and president of the University of Texas before coming to New York was expected to stand him well in the new work. If Woodrow Wilson still maintained scruples regarding nepotism, as his Secretary of the Navy Josephus Daniels later asserted,[14] they did not extend to the family of the President's confidant.[15] One son-in-law, Gordon Auchincloss, was at this time serving as Assistant to the Counselor of the State Department. Now Mezes, a brother-in-law (the husband of Mrs. House's sister) would administer and in effect direct the preparations for peace.

There were numerous candidates for positions with House's organization. At the time President Wilson approved of Mezes, he urged the Colonel to procure Walter Lippmann, youthful assistant to Secretary of War Newton D. Baker. From Felix Frankfurter, House heard of Wolcott H. Pitkin, then American political adviser to the Siamese government. Pitkin, according to Frankfurter, "was the one man in all the world who was most fitted for this kind of work." [16] With customary perception, House "looked over" Archibald Cary Coolidge, professor of Eastern European history at Harvard. Meanwhile, Croly was pushing James T. Shotwell, historian at Columbia University, then directing the Na-

14. Josephus Daniels, *The Wilson Era 1910–1917* (Chapel Hill, 1944), p. 359. Cf. Eleanor Wilson McAdoo, *The Woodrow Wilsons* (New York, 1937), p. 275.

15. Wilson to House, Sept. 24, 1917, Ray Stannard Baker MSS, Series I, Library of Congress. The President wrote: "I do not think that anyone could reasonably criticize your associating President Mezes with you . . . you certainly can do the work best with the assistance of men you know and trust."

16. Quoted in William Phillips to House, Oct. 6, 1917, House MSS, Yale.

tional Board for Historical Services, a wartime adjunct of the American Historical Association.[17] These men, considered in September, were all to become key members of the House commission.

Throughout all the conferences and conversations that accompanied his efforts, House assiduously avoided publicity. False optimism on the part of the public might follow should the news of the new organization leak to the press. Special precautions were therefore imposed to guard any knowledge of House's special assignment from getting out of control. Peace was always desirable copy for the press regardless of whether it was news or simply rumor. Was there really any possibility of maintaining the secret when so many persons not bound by the strict rules of the game became aware of the new project? At last one of these persons talked to a reporter, and the balloon burst. On September 27, Lincoln Colcord, Washington staff correspondent for the *Philadelphia Public Ledger,* created a sensation whose reverberation echoed across the continent and across the ocean. In part, Colcord's dispatch read:

> As is well known, both France and Great Britain have for some time been making active preparations in their own behalf for the Peace Conference. Many letters corroborating this fact have been received in important quarters in America during the last few months. It may safely be assumed that other and perhaps all of the belligerent governments in Europe are making their own preparations for the Peace Conference. Of course, there is nothing in these activities incompatible with the heartiest possible support of the war.
>
> Thus there has lately been felt to be a growing need in America for a series of similar activities unless we are to be greatly handicapped at the Peace Conference when it comes. In quarters where this need has been duly appreciated the knowledge that President Wilson has requested Colonel E. M. House to organize and direct American activities in this field meets with the most unqualified approval.[18]

For several days, news concerning America's sudden awareness of the necessity to plan in advance of the peace conference was splashed on front pages in metropolitan newspapers across the

17. Herbert Croly to House, Sept. 28, 1917, House MSS, Yale.
18. *Philadelphia Public Ledger,* Sept. 26, 1917.

United States and even in some foreign journals.[19] Denials, rumors, versions of interviews with House and with leaders at the State Department were all printed in turn.

Noticeably shaken by this unsolicited publicity, President Wilson immediately dispatched a protest to H. B. Brougham, editor of the *Public Ledger*. The danger, Wilson charged, with announcing the government's intention to begin the preparatory activity was that many readers might regard this action as signifying the official contemplation of an imminent end to the war. He underscored this by urging that a moratorium on all peace discussion be observed by the press for the best interests of the nation.[20] In contrast to the President's reaction, House and his son-in-law, Gordon Auchincloss, regarded the publicity as in no way injurious. Except for annoyances stemming from newspapermen prying for additional details, Colonel House saw in the unexpected publicity a most prudent technique for publicizing the President's plan. Auchincloss even speculated on how the publicity would quash rumors which might otherwise rise to the surface and disrupt American efforts to prepare for the peace settlement.[21]

Myths vied with facts in filling newspaper accounts. Ignace Paderewski, the Polish nationalist leader, was openly identified and associated with House's new assignment. Justice Louis Brandeis was said to be House's right-hand man. Rumors and more rumors made the rounds. In general, the editorial verdict well-nigh unanimously applauded the President's course. Those few "pro-German" newspapers, as House termed the opposition, though possibly slanting the news in order to jeopardize the nation's war effort, as many patriots claimed, did not succeed in the attempt.

19. *Chicago Evening American*, Sept. 28, 1917, p. 2; *New York Times*, Sept. 29, 1917, p. 1; *Los Angeles Evening Express*, Sept. 29, 1917, p. 1; *New York American*, Sept. 29, 1917, p. 1; *Chicago Examiner*, Sept. 29, 1917, p. 2; *Chicago Tribune*, Sept. 30, 1917, p. 1; *The Times* (London), Sept. 29, 1917, p. 5b.

20. Wilson to Brougham, Sept. 29, 1917, Wilson MSS, Series II, Library of Congress; also quoted in Ray Stannard Baker, *Life and Letters of Woodrow Wilson* (Garden City, 1922–23), 7, 287.

21. House to Wilson, Oct. 3, 1917, Wilson MSS, Series II; Gordon Auchincloss MSS Diary, Sept. 28, 1917, Yale. As a result of the publicity, House told Wilson, "the Jews from every tribe have descended in force, they seem determined to break in with a jimmy if they are not let in." According to House, the news leaked through Felix Frankfurter to William Bullitt of the *Philadelphia Public Ledger*.

The *New York Sun's* charge that Lansing had been kept ignorant of the President's decision could well be attributed to the manner in which the State Department casually denied the report at the outset.[22] From England, Ambassador Page wrote Lansing:

> the newspaper notice of House's quest for peace data . . . caused a little shudder here in spite of your explanation and his that it had no reference to making peace now but only to collecting information for the peace conference. Peace isn't a popular word here especially since London is now in the firing line.[23]

Though the publicity struck with surprising impact, by the end of October a calm had settled. The news had spent itself quickly, and there was barely a flicker pertaining to House's organization to be found in the nation's press during the balance of the war.

Publicity or no publicity, House and his lieutenants endeavored to keep the new organization and its staff hidden from the eyes of the curious. Headquarters were located, innocently enough, at the New York City Public Library, and were known only to the head librarian and one associate. Some name which would identify the organization for the initiated while at the same time pass unnoticed before the uninformed ear or eye was sought. Several were suggested, and before the end of October, the perfectly bland title, "The Inquiry," was adopted. James T. Shotwell, who took credit for suggesting the name, explained that it provided a "blind to the general public, but would serve to identify it among the initiated." When in November 1917 the Inquiry's headquarters moved to larger offices, at the American Geographical Society on Broadway at West 155th Street, Shotwell remembered that so much secrecy pervaded the move that Director Isaiah Bowman of the Society even decided against informing his entire Board of Directors about the new tenants. Secrecy brought in its wake guards, night watchmen, codes, and the customary cloak-and-dagger tensions.[24]

22. House MSS Diary, Oct. 3, 1917, Yale.

23. *Papers Relating to the Foreign Relations of the United States, The Lansing Papers* (Washington, 1939), 2, 47–48.

24. James T. Shotwell, *At the Paris Peace Conference* (New York, 1937), pp. 6–8.

The initial splash in the newspapers brought one definite by-product. A tide of letters arrived with scores of applications. Colonel House was literally besieged with office seekers. Democratic ward leaders, attorneys self-conscious about being left out of war work, and well-wishers desiring to join in the excitement were but a few representative types who solicited employment. Fairly typical was the application of D. C. Imboden, conveyed to Colonel House on October 1:

> I would be pleased to be your right hand man or one of your aides in your new work as I feel well qualified for same and I have the spirit of and love such work.
> Am initiator and organizer, and consider myself a close investigator of actual facts and of an analytical mind.
> The war, however, has upset my real estate business so that now my income is dependent upon my personal efforts.[25]

Another applicant was Barry Murphy, "a young man up the state who for many years has been active in Democratic politics"—so ran a letter from Robert Adamson of the New York City Fire Department in recommending "one of the best informed and energetic men in New York State." [26] Fortunately a good many letters from able scholars also arrived in response to the press notices. Had there been no newspaper spotlight, it is possible that such men as George Louis Beer, Manley O. Hudson, Sidney Fay, Henryk Arctowski, Stanley Hornbeck, Raphael Zon, and James McGuire would not so soon have come to the Inquiry's attention. Each of these men, reading in his newspaper about the formation of the commission, sent in an application and ultimately became associated with the Inquiry. George L. Beer's letter might be described as typical of letters written by scholars seeking service with House's organization:

> It is with some hesitation that I am writing these lines, but I trust that you will not misinterpret their motives. Briefly, I should like to offer you my services in the important work that you are now undertaking. I have for years been a student of these prob-

25. D. C. Imboden to House, Oct. 1, 1917, Mezes MSS, Columbia. Scores of application letters are to be found in the Mezes MSS and in the Inquiry Archives, National Archives.

26. Letter from Robert Adamson to House, Oct. 5, 1917, Mezes MSS, Columbia.

lems, and, since 1914, I have devoted my entire time to the questions involved in the war. I have followed the literature of the subject—books, magazines and press—very closely and have a good working knowledge of modern languages, French, German, and Italian. I should appreciate it very much if you could grant me the favor of an interview to discuss this matter. In this connection also allow me to point out that this offer of service is entirely independent of any question of remuneration. I am quite free to devote my entire time to this work regardless of compensation.

A letter from Henryk Arctowski asked specifically for the opportunity to "render good service in collecting and preparing the data concerning Poland and should like to have this work assigned to me . . ." And there was yet another kind of academic letter whose writer saw in the Inquiry the opportunity to place his son in patriotic service. President Edmund J. James of the University of Illinois wrote to Sidney Mezes in January 1918:

> I hope you won't forget if you see some good opportunity for a fellow to do an important service in the present great conflict, that my son, whom you know down in Texas, is a fellow equal to a job of that kind. He is practically out of the draft call. He is now over thirty-one, and owing to his being married and having a child, both wife and child being dependent upon him for support, he would go into the fourth class, I am quite sure. He is really anxious to do his bit in the war. He is doing it of course now, for I take it that every man who is helping to keep things steady in a patriotic spirit is doing an important work. But it is natural for a youngish fellow like him to want to be doing something which would be classed in the public mind with war work.[27]

Though Mezes responded politely to the request of a fellow college president, young James did not become associated with the Inquiry.

During October and November, the organizations of professional scholars placed their facilities and personnel at the disposal

27. For letters regarding employment, see Edmund James to Mezes, Jan. 13, 1918, Mezes MSS; George L. Beer to House, Sept. 29, 1917, House MSS, file 2-20, Yale; Henryk Arctowski to House, Sept. 29, 1917, Inquiry Archives; Sidney Fay to House, Sept. 29, 1917, Inquiry Archives; Raphael Zon to Walter Lippmann, Oct. 11, 1917, Inquiry Archives. There are about 80 letters of application to be found among the House MSS, Mezes MSS, and the Inquiry Archives.

of the Inquiry: the American Economics Association, the American Geographical Society, and the National Board for Historical Services. John R. Commons, president of the American Economics Association, learned about the American preparations for peace through the newspapers. He quickly notified Colonel House of the existence of a registry of American economists indicating their qualifications and special interests. Originally intended for the Civil Service Commission, the registry would be made available to House and his staff.[28] Isaiah Bowman, besides placing the third floor of the American Geographical Society Building at the disposal of the Inquiry, also offered his own personal services.[29] Bowman's generous donation was actually a boon for the Inquiry, for it provided spacious accommodations in an institutional setting camouflaged from prying reporters and unauthorized observers. Much of the fine map work performed by the Inquiry was created in the Society's laboratory, the work of the Society's cartographers. Bowman, too, served as an executive officer under Mezes, and eventually assumed practical leadership when Mezes lost effective control during the summer of 1918. The contribution from the American Geographical Society proved decisive for the Inquiry's entire program.

The National Board for Historical Services had been born on April 28, 1917 with a view to meeting the desire of American historians to "render useful public service during the war." Founded by John Franklin Jameson, then Director of Historical Research for the Carnegie Institution, the Board had three objectives: (1) to provide a means for placing the historical scholarship of the country at the disposal of the government; (2) to utilize historical scholarship for patriotic and educational ends, thus enlightening the general population on the issues confronting the nation; (3) to collect and preserve historical materials related to the war.[30] James T. Shotwell, chairman of the National Board (henceforth

28. John R. Commons to House, Oct. 1, 1917, Inquiry Archives.

29. John K. Wright, *Geography in the Making: The American Geographical Society 1851–1951* (New York, 1952), p. 199.

30. *Annual Report of the American Historical Association for the Year 1919*, 1, 161–70.

abbreviated to NBHS), also functioned as a member of the Inquiry. It was through Shotwell that the NBHS channeled its assistance to the efforts on behalf of peace.

On November 9, when the Executive Committee of the NBHS convened, Shotwell requested the group's assistance in the work of the Inquiry. He noted that publicity must be avoided, told his colleagues about the purposes and problems confronting the House commission, and appealed for recommendations on personnel. The upshot of this discussion was the formation of an advisory committee consisting of Frederick Jackson Turner of Harvard, William E. Dodd of Chicago, and William Dunning of Columbia. These men would meet periodically with officers of the Inquiry. Like the Geographical Society and the Economics Association in their respective disciplines, the NBHS operated as an advisory agency for the Inquiry's historical projects.[31]

As an institutional organism, the Inquiry grew slowly. During its earliest months it is difficult to know for certain how many persons were engaged in its activities. Personnel records and financial records were not maintained as efficiently as they were later. No classification of personnel according to the special tasks assigned was attempted before January 1918. That month, there were thirty-five persons on the research staff drawing salaries. Another sixteen persons working on research assignments were without salaries. This made a total of fifty-one research members of the Inquiry. At its maximum size, in October 1918, when personnel records were kept accurately, the Inquiry's roll, as carried on the official account books, numbered 126 executives and research collaborators (a term used extensively in the correspondence) and their assistants.[32]

The number 126 may or may not be significant, but breaking it into its component parts gives it additional meaning. The 126 persons were apportioned among the several research projects in this manner:

31. Shotwell to William E. Dodd, Dec. 10, 1917, Dodd MSS, Library of Congress.

32. Inquiry Account Book for October 1918, David Hunter Miller MSS, Library of Congress.

Project	No. of workers	Project	No. of workers
International law	8	Russia and Eastern Europe	15
Africa	4	Pacific Islands	1
Diplomatic history	14	Italy	1
Austria-Hungary	6½	Western Europe	5
Balkans	4½	Latin America	12
Far East	3	General research	10
Economics	6	Cartography	17
Western Asia	5	Reference and archives	11
		Executives	3

This allocation of personnel suggests that, despite what might be described as the presumed overwhelming importance of European questions in the eventual peace settlement, Europe was the unwanted stepchild in the Inquiry's family. Compared to the twelve persons assigned to the Latin American Division, only one person was formally responsible for studying the difficult problems of Italy. There was no division as such handling the complicated aspects of postwar German questions. That is not to suggest the Inquiry neglected Germany and Italy completely; rather, in terms of the distribution of personnel, the Inquiry seemed to focus attention on Latin America, Russia, and Eastern Europe at the expense of Central and Western Europe. Those very large auxiliary and technical projects—diplomatic history, reference and archives, and cartography—together accounted for forty-two persons, considerably better than one-third of the total staff. Fifty-seven persons were assigned to regional divisions, twelve of them in Latin American research. It should be borne in mind that members were not always assigned exclusively to tasks in a single division as the table implies. George Louis Beer, who concentrated chiefly on African problems, also studied the Pacific Islands. Clive Day's responsibilities spread from the Balkans to Austria to Western Europe, and he even contributed a report having to do with the commerce of the Dutch East Indies. Samuel Eliot Morison studied Finland, Estonia, and Italy. Ellen Churchill Semple conducted studies of the Austro-Italian frontier and then proceeded to study frontier conditions in the Middle East. Yet aside from these apparent exceptions the Account Book does afford some basis for a general classification of the Inquiry's personnel.

The procurement of qualified personnel was always one of the most serious problems confronting the Inquiry's officers during its entire life. Gradually, as the organization's duties enlarged, the scope of the preparatory work literally covered the globe with the exception of the arctic and antarctic recesses. Maps, charts, press translations, and innumerable reports touching on political, economic, social, and geographical aspects necessitated the hiring of a task force large enough to cope with the many complicated questions. Early in December 1917, Walter Lippmann optimistically had reported to his former chief, Secretary of War Baker, about the procurement of personnel, as follows:

> We are skimming the cream of the younger and more imaginative scholars, and although we have picked only on merit, it so happens that we are drawing on every section of the country. We have moved with greatest caution to avoid all publicity and yet when the work is done, I am confident that no important center of scholarship will be able to say it has not been allowed to contribute.[33]

Lippmann's statement did not entirely accord with the facts. Certainly, of the more productive members of the Inquiry listed on pages 53–68 below, the vast majority (about 65 per cent) were persons who had achieved their terminal academic degrees at just four institutions: Harvard, Columbia, Yale, and Chicago. And when it came to choosing personnel for the Inquiry, at least 50 per cent were recruited directly from five institutions: Harvard, Yale, Columbia, Princeton, and the American Geographical Society. It could therefore be presumed that some sections of the country were very definitely underrepresented in the enterprise. Virtually no representation was included from southern institutions, and institutions in the Middle West and Far West were not far from the bottom of the list. Lippmann's important centers of scholarship would have to be defined to encompass only a few private eastern universities. Six months later, in May 1918, the recruiting drive was not going so well, and Lippmann was pre-

33. Walter Lippmann to Newton D. Baker, Dec. 5, 1917, Newton D. Baker MSS, Library of Congress.

pared to confess how difficult was the task of discovering qualified talent:

> On many of the problems of first rate importance there is a real famine in men and we have been compelled practically to train and create our own experts. This is especially true of problems connected with Russia, the Balkans, Turkey and Africa. Those are lands intellectually practically unexplored. What we are on the lookout for is genius—sheer, startling genius and nothing else will do because the real application of the President's idea to those countries requires inventiveness and resourcefulness which is scarcer than anything. I have been reading lately with much perturbation about the way in which ignorance on the part of peace commissioners in the past has lost causes which have been won on the battlefield. It isn't difficult to win a war and lose the peace. England did it over and over again in the nineteenth century in regard to Turkey.[34]

What seemed bold, adventurous, and even simple at the outset changed after a few months to a sober realization of the magnitude of the task involved. The long years of isolation had left a heritage of ignorance which the United States found difficult to overcome in its new role as a great power.

Experts—men whose previous training and experience, publications, and teaching had developed in them certain highly specialized knowledge—there certainly were on the Inquiry's staff, though relatively few members of the Inquiry could at the outset have qualified as experts in the respective fields assigned them in the work of the Inquiry. A decade afterward, when Inquiry alumni met in reunion or gathered their recollections into volumes of memoirs, the tendency to exaggerate the intellectual prowess of members within the organization was pronounced. Men whose later reputations distinguished them in academic circles often observed that their reputations were antedated by the many writers who described the arrangements for peace.[35] Intellectual qualifi-

34. Lippmann to Baker, May 16, 1918, *Papers Relating to the Foreign Relations of the United States, Paris Peace Conference,* 1, 97–98.

35. Shotwell, *At the Paris Peace Conference,* Chap. I; Sidney E. Mezes, "The Inquiry," in *What Really Happened at Paris,* ed. Edward M. House and Charles Seymour (New York, 1921), Chap. I, are typical. See also George Creel, *The War, The World, and Wilson* (New York, 1920), pp. 157–59; H. W. V. Temperley, ed., *A History of the Peace Conference at Paris* (London, 1920–24), 1, 239–40.

cations are, however, relative. Judging from the abundant correspondence regarding personnel found in the Inquiry's archives, intellectual qualifications of prospective members were scrutinized by those officers who controlled the organization, but other factors also figured in the selection of personnel. Political affiliations or biases that cropped up from the applicant's background were definitely considered; a vigorous pacifist or socialist, an articulate opponent of the administration, anyone possessing a record attacking the nation's war effort or the President's pronouncements on the subject of future peace stood little chance to enter the membership. Ordinarily, the Inquiry did include Republicans (George Louis Beer, for instance, had listed himself in *Who's Who in America* as a Republican) as well as Democrats; within limitations, preparations for peace were not viewed as a partisan cause. Men were sought whose experience in research could be described as generally successful even though it had not focused squarely on the specific problem to be treated by the Inquiry. It also helped to have some friend or colleague already on the staff.

Following the initial period of organization, Colonel House and President Wilson only rarely interfered in matters affecting personnel. Appointments were handled by decision of the Executive Committee, usually acting on the advice of the particular division chairman with whom the neophyte would work. This meant, in practice, that personal contacts, previous professional or social connections, and institutional ties might prove decisive in the selection of personnel. Virtually the entire Latin American staff, for instance, had worked previously for Bowman at Yale or had served under him in one of his Latin American expeditions or was presently employed by the American Geographical Society of which he was director. The Inquiry's correspondence is replete with instances of members who brought in colleagues and friends rather than attempt seriously to comb American academic institutions in search of the best qualified talent.

To direct and administer the Inquiry, Colonel House chose a versatile quintet. Director Mezes, philosopher of religion and ethics, had risen through the ranks of university administration for fifteen years. In no sense, however, could Mezes be regarded as having a mind steeped in the study of international relations, and herein lay his most serious deficiency.[36] House might well have canvassed the field further in order to find an administrator who also had some broad knowledge of the subjects which the Inquiry would be treating. A sharp contrast to the often equivocal Mezes, Isaiah Bowman possessed a well-nigh authoritarian personality. With the passing months, his dominant leadership came to arrogate more and more of the responsibilities from the less confident Mezes. Bowman, a native of Canada (he was undoubtedly an American citizen in 1917 since his parents were "American stock" and he had spent his early years in Michigan), was a professional geographer who had taken the helm of the American Geographical Society in 1915. Alone among the Inquiry's leadership, Bowman's special interest had centered on Latin America and cartography as both writer of several monographs concerning that continent and leader of two scientific expeditions there. Perhaps his one personal triumph, if it can be so called, was the Inquiry's excursion into Latin American research. It was probably no coincidence that as Bowman's influence ascended in the Inquiry during 1918, the organization became steadily more immersed in Latin American research projects.

A third contrast in interests and temperament was the secretary, Walter Lippmann—youthful, dynamic, and quite intolerant of the painstaking detailed work involved in research. Whereas Mezes and Bowman were 54 and 39 years old respectively when the Inquiry was formed, Lippmann was a mere 28. In his undergraduate years at Harvard, Lippmann had delved deeply into politics and philosophy, and was already the author of three books concerned with politics and foreign relations. His forte, writing, combined with a liberal bent, had led him to associate with Herbert Croly in editing the *New Republic* when the liberal journal was founded in 1914. The war had brought Lippmann into government service first when he served as special assistant to the Secretary of War. His tenure on the Inquiry was cut short

36. For observations regarding Mezes, see Stephen Duggan, *A Professor at Large*, (New York, 1943), pp. 14–17. Duggan was a professor at the City College of New York where he was familiar with Mezes through the latter's connections both with the City College and with the Inquiry.

in the spring of 1918 when he resigned to take an overseas assignment with American military intelligence.

James T. Shotwell at 43 years of age was an anomaly among the Inquiry's officers. He came to the organization in the capacity of director of research with an extensive background in the general problems expected to confront the new organization. Since 1908, he had served on the history faculty at Columbia, and since about 1910 had been offering some courses in contemporary history. Years later, Shotwell reflected how his teaching of contemporary history had actually proved the decisive factor in his selection to serve on the Inquiry.[37] His Canadian birth might have been a disadvantage, but insofar as he could later recall there had been no criticism against allowing him to supervise the Inquiry's British Empire projects. The bulging Inquiry archives show the deep imprint which Shotwell carved on the preparations for peace. His hundreds of letters to scholars everywhere seeking their advice or services; his blunt critiques of Inquiry reports; his contributions to the administrative organization, and especially to the library, are all monuments to his gargantuan effort.

Qualifications or no qualifications, some members of the Inquiry applied themselves and learned their assignments well. At 42 years of age, David Hunter Miller had been a lawyer in New York. Miller's dive into the public arena had been facilitated by his law partnership with Gordon Auchincloss, Colonel House's son-in-law, forming the firm Miller and Auchincloss. Throughout the existence of the Inquiry, Miller served not merely as treasurer-keeper of the financial accounts, but also as major contributor in the Division of International Law. Here Miller served both the Inquiry and the Department of State in which he became employed early in 1917. Yet, despite these considerable responsibilities, Miller's record before 1917 had not been distinguished in the field of international studies. His chief asset was an uncommon ability to draft legal memoranda with artful polish; this, incidentally, had been the talent Colonel House had sought to capture for the Inquiry. When, after the war, the Senate Foreign Relations Committee started investigating the arrangements for

37. Author's conversation with Shotwell, early December 1954.

peace in the United States, Miller was called to testify. On that occasion, referring to his legal background prior to 1917, he asserted:

> MILLER: I have been connected with the State Department since the United States went into the war, or shortly afterwards . . . as special assistant in the Department of State. [Prior to 1917] I had a general practice in New York. To some extent it was European . . .
>
> SENATOR BRANDEGEE: Had you personally had any special experience as an international lawyer representing governments before commissions, making treaties or anything of that kind?
>
> MILLER: Not prior to my entrance into the State Department.[38]

These five men were, in effect, the Inquiry's personnel in microcosm. Their diverse interests, ages, and qualifications were reflected in the larger group. It was the drive, the spirit, the perseverance, the imagination which these five shared that stamped the Inquiry with a unique personality, an *esprit de corp* which endured in the minds of some members long after the peace settlement had brought the Inquiry to an end.

Any consideration of the rank-and-file personnel might logically revolve about each of the major divisions of the Inquiry.[39] It should be remembered that personnel attached to a given division was sometimes moved about to other divisions as the work required. There were likewise frequent changes, both drops and additions, in personnel from month to month. For the purposes of the following analysis of personnel, May 1918 and October 1918 are considered base months. As of May 1918, there were some sixty-three research-administrative members of the staff; in October 1918, the staff had doubled.[40] This analysis includes only those members who made substantial contributions and omits all persons whose relation to the Inquiry was strictly ephemeral. It is limited to those members who were carried on the organization's books during *either* May *or* October 1918, *and* who actually

38. 66th Congress, 1st Session, *Senate Document No. 106*, p. 385.

39. This organization is described in Mezes, "The Inquiry," in *What Really Happened at Paris*, p. 7.

40. All detailed personnel records are located in the David Hunter Miller MSS, Library of Congress.

submitted at least two reports. (One exception, however, has been made. William Lunt, in charge of the preparations with regard to Italy, has been included even though he completed but a single report.) Attention is concentrated upon the intellectual qualifications and experience brought by the members to their Inquiry assignments. Nativity is mentioned only where the individual concerned was not born in the United States. When such individuals did reside in the United States for at least five years prior to their Inquiry service, the presumption of American citizenship is made in the absence of evidence to the contrary. Such additional factors as age, terminal academic degree, position held at the time when he (or she) joined the Inquiry, and principal books published before 1918 are likewise included.

Northwest Europe, encompassing France, Western Germany, the Low Countries, and even Italy during the early months of the Inquiry, received the attention of five persons. Charles H. Haskins supervised the work of the division.[41]

Charles H. Haskins. Age 47. PhD., Johns Hopkins, 1890. Had specialized in American history as a graduate student. Was professor of medieval history and dean of the Harvard Graduate School at the time he joined the Inquiry. Published works before 1918 included several studies of the medieval church, medieval Latin literature, and medieval universities, and of the Renaissance.

Wallace Notestein. Age 39. Ph.D., Yale, 1908. Was professor of English history at the University of Minnesota at the time he joined the Inquiry. Books published before 1918: *History of English Witchcraft* (1913); *Source Problems in English History* (1915). Special assignments for the Inquiry were related to Alsace-Lorraine.

Lawrence Steefel. Age 23. A.M., Harvard, 1917. Was graduate student in German history at Harvard at the time he joined the Inquiry. No published volumes before 1918. Special work for the Inquiry concerned Luxembourg and North Schleswig.

Edward Krehbiel. Age 39. Ph. D., Chicago, 1906. Was professor of European history at Stanford at the time he joined the Inquiry. Books published before 1918: *The Interdict* (1909); *Syllabus of Lectures on International Conciliation* (1912); *Geographic In-*

---

41. Biographical data included in the personnel survey were obtained from the several volumes of *Who's Who in America* for the years after 1918 and from the *Directory of American Scholars* unless otherwise stated.

fluences on British Elections (1916). Major assignments with the Inquiry were concerned with possible plebiscites in Western Europe.

Hetty Goldman. Age 36. Ph.D., Radcliffe, 1916. Was excavator in Greek antiquities at the time she joined the Inquiry. Had specialized in Greek classical studies. No books published before 1918. Assignments with the Inquiry concerned Alsace-Lorraine.

It would seem that the major problem which the Inquiry expected to encounter in Western Europe was to be Alsace-Lorraine; three of the division's five members were engaged in studying these provinces. Only Krehbiel among this group had had intimate experience and study in the recent history of Western Europe. Prior to 1917, only Krehbiel had acquired any reputation as a specialist in the assigned subject. Charles Haskins, too much a scholar to boast of his expertness in twentieth-century problems, continuously lamented his inability to handle a vast assortment of problems when he began his association with the Inquiry.[42] Unlike some members of the organization, Haskins was alive to the fact that vast changes had shaped Western Europe over the centuries and hence a medievalist or classicist could not claim expert knowledge of a period so remote from his special interest. Hetty Goldman had just returned from several years of field work in Greece when she received her assignment with the Inquiry.[43]

In charge of the Eastern European Division, comprising Russia and its European provinces, was Archibald Cary Coolidge. After April 1918, when Coolidge went overseas, his place was taken by Robert H. Lord.

Archibald Cary Coolidge. Age 51. Ph. D., University of Freiburg, 1892. Studied in Paris and Berlin. Was professor of Eastern European and Middle Eastern history at Harvard at the time he joined the Inquiry. Books published before 1918: *The United States as a World Power* (1917); *The Origins of the Triple Alliance* (1917).

42. Haskins to Shotwell, Dec. 7, 1917; Haskins to Shotwell, Dec. 8, 1917; Archibald Cary Coolidge to Shotwell, Nov. 20, 1917, all in the Inquiry Archives.

43. Robert Lord to Walter Lippmann, June 12, 1918, Inquiry Archives: "Professor Ferguson has recently received a letter from Miss Goldman of Greece. Professor Ferguson has a high opinion of her work and wishes to take advantage of her good will, but thinks that it would be more desirable to transfer her work to another field."

Robert H. Lord. Age 32. Ph.D., Harvard, 1910. Had studied in Vienna, Berlin, and Moscow. At the time he joined the Inquiry was assistant professor of modern European history at Harvard. Specialty was Polish history. Book published before 1918: *The Second Partition of Poland* (1915). Special assignment with the Inquiry concerned Poland.

F. A. Golder. Age 40. Ph.D., Harvard, 1909. Had studied in Berlin and Paris. At the time he joined the Inquiry was professor of history at the State College of Washington (Pullman). Had conducted investigations in the Russian Archives for the Carnegie Institution during 1914–15 and early 1917. Published volumes before 1918: *Russian Expansion on the Pacific* (1914); *Guide to the Materials for American History in Russian Archives* (1917). Assignments for the Inquiry concerned the Baltic provinces and Siberia.

Sidney Fay. Age 41. Ph.D., Harvard, 1900. Studied in Paris and Berlin. At the time he joined the Inquiry was professor of modern history at Smith College. Published volumes before 1918: *A History Syllabus for Secondary Schools* (1904); *The Records of the Town of Hanover, N.H., 1761–1818* (1905). Special assignment for the Inquiry concerned the Baltic provinces and a brief report on the German colonies in Africa.

Henryk Arctowski. Age 46. Native of Poland. Had been living in the United States since 1911, and so was probably a U.S. citizen in 1917. Ph.D., University of Lemberg, 1912. Entire education in European universities. Was specially interested in geology. Had been in charge of the Belgian Antarctic Expedition of 1897–99. At the time he joined the Inquiry was chief of the Science Division, New York Public Library. Special assignments for the Inquiry concerned population problems of Poland. No published books before 1918.

I. M. Rubinow. Age 42. Native of Russia. Was probably a U.S. citizen by 1917. Ph.D., Columbia, 1914. Special interest was in the field of economic statistics. At the time he joined the Inquiry was statistician for the Department of Public Charities, City of New York. Books published before 1918: *Russia's Wheat Surplus* (1906); *Russia's Wheat Trade* (1908); *The Economic Condition of the Jews in Russia* (1908); *Social Insurance* (1913); *Was Marx Wrong?* (1914). Special assignment for the Inquiry concerned Russian economic problems.

Samuel E. Morison. Age 30. Ph.D., Harvard, 1912. At the time he joined the Inquiry was instructor in history, Harvard. Published volume before 1918: *Life of Harrison Gray Otis* (1913). Special interest had been in American history. Major assignments for the Inquiry concerned Finland and the Baltic states.

Vladimir G. Simkhovitch. Age 43. Native of Russia. Ph.D., Halle, 1898. At the time he joined the Inquiry was professor of economic history at Columbia. Book published before 1918: *Marxism versus Socialism* (1913). Work for the Inquiry consisted of producing studies of the western province of Russia; criticizing a variety of reports submitted by other persons; and supervising the Reference and Archives section of the organization.

This Eastern European Division included some of the best qualified persons on the Inquiry's staff. Coolidge had been the pioneer scholar in the field of Eastern European studies in the United States. Over many years, he had gained a facility with Slavic and Middle Eastern languages.[44] Golder and Rubinow, because of their European backgrounds, possessed not only linguistic tools but shared an intimate knowledge of the lands they were studying which could hardly be duplicated by an American, however brilliant and informed, who had never ventured into Eastern Europe. Arctowski, too, had the European background, but his highly specialized training in the sciences could hardly be expected to qualify him as an expert in political matters. His background was, however, ideally suited to deal with the complicated mineral problems of Silesia and Poland. Samuel Eliot Morison was to handle the question of Finland, and although his excellent training in American history could certainly have proven advantageous for various branches of historical research, it is indeed a far cry from American to Baltic studies. Coolidge, who had been mainly responsible for bringing together this coterie, seemed confident that he had recruited at least some of the best students for this work. He once said of F. A. Golder:

> I have not thought of any man better than Golder for Russia. He is a very conscientious worker and has been in the country recently. He has also worked in Washington and would know how to get at statistics that are there if need be.[45]

44. Harold J. Coolidge, *Archibald Cary Coolidge, Life and Letters* (Boston, 1932), pp. 158, 172–74, 193–99.

45. Coolidge to Shotwell, Nov. 3, 1917, Inquiry Archives; Charles Seymour to Clive Day, Oct. 29, 1918, House Inquiry MSS, file 33-161, Yale.

Austria-Hungary and Italy were treated by four members of the Inquiry family whose previous training and other qualifications varied considerably. Charles Seymour was placed in charge of the division.

Charles Seymour. Age 32. Ph.D., Yale, 1911. Was assistant professor of history at Yale when he joined the Inquiry. Had published before 1918: *Electoral Reform in England and Wales* (1915); *The Diplomatic Background of the War* (1916); and *How The World Votes* (1918). Special assignments for the Inquiry concerned nationalist problems within the Austrian Empire.

Robert J. Kerner. Age 30. Ph.D., Harvard 1914. Had studied and traveled in Austria, Germany, Russia, and France, 1912–14. At the time he joined the Inquiry was teaching modern European history at the University of Missouri. Author of the following volumes before 1918: *The Foundations of Slavic Bibliography* (1916); *The Jugoslav Movement* (1918). Credited with a facility in all principal Balkan languages plus French and German. Special Inquiry assignments emphasized nationalist problems within the Austrian Empire.

William E. Lunt. Age 35. Ph.D., Harvard, 1908. Traveled in Europe on a Harvard Fellowship in 1907–08 and 1911. Was professor of English history at Cornell at the time he joined the Inquiry. Had specialized in English medieval history. No books published before 1918. Had acquired some knowledge of the Italian language through early studies in Italy of Anglo-papal relations during the medieval period.[46] Special work for the Inquiry concerned Italy.

Austin P. Evans. Age 34. Ph.D., Cornell, 1916. Special interest was in medieval history. Was instructor of medieval history at Columbia when he joined the Inquiry. Author of several works on medieval history published before 1918. Assignments for the Inquiry concerned Austro-Italian frontier claims.

Of these four, only Kerner and Seymour presumably possessed sufficient specialized knowledge to qualify as experts on those Inquiry projects for which they were responsible. Throughout his tenure with the Inquiry, Kerner was regarded by his colleagues as predisposed toward the Slavs; at various times when objections were leveled against Kerner because of his strong bias, officers of the Inquiry maintained that Kerner's command of languages

46. Lunt to the author, Oct. 3, 1952.

more than balanced his partisanship.[47] When, in early May of 1918, an attractive opportunity almost enticed Kerner away from the Inquiry to teach at Clark University, the Inquiry's officers decided that he must be retained at all costs. Consequently, besides a substantial advance in salary, Kerner was awarded the singular honor of a written pledge—a pledge which, incidentally, no other member of the Inquiry was to receive:

> So long as the Inquiry continues, you will be a member of it at a salary of $266.66 per month. Colonel House will recommend you to the United States Government for the staff which it is expected the Government will require at the Peace Conference. If the work of the Inquiry will be discontinued, Mr. Lippmann and myself [Isaiah Bowman] will jointly assume the responsibility of securing a position for you which will cover the period up to the end of the academic year, 1918–1919.[48]

Kerner remained and followed up the commitment at the Peace Conference. The choice of Lunt and Evans, two medievalists, for the Italian work was either an indication of some gross underestimation as to the huge dimensions of the Italian question in the peace settlement or of the inability of the Inquiry to find a qualified student of modern Italian history in the United States. At least Evans later confessed to his extreme inadequacy when it came to writing the assigned reports.[49] Insofar as the Austrian-Italian divisions of the Inquiry were concerned, then, there were both experts and "experts."

Balkan Europe was another complex zone for the students engaged in preparations for peace. Clive Day was nominally in charge of personnel engaged in this research.

47. Coolidge to Shotwell, Dec. 8, 1917, Inquiry Archives; Charles Seymour to Clive Day, Oct. 29, 1918, House Inquiry MSS, Yale.

48. Bowman to the Inquiry Executive Committee, May 8, 1918, Inquiry Archives; Bowman to Kerner, no date (but on the reply from Kerner dated May 15, 1918, reference is made to the earlier letter's date as being May 8), Inquiry Archives.

49. Austin Evans to the author, Sept. 25, 1953: "My training was as a medievalist, and this particular job I had to work up from the very foundations. Also I was handicapped by a lack of knowledge of Italian. I submitted it with great reservations and was surprised and embarrassed a good many years later when Professor Lunt remarked to me in conversation that it had been useful in the work which he was doing."

Clive Day. Age 46. Ph.D., Yale, 1899. Studied in Germany and France. Special interest was in economic history. At the time he joined the Inquiry was professor of economic history at Yale. Author of two books published before 1918: *Policy and Administration of Java* (1904); *History of Commerce* (1907). Special assignments for the Inquiry emphasized commercial relations.

Max Handman. Age 32. Studied in France and Germany before receiving Ph.D. at Chicago, 1917. Native of Rumania. Was teaching sociology at the University of Texas at the time he joined the Inquiry. No books published before 1918. Special assignment for the Inquiry concerned Rumania.

William S. Monroe. Age 54. A.B., Stanford, 1894. Studied in Germany and France. Was professor of psychology, New Jersey State Normal School, Montclair, at the time he joined the Inquiry. Special interest had centered on educational psychology in which he had published extensively. Among his publications were a series of travelogues: *Turkey and the Turks* (1907); *In Viking Land* (1908); *Sicily, the Garden of the Mediterranean* (1909); *Bohemia and the Czechs* (1910); *Europe and Its People* (1911); *Bulgaria and Her People* (1914). Special assignments for the Inquiry concerned the political organization and international relations of the Balkans.

Paul Monroe. Age 48. Ph.D., Chicago, 1897. Studied in Germany in 1901. Special interest was in the history of education. Author of numerous studies pertaining to this special interest. At the time he joined the Inquiry was director of the School of Education, Columbia University. Special assignments for the Inquiry concerned educational problems in the Balkans.

Albert Sonnichsen. Age 39. No formal university education. Was newspaper correspondent in the Balkans from 1904–06. At the time he joined the Inquiry was an investigator of Slavic immigrants for the United States Immigration Commission. Published volumes before 1918 included: *Confessions of a Macedonian Bandit* (1909). Special work for the Inquiry concerned Macedonia.

William S. Ferguson. Age 42. Native of Canada. Was not an American citizen at the time he served on the Inquiry. Ph.D., Cornell, 1899. Studied in Germany and Greece during 1899–1900. Had resided and taught in Greece during 1913–14. Special interest was in ancient Greek history. Had published several works pertaining to this special interest. At the time he joined the Inquiry was professor of ancient history at Harvard. Work for the Inquiry concerned problems of Greece in the twentieth century.

Leon Dominian. Age 37. Native of Turkey. Had lived in the United States since at least 1912; hence was probably an American citizen. Had studied at Robert College, Constantinople, and the University of Liége, Belgium. Had traveled and explored in the American West. At the time he joined the Inquiry was a staff member of the American Geographical Society. Special interest was the geography and geology of Europe. Author of one published volume before 1918: *The Frontiers of Language and Nationality in Europe* (1917).

George R. Noyes. Age 44. Ph.D., Harvard, 1898. Studies in Russia during 1898–1900. At the time he joined the Inquiry was professor of classics at California. Special professional interest seemed to be comparative literature. Published volumes before 1918: *Carlyle's Essay on Burns* (1896); *Dryden's Poetic Works* (1909); *Selected Dramas of John Dryden* (1910); *Plays by Alexander Ostrovsky* (1913); *Tolstoy* (1918). Special work for the Inquiry concerned the Balkans.

These eight individuals responsible for reporting on the Balkans were essentially of two types: (1) native Americans drawn from various specialities but whose common qualification was in all cases a period of residence in at least one Balkan country (William S. Monroe's many publications relating to Europe, being in the *genre* of travelogues and written at a one-volume-per-year clip, would not necessarily qualify him as an expert on the area); (2) natives of the Balkan countries who later settled in the United States but whose training and experience had not provided any professional competency for handling or criticizing the source materials. Dominian, as much a scholar as any in this category, was constantly assailed by colleagues who complained of his Greek bias, thus discouraging him from any attempt to achieve scientific objectivity in his reports.

Ten persons formed the Western Asia (Middle East) section of the Inquiry. For much the greater part of the Inquiry's life, Dana C. Munro headed this division. Shortly before the armistice, William L. Westermann was named chief.

Dana C. Munro. Age 51. Had studied in Germany before taking the A.M. at Brown in 1891. Special interest was in medieval studies with some emphasis on the history of the Crusades. At the time he joined the Inquiry was professor of medieval history at Princeton. While a member of the Inquiry, he also served as research assistant to the Committee on Public Information (Creel Committee). Published books before 1918: *Medieval History* (1902); *Essays on the Crusades* (1902); *A Source Book of Roman History* (1904); *Medieval Civilization* (1904); *German War Practices* (1917); *German Treatment of Conquered Territory* (1918).

Dana G. Munro (son of Dana C.). Age 25. Ph.D., University of Pennsylvania, 1917. Special interest was Latin American history and politics. Had studied conditions in Central America under the auspices of the Carnegie Endowment for International Peace during 1914–16. Published books before 1918: *The Five Republics of Central America* (1918). Special work for the Inquiry concerned the organization of the Turkish government.

Arthur I. Andrews. Age 39. Ph.D., Harvard, 1905. At the time he joined the Inquiry was professor of history, Tufts College. No books published before 1918. Special studies for the Inquiry concerned the Transcaucasus.

Royal B. Dixon. Age 42. Ph.D. Harvard, 1900. Special interest focused upon the Indians of North America, but he did possess broad anthropological training. Published volume before 1918: *Oceanic Mythology* (1916). At the time he joined the Inquiry was professor of anthropology at Harvard. Special work for the Inquiry: Middle Asia, Turkestan, Tibet, Mongolia.

Ellen C. Semple. Age 54. A.M., Vassar College, 1893. Had studied in Germany. Special interest was the study of the influence of geographical conditions upon the development of society. Had published several volumes pertaining to anthropogeography before 1918. Special work for the Inquiry concerned Mesopotamia, the partition of Asiatic Turkey, and also the strategic character of the Austro-Italian frontier.

F. H. Newell. Age 55. Graduate of Massachusetts Institute of Technology in Mining Engineering, 1885. Special interest was hydrogeography. At the time he joined the Inquiry was consulting engineer for the U.S. Geological Survey. Author of several volumes before 1918 pertaining to his special interest. For the Inquiry, worked on studies of reclamation and irrigation relating to Asiatic Turkey.

David Magie. Age 40. Ph.D., University of Halle, Germany, 1904. Special interest had been classical civilization. At the time he joined the Inquiry was professor of classics, Princeton. For the Inquiry, assignments concerned Syria and Lebanon.

Abraham V. W. Jackson. Age 55. Ph.D., Columbia, 1886. Had studied in Germany. Special scholarly interest had centered on ancient

Persia. At the time he joined the Inquiry was professor of Indo-Iranian languages at Columbia. Had traveled in India in 1901 and 1911, and to Persia and Central Asia during 1903, 1907, 1910. Published volumes before 1918: *A Hymn of Zoroaster* (1888); *An Avestan Grammar in Comparison with Sanskrit* (1892); *Zoroaster, the Prophet of Ancient Iran* (1899). Inquiry assignment concerned twentieth-century Persia.

L. H. Gray. Age 42. Ph.D., Columbia, 1900. Special interest: ancient Persian linguistics and literature. At the time he joined the Inquiry was chief cataloguer and instructor in Indo-Iranian languages, Princeton. Published volumes before 1918: *The Hundred Love Songs of Kamal ad-Din of Isfahan* (1904); *Translation of a Sanskrit Romance* (1903). Work for the Inquiry concerned the commerce of the Near East, especially the Caucasus region.

William L. Westermann. Age 44. Ph.D., University of Berlin, 1902. Special interest: ancient history. At the time he joined the Inquiry was professor of ancient history, University of Wisconsin. Books published before 1918: *Story of the Ancient Nations* (1912). Work for the Inquiry concerned modern Turkish political administration.

Perhaps more than any other branch of the Inquiry, this division illustrated how the Inquiry's directorate selected men having special knowledge of ancient, classical civilizations and placed on them full responsibility for studies involving contemporary history. D. C. Munro, Jackson, Gray, Magie, and Westermann were authorities, to be sure, but in the Western Asia of at least one millennium preceding the Great War. D. G. Munro had only recently gained a specialized knowledge of Central America, while Ellen Semple's scholarly achievements had extended from studies of North America to the Mediterranean Basin. In later years, Arthur I. Andrews was to recall the words with which Archibald Cary Coolidge ushered him into the Inquiry: "'You know one Mohammedan from another' i.e., from others." [50] Similarly, and with little more rationale, Dana C. Munro very graciously offered gratis to the Inquiry the services of the entire history, politics, and sociology departments at Princeton. With these words, "all are ready to start work immediately without remuneration," Munro introduced these colleagues for employment in the Middle East section of the Inquiry:

50. Quoted in letter from Andrews to the author, dated Sept. 17, 1953.

Prof. W. K. Prentice to cover the field of northern Syria.

Prof. E. S. Corwin, a specialist in constitutional law, to make a study of guarantees of minority rights in Asiatic Turkey.

Prof. Christian Gauss to direct the reading of papers in Princeton Library bearing upon questions at issue. He is head of the modern languages department.

Prof. H. R. Shipman to make a study of English penetration in Western Asia.

Prof. Thomas Jefferson Wertenbaker to make a study of the French penetration of Western Asia.

Prof. R. W. Rogers to cover the general field of Mesopotamia with special reference to America's interest in Mesopotamia.[51]

Munro's offer failed to receive an appreciative response. Apparently the Inquiry directors thought that too many Middle Eastern "Experts" might spoil the broth.

The treatment of colonial problems was supervised by George Louis Beer and included the Far East and the Pacific area as well as Africa. Far Eastern research was first directed by Wolcott H. Pitkin, but after May 1918 supervision was exercised by Norman D. Harris and after September 1918 by Stanley Hornbeck. George Blakeslee was in charge of research pertaining to the Pacific Islands, while research on British Empire projects was handled by Preston Slosson and James T. Shotwell.

George L. Beer. Age 45. A.M., Columbia, 1893. Special interest had been the British Empire of the 17th and 18th centuries, with particular emphasis upon studies of imperial commerce. At the time he joined the Inquiry was engaged in private business. Had published several volumes on the old British colonial system and, more recently, the *English Speaking Peoples* (1917). Was one of the very few Inquiry members who listed his political preference for the Republican party. Claimed a facility in French, German, and Italian languages. Special work for the Inquiry concentrated upon colonial problems in Africa.

Nevin Fenneman. Aged 52. Ph.D., Chicago, 1901. At the time he joined the Inquiry was professor of geology at the University of Cincinnati. Books published before 1918: *Physiographic Divisions of the United States* (1912). Special interest was in geology. Assignments with the Inquiry concerned African problems.

Wolcott H. Pitkin. Age 36. Lawyer, having received the L.L.B., Harvard, 1906. Assistant United States Attorney, Southern District of

51. Memorandum, undated, no authorship indicated, in Shotwell MSS, Columbia.

New York, 1909–12. At the time he joined the Inquiry had been acting general adviser on foreign relations to the Siamese government since 1915. Insofar as can be determined, Pitkin had not traveled or lived extensively in any area of the Far East except for his two years in Siam. Possessed no facility in Asian languages.

Dorothy Kenyon. Age 29. Lawyer, admitted to the New York Bar in 1917. J.D., New York University, 1917. No evidence of any special interest in the Far East before being engaged by the Inquiry. In *Current Biography* for 1947, she wrote (p. 348): "Her first position after she was admitted to the New York Bar in 1917 was that of research specialist for a group of lawyers who were preparing studies for delegates to the 1919 Peace Conference. The first client assigned to her was the Kingdom of Siam." Special assignments for the Inquiry concerned India and the Philippines.

Norman D. Harris. Age 47. Ph.D., Chicago, 1901. Studied in England, France, Italy, and Germany. At the time he joined the Inquiry was professor of political science, Northwestern University. Published books before 1918: *History of Servitude in Illinois* (1904); *Intervention and Colonization in Africa* (1914). Special work for the Inquiry concerned China.

Stanley K. Hornbeck. Age 34. Ph.D., Wisconsin, 1911. Special interest was Chinese government. At the time he joined the Inquiry was professor of political science at Wisconsin. Books published before 1918: *The Most Favored Nation Clause in Commercial Treaties* (1910); *Contemporary Politics in the Far East* (1916). In 1917–18 was a special expert attached to the U.S. Tariff Commission. Work for the Inquiry concerned China.

W. W. McLaren. Age 40. Native of Canada. It cannot be ascertained whether he was a U.S. citizen in 1917–18. Ph.D., Harvard, 1908. Special interest was Japanese government and politics. Had taught in a Japanese university from 1908–14. At the time he joined the Inquiry was professor of economics at Williams. Books published before 1918: *Political History of Japan* (1916); Editor, *Japanese Government Documents* (1914). Special work for the Inquiry concerned Japanese politics.

Preston W. Slosson. Age 25. Ph.D., Columbia, 1916. At the time he joined the Inquiry was an assistant in history, Columbia University. Also served on the editorial staff of the *New York Independent*. Special interest was modern European history. Books published before 1918: *Fated or Free* (1914); *The Decline of the Chartist Movement* (1916).

George H. Blakeslee. Age 46. Ph.D., Harvard, 1903. Special interest was in the international relations of the Far East. At the time he joined the Inquiry was professor of history, Clark University. No books published before 1918.

One of the knottiest conundrums pertaining to the Inquiry's personnel is the reason for the selection of Wolcott H. Pitkin to direct research on the Far East. Nothing in Pitkin's background could suggest fitness for the position. He had had strong recommendations from close friends like Felix Frankfurter and Walter Lippmann. Nevertheless, his serious inadequacies provoked much adverse criticism within the Department of State. On October 27, 1917, Assistant Secretary of State Breckinridge Long sent a strongly worded letter informing House of Pitkin's record:

> Mr. Pitkin seems to have been assigned to study and obtain data on the Far East. The inquiries I have made concerning him have produced the information that he is not at all familiar with the Far East in general. He has some knowledge of Siam but his record in Siam is about this: that he was chosen, by the man he succeeded in office, as Adviser to the King; that he was not most efficient in that capacity and that he was demoted in rank and made Adviser to the Foreign Office. He has been serving in that latter capacity along with various other advisers, several Englishmen and Frenchmen. His knowledge of China and Japan is not extensive. In fact, he frankly stated, in the Department yesterday, that his knowledge of those countries was quite limited.
>
> I write you in this manner solely because I feel that you may not realize the limited knowledge and experience of Mr. Pitkin as regards Far Eastern matters.[52]

Despite such advice, Pitkin remained at his post with the Inquiry six months longer. Because the State Department's dissatisfaction with Pitkin resulted in a reluctance to supply him with essential information, Mezes took the problem to House in April 1918.[53] Mezes posed two alternatives: either the State Department should cooperate with Pitkin or he should be dropped from the Inquiry. By June, the latter course had been chosen. Here was one instance of State Department interference in the Inquiry's activities. With Pitkin went Dorothy Kenyon, who had entered the

52. Breckinridge Long to House, Oct. 27, 1917, House MSS, file 9-23, Yale. Letter also found in the Long MSS, Library of Congress.
53. Mezes to House, April 18, 1918, Mezes MSS, Columbia.

Inquiry at his invitation. Kenyon's qualifications were even fewer than Pitkin's.[54] Nevertheless, the younger lawyer supplied the Inquiry with sixteen reports on India plus a lengthy study of the Philippines, all produced during her less than three months with the organization—no mean feat even for the best Far Eastern experts.

Latin America received much attention from the preparatory organization during 1918. Consideration of the Latin American staff will also include the Inquiry's cartographers, all of whom were supervised by Isaiah Bowman.

Bailey Willis. Age 60. Hon. Ph.D., University of Berlin, 1910. Special interest was in geology. Worked with the U.S. Geological Survey from 1884–1916. Participated in geological explorations in China for the Carnegie Institution during 1903–04; consulting geologist to Minister of Public Works, Argentina, 1911–15. At the time he joined the Inquiry was professor of geology at Stanford. No books pertaining to Latin America published before 1918. Duties for the Inquiry concerned Latin America; he was chief of the Latin American Division.

Mark Jefferson. Age 54. Special interest was in Latin American geography. At the time he joined the Inquiry was professor of geography at Michigan State Normal College. Responsibility with the Inquiry was as chief of the Cartographic Division.

G. M. McBride. Age 41. Teacher, Instituto Ingles, Santiago, Chile, 1901–06. Teacher of geography and director of the American Institute, La Paz, Bolivia, 1908–15. At the time he joined the Inquiry was librarian, American Geographical Society. No published books before 1918.

Osgood Hardy. Age 27. Interpreter and Quartermaster, Yale Peruvian Expedition, 1912, 1914–16. No books published before 1918. At the time he joined the Inquiry was a graduate student at Yale. Special assignment with the Inquiry concerned Peru.

Frederick K. Morris. Age 32. Had been assistant geologist, Canadian Geologic Survey, summer 1912. At the time he joined the Inquiry was assistant lecturer and instructor in geology at Columbia. Before 1918 had been co-author of a chapter on engineering geology included in *Handbook for Highway Engineers,* edited by

54. Dorothy Kenyon's later comment: Pitkin had invited her to work with him on the Inquiry "instead of going into a law office immediately." Kenyon to the author, Oct. 10, 1953.

Blanchard (1915), and had written a volume, *Military Geology* (1918). Special work for Inquiry was as cartographer.

Armin K. Lobeck. Age 31. Ph.D., Columbia, 1917. Special interest was in physiography. No books published before 1918. Special work with Inquiry was as cartographer.

Douglas W. Johnson. Age 39. Ph.D., Columbia, 1903. Assistant in the U.S. Geological Survey during 1901, 1903–05. At the time he joined the Inquiry was an instructor in physiography at Columbia. Books published before 1918: *Lettre d'un Américain à un Allemand* (1916); *Topography and Strategy in the War* (1917); *Peril of Prussianism* (1917); *Plain Words from America* (1917). Special work for the Inquiry was as cartographer and as liaison with the Allied peace preparatory projects in England and France.

William Briesemeister. Age 22. Had been working for the American Geographical Society as a cartographer for about four years when he started in that capacity with the Inquiry.

Personnel working in the fields of international law and economics will be considered together.

A. A. Young. Age 41. Ph.D., Wisconsin, 1902. At the time he joined the Inquiry was professor of economics and finance at Cornell. Besides numerous articles had published *Outlines of Economics* (1908) before 1918. Work for the Inquiry was as chief of the Economics Division; also worked on the staff of the War Trade Board.

James C. Bonbright. Age 26. Ph.D., Columbia, 1921. Was a graduate student at the time he joined the Inquiry. Special work for the Inquiry was on the subject of tariff conditions in Central European trade.

Joseph P. Chamberlain. Age 44. Practiced law in San Francisco 1902–05. Lecturer in law at California, 1907–08. At the time he joined the Inquiry was a member of the Legislative Drafting Research Fund, Columbia University. Book published before 1918: *Index Digest of State Constitutions* (1915). Special work for the Inquiry concerned the international law of commerce.

Youth and lack of specific qualifications characterized the men and women who worked on the Inquiry. Their composite age was just under 41, but more significant was the large number of divisional directors and chief contributors who ranged between 25 and 33 years of age. Walter Lippmann was but 28, Robert H. Lord was 32, Charles Seymour was 32, Robert J. Kerner was 30, and

Preston W. Slosson was only 25. Although most members were native Americans, the organization was never reluctant to appoint naturalized citizens or even aliens who possessed some special knowledge thought to be useful. Besides this full-time staff, the Inquiry assigned numerous reports to various individuals at universities or in government service. Such persons were sometimes kept in ignorance as to the purpose of their efforts. A common subterfuge was to explain that the particular study was desired by the American Geographical Society or by the National Board for Historical Services. As will be noted below, a substantial portion of the Inquiry's work was actually performed by persons who had no official status in the organization.

Pecuniary considerations figured prominently at all times in the selection of personnel for the Inquiry. Occasionally the Executive Committee found it necesary to pass up the best qualified individuals because of its inability to offer a satisfactory salary.[55] Most members of the Inquiry interpreted their invitation to join the organization as a patriotic obligation, but some, less affluent, felt it necessary to receive some stipend adequate to meet their family financial obligations. Surprisingly enough, an exhaustive reading of all the Inquiry's correspondence has disclosed scarcely any reference to the question why the organization charged with preparing the government's case for the eventual peace conference was compelled to subsist on so small a budget. While some members received reasonably decent salaries for their services (see Appendix I), others were on leave from their academic employers and received their regular monthly salaries by prior agreement between the respective institution and the Inquiry. Only rarely were university administrations reluctant to cooperate with the government in this way, but one exception is worth some mention in passing. When the Inquiry asked Washington State College at Pullman to grant a leave of absence with salary to Professor F. A. Golder, President E. C. Holland explained his refusal as follows:

55. Robert J. Kerner told the author of several such instances in conversation on December 27, 1954. Other instances are cited in an undated note filed under "Byrne, Eugene H." in the Inquiry Archives. The note reads in part: "Mr. [William L.] Westermann is a decidedly better man than Mr. Byrne but if he were taken from Wisconsin University, it would cost the Inquiry $3500 per year and he would have to be employed for a whole year."

We have had many requests for assistance in increasing the agricultural production of the state and used up our appropriation in aiding the farmers of the Northwest. I am sorry that we must be the only exception in this matter.[56]

In spite of the college's inability to assume Golder's salary, in this case the Inquiry did find the necessary funds with which to employ the Russian scholar.

Where salary responsibilities were borne by the Inquiry itself, the compensation was not much below that of academicians in 1917–18. James T. Shotwell's salary of $541.66 per month represented the highest salary paid in the organization. Second in salary was Walter Lippmann with $500 per month. The general salary range for research directors and associates (collaborators, as they were called) extended from $150 to $400 including the periodic raises accorded various individuals. There was no apparent consistency in salary matters. Division chiefs in some instances (A. A. Young might be an example) often received less remuneration than did ordinary researchers.[57] Customarily the ancient law of supply and demand, compounded with persistent willpower, operated to the advantage of certain more highly regarded staff members. Let the reader merely recall what has already been related concerning the arrangements governing Robert J. Kerner's tenure. Notwithstanding the barrage of claims to the contrary emanating from members of the Executive Committee when corresponding with prospective recruits, the Inquiry did pay its staff reasonably well by the standards of the time. Somehow when dire need arose for the services of a scholar, the organization's treasury was able to scrape together the necessary funds. Money, however, did not represent the only obstacle which beset the Inquiry's quest for personnel.

Youth in wartime carries the responsibility of military service. A large percentage of the Inquiry's personnel was liable for military service. Draft calls, however, would have seriously disrupted the Inquiry's operations. One of the persistent responsibilities of

56. E. C. Holland to Mezes, Feb. 1, 1918, Mezes MSS, Columbia.
57. Inquiry financial records are to be found in the David Hunter Miller MSS, Library of Congress. There are also some records in the House Inquiry Reports, file 33-124, Yale.

the Executive Committee consisted of interceding with the War Department to obtain deferment for Inquiry members. A continuous stream of communications from the Inquiry's officers stressed the paucity of expert talent available in the United States, the special qualifications which the Inquiry's potential draftees possessed, and the significant work which these men were already contributing to the nation's war effort. A so-called "Black Book of Draft Exemptions" was compiled by the Inquiry staff on September 26, 1918, in which certain relevant documents were collected. Two typical entries read:

> Roland Dixon—one of an exceedingly small number of ethnographers in America. Has worked in Western Siberia, Turkestan, Mongolia, etc.

> William Lunt—It is exceedingly difficult to find a historian who is not already engaged in one form of war work or another who has knowledge of Italian. Lunt possesses knowledge of Italian. He has gone into the problem of the Trentino with enthusiasm and has produced results that indicate that he will be master of the problem in time for the peace conference.[58]

Scarcely a single Inquiry member was lost to the draft.

All wartime government agencies utilizing the services of specially trained persons tended to compete with each other in filling their complements. Besides ordinary demands from the military and naval establishments for historians, geographers, geologists, cartographers, lawyers, and other professionals, the expanded services of the State Department, the War Industries Board, the Central Bureau of Statistics, and the Commerce Department were drawing into patriotic employment the dwindling number of per-

58. Black Book on Draft Exemption Requests, Inquiry Archives. For other materials pertaining to Inquiry exemptions, see Statements to Draft Boards in House Inquiry MSS, file 33, Yale; Walter Lippmann to Ralph Hayes (Secretary Baker's assistant at the War Department), Nov. 16, 1917, Inquiry Archives; Mezes to Secretary Baker, Oct. 22, 1918, Mezes MSS, Columbia; Mezes to Secretary of State Lansing, July 24, 1918, Mezes MSS. Besides exempting eligible persons from the draft, the Inquiry succeeded in recruiting persons who were already serving in the military forces. Samuel E. Morison, for example, was a private in the army at the time he was recruited for service by the Inquiry—Conversation between Morison and the author, April 10, 1959.

sons with the desired talents. The Inquiry, formed some five months following American intervention in the war but actually filling its requirements for personnel seven to ten months after other government agencies had hired their staffs, encountered serious difficulties in obtaining a choice staff. University faculties, the basic source of talent for the Inquiry, were already overtaxed owing to manpower depletion to fill the needs of the military, the government wartime agencies, and private industry. By the time the Inquiry started bidding, it was not easy for university administrators to find replacements to fill staff vacancies. Hence there were instances when the person most eminently qualified to work on an Inquiry assignment could not obtain a leave of absence. Had the Inquiry been an official agency established by Congressional authority and comparable to other wartime agencies, far less difficulty might have been encountered in procuring personnel. The Inquiry's veritable shroud of secrecy was a handicap in this respect.

The work of a classified government agency having a code name and engaged in formulating the foreign policy of a great nation during wartime calls for the unqualified loyalty of all participating members. With respect to the Inquiry, loyalty became a pragmatic concept. Overt sympathy for the enemy was obviously suspect, but disloyalty was very loosely defined. Throughout its existence, there were seven cases in which charges of possible disloyalty were brought against members or prospective members of the Inquiry. These suspicions were brought to the attention of the Bureau of Investigation of the Department of Justice, which acted on all seven cases.

The Bureau of Investigation had been functioning within the Department of Justice since 1916. It served as a clearing house for the use of wartime government intelligence agencies. Once the United States had broken diplomatic relations with Germany, literally hundreds of complaints poured in upon the Bureau almost daily. Investigators from the Immigration Service and the "field forces" of the Post Office Department, Department of Agriculture, the Interior Department, and the Internal Revenue Service were relied upon to perform the routine investigations in the field.

71

Private agencies, such as the American Protective League, were also brought into the work.[59] It was this investigatory service that checked the loyalty of Inquiry personnel.

In November 1917, the Inquiry's officers endeavored to secure the services of a person qualified in the field of international law. The name of Alpheus H. Snow was suggested. Through his writings, Snow had made specific suggestions for a kind of international organization and was therefore regarded by colleagues and associates as being "forward looking." [60] Numerous scholars vouched for Snow's reputation and competence. Nevertheless, the Inquiry's director, Sidney E. Mezes, was dubious about Snow, for he sent off a letter to Attorney General Thomas W. Gregory in which he requested that an investigation be undertaken to determine how "he [Snow] stands with regard to the administration; that is, whether he deserves to be *persona grata* there and probably would be were his connections with the Inquiry known, in case his services should later on be used." Mezes did not, insofar as the evidence discloses, request such an investigation of all prospective members. It is not altogether clear, moreover, just why he asked for a probe of Snow at this time. Nevertheless, Attorney General Gregory proceeded almost immediately to conduct a confidential survey among various of Snow's acquaintances at the Washington Cosmos Club. From the several responses, Gregory summarized Snow's scholarly and social attainments in this way:

> The impression I gather is that on the basis of a good deal of attention to the work of the Hague Tribunal and a series of peace efforts that have grown out of that institution since 1899, he is more or less affiliated with men who could be termed, "Pacifists." I am informed that several years ago he expressed dissatisfaction with the policy of President Wilson. His wife has been somewhat bitter, to say the least, against our treatment of Germany before the declaration of war. She felt that in certain respects the English policy was very detrimental to the western world. Mr. Snow is a man who keeps his own counsel, and it is altogether

59. *Annual Report of the Attorney General of the United States for the Year 1917*, pp. 14–15, 82–87.
60. Alpheus H. Snow, "International Law and Political Science," *AJIL*, 7 (1914), 315–28.

probable that he would be able to hold his viewpoint in spite of his wife's avowed feeling.[61]

Pacifist, critic of the administration, his wife bitter regarding American policy toward Germany during the period of American neutrality and unappreciative of a government associated with the United States in the war—needless to say, the cards were stacked against Alpheus Snow. He did not receive any further serious consideration.

Almost simultaneously with the Snow investigation, Mezes had asked Attorney General Gregory's office to investigate another international lawyer also considered a good prospect for the Inquiry. Chandler P. Anderson, the subject of the probe, had been recommended by Secretary of State Lansing. Possibly with this in mind, Mezes proceeded cautiously in requesting the investigation. The Attorney General's findings ultimately reported several responses from sources which Gregory considered most reliable. Two samples follow:

> SOURCE No. 1—He [Anderson] unsatisfactorily filled the Office of Counselor of the Department of State for about two years. His failure to meet the requirements of that position arose from the lack of the qualifications that you seem to require.
>
> SOURCE No. 2—From information which came to me through mutual friends since the European War commenced, but prior to the entrance of the United States into the war, and as I recollect during the campaign of 1916, he was quite antagonistic to and critical of the administration. . . . I have heretofore rather looked upon him as distinctly reactionary in type.

Attorney General Gregory summarized the comments with this conclusion: "I think Anderson is a bright and shining example of pretty much everything you don't want." Early in February 1918, David Hunter Miller notified Anderson that his services would not be used by the Inquiry.[62]

61. Confidential Report to the Attorney General, unsigned, Nov. 8, 1917, quoted in letter from Attorney General Gregory to Mezes, Nov. 8, 1917, in Mezes MSS, Columbia.

62. Material pertaining to the investigation of Anderson is found in Mezes to Lansing, Nov. 2, 1917, Mezes MSS; Lansing to Mezes, Nov. 5, 1917, Mezes MSS;

Not only candidates but fully appointed members of the Inquiry were sometimes subjected to loyalty investigation. In November 1917, Edward Krehbiel of Stanford University was hired by the Inquiry to work on the political organization of certain European states. The record does not indicate the presence of any suspicion regarding his loyalty. Yet on December 6, a letter marked *Personal and Confidential* arrived for Mezes from Counselor Frank Polk at the State Department. Polk reported:

> A most reliable man connected with that institution [Stanford] had written us warning the Department against this man [Krehbiel] as a dangerous German sympathizer. This is not a case of gossip, but really came from a man in whose judgment I feel sure you will have some confidence.

A second ominous warning about Krehbiel was sent by Polk on the 14th. Though eminently satisfied with Krehbiel's work, Mezes was sensitive to such criticism and decided to terminate Krehbiel's services as of February 1. Meanwhile, Krehbiel was assigned to less delicate responsibilities. Whether he ever learned the reason for his suspicion is not clear from the record, for late in January President Ray Lyman Wilbur of Stanford withdrew the leave of absence which Stanford had accorded to Krehbiel, thus providing a suitable justification for revoking Krehbiel's connection with the Inquiry. As late as January 24, Mezes placed responsibility for the pro-German charge levied against Krehbiel on President Wilbur, but tangible evidence was never supplied. Severance of Krehbiel did not provoke any full-dress investigation. The pro-German accusation coupled with the recommendation from the State Department sufficed.[63] Here was another instance where

---

T. W. Gregory to Mezes, Nov. 20, 1917, with unsigned enclosure dated Nov. 17, 1917, in Inquiry Archives; Gregory to Mezes, Nov. 20 (#2) with enclosure unsigned dated Nov. 16, Inquiry Archives; David Hunter Miller to Anderson, Feb. 9, 1918, Inquiry Archives.

63. Material relevant to the investigation of Krehbiel is as follows: Frank Polk to Mezes, Dec. 14, 1917, Mezes MSS; Walter Lippmann to Krehbiel, Nov. 26, 1917, and Nov. 28, 1917, Inquiry Archives; Mezes to Frank Polk, Jan. 3, 1918, House Inquiry Correspondence, file 33-157, Yale; President Wilbur to Mezes, Jan. 1918 (wire), Inquiry Archives; Mezes to Wilbur, Jan. 22, 1918, Jan. 24, 1918 (2 letters), Inquiry Archives; Mezes to House, Jan. 24, 1918, House MSS, file 10-30, Yale; David Starr Jordan to Mezes, Feb. 16, 1918, Inquiry Archives; Krehbiel to Walter Lippmann, Feb. 4, 1918, Inquiry Archives; Krehbiel to Lippmann, April 26, 1918, Inquiry Archives.

the State Department intervened in the activities of the Inquiry.

The case of Arthur Pope, a distinguished authority on Persia, did require a government investigation. In March 1918, Pope was being considered for a position with the Inquiry. A newspaper report linked Pope to the Hindu conspiracy case which had attracted notoriety earlier in the year in San Francisco. Apparently the Hindu conspiracy developed as an anti-British, anti-war measure to publicize the cause of Indian independence. In any event, the Justice Department's investigation showed that Pope "has been closely associated with the most dangerous of the German Hindu agents, both those now in Germany, in Mexico, and those now on trial."

> Even at the time when it was publicly known that one of the most guilty of the defendants, Tarak Nath Das, was intimately connected with the German Government and in its pay, Professor Pope wrote a letter which was found among Tarak Nath's papers, showing close connection between the two and also referring to the fact that Pope had written a letter to Mexico (undoubtedly to another of the well known German Hindu agents there.)
>
> In view of the facts before me, I should say that it will be highly inadvisable that Professor Pope should be employed or used in any way in government work.[64]

Professor Pope was not employed or used by the Inquiry.

In May, another case involving a prospective employee resulted in a government loyalty check. When recommending to the Inquiry Charles Herz, a young man of Croatian descent, Frederick P. Keppel, who was assistant to Secretary Baker in the War Department, had mentioned that Herz's mother and brother, then living in Lexington, Kentucky, had been heard to utter unpatriotic remarks. Due to the Inquiry's need for someone having facility in Slavic languages, Mezes took the matter of Herz's loyalty before Attorney General Gregory. The case was referred to Chief Investigator A. B. Bielaski, whose report dated July 12 asserted:

> While employed at the War Trade Board, Herz never made any disloyal statements; nor did he ever openly take a strong stand in favor of his country. He was let out due to a letter received from

64. The Arthur Pope incident is cited in two documents: T. W. Gregory to Mezes, March 18, 1918, Mezes MSS; Gregory to Mezes, April 15, 1918, Inquiry Archives.

the Dean of the University of Kentucky containing information concerning the pro-German attitude of his mother.

Mrs. Mary H. Cochran, mother of the woman who conducts the flat [where Herz lived] stated that Herz . . . seemed to be a quiet, a well-behaved and gentle young man; and that he kept good hours and had but few friends and callers; that she had never heard him discuss the war . . .

Mrs. F. A. Vaile . . . wife of the British author, stated that she met Herz about 2½ years ago . . . that they often discussed the war and Herz was always very pro-ally.

Henry W. Geiger . . . stated that he had known Herz since about 1906 . . . that Herz is thoroughly American in every way, although about a year ago, after some German successes, Herz did remark to him that it seemed as though the Germans could not be beaten.

Professor J. T. C. Noe of the University of Kentucky stated that Herz had been in his classes for two years and was a very apt student . . . that he believes Herz is absolutely loyal to the United States . . .

In all, the government queried some twenty persons who had known Herz and his family in New York, Washington, and Lexington, Kentucky. Absolutely no evidence was uncovered which would implicate Herz as disloyal or even as a German sympathizer. In early August, it seemed to Charles Seymour, supervisor of the Austrian Division and the man who would take charge of Herz, that the investigation had cleared Herz of any taint of disloyalty. Nevertheless, on August 29, Mezes' secretary sent off to Herz final notice that his services would not be utilized. The only incriminating evidence against Herz had consisted of the statements alleged to be pro-German which had been uttered by his mother and brother.[65]

The final investigation case arose out of peculiar circumstances. It involved a scholar whose services later proved valuable to the government at the Paris Peace Conference. Albert H. Lybyer had

65. Correspondence relative to l'affaire Herz: F. P. Keppel to Lippmann, May 21, 1918, Inquiry Archives; Mezes to Attorney General Gregory, May 24, 1918, Inquiry Archives; Letter from A. B. Bielaski to Gregory, July 12, 1918, Inquiry Archives; Gregory to Mezes, July 24, 1918, Inquiry Archives; Charles Seymour to Clive Day, Aug. 7, 1918, House Inquiry MSS, file 33-161, Yale; Seymour to Day, Aug. 14, 1918, House Inquiry MSS, file 33-161; R. A. Ralston to Charles Herz, Aug. 29, 1918, Inquiry Archives.

been recommended for work with the Inquiry. Charles Haskins claimed, "There is no better authority in the country on Turkish history than Lybyer." He was to make a study of ethnographic maps which Charles McIlwain (professor of constitutional history at Harvard) had not felt competent to undertake. Three months passed before Lybyer's usefulness was cleared by investigation. The Greek minister in Washington, hearing that Lybyer was being considered for government work, had filed a protest with the State Department, declaring that Lybyer was ardently pro-Bulgarian. Though the United States was not at war with Bulgaria, the Bulgars were allies of Germany with which the United States was at war. A commotion was caused at the State Department and an immediate investigation ensued to ascertain whether Lybyer's presence on the Inquiry staff actually did constitute a threat to American security; whether Lybyer was in fact pro-Bulgar and consequently anti-Greek; and whether having pro-Bulgar sympathies was tantamount to being pro-German in the circumstances and context of the war. Since Lybyer was then teaching at the University of Illinois, the investigation centered in the community of Champaign. University President Edmund James denied what he described as irresponsible accusations that Lybyer was pro-German. Clive Day, who would supervise Lybyer's work on the Inquiry, noted how Lybyer's "constitutional prejudice in favor of the Bulgarians . . . will make it necessary to watch any work involving them very carefully." At Champaign, the post office inspector to whose lot the local investigation fell could not uncover any corroboration of the charge that during the previous winter Lybyer had delivered a public address in which certain strongly worded pro-Bulgarian statements had been aired, severely attacking the Greeks. Conversely, he reported, "no more loyal person to the United States and the cause of the Allies has lived in this vicinity." Similar testimonials came from Lybyer's colleagues. In view of the complete clearance, Lybyer became one of the territorial specialists accompanying the American delegation to the Peace Conference. This case, initiated by a foreign government toward which the United States could be expected to develop certain policies at the peace conference, actually revolved about alleged opinions which Lybyer had arrived at through systematic study. These opinions, interpretations, even conclusions, contrary as they might have been to the best interests of Greece, had been mistaken for national disloyalty.[66]

During some fourteen months of independent existence prior to the armistice, the Inquiry encountered serious personnel problems. It is possible that in its attempt to recruit the best qualified personnel to study the problems of peace, the Inquiry leaders tapped what could be classified as the best available personnel. Be that as it may, the majority of Inquiry workers were not in 1917 specialists or experts on their assigned topics. Experts were the exception rather than the rule. Most of the personnel had general knowledge of the geographical area, some had a basic knowledge of the economic, social, and political structure; a smaller percentage possessed some linguistic facility in the language of the area on which they were working. Had the Inquiry been merely an academic research organization, the outcome would not necessarily have been endangered; more time would merely have been allotted for the work. American peace preparations, however, were being punched on a time clock. Qualified or unqualified, each scholar worked according to a definite schedule, submitting his reports by scheduled deadlines. The peace conference would not be postponed because a member of the Inquiry had not turned in his report. Personnel qualifications then become crucially important in judging the end products of the Inquiry's work.

66. Material pertaining to l'affaire Lybyer: Charles Haskins to A. A. Young Aug. 10, 1918, Inquiry Archives; Edmund James to A. A. Young, Sept. 14, 1918, Inquiry Archives; Clive Day to William S. Ferguson, Nov. 25, 1918, House Inquiry MSS, file 33-150, Yale; Assistant Secretary of State Leland Harrison to Polk, Dec. 2, 1918, Harrison MSS, Library of Congress; Post Office Inspector Hal B. Mosby of Champaign, Illinois, to Harrison, Dec. 6, 1918, Harrison MSS; Postmaster Charles J. Mullikin of Champaign, Illinois, to Hal Mosby, no date, Harrison MSS; Mullikin to Mosby Dec. 11, 1918, Harrison MSS; Photostat letter from Professor Lawrence H. Larson to Evarts Greene, Dec. 12, 1918, Harrison MSS; Photostat letter from Lybyer to *Champaign News*, no date, Harrison MSS; State Department Solicitor Lester Woolsey to Harrison, Dec. 20, 1918, Harrison MSS; Woolsey to Polk and Phillips, Dec. 18, 1918, Harrison MSS.

Chapter 3

PLANS, OPERATIONS, ADMINISTRATION

AT ITS INCEPTION, a government bureau encounters the same hazards of life that face any newly established institution. Its practical administrative features, the *modus operandi,* must be determined by those who are supervising the infant organization. There are operational plans and programs to be devised; coordination is often essential in order that all component parts may function smoothly and the organization can operate efficiently in conjunction with other existing agencies of government. Effective coordination can prevent needless duplication of effort. Often, where there are numerous tasks to be performed, some system of priority must be established. The Inquiry, founded for the express purpose of preparing the American program for the eventual peace conference, was not only in dire need of qualified personnel; throughout its existence a continuous need was manifest for some well-defined method—an operating procedure with fixed priorities—by which the designated objectives would most likely be reached.

When Colonel House agreed to direct an independent commission having responsibility for the American preparations for peace, he and his associates shared only the haziest conception of what the project would entail. Questions involving fundamental policy decisions were raised, such as those posed by Secretary of State Robert Lansing: How far should the United States become involved in the determination of European boundaries? Should the

United States extend its authority beyond the point of either approving or disapproving future boundary arrangements desired by governments associated with the United States in the war? Should the territorial divisions be decided on the basis of race, language, religion, or previous political affiliation? Where two or more countries made conflicting claims to a particular territory, as was true in Macedonia, what should be the basis for a settlement? How far might conquest be weighted as constituting a basis for territorial settlement?[1] These questions were typical of those which confronted the Inquiry. The time that would be available to develop their solutions was always an unknown quantity. Moreover, the military and political conditions under which the peace would be restored, obviously so significant to any peace settlement, could only be hazarded with no promise of accuracy in the fall of 1917.

As early as October 1, 1917, Colonel House started canvassing ideas with regard to the method by which the Inquiry could best undertake its program. He approached several persons closely identified with American progressivism and internationalism. First, he conferred with the English pacifist and liberal, Norman Angell, author of several volumes having to do with the prevention of war, the best known of which was *The Great Illusion* (1910). Many of Angell's articles had been published in Herbert Croly's *New Republic* during the war years when Angell's many intimates in progressive circles easily afforded him an entrée to the Wilson administration.[2] Later, when writing his memoirs, he revealed how his status was decidedly less than *persona grata* to the British Foreign Office, a situation which was far from displeasing to the zealous Angell. As he recalled, "anything I wrote or discussed with the White House people should have no official colour and should be regarded for what it was—simply the contribution of a private and unofficial Englishman who happened to

1. Memorandum by Secretary of State Robert Lansing, no date, *Foreign Relations of the United States, Paris Peace Conference 1919* (hereafter referred to as *FRPPC*), *I*, 11–12.

2. Norman Angell's connection with the planning aspects of the Inquiry organization is cited in Angell to Colonel House, Oct. 1, 1917, House MSS, Yale; House MSS Diary, Oct. 2, 1917, Yale; Angell to Walter Lippmann, Oct. 12, 1917, and Oct. 14, 1917, Inquiry Archives.

have written books on international affairs." [3] Publicist that he was, Norman Angell's ideas were solicited by Colonel House for the benefit of the Inquiry, and he submitted two extensive memoranda containing suggestions as to the method by which the preparations for peace could best be undertaken.[4]

Norman Angell warned that massive accumulations of reports should be avoided. Given the Wilsonian conditions for peace, a tiny task force could select the best literature and source materials to implement the American objectives. Authors of important treatises could then be invited to appear before the Inquiry's staff and defend their views while at the same time explaining how in their opinion problems which they studied could be treated in accordance with the President's principles. Such a preparatory commission would thus serve merely as a clearing house for the collating and summarizing of pertinent, existing studies and would not itself undertake extensive research on subjects previously studied by reputable scholars. Later, after this first phase of the work reached completion, a corps of specialists could review the selected papers in order to formulate a statement of recommendations for United States policy. This statement, in turn, would be subject to review and criticism by diplomats, lawyers, and other professional specialists including the writers of the originally selected treatises. As a concluding process, Angell called for a concerted publicity campaign whose purpose it would be to obtain mass support behind the American recommendations at the peace conference. Throughout, Angell's plan emphasized the formulation of new principles rather than the collection of factual information. Top priority was to be placed on studying current world dynamics, not on historical precedents. In his words,

> . . . it would quite conceivably be a fatal handicap to really useful work in this department to allow it to be dominated by lawyers whose reputation is based upon their knowledge of the old rules. . . . It is a case again in which a mere "knowledge of the facts" would in truth stand in the way of a useful outcome, and tend to render the work of the organization sterile of really practical results.

3. Norman Angell, *After All* (New York, 1952), p. 203.
4. Norman Angell, "Memorandum on Methods of Preparation for the Settlement," Oct. 1, 1917, House MSS, Yale; Memorandum Regarding the Organization of the Inquiry, Oct. 14, 1917, Inquiry Archives.

Angell's prescription for success implied that experts were not really wanted; to the contrary, his plan called for the extensive use of non-experts. Youth, capable of concentrating upon the future order, unhampered by deep-seated commitments to past tradition, would best be able to translate the President's principles for peace into suitable provisos for the settlement. There is, however, no evidence to suggest that the Inquiry ever adopted this idea or made virtue out of necessity, because of the difficulties of recruitment, by arguing that non-experts were really desired. Norman Angell was but one of several liberal-internationalist publicists whose ideas were solicited in planning the operations of the Inquiry.

Early in October 1917, while the *New Republic*'s editor, Herbert Croly, was busily recommending personnel, the *New Republic*'s associate editor, Walter Weyl, was contributing his ideas on organization.[5] Weyl's design called for a central organization sufficiently flexible to allow for extensive cooperation and coordination. The Inquiry must be a cooperative project, for no single individual "could adequately supervise the entire work and because the best results are to be obtained by a free competition." Coordination would likewise be imperative if the different findings of the many staff members were to be composed. Any important, complex question, advised Weyl, must be treated from numerous vantage points. A pure geographical organization, dividing the Inquiry into regional groups, would not allow for a sufficiently comprehensive coverage. Serbian questions would then only be considered by some specialist on the Balkan Division. Since, however, Serbia's problems would certainly impinge upon the work of staff members handling Austrian and Italian problems, of economists and international lawyers and even ethnologists, there was a need for several approaches. In Weyl's view, the crucial problems would not be questions bearing upon territorial boundaries but rather questions involving general economic, political, legal, and ethnological conditions. Some methodological compromise must necessarily be effected, he believed, between the territorial approach and the substantive approach. To resolve this dilemma, Weyl recommended that an advisory board be established. On

5. Walter Weyl, "Proposed Organization for Research," Inquiry Archives.

this board would be specialists from various social science disciplines who would define each question as it was being considered, make the assignments, criticize and edit the complete reports. At the same time the specialists would coordinate the reports so as to avoid duplication and reconcile apparent contradictions. Centralized direction and multiple approaches to basic problems, then, provided Walter Weyl's principal recommendations to the planning of the Inquiry's work.

A third suggestion for the organization of the Inquiry was submitted by Stephen Duggan, an officer of the Carnegie Endowment for International Peace and professor of politics at the City College of New York.[6] Duggan proposed to divide the commission into several divisions, each supervised by a specialist. Over all the divisions would be a specialist on international affairs whose responsibility it would be to coordinate the work and to reconcile contradictory conclusions arrived at by the several divisions. Each division would arrange its own system of priority, so that the most pressing problems would be studied first. Of course, where research on particular questions had been conducted by some reputable institution like the Carnegie Endowment or the World Peace Foundation, the Inquiry would not duplicate it. The privately conducted research would be easily absorbed in the Inquiry's files. Each of these solicited memoranda contributed suggestions which were to prove valuable in the formation of the Inquiry's organization and method of work.

Sometime early in 1918, still another suggestion was offered for the management of the Inquiry's program. There is no date or mark on this memorandum to identify its authorship positively, but since reference is made to the Treaty of Brest-Litovsk and to the Treaty of Bucharest, it must be placed chronologically after these events. Penciled along one margin is the name Manley O. Hudson, so it might be presumed that he was its author.[7] Again, as with the earlier Angell memorandum, a deliberate attempt was made to minimize the collection of historical data. The peace con-

6. Stephen Duggan, Proposal, dated only October 1917, Inquiry Archives; James T. Shotwell to Duggan, Nov. 20, 1917, Inquiry Archives.

7. Memorandum on the Organization of a Political Service of the Inquiry, no date, Inquiry Archives.

ference, this later memorandum declared, would not be an historian's conclave, for it must deal with existing situations. The war had run its course, had altered conditions so drastically that the conference would find it futile to pick up the threads of political intercourse just where they were dropped in August 1914. Of even greater significance than those events which transpired prior to the war, insofar as the peace settlement was concerned, would be those events transpiring in the week just preceding the end of the war. It was the up-to-the-minute information, rendering necessary a virtual day-to-day communiqué, which would in the long run provide the basic requisite for American plenipotentiaries at the peace conference. The author believed, therefore, that a primary function of the Inquiry would be to gather current intelligence which would chronicle the rapidly changing social, political, and economic conditions in the critical problem areas of the world. Newspaper clippings could not be relied upon entirely to fill gaps in the Inquiry's files. This memorandum cited concrete instances illustrative of how inadequate were the United States government's sources of important information about conditions overseas. Five such concrete examples showed how information of importance for the drafting of the American program for peace was lacking in the United States:

(a) How many treaties were negotiated by the Central Powers and Roumania at Bucharest? Nobody on this side of the Atlantic knows. The State Department is unable to answer the question.

(b) What was the text of the Truce of Focsani of December 9, 1917? It cannot be obtained in America.

(c) What governments have been set up in the Caucasus? The best information service might not tell us, but its efforts would yield something.

(d) What has been done toward executing the provisions of the Brest-Litovsk peace treaty? Nobody in the United States is keeping up with this; nor can it be done as things stand.

(e) What is now going on in Poland? Have the Aaland Islands' fortifications been destroyed? This is being discussed in execution of the Brest-Litovsk treaty, but no one on this side of the Atlantic seems to know what has been done.

Besides advocating improved liaison with the various intelligence agencies already at work, this memorandum suggested establishing a special committee within the Inquiry to procure this needed current information. Working on the Inquiry's staff would be special agents attached to American embassies abroad who could gather information and dispatch it immediately to the appropriate members of the Inquiry in the United States. As grandiose sounding and ambitious as this scheme might have appeared in early 1918, before the war came to its end the Inquiry actually did dispatch intelligence agents to several crucial theatres of conflict where greater knowledge of prevailing conditions was deemed essential.

The Inquiry was never lacking in plans for its own organization; there were the manuals of method and procedure, the theories, and the general idealism which sometimes inspired its members. Yet, in the last analysis, what proved even more decisive were the practical, even harsh realities which often determined just how the theories would be implemented.

Early in November 1917, the recently formed Executive Committee of the Inquiry began considering proposals for the organization of the work. The first of the proposed plans, submitted by Walter Lippmann, bears the date of November 13, and divided the Inquiry's tasks into eleven separate divisions.[8] Division I, with a geographical orientation, was to have charge of gathering both official and unofficial declarations of peace objectives in all the belligerent countries. These declarations would include government statements, newspaper editorials, speeches, and articles concerned with territorial settlements. One month was allowed for the gathering of this material. Division II, a bibliographical project, was to gather on cards a list of official source materials bearing on the diverse claims which each belligerent could be expected to press at the peace conference. It would be necessary to scrutinize and catalogue the various sources of government statistics and private surveys in order to note the location of these materials in the United States and abroad. All standard reference guides would be checked, and in a separate critique any biases or inaccuracies would be noted. For these painstaking tasks, Lipp-

8. Memorandum from Walter Lippmann to Sidney Mezes Regarding the Organization of the Inquiry, Nov. 13, 1917, Shotwell MSS, Columbia. This memorandum is presented here as Appendix III.

mann allowed Division II only a single month. Cartography, the responsibility of Division III, consisted of the preparation of elaborate maps of uniform and adjustable scale capable of showing all boundary claims registered by the contending governments, subject peoples, and miscellaneous factions. Considering all the varied data intended for inclusion, the one- to two-month time limit imposed by Lippmann seemed a little optimistic. Similarly, Division IV, to be in charge of gathering data pertaining to the economic problems of European territories over which disputes raged, was given only two months to assemble its data concerning public debts, revenues, property ownership, capital value, land tenure, property destruction, school facilities, legal and political inequalities, and even political parties. And Division V, studying scarcity and monopoly, was not to be treated any more leniently, with its February 1 deadline, at which time its surveys and analyses of the condition and distribution of vital raw materials, key industries, and the manner in which industrial organization would be affected by several projected transfers of territory were to be completed. As for Division VI, considering international trade in terms of government regulations, national needs, sources of supply, storage and related problems, a deadline of March 1 was imposed. Division VII was to assemble all important texts on the subject of international law and prepare digests of materials concerning those governments defined as less than sovereign. This work was scheduled for completion before February 1, 1918. Division VIII, charged with gathering data about the "great powers," their political parties, political leaders, constitutional features, and the political interests of leading economic groups, was also given until February 1. The assignment of Division IX, considering neutral countries, was to emphasize the degree of their dependence on the several belligerents in order to "estimate the political significance of German concessions and the nature of desirable counter concessions on the part of the allies." At this point the memorandum conceded that Division IX would not be able to cope with these responsibilities without direct assistance from the State Department. Here then is another instance where the Inquiry's leaders were prepared to lean upon the State Department. Apparently no special urgency was attached to the work of Division IX, for no special deadline was stipulated.

Lippmann's proposal was considered by the Inquiry's Executive Committee on November 24.[9] Three days later, Mezes informed Lippmann that an abbreviated and somewhat modified version had been tentatively accepted.[10] Under the approved program, the organization's activities would be divided among four general categories: (1) planning; (2) collecting; (3) digesting; and (4) editing the raw data. Moreover, the number of divisions was to be reduced to seven; these would be: politics and government; geography; history and social science; economics and business; international law; strategy; and bibliography. Each division was expected to concentrate its attention, regardless of topic being studied, upon the interests of those nations associated with the United States in the war, the interests of the enemy states, and then the neutral states. Top priority would be given to the task of collecting source materials. Not until early December 1917, however, did Walter Lippmann propose a priority of subjects which members of the Inquiry were to study before February 1, 1918, with the order of urgency indicated, as follows:

I. Declarations and proposals [regarding the peace, emanating from the belligerents and other interested nations]; studies of political parties and a Who's Who of the principals.

II. Physical, racial and economic maps for territory from the Baltic Sea to the Persian Gulf. Economic and political map of Africa. Boundary maps to be superimposed indicating tentative solutions for Poland, Balkans, Asia Minor, and Africa. Economic maps of Alsace-Lorraine and occupied area of France.

III. A small and authoritative library on all moot questions.

IV. Tables and charts of (a) immediate civil and economic needs in Europe; (b) available tonnage; (c) credit position [of belligerent nations].

9. Mezes to Shotwell, Dec. 5, 1917, Mezes MSS, Columbia. Although the letter does not specify which plan received consideration, the proposal of November 13 was the only proposal submitted before the twenty-fourth of November.

10. Sidney Mezes to Walter Lippmann, Nov. 27, 1917, Mezes MSS, Columbia. This plan can be found in Appendix IV.

V. Analysis of "freedom of the Seas."

VI. Social data for (a) Baltic Provinces; (b) Poland; (c) Serbia; (d) Macedonia; (e) Palestine; (f) Italia-Irredenta.

VII. Analysis of German, French and English commercial relations to (a) Antwerp, and (b) Belgian railroads and canals.

VIII. Method of estimating reparation.

IX. Tentative proposals for internationalizing Bagdad Railroad and the Straits.

X. Tentative proposals for preventing undue economic penetration especially in Russia.

XI. The relation of the Monroe Doctrine to the Settlement.[11]

It is worthy of note that here Lippmann placed commercial considerations and "freedom of the seas" on a higher priority than questions of new states and boundary solutions. It is also noteworthy that problems involving the German colonies, Austria-Hungary, and the Far East had no priority.

Throughout these multifarious plans was an apparent conflict over just where the paramount emphasis should be placed. Given a geographical orientation, those members of the staff working on one region might have only slight awareness of research in progress on another, possibly related area. Where the research could be sufficiently localized by area, this procedure might prove effective, but real difficulty could arise when the given problem transcended national or regional frontiers. Once the Inquiry's work progressed to the point where complications developed over the application of principles of self-determination, freedom of the seas, and territorial transfers, it would not be easy to isolate the various issues on the basis of arbitrary geographical divisions. And there was still unresolved the question whether the Inquiry's paramount contribution to the peace conference would stem from its reports or would emerge from the training of expert consultants capable of providing accurate information at the conference. These functions, while related, were not identical, and early in the Inquiry's existence one of its leading members ventured to criticize the plans.

11. Walter Lippmann to the Executive Committee, Dec. 7, 1917, Shotwell MSS, Columbia.

Wolcott Pitkin, head of the Far Eastern Division, argued in December 1917 that the Inquiry's members were too closely attached to a particular geographical frame of reference. Though the members might presumably become highly specialized in terms of special regions, they would be in danger of lacking whatever balance of judgment might be gained from a broad acquaintance with world politics. In Pitkin's view, the narrow specialist would not make the most appropriate adviser at a peace conference. Questions might arise, he reasoned, which would call for decisions cutting across geographical divisions and at the same time be so complex that scientific methods alone would not suffice in reaching solutions. Surely American commissioners would prefer men capable of supplying answers to pressing questions based on trustworthy information. A maze of detailed information might have value, but in the end the generally informed consultant would make the best adviser for the nation's plenipotentiaries. Bringing his argument down to his own work with Far Eastern problems, Pitkin commented:

> That my correspondence with the Inquiry has been called for with the ultimate objective of performing some such task as this, seems obvious from the fact that my training has all consisted in giving advice, at first privately as a lawyer and later in practical politics. It is perhaps not irrelevant to suggest that if my cooperation is desired only in securing data for the Far East which is to be utilized in the general scheme, then the Inquiry might do better by securing the services of some one better trained than I am in research and better grounded to begin with in Far Eastern matters.[12]

Two days later, in its report of progress of December 15,[13] the Inquiry's Executive Committee displayed some awareness of this conflict in objectives but at the same time expressed little optimism about solving the dilemma. Until February 15, 1918, the Inquiry was principally involved with gathering data. The area of the world to which it attached greatest urgency extended through central Europe from the Baltic provinces to the Mediterranean, then southeastward through the Turkish provinces to the

12. Wolcott H. Pitkin to Mezes, Dec. 13, 1917, Mezes MSS, Columbia.
13. The Inquiry, Report of Progress to December 15, 1917, *FRPPC, 1*, 34–39.

Persian Gulf. Second in priority came the colonial questions of central Africa. But the question remained: how were the staff members of the Inquiry, inadequately prepared for the most part to undertake specialized studies, to tackle the complicated, thorny questions involved and recommend their solutions in so limited a period of time? From the outset, Inquiry leaders kept urging the staff of scholars to avail itself of standard reference works such as the *Encyclopedia Britannica*.[14] Later, scholars might find time for more elaborate treatises, but in the meantime the preliminary reports were to be hasty compilations of data "into the briefest possible form so as to be both readable and graphic." [15] Then, from these boiled-down statements, the Executive Committee could draw its information and formulate briefs with regard to the special issues that might be expected to concern the peace conference. This plan called for the Executive Committee to synthesize the projects of numerous "specialists" with the object of bringing the mass of information to focus upon the pertinent international problem.

By mid-March 1918, Mezes and the Executive Committee declared the paramount responsibility of the Inquiry to be gathering material and arranging it in such flexible form that its utility would be assured regardless of how or in what order the questions at issue would be introduced at the peace conference. An Inquiry report, written that month, emphasized the technical challenge confronting the organization in this regard:

> No one can foresee at this time the order in which data will be requisitioned, nor the ideas about which the data will have to be grouped in the course of the negotiations. Whatever facts are assembled must clearly be under such control that they can be arranged and grouped and presented in almost any form at the shortest possible notice.[16]

Statistical tables in themselves might have little practical value at the peace conference unless the student collecting the statistics was completely alive to the history and circumstances under which

14. Mezes to Shotwell, Dec. 14, 1917, Shotwell MSS, Columbia; Mezes to A. A. Young, Dec. 12, 1917, Inquiry Archives.
15. The Inquiry Report of Progress, December 15, 1917, *FRPPC, 1,* 34–39.
16. Report on the Inquiry, Its Scope and Method, March 20, 1918, ibid., 55–72.

the data had originally been gathered and even published. To have this statistical information in such form that it could be made useful for any relevant question arising at the peace conference often meant asking for the impossible.

Still another enormous task was the collection of a library of basic reference works. Here again, the Inquiry endeavored to locate and catalog the most valuable literature with the hope that within a two-week period all books could be quickly assembled as needed. So effective a mastery over their materials were Inquiry members expected to acquire that later at the peace conference any question of fact could be verified or ascertained authoritatively and completely in a period of less than two hours. Such at least were the ambitious plans of the Executive Committee.

Of equal importance to the written reports was the projection of data upon base maps in order to show graphically the geographic relationships, quantitative information, and political frontiers. Sheets containing population statistics, the location of economic resources, and the distribution of other kinds of data would be prepared according to a uniform scale and designed so that the diversified information could be superimposed upon base maps. An enormous amount of information could in this way be made serviceable when territorial questions arose for discussion during the peace negotiations. The report of March 1918 expressed the importance of graphic materials as follows:

> Besides maps, the Inquiry is planning charts and graphs showing various relationships, as, for example the dependence of Austria upon the Port of Trieste or the relations of the trade of an independent Poland to Germany and to Austria. Provided there is a sufficient expert staff to control the underlying source material adequately, and provided sufficient draftsmen and cartographers are available, the Inquiry ought to be in a position to furnish the American negotiators with graphic representations of sets of facts in their relationships upon very short notice.

Always vying for attention would be the various interests—national, religious, and class. "Wherever possible," the report reminded the staff, "it is important that the interests of each nation should be visualized as concretely as possible and traced home to its source."

Throughout the fall, winter, and spring of 1917–18, the Inquiry organization was evolving and wheels were grinding, but the results were frequently disheartening. Scheduled deadlines were disregarded more often than not; submitted reports frequently seemed no better than sketchy drafts. Dana Munro kept complaining about difficulties that had upset the work on the Turkish Empire. Several men had utterly failed to complete their assignments; others had taken ill. Some of the completed reports, Munro revealed, bore the marks of superficiality rather than solid scholarship. "I gathered the impression that you [Isaiah Bowman] wanted something on hand which might serve as an introduction." [17] And, according to Archibald Cary Coolidge, the Inquiry organization was developing several contradictory and improperly conceived functions and methods. What was the necessity, asked Coolidge, for using persons having some specialized knowledge if the Inquiry staff was simply amassing data? Certainly a specialist engaged on an assignment could not be expected merely to copy statistics or paraphrase his findings in reference books. Coolidge was raising a matter of procedure which struck at the very roots of the Inquiry's method:

> I am not quite sure that I understand what you [Coolidge was addressing James T. Shotwell] mean about the men here confining themselves for the present to the "gathering of data in the historical field." In questions of nationalities such as the people here have been working over, the story of the different theories and claims, the basis on which they rest and the arguments put forward in support of them are an important part of the subject. If we are to have trained men to handle such things we expect from them a certain amount of sifting and we shall evidently get a certain expression of their views. These views we are not bound to accept any more than the future representatives of the United States are bound to accept our views, but I do not feel that when we get a man like [Robert] Lord who is the only one in the United States who really knows anything about Polish history, that we can ask him to confine himself to compiling statistics. [18]

The accumulation of factual information would, in the view of the Executive Committee, avoid the pitfalls of subjective impres-

17. Dana Munro to Isaiah Bowman, May 9, 1918, Inquiry Archives.
18. Coolidge to Shotwell, Nov. 28, 1917, Inquiry Archives; for another criticism, see Coolidge to Lippmann, April 5, 1918, Inquiry Archives.

sions, interpretations, and judgments. Moreover, there was concern that at the peace conference the commissioners might be seeking only facts, and impressions, interpretations, or judgments submitted by the Inquiry staff might tend to confuse. Perhaps due to Coolidge's insistence, the Inquiry's reports were henceforth to be of two varieties: (1) the statistical, largely descriptive report heavily laden with facts but lacking in overt interpretations, conclusions, and definite proposals; (2) an interpretive, analytical report containing conclusions and even recommendations.[19]

By early May, the Inquiry's operations were divided into twenty-nine divisions, twelve of which were called "analytical territorial divisions" while seventeen were simply referred to under the category, "synthetic research." The report of May 10 suggests the several directions in which the work was leading. Instead of an Italian division, there was a division titled, "the head of the Adriatic—the Trentino, the Isonzo, Istria, and Trieste, the Dalmatian Coast." In the absence of a separate German division, there now existed an administrative unit called "the Western Front," though the only section of Germany which was to receive explicit study according to this report was Alsace-Lorraine. Rumania and Bessarabia were to form the subject of a separate division in the Inquiry's organization as would Persia, Afghanistan, and Beluchistan together. Finally, Section 12 of the report dealt with projected research concerning South and Central America. Regarding the latter project, the report announced:

> The research will be directed by Dr. Isaiah Bowman. As the authorization for this work was not secured until approximately May 1st, it is entirely in its preliminary stages. General plans have been drawn, and Professor Bailey Willis of Stanford University has been selected to do the economic and scientific part of the research. The active cooperation of Mr. J. H. Stabler of the Division of Latin American Affairs of the Department of State has been secured on the political side.[20]

The inclusion of Latin America within the scope of the Inquiry's activities not only brought forth a new dimension for the organiza-

19. Report on the Inquiry, Its Scope and Method, March 20, 1918, *FRPPC, 1*, 55–72.

20. Report on the Inquiry, May 10, 1918, *FRPPC, 1*, 82–97. Part I is quoted in Appendix V. For extended consideration of the Latin American Inquiry see infra, pp. 101 ff. and also Chap. 9.

tion's research, but also reflected a far-reaching alteration in the administrative direction of the Inquiry. There was henceforth a greater degree of supervision provided by the Department of State, and at the same time Sidney Mezes' position as director was openly endangered.

In the summer of 1918, latent criticism of Mezes' leadership which had pervaded the Inquiry for many months at last burst forth into the open. The dissension arose out of the charge that Mezes had been disregarding the Inquiry's Executive Committee, which was supposedly supervising the Inquiry's operations. Mezes was, his critics charged, acting independently of the Committee, arrogating the latter's authority for himself. Whether his action was justified or not, several officers regarded it as unjustified and highhanded and they thought Mezes was attempting to dictate to the organization. The critics also pointed out that numerous memoranda had been issued from time to time which seemed contradictory, and that division chairmen as well as staff members generally were often unsure of their proper functions. Morale, too, was said to be declining measurably, and by July 1918 there was grave danger the Inquiry would suffer seriously through wholesale resignations.[21]

Two principal records of this administrative revolution throw the issues into bold relief.[22] Both documents were apparently the work of the leading spirit in the rebellion, Isaiah Bowman. There are, however, certain difficulties in the way of accepting these documents as entirely reliable. First of all, the two memoranda bear different dates—November 30, 1918, and March 14, 1932. Secondly, whereas both recount much the same events, there are highly significant variations. According to both, the crisis within the Inquiry's organization was so serious that Colonel House was asked to intercede. In the earlier memorandum, Bowman directed criticism to the Inquiry's inefficiency, its utter dependence upon the American Geographical Society, and the Executive Committee's attempt to impose an "insane" individual (James McGuire of the

21. Bowman to Mezes, July 13, 1918, Shotwell MSS, Columbia; Author's interview with Shotwell, December 1954.

22. Bowman's notes on the Inquiry, Nov. 30, 1918, Shotwell MSS, Columbia; Memorandum from notes dated March 14, 1932, Shotwell MSS, Columbia. The two memoranda will be found as Appendix VI and Appendix VII respectively.

Coast and Geodetic Service) upon the cartographic section of the Inquiry. Moreover, in this first memorandum Bowman emphasized how his proposed program of work, submitted on May 1, 1918, was "disregarded" until August 1 and approved then only in modified form. During May and June, Bowman continued, the state of disorganization had proceeded so far that half of the principal scholars had announced privately their intention of resigning. Meanwhile, before the resignations materialized, Bowman went on vacation for a period of three weeks, not returning to his office until July 16. On that date he conferred with Mezes about the need for some drastic administrative changes. Following this exchange, Mezes consulted with David Hunter Miller who subsequently invited Colonel House's intercession. The Colonel, Bowman recalled, "asked me [Bowman] to become executive officer of the Inquiry, and Dr. Mezes asked me to be responsible for men, money and plans of the Inquiry from that time."

By way of contrast, the second memorandum, bearing a date some fourteen years after the events being described, reveals quite a different version. Conditions were deteriorating in the Inquiry during the early summer of 1918. Toward the end of July or the beginning of August (Bowman is far less definite in this second memorandum), David Hunter Miller called to notify Bowman that Colonel House desired to see him. A conference was at once arranged and it was House personally (not Mezes) who placed Bowman in charge of "men, money and plans." Of greater significance, however, is the implication in the second memorandum that from August to October 1918 Mezes was clearly on the sidelines of the Inquiry organization. Colonel House, in the words of the later memorandum, had placed Bowman in "complete charge." To make the matter even clearer, the memorandum adds, "As Dr. Bowman could not think of anything this did not include, he accepted." Then, "For the first time, the work became orderly and effective and constructive." A research committee consisting of Haskins, Young, Shotwell, and Bowman gradually assumed full direction and shunted Mezes into the shadows.[23] The formation of the Research Committee in very early August seems to bear out

23. Bowman announced the formation of the Research Committee in his letter to Charles Haskins, Aug. 3, 1918, *FRPPC, 1*, 103–04.

Bowman's argument in the second memorandum that he assumed control at that time rather than at the end of August.

One possible consequence of this administrative *coup* was the severance of Walter Lippmann's connection with the Inquiry. Lippmann resigned in the midst of the turmoil to accept a commission as captain in Military Intelligence. Otherwise the administrative shakeup did not affect the Inquiry's personnel. From the start of the reorganization, Bowman expressed reluctance to assume responsibility for "men, money and plans" unless this responsibility was to be fully shared by all members of the new Research Committee. He considered each member of the committee to be a man about whom "there can be not the slightest question," by which he probably meant that each possessed an outstanding scholarly reputation.[24]

As far as Mezes was concerned, his inability to convince his associates that he possessed a real capacity for directing studies in international relations was undoubtedly an important ingredient contributing to the "rebellion." [25] On the other hand, it does not seem that Bowman's ascendancy within the Inquiry's high command was in any way accompanied by Mezes' removal from the position of leadership despite the implications of the two Bowman memoranda. As a matter of fact, Mezes continued to communicate with Colonel House concerning the organization's operations all through the months of August, September, October, and November. Mezes even continued to relay House's instructions to members of the Research Committee. For instance, on August 6 Mezes wrote to House:

> There has been nothing much to report for the last week or two as we were engaged in laying out a program of work for the interval between now and November 1st, and effecting an organization of the staff. These tasks have now been completed, and I am enclosing two memoranda which show what we have been doing in this respect.[26]

24. Bowman to House, Aug. 17, 1918, House Inquiry MSS, file 33-140, Yale.
25. Shotwell, *At the Paris Peace Conference* (New York, 1937), pp. 5–6; Author's interview with Shotwell, December 1954; Author's interview with Robert J. Kerner, Dec. 27, 1954.
26. Mezes to House, Aug. 6, 1918, House Inquiry MSS, file 33-157, Yale.

Again on September 18, Mezes dispatched to House news of the Inquiry's progress. In this letter, however, it is evident that Mezes fully realized the extent to which his influence in the organization had fallen, for he thought it necessary that House "ask the force of the Inquiry to prepare [a series of reports] as I suggested the other night." [27] Over House's signature the directive could then be carried by Mezes to Bowman and the Research Committee. It followed, therefore, that on September 23 Mezes presented to Bowman certain suggestions received from House concerning the Inquiry's work:

> Colonel House would like us to prepare reports as outlined in general in the memorandum I am enclosing. Won't you be good enough to start the work, as he would like the reports as soon as possible.[28]

Sidney Mezes apparently accepted the change in administrative leadership with outward calm, but on at least one occasion his temper did flare. In the middle of August, he wrote to House:

> When you get time to look over the new organization of the Inquiry, you will of course see that somewhat academic and impractical results are to be expected from Bowman and his professorial assistants especially as he, while a manly fellow, *can't* do things any way except his own, and has to be given his way to work well or not at all. I don't think the price is too high for his fine house [the American Geographical Society Building] and exceptional geographical competence.[29]

Whether or not Mezes was actually stripped of effective leadership over the Inquiry's organization during August, as the two memoranda suggest, it can be ascertained that Bowman's influence did become far greater in the months just before the armistice. The rivalry and conflict between Mezes and Bowman were all the more important because for all intents and purposes the Inquiry's administration was completely autonomous, only rarely affected by Colonel House and the President.

27. Mezes to House, Sept. 18, 1918 Mezes MSS, Columbia.
28. Mezes to Bowman, Sept. 23, 1918, Mezes MSS, Columbia.
29. Mezes to House (handwritten), Aug. 18, 1918, House Inquiry MSS, file 33-157, Yale.

Colonel House did oversee some of the Inquiry's operations. He had exercised some influence upon the selection of key personnel, but aside from the leadership, the selection of other staff members did not trouble him. House had taken some interest in the administrative struggle which transpired during the summer of 1918, and from time to time even commented upon the various plans for the organization. But House, like the President, was deeply involved in a myriad of other responsibilities; other matters were constantly pressing for his attention. To judge by the infrequent references to the Inquiry in his diary, House's supervisory obligations with respect to the Inquiry occupied very little of his time and attention prior to the armistice.

It cannot be determined which of the Inquiry's reports and memoranda were transmitted to the White House. Probably all of the organizational charts and at least some significant memoranda were brought to the President's attention. As a rule, the President, if he actually read the papers, provided no direct response. In November 1917, Wilson politely thanked Mezes for the Outline of Inquiry subjects and even went so far as to recommend the inclusion of additional topics. The President's note read:

> Thank you for the preliminary and brief outline of the subjects to be dealt with in the Inquiry. It seems to me to suggest most of the chief topics that will have to be studied, though it occurs to me that there is one omission, though it may be only apparent.
> It seems to me that it will be necessary to study the just claims of the larger states, like Russia and Austria, and Germany herself, not only to an assured access to the sea and the main routes of commerce, but to a reasonable access to the raw materials of the world which they themselves do not produce.
> Of course, what we ourselves are seeking is a basis which will be fair to all and which will nowhere plant the seeds of such jealousy and discontent and restraint of development as would certainly breed fresh wars.[30]

If the President entertained any reservations about the Inquiry's failure to carry through with his concept of its function, no communications were forthcoming from his office or from his re-

30. President Wilson to Mezes, Nov. 12, 1917, Wilson MSS, Series II, Library of Congress. Reference is made to a conference with the President in Mezes to Coolidge, Nov. 19, 1917, Inquiry Archives.

nowned typewriter. The leaders of the Inquiry naturally consulted with House more frequently. In June 1918, Mezes sought
House's opinion as to whether the reports already produced by
the Inquiry were satisfactory:

> Won't you let me know at your convenience whether the re-
> ports being sent are what you want? They are our best guess as
> to what would be useful. Let me know what is surplus and, what
> else, if anything, you would like to have included, and whether in
> form you prefer Bowman's detail in staccato without explana-
> tions, or Lippmann's more flowing form with explanations.[31]

The next day, June 8, House confided to his diary his intention
to spend more time keeping *au courant* with the Inquiry's operations.[32] At least by October, House found time to read some of the
reports and even offered occasional comments with suggestions
for their improvement.[33] By and large, however, he contented
himself with mediating when necessary, making modest suggestions, and delegating authority for the responsibility to his chosen
subordinates.

A greater measure of Presidential supervision might not have
altered the course of the Inquiry's operations markedly, but the
perpetual financial distress under which the Inquiry suffered
could well have been alleviated. As an independent commission
established solely by executive action, the Inquiry never received
any Congressional recognition such as a separate appropriation
with which to carry on its work might have afforded. Throughout
its existence, the Inquiry drew its operational expenses directly
from the President's special contingency-reserve fund for national
security and defense. This fund, consisting altogether of $150,000,-
000, had been placed at the President's disposal by two separate
Congressional enactments.[34] In granting these funds, Congress

31. Mezes to House, June 7, 1918, Mezes MSS, Columbia.

32. House MSS Diary, June 8, 1918, Yale.

33. Bowman to Charles Seymour, Oct. 2, 1918, House Inquiry MSS, file 33
misc., Yale; Bowman to Shotwell, Oct. 2, 1918, Inquiry Archives.

34. President Wilson to Representative John J. Fitzgerald (chairman of the
House Appropriations Committee), Dec. 5, 1917, Wilson MSS, Series II, Library of
Congress. The President requested that the unused balance from the previous year
be made available for 1918.

had probably authorized all the money requested by the President.[35] Following customary practice, no particular purpose was specified by Congress for the use of the funds; they were to be expended at the discretion of the Commander in Chief. In practice, it must be noted, the White House submitted a weekly report covering the expenses drawn from this fund.[36] These weekly, plus other monthly, financial reports were compiled by the Treasury, then sent to the White House, after which they were submitted to the House of Representatives. Each of the reports regularly stipulated the allotment specified for use by the Inquiry.[37] Once again it is noteworthy that although the Inquiry's allotment was drawn directly from the President's Fund for National Safety and Defense, it was Secretary of State Lansing who made the formal requests for the money. Lansing, not Colonel House, directed requests for Inquiry funds in January 1918 and in February 1918. Later, on May 1, 1918, when Latin American studies were undertaken by the Inquiry, all funds for this project were provided by the Treasury, first to the State Department and only then to the Inquiry.[38]

Throughout the Inquiry's independent existence, recorded in the financial books from October 27, 1917, to January 31, 1919, the organizational operating expenses, its entire allocation of funds, totaled $241,200.[39] This amount included expenditures both for

35. Moorfield Storey to Lord Bryce, Dec. 26, 1917, quoted in Mark A. de Wolfe Howe, *Portrait of an Independent, Moorfield Storey 1845–1929* (Boston, 1932), pp. 318–20.

36. United States Congress, 65th Congress, 2d Session, House Report 212.

37. Treasury Department Weekly Reports concerning the use of the fund for national security and defense are found in the Wilson MSS, Series II, Library of Congress.

38. Lansing to Wilson, Jan. 8, 1918, Wilson MSS, Series VI; Wilson to Lansing, Jan. 9, 1918 (approved the request for funds), Wilson MSS, Series VI; Lansing to Wilson, Feb. 23, 1918, and Wilson to Lansing, Feb. 25, 1918, Wilson MSS, Series VI; Treasury Department Weekly Report May 1, 1918, provides funds for Latin American studies by Mezes, Wilson MSS, Series II; Lansing to Wilson, April 30, 1918; Wilson to Lansing, May 1, 1918, Wilson MSS, Series VI, Library of Congress.

39. Inquiry Account Book, David Hunter Miller MSS, Library of Congress; Financial Reports of the Inquiry, House Inquiry MSS, file 33-119, Yale. Complete financial records including canceled checks, account books, and correspondence concerned with expenditures are located in the David Hunter Miller MSS. Unless

material and for personnel. The average monthly budget thus approximated $17,000. Until July 1918, however, the Inquiry's monthly expenditure did not exceed $15,000.

Ordinarily, 65 per cent to 75 per cent of the total budget went for salaries of the research staff while the balance was used for purchasing supplies, travel expenses, and for payment of clerical assistance. During February 1918, for instance, of the $11,157.29 used by the Inquiry, $6,511.10 went directly for research salaries. In March, a total of $13,110.33 was spent, with $7,427.98 going for research. From October 1917 to June 30, 1918, a total of $88,-464.43 was spent, of which $53,514.17 was earmarked for research per se. Of the total expenditures made by the Inquiry from October 1917 through January 1919, $139,895.08 was paid on research salaries. When it is recalled that the Inquiry's staff numbered at least 125 members in various research capacities, it is clear that this money must have been stretched to the maximum.

No analysis of expenditures of Inquiry funds would provide the sole criterion for reckoning the relative importance attached to the several research projects by the executive leadership of the organization. Nevertheless, percentages of the total budget allocated for different projects can furnish one yardstick for assessing the importance of the different divisions. Presumably, consideration of Latin America had not been part of the President's original proposal for the Inquiry's operations. Additional money was, however, made available for this responsibility when it was assumed.

The degree of importance attached to Latin American research by a commission ostensibly designed for the purpose of preparing the American case in time for the peace negotiations should be noted. As of August 1918, for instance, when the Inquiry was spending (on salaries) $1,024.98 for research on Austria-Hungary; $406.72 on the Far East; $26.79 on Italy; $2,014.45 on Russia; $57.21 on the Pacific Islands; $387.54 on the Turkish Empire, and $1,109.69 for completion of the Diplomatic History Project, it was allocating $4,070.63 for the study of Latin American problems.

---

otherwise stated, statistics and other financial information pertaining to the Inquiry are based upon materials in the Miller collection.

More money was in fact spent on Latin American research during August 1918 than was allocated for all other regional problems combined. The table below shows how research funds were distributed among the several divisions in September 1918:

Africa	$ 255.59	Western Asia	$ 638.42
Austria-Hungary	1,594.53	Western Europe	436.50
Balkans	43.00	Diplomatic history	2,170.74
Far East	499.34	Economic studies	1,556.72
Pacific Islands	87.08	International law	2,476.77
Russia	1,616.61	Latin America	4,409.22

Even as late as November 1918, the month of the armistice, fully half of the Inquiry's total allocation for regional research was channeled into Latin American projects. Once Bowman ushered in his regime of orderly efficiency, directing "men, money and plans," barely a trickle of the regime's budget was used for studies of the Far East, Italy, Austria, and Western Europe. Though the Inquiry was in constant need of funds, the available money went into projects mainly concerned with Latin America, projects which could have only the most remote relationship to the peace settlement. During the months of August and September 1918, when the whole Inquiry budget barely exceeded $15,000 per month, more than 25 per cent of its funds went for Latin American research.

Appendix IX shows how the total budget of $241,200 was spent. These figures illustrate several curious relationships. The $35,000 for Latin American studies exceeded by some $7,000 the *total funds made available for all other regional research*. The cartographic program's $16,000 and the international law program's $9,932.11 together totaled as much as the entire regional research program exclusive of Latin America. In November 1918, out of a budget of $30,258.43, international law was allotted $2,302.09; the map program, $3,345.19; and Latin America $4,654.13. Inquiry documents do not indicate in any conclusive fashion whether Isaiah Bowman personally inspired this strange use of funds by a peace preparatory commission. Nevertheless, the curious emphasis upon Latin American projects—certainly at variance with President Wilson's definition of the Inquiry's functions—was instituted in May 1918 and gathered momentum after the reorganization of August placed greater operational control with Isaiah Bowman, a man whose special professional interest had been Latin American geography.

From its headquarters at the American Geographical Society in New York City, the Inquiry's organization sprawled northward and southward like so many tentacles. The Eastern European Division maintained its office at Harvard University; the Austrian Division operated at Yale University; while Turkish Empire studies were handled at Princeton; and economics research was coordinated at Washington, D.C. Integration of these projects necessitated constant meetings to bring staff and division chairmen together so as to coordinate their activities. As a rule, there was a monthly Executive Committee meeting which brought the research directors together in New York. At these meetings, principal papers were discussed, occasional speakers were heard, criticism was aired, and new directives were announced. In one important sense, the decentralized locations offered at least one advantage whose importance undoubtedly went unnoticed at the time: it encouraged a continuous flurry of correspondence clarifying the operations of the organization for the benefit of the later historian. From a practical standpoint, decentralization allowed the various Inquiry divisions to make use of the excellent library resources in the respective universities and in the national capital.

Operating as it did on so slender a budget, the Inquiry from the beginning of its existence endeavored to obtain the cooperation of existing government departments, private research organizations, and private business firms. Persons employed by these organizations were asked to compile reports for the Inquiry, in most instances without being informed of the intended purpose of their studies. In almost every case, these supplementary reports were prepared as a patriotic service by the writer, without remuneration from the Inquiry. One fundamental advantage of "farming out" reports in this fashion was that it allowed the Inquiry to make use of the part-time services of specialized talent which had already become committed to government or private employment. Fully 50 per cent of all Inquiry reports were the products of this "farming out" system. On October 1, 1918, the Inquiry Research Committee listed the government agencies with which the Inquiry had made liaison for the purpose of obtaining reports:

1. Military Intelligence Division, Army General Staff.
2. Bureau of the Census, Department of Commerce.
3. United States Geological Survey, Department of Interior.
4. United States Forest Service, Department of Agriculture.
5. Bureau of Soils, Department of Agriculture.
6. Bureau of Plant Industries, Department of Agriculture.
7. Division of Foreign Tariffs, Bureau of Foreign and Domestic Commerce, Department of Commerce.
8. Division of Latin American Affairs, Department of State.
9. Foreign Trade Adviser, Department of State.
10. Bureau of Research, War Trade Board.
11. Division of Planning and Statistics, War Industries Board and United States Shipping Board.
12. National Research Council (Anthropological Committee, Medical Research Committee).[40]

Private research agencies cooperating with the Inquiry were the National Board for Historical Services, the National Geographical Society, the Carnegie Institution, and the Carnegie Endowment for International Peace.[41] Private business firms, which mainly contributed economic data reports, included the War Service Committee of the Rubber Industry, the General Rubber Company, the Standard Oil Company of New York, and the American Tobacco Company.[42] The American Board of Foreign Missions, through its president, James L. Barton, was authorized to gather material pertaining to mission problems after the war, and this material was incorporated in the Inquiry files.[43] Representatives

40. Confidential letter from the Research Committee of the Inquiry to divisional chiefs, Oct. 1, 1918, Inquiry Archives. There is a vast quantity of correspondence in the Inquiry Archives touching upon coordination with each government bureau concerned.

41. Shotwell to David Hunter Miller and A. A. Young, Nov. 27, 1918, Inquiry Archives.

42. A. A. Young to B. G. Work, chairman of the War Service Committee of the Rubber Industry, May 8, 1918; B. G. Work to Young, May 14, 1918; Mezes to Robert S. Woodward, president of the Carnegie Institution of Washington, May 23, 1918; Bailey Willis to William Boss, general manager, General Rubber Company, June 18, 1918; W. K. Prentice to the American Tobacco Company, July 29, 1918, Inquiry Archives.

43. James L. Barton to Mezes, May 23, 1918; May 25, 1918; Mezes to Barton, June 4, 1918, Inquiry Archives.

from Zionist groups, European ethnic and nationalist associations desiring to gain American assistance at the peace conference, all contributed "studies" to the Inquiry's growing eclecticism.

The Inquiry did not always exploit these relationships for its exclusive advantage. The Inquiry was anxious to obtain current intelligence information from the War Department for the benefit of those at work on frontier studies,[44] while the War Department in turn borrowed numerous Inquiry reports. One request for a loan from the Inquiry consisted of twenty-nine typewritten pages just listing the titles of Inquiry reports desired by the War Department staff.[45] These examples of cooperation were extensive before the Inquiry's work was concluded.

Among all the government agencies with which the Inquiry cooperated, the Department of State was the one with which there was the closest and most frequent association. There already existed within the Department of State certain channels through which the American government acquired knowledge of political intelligence. It was therefore important for the Inquiry to gain access to this intelligence service if its reports were going to be based upon the best available information. As early as November 5, 1917, Sidney Mezes started exploring techniques to determine how the State Department could assist the Inquiry.[46] Reports from the far-flung network of American consulates were regularly turned over to the appropriate divisions of the Inquiry. Periodically, division leaders from the State Department visited the Inquiry headquarters in New York, and Inquiry leaders made regular pilgrimages to the State Department to read Department files and consult with Department specialists.[47] Despite this attempt at

44. Bowman to Captain Lawrence Martin, Army War College, Feb. 21, 1918, Inquiry Archives.

45. Stephen Bonsal, Office of the Chief of Staff, letter to Walter Lippmann, March 19, 1918; Lippmann to Bonsal, March 28, 1918; Captain Herbert B. Blankenhorn to Lippmann, June 14, 1918; Lippmann to Colonel House, June 20, 1918, Inquiry Archives; Lippmann to Secretary of War Newton D. Baker, Dec. 17, 1917, Baker MSS, Library of Congress.

46. Mezes-Lansing Correspondence, Nov. 5, 1917, and Nov. 9, 1917, *FRPPC, 1,* 14–15.

47. Mezes to Gordon Auchincloss, Feb. 1, 1918, Mezes MSS, Columbia; Mezes to Auchincloss, May 9, 1918, Auchincloss MSS, file 265, Yale; State Department Counselor Frank Polk to Mezes, Nov. 24, 1917, Mezes MSS; Mezes to Wolcott

coordination, some persons familiar with the arrangement never felt that a high degree of smooth cooperation was ever achieved.[48] Writing in London during November 1918, Walter Hines Page observed:

> There's an amateur touch at Washington as regards foreign affairs. Else of course Lansing would come here himself. The President would send him instead of sending House. The civilian members of the House Commission have no coordination with the State Department. When we showed them at the chancery the information and documents that I have sent to Washington (to the State Department, of course), they exclaimed: "Why we never saw them. Why don't they come to us?" And several of them especially asked if I couldn't henceforth communicate with them direct. In a very important sense, there is no State Department.
>
> The civilian members of the Commission are of course trying to formulate policies—trying after a study of each subject, to recommend lines of action to the President . . . The whole management of foreign relations has an uncoordinated amateur touch.[49]

Ordinarily, Inquiry members received from the State Department information they requested; it was not furnished voluntarily.

If there was any personal antagonism on the part of career State Department officers, some of whom at least viewed the Inquiry as usurping a function properly belonging to the Department, the record does not bear it out. The Inquiry entered the intelligence field not because the State Department was uncooperative in supplying current reports, but rather because the

---

Pitkin, Nov. 27, 1917, Mezes MSS; Mezes to Lippmann, Dec. 15, 1917, Mezes MSS, Columbia.

48. Shotwell, *At the Paris Peace Conference* (New York, 1937), p. 12. Contrary evidence showing the effective efforts at cooperation by the Department of State and the Inquiry can be found in Telegram from Department of State to all American Consuls General and Consuls signed by Secretary Lansing, May 17, 1918, House Inquiry MSS, file 33-26, Yale; Requests for current economic information can be found in Memorandum from William C. Bullitt to William Phillips, June 13, 1918, Bullitt MSS, file 51-11, Yale. These requests contain instructions to ambassadors and ministers and consular officials to facilitate the work of the peace preparations. There is literally a small mountain of correspondence which throws light upon the attempts of the State Department to aid the Inquiry. Much of this documentation is in the Inquiry Archives.

49. Diaries and Embassy Notes, Nov. 24, 1918, Walter Hines Page MSS, Harvard.

State Department did not possess the kind of information needed.

During January 1918, Allen Dulles, attached to the American Legation in Berne, Switzerland, suggested to the State Department the advantages of having a group of American scholars stationed in Switzerland for the purpose of studying "at first hand the problems of nationalities and to determine where justice lies in the various claims of the European races and nations, especially the Slavs." [50] Dulles continued, "Here at the Legation we are barely able to keep up with political developments in Germany and Austria day by day, and could not possibly undertake such a study as these problems involve, but could help others to get in touch with the sources and the persons from which they could obtain the necessary information for their study." Even while Dulles was writing these words, Remsen Whitehouse, a Department aide, was en route to Berne for the avowed purpose of opening an American propaganda bureau, but in his briefcase was a memorandum from Isaiah Bowman covering certain intelligence which Whitehouse was to procure and transmit to the Inquiry. The list of materials which Bowman requested included the following:

1. Eugene Romer's atlas of Poland, published in 1916 (urgent).

2. Recent geographical publications in the Central Powers, particularly seventeen German volumes [names listed].

3. Pamphlets and separates of papers published in Austria and Germany on the individual peoples within the field of military domination of the Central Powers. We suppose that quite a number of these have been issued. They are studies by German geographers and ethnographers on the ethnography and economic resources, etc., of the people.

4. (a) After the German occupation of Riga and the overrunning of Lithuania the German military authorities made a census of the population of Lithuania. This census was published in the German papers and abstracts of it have reached this country but cannot be found by the Inquiry. It will be a great service to secure this census for our use. (b) Doubtless censuses have been taken of other areas occupied by Teutonic force, for example, Roumania, Serbia, Montenegro, etc.

5. German peace maps, etc.[51]

50. Allen Dulles to Robert Lansing, Jan. 17, 1918, Paris Peace Conference, American CTNDQ, file 182/8, State Department Archives, National Archives.

51. Lippmann to Remsen Whitehouse, Jan. 22, 1918, with enclosure; Whitehouse to Lippmann, Jan. 23, 1918, Inquiry Archives.

Through Whitehouse, the Inquiry obtained vital European books, especially from Germany.[52]

While Whitehouse was gathering information in Switzerland, James F. Abbott, a zoologist from Washington University (St. Louis) then on duty with Military Intelligence, went off to Japan to obtain data for the Far Eastern Division of the Inquiry. According to instructions sent to Abbott by Wolcott Pitkin, the Inquiry was anxious to obtain "all the information you may find it possible to lay your hands upon relating to organizations like the South Manchurian Railroad Company, the Nippon Yusen Kaisha, the Yokohama Specie Bank, and the Mitsui Company which would tend to throw any light upon the relationship between these companies and the Japanese Government or the controlling element in the Japanese Government, the extent of control which they, or the controlling element are in a position to exercise upon the Japanese Government itself and methods by which they are utilized in carrying forward Japanese imperialism." [53] Archibald Cary Coolidge was sent to Scandinavia to transmit needed German publications. Toward the end of the war, Roland Dixon, whose work for the Inquiry focused upon Central Asia, was preparing to lead a caravan expedition into Central Kashgar for the purpose of obtaining information. Though Robert Lord expressed opposition to Dixon's plan and even urged that military intelligence agents be used to extract the needed information, Isaiah Bowman was enthusiastic about Dixon's proposed field trip and declared to Dixon: "Lord reported to you without authorization from the Inquiry." [54] Nevertheless, when the armistice was signed on November 11, Dixon wrote to Bowman that he was "cheated" out of his expedition by twenty-four hours.[55] There is certainly room for some speculation as to what Bowman and Dixon expected to learn, that would be of service to an American delegation at the peace conference, by resorting to a caravan expedi-

52. Remsen Whitehouse to Lippmann, Feb. 26, 1918; Lippmann to Whitehouse, May 28, 1918; Whitehouse to Lippmann, June 21, 1918, Inquiry Archives.

53. Pitkin to James F. Abbott, Jan. 21, 1918, Inquiry Archives. Also relevant is Pitkin to Mezes, Jan. 18, 1918, Inquiry Archives.

54. Bowman to Roland Dixon, Oct. 24, 1918, Inquiry Archives. See also Dixon to Bowman, Oct. 24, 1918, Inquiry Archives.

55. Dixon to Bowman, Nov. 12, 1918, Inquiry Archives.

tion into Central Kashgar, which had not been involved in the war.

By all odds the most dramatic attempt by the Inquiry to employ an independent intelligence agent occurred in October 1918. Carl R. Blegen was an American citizen whose scholarly interests in classical archaeology had taken him to Greece just before the war as secretary to the American School of Classical Studies. On September 21, 1918, at a meeting of the Balkan Committee of the Inquiry, William S. Ferguson proposed that Blegen be employed by the Inquiry to "visit the disputed region of the northern frontier of Greece (Albania, Macedonia, Thrace) and report concerning:

> 1. the movements of population in those territories since 1912–1913.
> 2. the attitude of the people in each section toward claimant states.[56]

Additional instructions were to be supplied through Ferguson. These specified:

> 1. To what extent the Bulgarian element has been withdrawn recently (1918) from the Sari Chaban-Drama-Kavalla region and from the Demir-Hissar-Serres region and to what extent the Greek element, evacuated therefrom in 1916–1918 is being restored; to what districts specifically, and, if possible, to what occupations. The Struma valley region should be reported on separately.
> 2. To what extent the Bulgarian population has disappeared from the district between Salonica and the Vardar-Rupel frontier given to Greece in 1913. Did the Bulgarians driven from this region by the Greek army on its advance in the Second Balkan War ever get back again? How complete was the expulsion effected at this time?
> 3. The effect of the advance and subsequent withdrawal of the Bulgarian army in the region west of Lake Ostrovo in 1916 in evacuating from that region (Florina Castoria, etc.) the Bulgarian partisans.
> 4. What is the present strength of the Greek party in Monastir and its environs; the Greek party in Koritza and its district, and those districts under Italian occupation.[57]

56. The Balkan Committee of the Inquiry to Isaiah Bowman, Sept. 21, 1918, House Inquiry MSS, file 33-144, Yale.

57. William S. Ferguson to A. A. Young, Oct. 17, 1918, Inquiry Archives; Young to Clive Day, Oct. 9, 1918, Inquiry Archives.

Blegen was to start in the east and proceed in the direction of Santi Quaranta, arranging to meet Archibald Cary Coolidge who was then traveling in southeastern Europe. Coolidge would contact Blegen through the American minister at Athens. On October 24, Blegen cabled that he was proceeding as instructed, disguised as a member of a Red Cross commission.[58] No further communications were received from Blegen, although on December 27, Clive Day addressed to Blegen a request that he submit all information obtained on his mission.[59]

These few instances in which the Inquiry's professorial staff endeavored to obtain first-hand information on its own initiative offers some indication of how inadequate were the orthodox intelligence channels at the command of the United States government during the war years. The use of academicians for intelligence-gathering purposes was also symptomatic of a deep-seated conviction among the Inquiry's leaders that the Inquiry must take no chances; it must gather as much data as time and resources could permit. In carrying out their function, they thought it necessary to anticipate numerous complications. Although Latin America seemed remote from the peace settlement, for example, the American commissioners would have to be prepared should Latin American questions arise for discussion. Similarly, if Turkestanese questions should be considered, the American commissioners would look to the Inquiry for pertinent information. No one could possibly foretell exactly what information would be required.

In all, the Inquiry and coordinate agencies compiled about 2,000 separate reports dealing with peace problems. If this material were to be usable before and during the peace conference, an efficient, systematic reference and filing arrangement was essential. Staff members were expected to adhere to a prescribed format in preparing their reports. They were advised to include bibliographies plus whatever maps and other graphic illustrations were important to convey the report's message. Ideally,

58. Diplomatic Cable from Carl Blegen in Athens to William S. Ferguson via the State Department, Nov. 2, 1918, Inquiry Archives. Instructions to Blegen in regard to the secrecy of his mission and funds for the purpose are found in a letter from Bowman to Gordon Auchincloss, Nov. 6, 1918, Inquiry Archives.

59. Clive Day to Blegen, Dec. 27, 1918, House Inquiry MSS, file 33-149, Yale. That Blegen completed his mission and submitted a report is verified in letter from Blegen to the author, Oct. 23, 1957.

monographic reports were to be written in such a fashion as to be comprehensible to the nontechnical reader.

> Reports should not be clogged with too much detail, but at the same time they should not be without specific references to the more detailed studies, and monographs on each topic touched upon. They should have a limited number of footnote references, enough to enable the reader to pursue his investigations along any topic touched upon or covered in the survey. . . . Writer's opinion should be stated in separate paragraph.[60]

Though the length of Inquiry reports commonly ranged from one to thirty pages, a 400–500-page monograph was no oddity. Despite instructions to the contrary, many Inquiry reports were truly cluttered with data, often with highly valuable statistical information. Collaborators learned quickly how difficult, if not well-nigh impossible, was the task of describing complex relations within the confines of one or five pages. Brevity was especially difficult because the pressure of haste did not allow for much editing or compression.[61]

Members of the staff were required to prepare their reports in quadruplicate: one copy to remain with the author and three copies to be submitted to Inquiry headquarters. One copy was filed under alphabetical arrangement by author. A second copy was filed under a geographical arrangement by region. When it was necessary, reports encompassing more than one region were broken up and filed separately. The third file was a classification by topic.[62] For example, a study dealing with the mineral resources of Germany would be filed under minerals.

Each Inquiry report was submitted by the writer to the chairman of his division, who presumably read the report before sending it on to headquarters. Upon arrival at headquarters, reports were supposed to be scrutinized and criticized by at least one member of the executive staff—Mezes, Shotwell, Lippmann, Bow-

60. Memorandum of the Editorial Committee on the Kinds of Reports, no date, House Inquiry MSS, file 33-5, Yale. Also relevant is Memorandum on the Physical Makeup of Reports, no date, House Inquiry MSS, file 33-3, Yale; Memorandum on the Physical Makeup of Reports for the Inquiry, no date, William E. Dodd MSS, Library of Congress.

61. Mezes to A. A. Young, Jan. 22, 1918, Inquiry Archives.

62. Mezes to Shotwell, Dec. 6, 1917, Mezes MSS, Columbia.

man, or Miller. As the work proceeded and the number of reports mounted, the criticism, editing, and revision processes were largely suspended. A large percentage of reports, therefore, never received any critical analysis before entering the archival files.[63]

As first director of the library and archives section, the Inquiry obtained the services of Andrew Keogh, librarian of Yale University. With Florence Wilson, borrowed from the Columbia University Library, and the part-time services of Shotwell and Vladimir Simkhovitch, Keogh attempted to organize a select reference library, which was located on the top floor of the Geographical Society headquarters. Atlases, a gazetteer, biographical reference volumes, and many yearbooks containing statistical data were gathered. Encyclopedias and dictionaries were collected as needed. Other books and serials were acquired when requested by the research workers. Files of Inquiry reports included special reports from government bureaus, newspaper and magazine article clippings and extracts, statistical charts, graphs, and map work. All was filed in the library. Once this material was received, the librarians prepared elaborate indexes and catalogue cards so that the data would not only be filed but would be accessible at a moment's notice. At all times, Inquiry personnel was able to consult the files directly, with a minimum of restriction, except for some few files marked confidential to which access was more restricted. In the event of fire, provision was made for the conveying of the archives to the roof of the building where the materials would be lowered to safety.[64] The two tasks confronting the Reference and Archives Division were aptly described by Keogh:

> One is that of an effective service to the workers of the Inquiry in their present daily needs; the other task is that of preparation for the future—the organization of the staff, and the organization of material to stand the test that the Reference and Archives Division must meet in the future.[65]

63. This generalization is based on the few critiques uncovered for the six-month period preceding the armistice.

64. Andrew Keogh to Executive Committee of the Inquiry, Dec. 27, 1917, Inquiry Archives; Mezes to House, June 21, 1918, House Inquiry MSS, file 33-129, Yale.

65. Report from the Reference and Archives Division to the Research Committee of the Inquiry, no date, House Inquiry MSS, file 33-121, Yale.

Plans thus changed considerably during the Inquiry's first six months of operations. Attempts were abandoned to restrict the Inquiry within the confines envisioned in the President's letter to House, September 2, 1917, which had started the peace preparatory work.[66] Gradually more and more subjects pressed for inclusion on the Inquiry's agenda. The scope of its effort was extended to include the whole world. Coordination with private research foundations and a long list of government agencies was established to relieve the undernourished budget and to make use of specialists occupied elsewhere. Inadequate, weak supervision from above greatly affected its activities. The organization was permitted to go its own way. Neither Colonel House nor President Wilson assumed any effective supervision. As for the Department of State, it cooperated but exercised no effective controls. The Inquiry's operations frequently reflected lack of money, but also lack of foresight. Bulging files did not receive the critical attention which would have made them more serviceable. Too much was attempted. There did not exist enough in the way of adequate human or material resources to achieve the grandiose objectives.

66. Supra, p. 30.

Chapter 4

THE INQUIRY AND THE ALLIES

WARTIME SELF-INTEREST might logically dictate a national policy of cooperation with allies and associates in a common struggle. There is a special incentive for unity when the balance of power is delicately poised. Yet, in an age of hyper-nationalism, a Machiavellian independence of action ever watchful of advantage gained by friend as well as foe is operative. Even when governments are solemnly united in alliance, their historical relations may evoke distrust and suspicion. Differing war aims, assuming the coalition triumphs, can also account for ineffective coordination between participating nations. Hence the pursuit of victory is characteristically accompanied by the jealous defense of national interests, a condition which assumes the same importance in war as in peace.

In April 1917, when President Wilson affixed his signature to the American declaration of war, America became an active belligerent in the war against Germany. The new status of belligerency did not, however, lead to a new relationship between the United States and the existing coalition against Germany. A long tradition of separation from European politics would not countenance an immediate alliance. American memory of British and French imperialist exploitation, real or imaginary, did not augur well for a policy of unified action by the United States. Too many tangible and intangible wounds from the previous years of American neutrality were still perceptible. The scars from British attempts to restrict American neutral rights, memories of the black-lists, violations of sacred postal service, as well as the operations of the Allied blockade, all could not be forgotten at once. Compounded with these, the highly intangible but nevertheless real Anglophobe passions exerted upon the Congress and the President by Irish and German pressure groups in the United States did not exactly dispose the American government to favor entering the formal alliance against Germany.

American policy-makers were beset from the earliest months of the nation's military involvement with the problem of defining the relationship that would exist between the United States and the other nations already engaged in the war against the Central Powers. From the first month, President Wilson and his trusted advisers had become familiar with the most important of the Allied governments' secret treaties. The Allies' reluctance to commit themselves to a peace without aggrandizement contributed to President Wilson's insistence that America must pursue a definitely independent course, one not dependent upon the avaricious policies of England, France, Italy, and Japan. Knowledge of Allied war objectives coupled with reports that the British and French governments were already preparing programs for the eventual settlement had inspired the President to establish an American commission to prepare for the peace conference. Although the Wilson administration provided enthusiastic financial and material cooperation, mounted an American expeditionary force for the Western Front, and was willing to coordinate the war efforts, the months following American intervention also witnessed President Wilson's insistence that America should not become anything more than an equal partner in the coalition. Throughout the months of American involvement, the administration refused to enter into the structure of alliances, and the President was particularly careful to use the term "associate" in referring to the American relationship toward the Allies. At no time did the President affirm, recognize, or condone Allied war objectives as in any respect identical with American objectives. His reluctance to permit American troops to be fully integrated into a general Allied command provided still another reflection of his desire to follow an independent course. Nowhere was the imprint of this policy more evident than in the formation of the Inquiry. In his letter to House initiating the organization, President Wilson had specified its function to be the study of Allied objectives in the war and the establishment of an American case either for or against these objectives.

By entrusting this task to Colonel House, Woodrow Wilson had placed the commission under the control of a confirmed Anglophile. No member of the Wilson Cabinet was as intense in his desire to cooperate with the British and French governments as was Colonel House. Critical of his chief's insistence upon an independent course of action, House was always anxious to minimize tensions which might possibly disrupt American-Allied cordiality.[1] Winning the war, in House's view, might demand the sacrifice of certain national interests to the common advantage of the entire coalition. His strong feelings on this subject during the months before the peace conference can be perceived readily in the pages of his voluminous diary.[2] Whether President Wilson was familiar with House's inclinations is questionable. It was a matter of pride with House that he knew the Chief Executive so well that he would tell him only what Wilson wanted to hear.[3]

British and French officials were not unaware of House's long-standing sympathies for the Allied cause. It was through the intermediary of Colonel House that British and French leaders expected to influence the White House. Very soon after the United States entered the war, the British government sent to the United States a young (age 32) military officer, Sir William Wiseman, to serve as chief of British Military Intelligence. Neither American Ambassador Walter Hines Page in London nor British Ambassador

1. House MSS Diary, Aug. 20, 1918, Yale: "In talking with the President the other day, I called his attention to the necessity of not offending the British Government in a way that would offend the entire British nation."

2. House MSS Diary, July 2, 1917, Yale: "Have been working assiduously in my effort to adjust the differences between the United States and the British Government in regard to finances. I am in touch with every phase of the situation and am advising from three or four angles but always under cover, so that one group does not know I am advising the others. In this way, I have the whole picture before me and can act to the best advantage without creating friction."

3. Supra, Chap. 1. House MSS Diary, Aug. 27, 1918. "[William Phillips, Assistant Secretary of State, called on House.] Phillips thinks the President and Lansing are so prejudiced against the British Government that there is danger of serious complications."

Sir Cecil Spring Rice in Washington had been successful in transacting the delicate business of Anglo-American negotiations.[4] Wiseman was sent across the Atlantic to act as personal liaison between Downing Street and the White House. He quickly gained the confidence of Colonel House. House even started coaching the young Englishman on the most effective means of dealing with the President.

> The President easily gets annoyed and allows policy to be swayed by annoyance. . . . Never begin by arguing. Discover a common hate, exploit it, get the President warmed up and then start in on your business.[5]

Wiseman was soon devoting much time to cultivating his close relations with Colonel House. During August 1917, he engaged a flat in the same New York City apartment building where House resided. The older man dwelled on the ninth floor, Wiseman on the second. In October, Wiseman wrote his superiors in London:

> I am able to see him [House] several times a day, and we are working together even more closely than previously. As you know he has a private telephone to the State Department and the White House, so I could not be in closer touch if I were in Washington.[6]

From the fall of 1917, when House traveled abroad, he sometimes sought permission for the amiable Wiseman to accompany him.[7] He even shared restricted communications with this likeable agent.[8] Wiseman took his job very seriously, and in August 1917 his duty was to apply himself to two problems:

> 1. How to assist and encourage the United States to bring the full might of their power to bear upon the struggle as quickly and as effectively as possible.

4. Arthur Willert, *The Road to Safety: A Study in Anglo-American Relations* (London, 1952), pp. 61–62. House MSS Diary, Aug. 24, 1918, Yale.

5. Quoted in Willert, *The Road to Safety*, p. 63.

6. Ibid., p. 64. Cf. House MSS Diary, Dec. 17, 1918. "I am in constant touch with Sir William Wiseman who is working earnestly and intelligently for the best interests of all."

7. Willert, *Road to Safety*, p. 65.

8. Wiseman to Lord Robert Cecil, July 19, 1918, Wiseman MSS, Yale.

2. How to promote a full agreement between the two countries both upon *War Aims and Terms of Peace*.[9]

Wiseman learned quickly that Colonel House was susceptible to flattery. There was almost a continuous bombardment of beguiling compliments showered upon the Texas colonel. Typical was the following comment, which House doubtless liked for he recorded it in his diary:

> Wiseman has just arrived and I have had a few minutes talk with him. He opened the conversation by saying: "You have no conception of the influence you have with the British Government. There are only three nations to be considered in this war, Prussia, Great Britain, and the United States, and the strings are all being pulled at Magnolia." [10]

9. Final draft of Memorandum on Anglo-American Relations, August 1917, Wiseman MSS, file 90-5, Yale.

10. House MSS Diary, Sept. 12, 1917, Yale. Wiseman's extravagent praise for House and for the Inquiry continued even after the war and the peace conference. See, for example, the memorandum by Wiseman dated June 5, 1928 in Seymour, ed., *Intimate Papers of Colonel House*, 3, 170–73:

"It has therefore been sometimes assumed that the American delegation came to Paris ill-prepared, and that Wilson had not the benefit of the research and skilled advice afforded to the other heads of missions. This is not true. Colonel House foresaw very clearly the need for preparation, and as early as the summer of 1917 suggested a plan to Wilson which at once appealed to the President's scholarly and orderly mind. Colonel House proposed that an organization be created which was called the Inquiry. . . .

"This earnest and scholarly group of men gave deep and impartial study to the tremendous and complicated problems arising from a war which shattered the remnants of the Holy Roman Empire, dissipated the dreams of Bismarck, and left the great Russian Empire chaotic and impotent.

"The members of the Inquiry conferred freely with anyone—American and foreign—who could speak with authority and knowledge of any pertinent matter. Facts, opinions, prejudices, were patiently considered and carefully analyzed. The results of their work, their conclusions, their best advice, were summarized and submitted to the President by Colonel House, together with his own wise observations.

"Wilson often surprised his colleagues in Paris by his deep knowledge of the affairs of the Balkans, the bitter political struggle in Poland, or the delicate questions of the Adriatic. If Wilson's theories seemed strange and impractical to the realists of Europe, at least they could find no fault with the accuracy of his facts.

"Among the many services which the American Nation rendered to the world during this crisis in its history, the work of the Inquiry is by no means the least important and the record of the Inquiry, so little known to the public, remains a fine example of a difficult task, well accomplished and most modestly."

Information was transmitted to House from the British Foreign Office through Wiseman, but certainly there was discretion exercised as to what was divulged. Yet House reported on October 10, 1917, perhaps naïvely:

> Practically all the information which the British Foreign Office receives that is of value comes to me either directly or through Wiseman or Reading for me. Many of these cables are attached to the record, others I destroy.[11]

At all times, Wiseman endeavored to keep abreast of the work carried on by the Inquiry. Among the Wiseman papers, there is a folio marked "confidential" in which a copy of the Inquiry report of progress to January 15, 1918, is included. Wiseman sent this report off to his superiors in London, retaining a copy for himself.[12] Acting through House, Wiseman attempted to influence the preparation of Inquiry reports so that the latter might better suit British territorial aspirations after the war. In fact, during the summer of 1918, Wiseman could write to Lord Robert Cecil that the President had turned over the matter of the League of Nations to Colonel House to study, and House in turn

> is making use of the organization which he has created to prepare the American case for the peace conference. *It is, as you know, my chief duty here to keep in the closest touch with House and this organization of his.*[13]

Two questions involving the Inquiry particularly attracted the interest of Wiseman and his superiors. Wiseman expended much effort to influence Inquiry reports relating to the German colonies in Africa and the reports on the League of Nations. He was ordered to bring the British case for retention of the African colonies to the attention of Inquiry scholar George Louis Beer. Early in

11. Report of Conversation between Colonel House and President Wilson, Oct. 10, 1917, House MSS Diary, Oct. 13, 1917, Yale.

12. Lord Eustace Percy to Wiseman, July 5, 1918, Wiseman MSS, Yale. Folio containing the Inquiry report is located in the Wiseman MSS, File 90-57, Yale. Wiseman also transmitted the American Memorandum on the League of Nations prepared in July 1918 to the Foreign Office; see Wiseman to Lord Robert Cecil, July 19, 1918, Wiseman MSS, Yale.

13. Wiseman to Lord Robert Cecil, July 19, 1918, Wiseman MSS, Yale. Italics inserted by the author.

June 1918, Wiseman requested information about the possible use of East Africa for British Indian immigration. "Such use would make a good argument for retention of German colonies in eyes of U.S. public."[14] German misgovernment in the past and the difficulties in discovering the wishes of native peoples were to be the strongest elements in the British case. Wiseman was to allow Beer to "have a sight" of the British memorandum on the African colonies.[15] Likewise, he was authorized to show British memoranda to members of the Inquiry, *"in cases where we know his* [House's] people are 'on to' such questions."[16] He advised Lord Eustace Percy that British policy as it concerned the eventual peace settlement should be limited in the United States to "laying the facts before some of the leading men here, including of course, Colonel House's Inquiry."[17] Wiseman also attempted to make good use of personal contacts with influential members of the Inquiry. All of these techniques were followed up by the dispatch of certain Inquiry reports for the benefit of British Intelligence.

The British government manifested interest in American plans for the League of Nations in a similar fashion. Starting in February 1918, Wiseman's communications with London kept his superiors informed about American planning for an international organization.[18] Wiseman and his British associates consulted privately with such Inquiry stalwarts as Walter Lippmann and reported their conversations to London. During the summer of 1918, for instance, Lippmann, then in London but no longer a member of the Inquiry, told William Tyrrell in private conversation that President Wilson did not conceive of a League of Nations without German membership. London then cabled Wiseman:

14. Memorandum of William Wiseman, dated only June 1918, Wiseman MSS, Yale; cf. Wiseman to Lord Eustace Percy, July 19, 1918: "Many thanks for your interesting letter of June 18th. It seems we have a strong case for the retention of the German colonies, and I do not believe that there would be very serious opposition in this country if we go about it in the right way." Wiseman MSS, Yale.

15. Lord Eustace Percy to Wiseman, June 18, 1918; Memorandum of Wiseman dated only June 1918, Wiseman MSS, Yale.

16. Lord Eustace Percy to Wiseman, July 5, 1918, Wiseman MSS, Yale.

17. Wiseman to Lord Eustace Percy, July 19, 1918, Wiseman MSS, Yale.

18. Correspondence between Eric Drummond and William Wiseman, Feb. 9, 1918, and Feb. 14, 1918, House MSS, file 16-5, Yale.

Without giving away Lippmann, can you let me have your views on above remarks? To what extent is Lippmann in COLONEL HOUSE'S confidence? [19]

And Wiseman's response:

No one knows exactly the President's attitude because he himself has not yet decided what is the best way to proceed with the idea of a League of Nations. Both the President and House would probably be opposed to constituting a League of Nations without Germany.

I would not say that Lippmann is very closely in House's confidence.[20]

As he traveled about London and Paris during August and September 1918, Walter Lippmann was surprised to discover how much better the British were acquainted with the Inquiry than were Americans. Lippmann inferred the reason to be that Europeans maintained the "minutest interest in Colonel House's doings." [21] A more likely reason was that the confidential character of the Inquiry screened the American organization and its work from all save the favored few. Guards patrolled Inquiry headquarters night and day. Reports of Inquiry progress were not circulated in the press. Wiseman, however, was given access to confidential Inquiry reports, and, through personal contacts with House, became intimately acquainted with the operations of the Inquiry. Knowledge of American peace preparations never made available to American Congressmen could be procured by authorized British personnel at the Foreign Office in London.

All the major European belligerents—England, France, even Germany—had been busily developing elaborate preparations for the eventual peace settlement. Like the Inquiry, the Allied governments predicated their preparatory efforts on alternative assumptions of (1) total military victory, (2) a negotiated settlement. The British government, during the fall and winter of 1916–17,

19. Arthur Murray to Wiseman (cablegram), Aug. 8, 1918, Wiseman MSS, Yale.

20. Wiseman to Arthur Murray (cablegram), Aug. 10, 1918, Wiseman MSS, Yale.

21. Walter Lippmann to Sidney Mezes, Sept. 5, 1918, House MSS, file 10-30, Yale.

had established a commission to prepare for the peace conference at the instigation of Prime Minister David Lloyd George. Control over the British preparatory commission was exercised directly by the Foreign Office. In fact, the British commission was an adjunct of the Foreign Office. Various specialists from British university faculties were recruited to perform the necessary research.[22] Every corner of the globe was touched, and, in the end, the British preparatory commission produced—and later published (1920)—a total of 163 volumes composing a series known as the British Peace Handbooks.[23] These handbooks dealt with questions deemed by the Foreign Office to be relevant to the peace settlement. Economic questions, boundary questions, and strategic considerations all fell within the purview of the commission's work. As with the Inquiry, the British counterpart attempted a program of intensive coordination with existing government departments in Britain. The geographical section of the General Staff supplied necessary maps; a special section of the Admiralty took charge of geographical studies; while the War Trade Division and Intelligence Division provided current economic and political data respectively. Work on the formulation of military and strategic frontiers was coordinated by the General Staff.

Throughout its existence, the British peace preparatory commission suffered from an administrative defect familiar to the Inquiry. There was all too little consultation between and among persons responsible for the many related projects. Again, like the Inquiry, the British group encountered continuous conflict between theory and practice, between what seemed desirable and what was practical. The maze of British factual reports embraced a tremendous quantity of information, and circumstances later proved them superfluous to the needs of the peace conference. In conformity with the philosophy shared by the Inquiry, British leaders wanted to anticipate every possibility so that British rep-

22. H. W. V. Temperley, et al., eds., *History of the Peace Conference at Paris* (London, 1920–24), *1*, 240–41; Douglas Johnson, Confidential Report on Arrangements Made by the British Government for Collecting Data for the Peace Conference, May 1, 1918, Manuscript in House Inquiry MSS, file 33, No. 8, Yale.

23. The Library of Congress Card Catalogue lists 163 volumes in all, of which 157 were published in 1920. Six volumes were apparently suppressed and have never appeared in published form.

resentatives at the peace conference would not suffer in the discussion of any question that might arise.

Despite these possibly inevitable difficulties, the British preparatory commission was able to develop some fundamental recommendations for use at the peace conference. Sir George Prothero, an historian, headed the historical section of the Foreign Office which was responsible for the peace preparatory work. Henry N. Dickson of Reading College directed the Naval Intelligence Division which worked closely with the Foreign Office. Early in 1917, the British commission submitted to the Cabinet a series of recommendations, including the following:

1. Freedom and security for the development of all states.
2. The principle of nationality to guide the formulation of a territorial settlement. In cases of conflict between "nationality" and other principles, British interests should influence the decision.
3. Belgium to be restored and indemnified. A permanent alliance among France, Belgium, and Britain was urged.
4. Opposition to any extensive annexation of German territory by France on the grounds of "strategic exigencies."
5. Incorporation of Luxembourg and Belgium.
6. No present statement regarding the future status of Heligoland and the Kiel Canal.
7. Creation of a Polish kingdom to serve as a buffer between Germany and Russia.
8. Dissolution of the Austro-Hungarian Empire.
9. Germany to yield its coal fields in Silesia to Poland.
10. Allies were bound by Russian pledge to Rumania; Bukovina to be assigned to Rumania.
11. Respect for the Allied treaty with Italy even though it violated the principle of nationality.
12. Montenegro to be absorbed by Serbia.
13. Britain should encourage the union of the South Slavs.
14. Austrian provinces should be annexed by Germany. This would increase Catholic influence in German politics.
15. Three alternative suggestions regarding Bohemia:
    a. Independence.
    b. Absorption into a South Slav confederacy.
    c. Absorption into a new Polish State.
16. An independent Magyar Hungary.
17. Creation of a League of Nations based upon force to deter aggression.[24]

24. David Lloyd George, *The Truth About the Peace Treaties* (London, 1938), 1, 31–50.

These recommendations were suggestive of the European problems with which the British were most seriously concerned. Worldwide colonial problems were also systematically studied by the British group. Like those of the Inquiry, most of the British studies were in essence compilations of factual information rather than the considered recommendations of scholars. Presumably British representatives having access to the facts could better counter opposing arguments in debate while arriving at decisions safeguarding British interests in the peace settlement.

In Paris, three organizations had been established in 1916 and early 1917 for studying the special interests of France at the peace conference. These organizations were (1) the *Comité d'études;* (2) a special committee of economists directed by Jean Morel; and (3) a special committee created to coordinate and edit reports and at the same time to formulate definite policies and conclusions. This last committee was headed by André Tardieu.[25]

The *Comité d'études,* the French equivalent to the Inquiry, was formed on February 17, 1917. At its first meeting, Director Ernest Lavisse announced that the commission's purpose would be the preparation of reports "which would be useful to those who would have the responsibility of representing France at the peace conference."[26] In contrast with both the British and American projects, Lavisse's group confined its activities to carefully selected areas and problems. Questions pertaining to Europe would be examined, but aside from a consideration of the Turkish Empire in Asia, colonial matters per se were not regarded as germane. In contrast to the scores or even hundreds of reports assembled by the British and American commissions, the accumulated output from Lavisse's *Comité d'études* fitted neatly into two oversize volumes replete with basic maps.[27] Highest priority was placed upon questions involving the northeast frontier of France. Second priority was given to questions of interest to France's allies. The *Comité* was a compact organization[28] which did not at-

25. André Tardieu, *The Truth About the Treaty* (Indianapolis, 1921), pp. 85–86. Also see Temperley, op. cit., 239–40; Charles Haskins and Robert Lord, *Some Problems of the Peace Conference* (Cambridge, 1920), p. 23.

26. *Comité d'études, Travaux du comité d'études* (Paris, 1918–19), *1*, iii–v.

27. Ibid., Introduction, Vol. I.

28. Ibid., For names of personnel in the *Comité,* see ibid.

tempt extensive cooperation with numerous French governmental bureaus.[29] Only topics assigned by the French Foreign Office were studied. Furthermore, to avoid difficulties arising from failure of members to consult each other and failure to provide satisfactory criticism for the scholarly reports, Lavisse instituted the seminar procedure. At its weekly meetings in the Salle des Cartes of the Institut de Géographie at the Sorbonne, all members convened to hear and criticize completed reports. In this way, the membership became cognizant of what was being produced in the organization.

While Wiseman was gathering the Inquiry's reports for transmission to England, the Inquiry in turn was receiving certain materials from the British and French commissions. Some studies procured from the Allied governments reached the Inquiry, it is worthwhile to mention, via State Department channels. The French commission's studies relating to the eastern frontier of France arrived on February 14, 1918.[30] Lord Robert Cecil indicated Britain's willingness to exchange ideas on the subject of postwar international organization in early June.[31] French materials pertaining to proposed Italian frontier settlements were received by the Inquiry in late May.[32] While in Paris, Archibald Cary Coolidge received other reports directly from the *Comité*. Sir William Wiseman turned over to House additional British data in June.[33] By the time of the armistice, the American Inquiry had accumulated a vast quantity of material from both the British and French organizations.

Although the United States government was receiving considerable information from the two Allied governments through these exchanges, American officials made no attempt to influence

29. Ibid.

30. Isaiah Bowman to Charles Haskins, Feb. 14, 1918, Inquiry Archives.

31. Robert Lansing to Sidney Mezes, June 7, 1918, Lansing MSS, Library of Congress; House to Mezes, June 3, 1918, Inquiry Archives.

32. Charles Haskins to Walter Lippmann, May 29, 1918, Inquiry Archives. See also Secretary Lansing to Sidney Mezes, June 7, 1918, and Mezes to Lansing, June 10, 1918, *Foreign Relations of the United States, Paris Peace Conference, 1,* 98–99.

33. House to Mezes, June 3, 1918, Inquiry Archives; Mezes to House, June 29, 1918, Mezes MSS, Columbia.

the writing of the Allied reports or the conclusions and recommendations therein. In contrast, Sir William Wiseman's efforts in the United States, as has been previously emphasized, were geared not merely toward securing and transmitting the Inquiry's studies to London; they were directed also toward influencing the preparation of reports and recommendations.

Until the spring of 1918, the United States government did not have any agent in Europe who could act as intermediary between the Inquiry and the Allied preparatory commissions. As early as November 1917, the Inquiry's leaders considered the desirability of sending an American liaison agent to Europe. Douglas W. Johnson, a geographer on the faculty at Columbia University, was selected to go abroad in the spring of 1918. Johnson's objectives were not all directly related to the work of the Inquiry. His first project was to study the relationship between physical geography and military strategy for the benefit of the American Geographical Society. This work would involve the preparation of maps, diagrams, photographs, and explanatory articles. Second, Johnson's work for the Inquiry would attempt an analysis of the relation of national military strategy to the creation of national frontiers and how this relationship would affect the settlement of postwar national boundaries. Third, Johnson was to inspect the work of Allied preparatory commissions when possible, and to confer with the leaders of these projects.[34]

On March 15, 1918, Douglas Johnson departed for Europe. Equipped with the military rank of major and formal credentials from the Intelligence Office of the Army War College, Johnson was to send regular dispatches to the Intelligence Office, to the Inquiry, and to the Department of State. Members of the American embassies in Europe were instructed by the State Department to cooperate with Johnson's endeavors. How Johnson was to operate and what method would be used in his work were left to his personal discretion.[35] One reaction to the Johnson mission, from the diary of American Ambassador Walter Hines Page in London, is worthy of mention:

34. Isaiah Bowman to Walter Lippmann, Nov. 27, 1917, Inquiry Archives; Bowman to Lippmann, Feb. 28, 1918, Inquiry Archives.
35. Frank Polk to Douglas Johnson, March 6, 1918, House Inquiry MSS, file 33-159, Yale.

> Here comes an Army officer, Professor Johnson of Columbia, a very nice fellow who doesn't at all see the absurdity of his errand—to report in preparation for the Peace Conference on the Geography of Europe. This is House, of course, to whom he is instructed to report. House and Evangeline are innocent twins.[36]

Before August 1918, Douglas Johnson had succeeded in meeting many of the chief architects of the Allied organizations. He observed their methods and read many of their reports. Therefore he felt qualified to report and render fundamental suggestions to the Inquiry leadership in New York.[37] The Inquiry, he believed, should endeavor to coordinate its work more closely with the Allied commissions. In London, Johnson learned that British workers on peace preparations were "entirely ignorant" of the comparable projects in Paris. There were many Englishmen in the London Foreign Office who pleaded complete innocence of any knowledge that France was even attempting preparatory studies. Johnson heard the British tell how a Mr. Le Roux, possessing highly impressive credentials from the French government with offers of reciprocity had appeared in London, made a noticeably bad impression but nevertheless secured "all the data" he could about British preparations. Upon his return to Paris, the French failed to transmit any reciprocal data pertaining to their plans for peace. British suspicions had become aroused; they thought the French were trying to profit by British preparatory efforts. Still another theory was that while the French were working in secret they were attempting to exploit information obtained from their allies.

In Paris, Johnson heard a different version. Members of the *Comité d'études* revealed no knowledge of a British organization studying the problems of future peace. The Mr. Le Roux had no connection whatsoever with the *Comité;* in fact, he acted without any authority in his representations to the British Foreign Office. Furthermore, he could not have communicated any French reports to the British for he had no access to such reports. Yet, mused Johnson, the British and French commissions seemed most

36. Walter Hines Page MSS Diary, April 13, 1918, Harvard.
37. Johnson to Colonel House regarding Confidential Report on Arrangements Made by the British Government for Collecting Data for the Peace Conference, May 1, 1918, House Inquiry MSS, file 33, No. 8, Yale.

anxious to learn what work was in progress across the Channel. At all times he tactfully refused to reveal to one or the other any information given him in confidence.

> In each instance I made it evident, as delicately as I could, that it was impossible for the representative of a third commission to be the medium of communicating to one commission confidential information given by the other.[38]

Among the preparatory commissions, Johnson observed, the Inquiry occupied a unique position. It possessed fairly detailed reports of the operations of both the British and French commissions. At the same time, there was a noticeable attitude of suspicion and even distrust between London and Paris regarding the preparations for eventual peace. The one hope lay in cooperation and coordination among the several Allied and Associated governments attempting these studies in advance of the peace conference. At London, Paris, and New York, different students were studying the same problems independently with a view to establishing fundamental facts upon which policies would be based. Despite the common concern with the same problems, these independent studies were producing different compilations of statistics, different methods for evaluating and weighing such data, and hence entirely contrary conclusions. In the absence of any correlated methods, British, French, Italian, and American negotiators were most likely to arrive at the peace conference with conflicting statements of facts and figures. The enemy—meaning Germany—on the other hand would arrive for the negotiations possessing a coherent program and a unified body of information. This situation would place Germany's opponents, regardless of the military outcome of the war, at a serious disadvantage.

Douglas Johnson advanced the idea of maintaining a center where accredited representatives from the British, French, and American commissions could correlate their respective national programs, at least insofar as facts and figures were concerned, in

38. Douglas Johnson to Inquiry, Suggestions for a Plan for the Closer Cooperation of the Several Commissions engaged in Assembling Data for the Use of the Peace Conference, no date except on endorsement from David Hunter Miller to House where the date of August 14, 1918 appears. House Inquiry MSS, file 33, No. 9, Yale.

advance of the peace conference. Such a central committee would be devoted continuously to the task of establishing the fundamental facts for each major problem requiring solution. Each problem would thus be subjected to critical analysis and basic differences thrashed out before the Allies and the United States presented their bargaining position to the German representatives. Maps, statistics, facts submitted by each commission would be checked and compared. Where information was lacking, recommendations for further study could than be made.

> In such a problem as the distribution of nationalities in Austria-Hungary, or in the Balkans, the Central Committee would compare the maps and reports prepared under the direction of each inquiry, note where divergence of opinion as to the facts existed, critically study the value of the authorities used and the methods of interpreting statistics employed by each investigator and endeavor to reach substantial agreement as to which authorities and interpretations seemed most worthy of confidence. On the basis of such a study the committee could then report back to the several inquiries (1) that the allied representatives were unanimously agreed that the validity of such and such fundamental facts were fully established and could be relied upon by negotiators as a secure basis for determining actions and policies. (2) that further investigation by the several inquiries . . . was necessary before agreement could be reached. (3) that in regard to such and such other matters, substantial agreement as to what were the true facts could not be reached.[39]

In frank discussions, suspicions and distrust would tend to vanish, Johnson thought. The principle of independent investigation would be retained, but to it would be added the advantage of critical comparison of expert views. Better results might flow from the knowledge that each inquiry's findings would be subjected to the scrutiny of experts from other countries. There would be serious difficulties for the national commission which attempted to manipulate facts to serve national interests. Through cooperation, President Wilson's "open covenants" would achieve realization even before the war's end. Objections would undoubtedly be expressed (1) that such cooperation would constitute a virtual peace conference before the constituted peace

39. Ibid.

conference convened; (2) that disunity rather than unity would prevail when the respective peace programs were discussed, and that this would weaken the effect of allied-American relations rather than strengthen them; (3) that members of Allied commissions who were governmental officials might find it difficult if not impossible to divest themselves of their official status for the purpose of cooperating in the peace preparations with other national commissions.

Despite these possible objections, Johnson was convinced that the difficulties could be overcome. Leading members of the *Comité d'études* with whom Johnson discussed his proposal expressed private sympathy with the plan but were unsure that support would be forthcoming from their superiors. In any event, Johnson considered the "disinterested" United States Inquiry as the instrument most likely to bring an accord among the different preparatory organizations so that the diverse findings could be correlated for the common advantage of the Allied and Associated Powers. Nevertheless, the Johnson proposal never won official recognition or support from the several governments engaged in preparations for peace. In his zealousness for cooperation Johnson overlooked the fundamental differences dividing the Allies and separating American war and peace objectives from those of the Allied governments. While aspiring to effect greater efficiency in the operations of peace preparations, he underestimated the intensity of nationalism and of national interests. Through the Allied secret treaty network, the British and French governments were committed to a kind of peace settlement which President Wilson was not prepared to accept. All that could be expected from American-Allied preparatory relations was a more systematic exchange of views, but national interests prevented even this from being entirely feasible.

France and Britain were not alone in their attempt to influence the work of the Inquiry in the United States. Leaders of several European ethnic groups aspiring to independent national existence after the war made it a standard operating procedure to meet with Inquiry members responsible for studying problems relevant to their national aspirations. In turn, Inquiry members welcomed the opportunity to hear the arguments and obtain pertinent information and the nationalistic rationale for statehood prior to the convening of the peace conference where such matters would most likely be decided. Later, when writing his memoirs, the Czech patriot Thomas Masaryk remembered and recorded his activities in the United States during the anxious months prior to the armistice:

> Naturally, I sought to get a grasp of the American political situation without delay. This meant, in practice, making the acquaintance of the most influential people in the government, in Congress and in Society . . . Finally, through the good offices of Mr. [Charles] Crane, I came into touch with Colonel House and President Wilson. Our task was to gain the favor of the public and in this we succeeded. Before long . . . I was able to establish personal relations with prominent writers of all opinions . . . I had too the advantage of knowing the Preparatory Committee which under the Chairmanship of Professor Mezes was working upon material and memoranda in view of the peace negotiations and for the President. On behalf of the Czechs, Professor Kerner worked with him.[40]

Besides Masaryk, House brought other nationalistic leaders into contact with the Inquiry.

> Milenko Vesnitch, head of the Serbian mission was one of my callers. The President had asked him to see me and confer about writing a memorandum on the Serbian and Balkan question for our Peace Inquiry. I was glad to give him the opportunity. I put him in touch with Mezes and asked him to give Vesnitch every facility.[41]

Polish nationalist leader Ignace Paderewski was also placed in touch with Inquiry members dealing with the Polish question.[42] Charles Haskins, who had charge of studies on Belgium, maintained contacts with the official Belgian Information Service. Haskins and George Louis Beer, preparing reports dealing with the Belgian Congo, obtained information from Belgian sources through colonial specialists like Professor Edmond Leplae in Bel-

40. Thomas G. Masaryk, *The Making of a State: Memoirs and Observations 1914–1918* (London, 1927), pp. 235–36.

41. House MSS Diary, Feb. 7, 1918, Yale.

42. Rom Landau, *Ignace Paderewski: Musician and Statesman* (New York, 1934), pp. 113, 117–18.

gium. Leplae was at work on an official study for the Belgian government dealing with the implications of war and eventual peace for Belgium's colonial possessions.[43] From the Italian ambassador in Washington, the Inquiry received via the State Department information pertaining to Italy's postwar claims.[44] So much information arrived at the Inquiry and at the Department of State from European governments and ethnic organizations that House was moved to dispatch the following note to President Wilson and Secretary Lansing during the closing days of hostilities:

> We are getting a mass of information respecting present conditions in Austria, Bohemia, and the Ukraine, practically all of which is being furnished us by the English, French, and Italians. We have no American sources of information. The reports received are often colored by the self interest of the persons furnishing them. I regard it as exceedingly important that we send at once to these countries agents who will be in a position to furnish us with accurate and unbiased information respecting conditions.[45]

Colonel House and his associates directing the Inquiry's operations endeavored to close the gap which divided the United States from the Allies. Their motive was based on a sincere desire to effect a unified military effort and a unified peace program with a minimum of discord. A close working arrangement with Sir William Wiseman and exchanges of materials with the *Comité d'études* in Paris and its counterpart in London were among the measures calculated to plane smooth the rough edges and relax the tensions that existed or might arise prior to the peace conference. Colonel House was continuously actuated by an intense desire to mediate and compromise differences that could cause a rift between the United States and the Allies. For House, United States national interests in war and later at the peace conference would be served best by the closest possible cooperation.

43. P. Van den Ven, director of the Belgian Information Service to Isaiah Bowman, Oct. 21, 1918, Inquiry Archives.

44. Gordon Auchincloss to Sidney Mezes, Oct. 15, 1918, House Inquiry MSS, file 33-140B, Yale; Frank Polk MSS Diary, Nov. 18, 1918, Yale.

45. Telegram from Colonel House for the President and the Secretary of State, marked "secret," Nov. 8, 1918. Quoted in full in Gordon Auchincloss MSS Diary, Yale.

Fortunately or unfortunately, President Wilson and Secretary of State Lansing were not willing to compromise American objectives for the sake of cooperation with the Allies. House's persistent criticism of the President on this score would indicate that the President did not see eye to eye with his Texan confidant. A definite program for peace resting upon his Presidential pronouncements represented Woodrow Wilson's unequivocal objective. If necessary, the United States would do battle with the Allies at the peace conference. American interests would not be served by fusing them in a potpourri called Allied interests. In the summer of 1918, Robert Lansing succinctly expressed this view in a letter to the President:

> The allies are constantly seeking to have us act jointly with them in political matters, and this is another effort [a proposed joint note] in that direction. I believe that to keep our hands free and to act independently is our best policy since we can in that way avoid taking sides in the conflict of interests.[46]

46. Robert Lansing to Woodrow Wilson, June 29, 1918, Wilson MSS, Series II, Library of Congress. Cf. Frank Polk MSS Diary, Nov. 2, 1918, Yale: "Told Secretary [Lansing] I thought we should be very careful at this time not to commit ourselves on peace terms."

Chapter 5

THE INQUIRY AND THE FOURTEEN POINTS

YEARS AFTERWARD, when writing his memoirs, William Phillips, Assistant Secretary of State during the Wilson administration, described how he had first learned of President Wilson's intention to deliver his major address on American peace objectives, the well-known Fourteen Points Message of January 8, 1918. Early that morning, Phillips had been attending a Congressional committee hearing. Suddenly, without previous notice, a courier brought tidings which announced the President's intention to appear before both Houses of Congress and deliver an important message. The President's announcement also found several members of the Cabinet unaware that a declaration of foreign policy was about to be made. Phillips commented:

> It was such an unexpected move on his part that four members of the Cabinet . . . were unaware of his intention and failed to be present. This lack of proper liaison was one of the leading weaknesses of the administration.[1]

Phillips' testimony contributes additional evidence of the failure of President Wilson to coordinate fully the resources and personnel of the State Department in the formulation of American policy toward ultimate peace. Secretary of State Robert Lansing's principal criticism of the President's handling of peace arrangements was that Wilson failed to discuss the nation's policy with his associates on the peace commission in 1919.[2] In testimony before

1. William Phillips, *Ventures in Diplomacy* (Boston, 1952), p. 92.
2. 66th Congress, 1st Session, *Senate Document No. 106*, p. 162.

the Senate Foreign Relations Committee, investigating the administration's handling of peace negotiations, Lansing asserted that the Fourteen Points, the foundations of American peace policy, were never discussed by United States delegates to the peace conference. The fundamental weakness of the American position, Lansing insisted, was that there was no overall program, no agreement on policies to be pursued by the various American commissioners.[3]

Failure by the President to consult with the Department of State and the Cabinet prior to the Fourteen Points Address did not mean that he neglected to seek any advice. As in other aspects of peace preparations, the President relied upon Colonel House and the newly created organization operating under House's supervision, the Inquiry, for counsel and ideas.

Within a month after making the initial arrangements for the organization of the Inquiry, Colonel House went off to Europe as an American representative on the Supreme War Council. While in Europe, House urged the Allied governments to join with the United States in formulating a broad declaration of war aims. Such a declaration would, in his view, knit together all the peoples in coalition against the Central Powers. Despite House's efforts, however, the British and French governments refused to issue a common statement with the United States. This refusal provided President Wilson with the opportunity to issue a unilateral American statement of peace objectives.

By the middle of December 1917, the President had decided upon this course. A statement of American peace objectives might inspire liberals and socialists in Europe as well as in the United States if it urged a peace settlement based on justice rather than on conquest. The President also shared with House a desire to persuade the Bolshevik leaders in Russia of America's interest in a just settlement, which might serve to prevent Russia's withdrawal from the war.[4] Mixed motivations, therefore, led to the President's decision. Delivered on January 8, 1918, the address

3. Robert Lansing, *The Peace Negotiations, A Personal Memoir* (Boston, 1921), pp. 190–92.

4. House MSS Diary, Dec. 18, 1917, Yale. See also House's comments in MSS Diary, Jan. 3, 1918, Yale. The armistice between Russia and Germany was signed, however, on December 15, 1917.

illustrated clearly how far the President was prepared to go to prevent any rupture among the nations at war with the Central Powers and how anxious he was to shorten the war through a statement of liberal peace objectives.

As of the middle of December 1917, the Inquiry had been functioning for barely two months. During this period, the organization had been largely engrossed with the problems of recruiting personnel, of planning its assigned reports, and with the general responsibilities of setting up shop. Hardly any of the assigned reports were yet in the hands of the Executive Committee.[5] At the instigation of Colonel House, however, the Inquiry's Executive Committee compiled a memorandum containing specific recommendations for the postwar settlement.[6] The lengthy memorandum carried the date of December 22, but before it was submitted for the consideration of the President, it was further revised and enlarged. In its amended form, the memorandum bore the title, "A Suggested Statement of Peace Terms," and it was dated January 2, 1918.[7] When Colonel House visited the White House on January 4 for the purpose of advising and aiding President Wilson in drafting the message to Congress, he brought with him this Inquiry memorandum.[8]

5. National Archives, "Preliminary Inventories No. 89," Records of the American Commission to Negotiate Peace, compiled by H. Stephen Helton. This list of Inquiry reports in the collection of the National Archives does not list a single report written by a member of the Inquiry staff which bears a date of submission earlier than January 1, 1918. There were, presumably, preliminary drafts of reports in existence by that date.

6. Members of the Executive Committee who were responsible for the memorandum were Sidney Mezes, David Hunter Miller, and Walter Lippmann. There are no authors listed as such on either the draft of December 22 or on the revised version of January 2. In the introductory section of the latter appears a statement, in parentheses: "(Miller dissents from Mezes and Lippmann)" thus suggesting that these were the three authors.

7. A Suggested Statement of Peace Terms Revised and Enlarged from the Memorandum of December 22, 1917, dated Jan. 2, 1918 (hereafter cited as "Memorandum"), typescript copy in Wilson MSS, Series II, Library of Congress. The initial version of this memorandum, dated Dec. 22, 1917 (hereafter cited as "Draft") is more accessible in its published form in Foreign Relations of the United States, Paris Peace Conference 1919 (hereafter referred to as FRPPC), 1, 41–53.

8. House MSS Diary, Jan. 4, 1918, Yale. Victor Mamatey in The United States and East Central Europe (Princeton, 1957), p. 173, relates: "House assured him [Wilson] that a memorandum was unnecessary [from the Inquiry] because he

The subject matter of the memorandum was confined to questions of territorial arrangements after the war. There was no discussion of the general propositions which would later form the first five points in the address of January 8. A brief suggestion concerning the League of Nations (the term "League" rather than "Association of Nations" which Wilson used on January 8 is found in the Inquiry memorandum) was also included. Hence the Inquiry's recommendations dealt with the subjects covered in the President's address as Points VI to XIV inclusive. Concerning Russia (Point VI), the memorandum was firm in its conviction that a Bolshevik Russia would not be easily dominated by Germany. Anti-capitalist tendencies in Russia, "a religious love of Russia which is spiritually antagonistic to Protestant Germany," and powerful Russian nationalistic sentiment especially among the moderates could all be expected to act as a deterrent to any attempt by Germany to capitalize upon the chaotic situation in Russia.[9] The Inquiry's memorandum was highly dubious of Germany's ability to take advantage of the revolutionary situation in Russia. Toward Russia, the memorandum affirmed, a successful American policy must include a willingness to state war aims, an enthusiasm for a League of Nations, and "a demonstration to them that the diplomatic offensive is in progress, and that the Allies are not relying totally upon force."[10] The Inquiry's memorandum did not contain specific information or advice, but may have affected the President's emphasis in Point VI upon justice and cordiality:

> The evacuation of all Russian territory and such a settlement of all questions affecting Russia as will secure the best and freest cooperation of the other nations of the world in obtaining for her an unhampered and unembarrassed opportunity for the independent determination of her own political development and national policy and assure her of a sincere welcome into the society of free nations under institutions of her own choosing; and, more than a welcome, assistance also of every kind that she may need and may herself desire. The treatment accorded Russia by her

had all the data needed 'in [his] head' but when the President insisted, he asked his friends and proteges in the Inquiry, Sidney E. Mezes, David Hunter Miller, and Walter Lippmann to prepare one."

9. "Draft," *FRPPC, 1,* 46.

10. Ibid., 48.

sister nations in the months to come will be the acid test of their good will . . . of their intelligent and unselfish sympathy.[11]

In contrast with the somewhat general observations concerning Russia, the Inquiry's memorandum was quite explicit on the subject of Belgium. The evacuation of Belgian territory by the German armies was made a virtual *sine qua non* for any settlement with the Central Powers. Under no circumstances should Belgium be treated as a pawn for diplomatic bargaining purposes. Germany, by the act of evacuating and paying for the restoration of Belgium, would in effect be acknowledging guilt for bringing on the war. Any financial indemnities and reparations received by Belgium would be less important than such an acknowledgment. The language of the first draft of the memorandum was far weaker and briefer than the revised version. The first draft merely called for the evacuation and restoration of Belgian sovereignty by Germany, while the later draft stated:

> Belgium—Evacuation and restoration is not to be treated as part of any bargain. Belgian restoration is a prime precondition of negotiations because by accepting it Germany will say *peccavi* in act, and it is essential that she should say it in act, since it is no doubt impossible to force her except by crushing defeat to say it in words. Moreover, the innocence and sufferings of Belgium and the world sympathy for her will give strong backing in democratic public opinion everywhere to our insistence; that the financial amounts involved are less important than the acknowledgment of wrong involved in Germany's consent to rehabilitate the country.[12]

The President's Point VII is certainly more comprehensible in the context of the Inquiry's memorandum. His Point VII read as follows:

> Belgium, the whole world will agree, must be evacuated and restored without any attempt to limit the sovereignty which she enjoys in common with all other free nations. No other single act will serve as this will serve to restore confidence among the nations in the laws which they themselves set and determine for the government of their relations with one another. Without this heal-

11. Ray Stannard Baker and William E. Dodd, *Public Papers of Woodrow Wilson, War and Peace* (New York, 1927), *1*, 159–60.
12. "Memorandum."

ing act the whole structure and validity of international law is forever impaired.[13]

In view of the whole controversy about war guilt and reparations that arose later at the peace conference, the connection of war guilt with the restoration of Belgium, drawn by both the Inquiry and by Wilson, assumes considerable significance.

Wilson devoted Point VIII to French territorial problems. In the Inquiry's memorandum, northern France, meaning that section invaded by German military forces, and Alsace-Lorraine were treated separately. Northern France had been invaded in consequence of Germany's violation of its pledge to honor Belgian neutrality. The ravages perpetrated by the German army in northern France could not legally be considered proper methods of waging war. Had the invasion of northern France been consummated through the Franco-German frontier, there might have been no justification for demanding German reparations and/or indemnity in the area. In other words, Germany's invasion of northern France via Belgium had placed that region in the same legal status as Belgium. The French government was therefore justified in demanding full compensation in order to restore the status quo ante. The revised memorandum did not differ materially from the earlier form; it served to amplify the terse statement found in the draft of December 22: "Northern France must be evacuated and restored." [14] President Wilson used almost the same language in his Point VIII: "All French territory should be freed and the invaded portions restored . . ." [15] Here the language was clear and unequivocal.

The more extensive treatment of Alsace-Lorraine by the Inquiry's memorandum was deliberately phrased to avoid making the return of these provinces a paramount objective of the United States. Returning the provinces to France was deemed to be a highly desirable, perhaps even an essential condition for French economic recovery. Similarly, Germany's relinquishment of the

13. Baker and Dodd, op. cit. *1*, 160.
14. "Memorandum."
15. Baker and Dodd, op. cit., *1*, 160. Cf. Wilson marginal notes on the Inquiry report: "All the French territory must be freed and invaded portions restored." Quoted in Ray S. Baker, *Woodrow Wilson and World Settlement* (hereafter referred to as *World Settlement*) (Garden City, 1922), 3, 34.

two provinces might act as a "final seal upon the destruction of German militarism." [16] Nevertheless, the Inquiry's memorandum —both drafts—did not recommend any American commitment for continuing the European war in order to force the German government to restore these two provinces. Were a plebiscite held in the two provinces as a whole, the Inquiry recognized the strong possibility of a preponderant preference for German sovereignty. If plebiscites were conducted in each Reichstag district, there was a possibility of as many as three districts in Lorraine choosing French sovereignty. The fate of the three districts in upper Alsace would be highly doubtful under a gerrymandered-districted plebiscite. Lower Alsace was sure to favor Germany. Should Alsace and Lorraine be polled separately, Lorraine except for Metz was likely to support France while lower Alsace was believed certain to register a strong German vote. Under a rigged plebiscite arranged for the benefit of France, the latter would regain Lorraine with its valuable iron and coal districts. Such a plebiscite might achieve a settlement of a thorny historical dilemma. There was also the opportunity for France to "regain her lost population . . . [and achieve] a less menacing economic situation as between herself and Germany." [17] On the other hand, a plebiscite could offer legal recognition of Germany's annexation of the two provinces in 1871, and would in effect accept the results of overt German efforts at Germanization during the intervening years. The Inquiry's memorandum offered no definite recommendation for or against a plebiscite.

The failure of the Inquiry's Executive Committee to assume a strong stand on Alsace-Lorraine prompted one member to file a report dissenting from the majority. David Hunter Miller's individual report was far more forthright. An essential part of any American plan for peace, Miller pleaded, must seek to destroy Germany's potential either to dominate the world politically and economically or to terrify the world with the threat of such domination. Alsace-Lorraine must be *wholly restored to France with-*

16. "Draft," *FRPPC, 1,* 50.

17. "Memorandum." In the earlier "Draft," *FRPPC, 1,* 49, appears the following sentence: "For the sake of the morale of France, it will perhaps be wise to indicate an interest in the solution of the problem of Alsace-Lorraine."

out plebiscite, he contended.[18] More than any Allied country, France was quickly approaching economic ruin as a result of the war. In contrast with Germany, France was not likely to constitute a menace to world peace even with the inclusion of Alsace-Lorraine. Its economic recovery would be slow even with the benefit of the rich mineral resources from the two provinces; without them, economic recovery would be "almost impossible." The restoration of the two provinces to France, announced as an American war aim, would measurably raise faltering French national morale, so necessary to the assurance of Germany's military defeat.

President Wilson accepted the majority position in the Inquiry's memorandum, and, allowing for the shifting of words, followed the recommendations implicitly. Even in the matter of language, the influence of the Inquiry is apparent:

Inquiry Memorandum	*Wilson's Point VIII*
Every act of Germany towards Alsace-Lorraine for half a century has proclaimed that these provinces are foreign territory, and no genuine part of the German Empire. Germany cannot be permitted to escape the stern logic of her own conduct. The wrong done in 1871 must be undone.[19]	. . . the wrong done by Prussia in 1871 in the matter of Alsace-Lorraine which has unsettled the peace of the world for nearly fifty years, should be righted in order that peace may once more be made secure in the interest of all.[20]

Whether the President was thinking of holding a plebiscite or favored the direct restoration of Alsace-Lorraine to France was not made clear.

Wilson's Point IX provided a terse statement to the effect that Italy's frontiers should be readjusted on the basis of nationality. This was an application of the principle of "self-determination"

18. David Hunter Miller, Minority Report on Suggested Peace Terms, n.d., Wilson MSS, Series II, Library of Congress. Mention is made of the Miller minority report in *FRPPC*, *1*, 50.

19. "Draft," *FRPPC*, *1*, 49.

20. Baker and Dodd, op. cit., *1*, 160. Cf. Wilson's marginal note on the Inquiry report: "Alsace-Lorraine must be restored to France without excluding Germany from the use of the economic resources of these provinces." Quoted in Baker, *World Settlement*, *3*, 34.

which had become the favorite solution advocated by the President for settling Europe's boundary problems. The Inquiry's memorandum treated Italian questions in far greater detail, weighing economic and strategic considerations along with ethnic facts. The first draft recognized Italy's "right" to rectifications of its boundaries on the basis of a just balance of defensive and nationalist considerations. Trieste, a land-locked island of Italians surrounded by a sea of Slavs "should be commercially free . . . and the inhabitants of the city deserve their cultural autonomy." [21] Optimistically, the writers of this first draft concluded with the expectation that Italy's just demands would be met "without yielding to those larger ambitions along the eastern shore of the Adriatic for which we can find no substantial justifications."

Apparently the Inquiry's Executive Committee was not entirely satisfied with this general statement. In the revised form, the memorandum divided the Italian questions into three categories: (1) the Trentino; (2) Trieste and the Istrian Peninsula; (3) Dalmatia. In each region, Italy's strategic needs for improved defensive positions were to be balanced against the ethnic composition of the population. For the Trentino's mountainous districts where the population dwelled in valleys, the ridges offering superior defensive fortifications were to be ceded to Italy while the predominantly Austrian population continued under Austrian dominion. Trieste, following the earlier draft, was to have international status as a free city. When it came to Italian claims to the Dalmatian coastal regions, the revised memorandum asserted in no uncertain terms that there was no justification for extending Italian sovereignty to the alien Slavic majority inhabiting the Dalmatian coast. Moreover, the Inquiry's memorandum expressed a fear of Italian expansion in the Balkans:

> The establishment of Italian rule on the whole Adriatic littoral would menace the independence of Austria, Montenegro, Serbia, and Greece. It would put into the hands of Italy a commercial power out of all proportion to her commercial and industrial importance in the region. The demand represents no legitimate need of Italy's, as she is obviously abundantly supplied with means of access to the sea.

As Italy has neither an economic nor a nationalistic claim to

21. "Draft," *FRPPC, 1,* 50.

the eastern shore of the Adriatic, her demand must be looked upon as primarily aggressive. Once established on that coast, the logic of strategic security would call for an advance into the hinterland and an extension of Italian imperialistic influence among the Balkan states.[22]

Compared with the Inquiry memorandum, Wilson's Point IX politely skirted over the controversial, complicated aspects of Italy's claims.

When considering the problems of Austria-Hungary within the framework of the future peace settlement, President Wilson again trod delicately. In Point X he simply advocated an autonomous status for the various ethnic groups within that empire. Again, the Inquiry memorandum was far more explicit. It recommended the following approach to the Austrian nationality question:

> Towards Austria-Hungary the approach should consist of references to the subjection of the various nationalities, in order to keep that agitation alive, but coupled with it should go repeated assurances that no dismemberment of the Empire is intended, together with allusions to the humiliating vassalage of the proudest court in Europe.[23]

The first draft would have had the President draw attention to the "huge debts" which bound Austria-Hungary to Germany. No suggestion of cancellation should be implied, but some mention of the indebtedness might well "produce a useful ferment." Some ferment might also rise to the surface were the President to discuss the question of disarmament, then receiving much popular support in Austria. American policy, the memorandum insisted, should endeavor to stir nationalist discontent within the Dual Monarchy but at the same time refrain from any declaration which seemed to endorse the dismemberment of Austria-Hungary.[24] There was a point to this apparent inconsistency; by seeming to

22. "Memorandum." Cf. Wilson's marginal note on the Inquiry report: "That is the readjustment of the frontiers of Italy along clearly recognized lines of nationality." Quoted in Baker, *World Settlement*, 3, 35.

23. "Draft," *FRPPC*, 1, 48.

24. Ibid., 45. Wilson's marginal note on the Inquiry report asserted: "The peoples of Austria-Hungary, whose place among the nations of the world we wish to see safeguarded and assured must be accorded the freest opportunity of autonomous development." Quoted in Baker, *World Settlement*, 3, 38.

encourage the several nationalist threats to the empire while at the same time holding out the possibility of the empire's preservation after the war, Austro-Hungarian resistance could be "reduced to a minimum," with the chance that the Austro-Hungarian government might make some early overture toward ending the war.

Wilson followed the general idea developed in the Inquiry's memorandum. His allusion to the self-determination of ethnic groups within the empire did not extend to supporting the dissolution of the empire. The President was also prudent enough to refrain from involving himself in the many specific issues suggested by the Inquiry's memorandum, preferring to maintain his discussion of war and peace objectives on a more general level.

About the same comparison can be drawn between the Inquiry's memorandum and the President's Point XI, which treated the Balkans. Wilson dealt with general problems, but his language was direct. Rumania, Serbia, and Montenegro were to be evacuated; those territories occupied by enemy forces were to be restored; Serbia was to be accorded free and secure access to the seas; the relations of the several Balkan states with each other were to be determined "by friendly counsel along historically established lines of allegiance and nationality"; and international guarantees of the political and economic independence and territorial integrity of the several Balkan states were to be provided.

The Inquiry's advisers were more specific. Their memorandum expressed dissatisfaction with the Treaty of Bucharest, describing it as a "product of the evil diplomacy which the peoples of the world are now determined to end." [25] A just settlement must begin, the memorandum continued, with the evacuation of Rumania, Serbia, and Montenegro. Any equitable settlement in the Balkans must be based upon a balance of nationalistic and economic considerations. The Dobrudja, then occupied by Rumanian military

---

25. *FRPPC, 1,* 50. Presumably the Treaty of Bucharest to which the Inquiry referred here was that of August 1913 which ended the Second Balkan War. Cf. Wilson's marginal notes on the Inquiry report concerning the Balkans: "Roumania, Serbia, and Montenegro must be evacuated; occupied territories restored; Serbia accorded free and secure access to the sea; and the relationships of the several Balkan states to one another determined by friendly counsel along historically established lines of allegiance and nationality. International guarantees should be entered into of the political independence and territorial integrity of all the Balkan states." Quoted in Baker, *World Settlement, 3,* 36.

forces, was predominantly Bulgarian in its population and should therefore be returned to that country's dominion. The international boundary separating Turkey and Bulgaria should extend along the Enos-Midia line in accordance with the decision of the London Conference of 1913. Bulgaria's territory should legitimately extend to the Aegean Sea, along the coast from Enos to the Gulf of Orfano. Serbia should be allowed access to the sea through the port of Salonika. As for Macedonia, its future should be decided later after additional studies were completed. On the other hand, definite recommendations were made to Albania, "almost certainly an undesirable political entity." [26] Insofar as Balkan affairs were concerned, the Inquiry memorandum observed, economic factors outweighed in importance the ethnic affiliations of population groups. Hence, in arriving at territorial boundaries for the Balkans, economic factors should be given paramount consideration.

Between December 22 and January 2, the interim between the first and second drafts, various clarifications and revisions were made. Salonika was suggested as the port for Serbia; it would, however, be internationalized. The partition of Albania was urged on the ground that the principality represented the "meddling of the Great Powers." [27] Accordingly, Scutari would pass to Montenegro, Durazzo to Serbia, and Avlona to Greece. It is quite plain from these recommendations that the Inquiry did not at this time envision the formation of any south Slav political federation. The memorandum (both drafts) anticipated a continuation of the prewar political divisions in the Balkans except where specified. President Wilson walked the Balkan tightrope very gingerly, only pausing to urge that Serbia be granted free and secure access to the sea, as the Inquiry had recommended.

Point XII described the President's proposals for the Ottoman Empire:

> The Turkish portions of the present Ottoman Empire should be assured a secure sovereignty, but the other nationalities which are now under Turkish rule should be assured an undoubted security of life and an absolutely unmolested opportunity of autonomous

26. FRPPC, *1*, 51.
27. "Memorandum."

development, and the Dardanelles should be permanently opened as a free passage to the ships and commerce of all nations.[28]

There was a striking similarity between the Inquiry's recommendations for the Ottoman Empire and those for the Austrian Empire. Turkey proper "must be justly treated and freed from economic and political bondage." [29] The latter referred to the Turkish war debts owed to Germany and for which the Inquiry urged complete cancellation as a condition for peace. Turkish economic independence could also be assured if some adjustment were allowed for losses of territory. Furthermore, some arrangement was suggested for the extension of credit after the war for the economic rehabilitation of the country and the improvement of educational and sanitary facilities. "Thus Turkey can be freed from intermeddling and enabled to develop institutions adapted to the genius of her own people." [30] This was undoubtedly what the President had in mind when he urged that the Turkish portions of the Ottoman Empire should be assured a secure sovereignty.

In regard to the non-Turkish provinces and the Straits, the Inquiry's memorandum stressed the necessity to "free the subject races of the Turkish Empire." At the very least, autonomous status was to be granted Armenia and "protection . . . by the civilized nations" provided for Palestine, Syria, Mesopotamia, and Arabia. And the Inquiry's memorandum was forthright on its recommendation for the Straits, for it provided, "It is necessary also to establish free intercourse through and across the Straits." [31] Thus, in all three aspects of Point XII—Turkey proper, the subject nationalities, and the Straits—the President relied heavily upon the proposals found in the Inquiry's memorandum.

This memorandum in its original version of December 22 classified Poland as "by far the most complex of all problems to be

28. Baker and Dodd, op. cit., *1*, 160–61. Cf. Wilson's marginal phraseology on the Inquiry report: "The Turkish portions of the present Turkish Empire must be assured a secure sovereignty and the other nationalities which are now under Turkish rule must be assured full opportunity of autonomous development." Quoted in Baker, *World Settlement, 3,* 39.

29. "Draft," *FRPPC, 1,* 52.

30. Ibid.

31. Ibid.

considered." [32] The establishment of an independent and democratic Poland was recommended. At the same time (and seemingly inconsistently with the first recommendation), the Inquiry proclaimed, "The form of Poland's government . . . should be left to the determination of the people of Poland acting through their chosen representatives." [33] A democratic state was deemed essential to prevent internal friction among the several minority groups from allowing Poland to be rendered "impotent in the presence of Germany." Other complexities in the Polish situation stemmed from the difficulty of drawing effective boundaries around clusters of Polish-speaking groups without including sizable numbers of non-Poles. Ethnically determined lines did not conform with desirable economic boundaries, for Poland's access to the sea would necessarily cross lands largely populated by German-speaking people. There was the additional complication of East Prussia, an area incontestably German, but which would be separated from Germany proper by lands designated for the new Polish state. The draft of December 22 phrased the dilemma in this way:

> The present distribution of Poles is such as to make their complete unification impossible without separating East Prussia from Germany. This is probably not within the bounds of practical politics. A Poland which consists essentially of Russian and perhaps Austrian Poland would probably secure its access to the sea through the Vistula River and the canals of Germany which run to Hamburg and Bremen. This relationship would very probably involve both the economic subjection of Poland and the establishment of an area of great friction.[34]

Before the second draft was completed on January 2, the Inquiry's leaders had changed their minds because of the grave complications involved. Again, the difficulties are mentioned:

> The present distribution of Poles is such as to make their complete unification impossible without separating East Prussia from Germany. This is probably not within the bounds of practical politics. The consequence of this is that in establishing a Polish state we are confined to a territory which does not touch the sea,

32. Ibid., 51.
33. Ibid.
34. Ibid.

which has no natural boundaries, and which does not contain within it that vigorous part of the Polish nationality now within Germany.[35]

Internal friction among Poles, Ruthenians, and Jews was regarded as potentially explosive. The grave difficulties of drawing practical boundaries which would not leave a serious irredentist problem likewise contributed to the revised recommendation. In default of granting independence, the next best solution would be some kind of federation. On this point the January 2 Inquiry recommendation declared:

> In our opinion the best solution of the Polish question, both economically and politically, would consist in the inclusion of Poland as a federal state in democratic Russia. The second best solution would probably be the unification of Russian and Austrian Poland as an autonomous state within the Austro-Hungarian monarchy. It is believed that the effect of the inclusion of so large a number of independent Slavs might do more than any other thing to upset the existing German Magyar ascendancy, might release the Czechs and south Slavs, might result in a reorganization of the Dual Monarchy on the federal principle with Slav preponderance, and might consequently break the ascendancy of Berlin over Vienna.[36]

In other words, a Polish settlement could serve dual ends. In addition to achieving a degree of Polish autonomy, the settlement might stabilize a tottering Austrian monarchy and offset German influence upon the Austrian Empire. The recommendations in the Inquiry's two drafts, written less than two weeks apart, were thus quite different. This underscores the great difficulty the Inquiry had in making recommendations so early in its existence on the basis of only incompleted studies. When the President finally considered the Polish dilemma, his language was strong, and his intent conformed to the recommendation found in the first Inquiry memorandum. Point XIII provided:

> An independent Polish state should be erected which should include the territories inhabited by indisputably Polish populations, which should be assured a free and secure access to the

35. "Memorandum."
36. Ibid.

sea, and whose political and economic independence and territorial integrity should be guaranteed by international covenant.[37]

In spite of the grave obstacles, President Wilson chose to invoke the doctrine of "self-determination" and to support an independent Polish state.

The two drafts of the Inquiry's memorandum were exactly the same on the subject of the proposed League of Nations. Actually, the Inquiry's proposals for the League were unusually noncommittal. Mention was made of growing sentiment, in the countries at war with Germany, in favor of "a League of Nations for common protection," and this was followed by the assertion that a League was necessary for the peaceful settlement of international disputes and to assure economic prosperity. But then came what would have made a realist in international politics rub his eyes with disbelief. A connection was drawn between the form of the League and the political organization of postwar Germany. The memoranda advised:

> Whether this League is to remain armed and exclusive, or whether there is to be a reduction of armaments and a cordial inclusion of Germany, will depend upon whether the German Government is in fact representative of the German democracy.
> This is of course simply another statement of the alternative before Germany.[38]

Since Germany's future was so intimately bound to the proposed League of Nations, the Inquiry report advised the President about certain coercive weapons which the United States and the Allies could exert in order to bring about desired changes in postwar Germany. The coercive weapons were to take the form of economic sanctions of one kind or another. Until such time as Germany consented to Allied and American arrangements for peace,

37. Baker and Dodd, op. cit., *1*, 161. Cf. Wilson's marginal note by the Inquiry's Memorandum concerning Poland, which reads as follows: "An independent Polish State must be established, whose political and economic independence and territorial integrity shall be guaranteed by international covenant. It shall include the territories inhabited by an indisputably Polish population and shall be granted a free and secure access to the sea." Quoted in Baker, *World Settlement, 3,* 37.
38. "Draft," *FRPPC, 1,* 53.

it could be barred "indefinitely from access to supplies and to protract the negotiations at her cost and at our own benefit." This section of the memoranda continued:

> We emphasize our belief that no surrender of this power, even by inference should be considered until all the terms stated above are definitely agreed to in detail as well as in principle, by Germany at the peace conference. This involves adopting as our policy the reserving of the discussion of economic peace until our political, social, and international objects are attained. We might well adopt as our slogan, "No economic peace until the peoples are freed." [39]

These were weapons which the victors could use in order to compel acceptance of the peace terms by the vanquished or defeated governments.

For his part, Woodrow Wilson offered the "general association of nations" as the crowning climax to the Fourteen Points. His choice of words on this score was definite and unequivocal. The general association of nations "must" be formed for the purpose of affording mutual guarantees of political independence and territorial integrity to great and small states alike. To achieve all the objectives of the Fourteen Points, Wilson warned, the American people would be willing to fight continuously and unceasingly. Finally, Wilson served notice upon the German government that democratic reforms were imperative, that a German government must be responsive to the will of the German people. Before the United States and its co-belligerents would negotiate with the German government, it was necessary for them to know just whom the German government actually represented. [40]

Thus in formulating some of the Fourteen Points Wilson drew heavily upon the Inquiry's recommendations while in other instances he relied upon his own resources. Certainly the Inquiry had no share in the formulation of Points I–V. As for the remainder, the Inquiry's authors were far more specific than the President. Wilson relied more strongly upon the principle of self-de-

39. Ibid.
40. Baker and Dodd, op. cit., *1*, 161–62.

termination than did the Inquiry, which was prone to emphasize economic and strategic factors.

Colonel House revealed in his diary how depressed the President was after reading British Prime Minister Lloyd George's speech of January 5, at Caxton Hall, London, which set forth Britain's war and peace objectives. Wilson regarded the Prime Minister's terms so similar to his own that he thought it would be impossible for him to go before Congress on January 8. In reply, House insisted that Lloyd George "had cleared the air," making it even more necessary for the President to deliver his address. House concluded his account of the incident in his inimitable fashion:

> I also insisted that after the President had made his address, it would so smother the Lloyd George speech that it would be forgotten and that he, the President, would once more become the spokesman for the Entente, and, indeed, the spokesman for the liberals of the world. The President was greatly heartened by this opinion, and set to work again with renewed zest.[41]

Through the Fourteen Points, especially those clauses pertaining to the territorial settlement, President Wilson gave notice that the United States was henceforth taking a strong interest in the fate of European peoples if for no other reason than to safeguard the peace of the world. Colonel House feared this precedent might lead some European states to propose countermeasures in the form of territorial changes in the Western Hemisphere. The President responded that the American people would have no objection if the same principles were applied in the Americas.

In the process of drafting the Fourteen Points, a major declaration of American foreign policy, the President had depended on House and the Inquiry and in the process had neglected the State Department. Secretary Lansing, on January 10, confided to his notebook some strong comments on the Presidential address of two days earlier. Foremost in Lansing's mind was the apparent impossibility of reconciling the secret treaties arranged by the Allies earlier in the war with the principles of justice advanced by the President. How could the principle of self-determination be

41. House MSS Diary, Jan. 6, 1918, Yale.

applied to a settlement of colonial questions when many of the inhabitants were "too low in the scale of civilization to be able to reach an intelligent decision"? Italy's security in the Adriatic could not be achieved without control of Dalmatia and even of Albania unless international machinery strong enough to provide national security was created. Lansing was dubious, furthermore, about the efficacy of settling Balkan problems on the basis of self-determination. There were just too many complications—ethnic, economic, and historical—to achieve a lasting settlement on the terms envisioned by the President. The point Lansing regarded as most unfortunate was the proposal for Austria-Hungary (Point X). Any announcement which expressed an intention to perpetuate the Austro-Hungarian Empire was, in Lansing's view, most unwise. Instead, the Secretary urged:

> I think that the President will have to abandon this idea and favor the erection of new states out of the imperial territory and require the separation of Austria and Hungary. This is the only certain means of ending German power in Europe. Convinced of this, I think we should encourage the erection of a Polish state, a Czech state, and possibly a Ruthenian state. Then would come the union of Croatia, Slavonia, Dalmatia, Bosnia-Herzegovina, Montenegro, and Serbia under one sovereignty. There should also be considered the annexation of the Roumanians of Transylvania to Roumania and of the Italian provinces to Italy. Finally, to complete the dismemberment, the Austrian Empire and the Kingdom of Hungary could be separated. These independent states would present an insuperable barrier to German ambition . . . I shall await an opportune time to lay this last question before the President.[42]

By comparing the President's address of January 8 with Lansing's contemporaneous comments, it is possible to surmise what changes might have been instituted had Lansing rather than House advised the President in the formulation of American objectives.

Ten months prior to the armistice, then, President Wilson had set forth in a public address the fundamental elements of the

42. Robert F. Lansing, Private Memorandum on the President's Statement of War Aims on January 8, 1918, which are Open to Debate, dated Jan. 10, 1918, Lansing Confidential Files, Lansing MSS, Library of Congress. Cf. Memorandum by Lansing, Sept. 21, 1918, defining a proposed American program for the peace settlement. It is published in Robert Lansing's *The Peace Negotiations*, pp. 190–92.

American program for peace. His lack of precision on some issues did not result from any lack of confidence in an ultimate Allied-American military victory. His failure to spell out the objectives more clearly did not even reflect upon the inadequacy of the Inquiry's research as of the end of December 1917. In being vague or general in his proposed solutions, Wilson showed an unwillingness to break with the Allied governments, bound as they were to their network of secret treaties. So the President wisely talked in terms of general principles except where there was no major controversial issue between Allied interests and American interests, and here—Point VII in regard to Belgium, for instance—he could afford to be specific. It is clear that in the formulation of the Fourteen Points, the Inquiry's memorandum exerted much influence.

Chapter 6

THE INQUIRY MOVES TO PARIS

DURING THOSE AUTUMN DAYS of 1918, Colonel House, sitting in Paris on the Supreme War Council, could well understand the meaning of the Allied and American military offensive. He arrived in the French capital on October 26. Intermittent conferences with ranking representatives from every Allied capital, along with daily communications with the White House, allowed him to gaze with olympian perspective over the wide vista of war and to take stock of the prospects for peace. Few observers were so favorably situated. He could see that the cessation of conflict would lead with hardly a pause to the convocation of the peace conference. And he could see also that American leadership at the conference could easily depend upon the fundamental decisions President Wilson had to make in the weeks between the armistice and the start of the conference. Among these decisions were the choice of conference location and the mechanical-procedural organization. The selection of American personnel from plenipotentiaries down to advisers and clerks would be highly significant for the outcome of the peace settlement. Separated from House by an ocean and by the burden of full responsibility, President Wilson and Secretary Lansing also pondered long over these matters. The Inquiry figured prominently in all the American plans.

Austria's collapse at the end of October proved to be the prelude to the general capitulation of the Central Powers. While the German high command and a reorganized German government

154

were busily endeavoring to sue for an armistice on the basis of the Wilsonian Fourteen Points, Colonel House proceeded to line up Allied support behind the President's peace program. Early in November, House sent notice to Washington that the Belgian and Italian governments had offered protests to Points III, V, and IX concerning the removal of economic barriers, the impartial adjustment of colonial claims, and the readjustment of Italy's frontiers.[1] Trying hard to minimize the Allied-American dissension over the peace program, House sent notice that Lloyd George's government was not receptive to the freedom-of-the-seas plank. Nevertheless, House saw reason for optimism in the British and French approval of the League of Nations principle, the foundation of the Wilsonian structure for peace.

After more than four years of costly conflict, the armistice with Germany was signed on November 11, 1918. The guns were finally silenced. There was now an opportunity to put the plans from the drafting boards into operation. Every important belligerent including Germany had been making plans for the eventual peace settlement.[2] Between November 11 and January 18, 1919, the day on which the peace conference commenced, delegations were appointed, plans were revised where necessary, and each belligerent government made ready to do battle on a different kind of battlefield. Insofar as the American government was concerned, this interim period was of crucial importance to the later events of the conference and settlement. It was during this two-month period that the strengths and weaknesses of the American preparations for peace emerged in bold relief.

Even before the armistice, President Wilson and Secretary Lansing concurred in the wisdom of holding the peace conference in the French capital rather than in some neutral city in Switzerland, a proposal which they had at first considered advantageous.

1. House to Wilson, Nov. 3, 1918, *Foreign Relations of the United States 1918, Supplement 1, the World War, 1,* 448. House's statement regarding the Austrian surrender as a prelude to a general armistice is found in his MSS Diary, Oct. 29, 1918, Yale. House's conversations with British officials relevant to the Fourteen Points are dealt with in House to Wilson, Nov. 5, 1918, Wilson MSS, Series II, Library of Congress.

2. The best statement, though far too brief, concerning German preparations for peace is found in Alma Luckau, *The German Delegation at the Peace Conference* (New York, 1941), pp. 27–63.

Although a Swiss city would provide a location where negotiations could proceed in an atmosphere free from wartime hysteria and popular commitment to any program, Switzerland still carried the aura of espionage center of Europe. The Swiss cities were gaining in reputation, moreover, as citadels seething with revolutionary activity. Bolshevik influences were reported to be rampant in Lausanne and Geneva, the two Swiss cities most seriously considered as sites for the peace conference. Secretary Lansing had summed up the advantages and disadvantages of Paris and the Swiss cities respectively in a cable to House, November 9, 1918:

> I quite agree with the President that we should hold the peace conference at Versailles instead of in Switzerland. The fact that Headquarters of Bolsheviks and other revolutionaries is in Switzerland makes it to my mind impossible for the President to go there. Besides there would be hostile influences constantly exerted. Moreover, we would not at Versailles be in constant danger of the activity of spies.[3]

Other facts doubtless contributed to the ultimate choice of Paris. It is noteworthy that the American government was not opposed to holding the peace conference there.

Plans for the organization of the peace conference did not await a decision on the conference site. Early in September, Inquiry leaders were busily investigating the techniques, procedures, and organizational administration of the conference. On September 1, a memorandum was completed in which the principal responsibilities and work of the Inquiry at the peace conference were conveniently enumerated.[4] It seems clear from this memorandum that Inquiry leaders conceived their work in the peace negotiations to encompass virtually every aspect of the settlement. Frontier boundaries were to be rearranged in tension areas; new economic arrangements would be devised; where applicable, new governments would be formed; international law would be vastly modified or rewritten. Certainly the Inquiry cannot be accused of underestimating the herculean tasks which would confront the

3. Full text quoted in Gordon Auchincloss MSS Diary, Yale.
4. Memorandum on the Practical Tasks of the Conference in which the Inquiry Can Help, Sept. 1, 1918, House Inquiry Reports, file 33-10, Yale. This memorandum is presented as Appendix IX.

architects at the conference or of undue modesty in assigning responsibilities to itself.

Some ten days later a second memorandum was produced.[5] Of greatest importance was the observation that agreement among the Allied and Associated governments must be a necessary prerequisite at the conference, to be reached before the negotiations began. Some decisions on points of agreement must precede the peace conference. Otherwise the vanquished nations could easily adopt the strategy of driving a diplomatic wedge between their military opponents, creating discord among members of the victorious coalition. Using such tactics, the Central Powers might stand to reap the victory denied them on the battlefield. Once the opposing groups of belligerent representatives convened and submitted their proposals and counterproposals, the Inquiry memorandum continued, the conference should then adjourn and a "Permanent Allied Organization for Unity of Aim" consisting of foreign secretaries should meet in separate, closed sessions for the purpose of reaching agreement before again confronting the German delegation. Throughout the conference, this assemblage of Allied-American representatives should strive to achieve unanimity on all major terms to be included in the settlement.

For its part in the negotiations, the United States government would have the services of a large delegation which would be known collectively as the American Commission to Negotiate Peace. At the head of the commission would be the American plenipotentiaries. The entire commission would be carefully selected to assure its smooth, efficient operation. Members of the commission's advisory staff would naturally—considering the advance work of the Inquiry—be drawn from the Inquiry's research committee, with the possible addition of Edwin F. Gay, distinguished economist then serving as director of the Central Bureau of Research and Statistics for several wartime agencies in Washington. Presumably other military and scientific branches of government would also be represented. The assumption, however, was that the hard core of technical advisers would be members of the Inquiry.

5. Memorandum on the Organization and Working of the Peace Conference, Sept. 10, 1918, no authorship cited. Shotwell MSS, Columbia.

These two memoranda of September 1918 revealed several underlying assumptions with which Inquiry leaders were approaching the problems of the peace settlement. The Inquiry's scholars had brought to their studies, looking toward a new international policy, much the same perspective that an engineer brings to his design for a new construction project. The world, like some bridges, had suffered from imperfect construction; a new blueprint was needed, a new design effected by an expert staff of social engineers. Out of the embers of war, Inquiry scientists and engineers were ready to fashion a new world order—boundaries, governments, economic arrangements, international law and organization. There was the tacit assumption that while the peace engineers went about their tasks of manipulating and directing the institutional changes, the existing nations and societies would remain stable, pliable, accepting these changes without complaint. That the peoples of east-central Europe, the Middle East, Africa, and elsewhere would not acquiesce and readily approve the design offered by the engineers was never given serious consideration. The Inquiry leaders seemed ready to believe that once the peoples concerned and the representatives of the great powers were enlightened by the facts and arguments advanced in their support there would be no genuine opposition to the proposals set forth by the planners. The economic and military preponderance clearly on the side of the planned settlement would further discourage opposition. The peace conference was to take on the appearance of a huge laboratory whose director would be the American president. Its purpose would be the creation of a world freed from the bondage of war. Though such an assumption was implicit in a good many Inquiry reports, it is manifest clearly in the memoranda describing the work to be done by House's aides at the peace conference.

In the closing months and weeks of the military conflict, Inquiry leaders were also making arrangements for the assignment of personnel to the conference. To an extent far greater than operational planning, personnel planning brought out into the open the latent antagonisms between Secretary Lansing's State Department and Colonel House's Inquiry. The administrative conflict when reduced to its essentials could be defined in this way:

whichever organization obtained the President's consent to select the personnel of the American delegation would play the dominant role at the peace conference, leaving to the other organization a subordinate status. Presidential intervention was necessary to decide the issue.

During the final weeks of the war and the first days after the armistice, Colonel House was in Paris, and the Inquiry had little influence on the important policy decisions being made by the President. Work on the formulation of the armistice terms had been delegated to military advisers. So it went also with the organizational arrangements for the peace conference, which President Wilson had turned over to the State Department. Meanwhile, the Inquiry remained behind the scenes awaiting its cue.

On November 30, the nation's press carried news of the President's selection of American plenipotentiaries. The inclusion of the President himself, Lansing, and House was accepted if not actually approved by the public. To judge from Secretary Lansing's description of the notification of Henry White of his appointment, it would appear that the selection of White and Tasker Bliss was characterized by casualness rather than serious forethought. Lansing's cryptic account was as follows:

> Henry White at my house. Asked him as to his attitude re 14 Points. Said he was in entire sympathy. Tendered him place on Peace Conference.[6]

Colonel House would have chosen differently. The observation in his diary on what would constitute the ideal American leadership at the peace conference is a jewel:

> I wish in my soul the President had appointed me as Chairman of the Peace Delegation with McAdoo and [Herbert] Hoover as my associates. I could have attended to the political end, McAdoo to the financial, and Hoover to the economic end. The distribution politically would have been perfect: Texas, New York and California with Hoover as the Republican member. If I could have had these two men as associates and only these, I would have been willing to guarantee results.[7]

6. Lansing Date Book, Lansing MSS, Library of Congress.
7. House MSS Diary, Dec. 3, 1918, Yale.

With the President at the helm of the commission, the choice of plenipotentiaries was not exactly tantamount to a shattering of precedent but was nevertheless highly controversial. The selection of Colonel House was logical because of his intimate knowledge of wartime problems and his special direction of peace preparations as responsible director of the Inquiry. Lansing, as Secretary of State, would naturally be one of the plenipotentiaries. Henry White's qualifications did not rest on his affiliation with the Republican party; he was perhaps the most experienced American diplomat of the twentieth century. His knowledge of international politics and statesmen was probably more intimate than that of any other American of his generation, and, what was equally significant, White was considered by the President to be a moderate in his attitudes toward the peace settlement. The choice of Tasker Bliss, former Army Chief of Staff, could be easily explained by the importance that disarmament and military occupation would assume at the peace conference. Admittedly President Wilson could have appointed plenipotentiaries more clearly reflecting the national political complexion. There was, nevertheless, sound rationale behind his selections.

As early as June 1918, Sidney Mezes had conferred with House about the choice of Inquiry advisers whose services would be required at the peace conference.[8] Six names were mentioned: Charles Haskins, Robert Lord, Clive Day, Charles Seymour, Robert Kerner, and A. A. Young. Day and Seymour, Mezes suggested, could work cordially together, while Kerner's facility with the Slavic languages tended to offset his decided Slavophile bias. Bowman's name was noticeably absent from this first list. There is no record that the subject was again discussed until October when the personnel question loomed large. On October 25, Mezes sent to the Secretary of State an organizational chart showing his expectation of the Inquiry's role at the peace conference.[9] At the same time, Mezes informed Lansing of House's opinion that the Inquiry force should be composed of some 75 or 80 members. While this large force was not absolutely essential for the earliest

8. Mezes to House, June 14, 1918, House Inquiry Report, file 33-135, Yale.
9. Confidential letter from Mezes to Lansing, Oct. 25, 1918, Mezes MSS, Columbia.

phases of the work, House deemed it necessary to preserve it intact because of the grave difficulties attending any later reconstruction of the organization.

On October 24, Mezes conferred with Secretary Lansing on this subject. As Mezes recorded the conversation for the benefit of House, who was in Paris, the meeting clearly showed Lansing's antagonism toward the Inquiry. "His feeling," Mezes said, "seemed to be that our Inquiry force was inexperienced in practical dealing with foreign questions which is true, and that he had better men on his force, which I doubt. He specifically mentioned his man [R. S.] Miller for the Far East, and evidently had in mind others he'd like to take over—unnamed." Certainly the Secretary General of the American commission should be a person of practical experience in international affairs, and obviously such a person could only be found in the ranks of the State Department. In Mezes' words, Lansing concluded on this note:

> Lansing spoke of talking over the whole question of personnel with the President. He *may* try to get more of his men and to influence the composition of the secretariat. He agreed that technical advisers should be sent for as needed. He also agreed that the Inquiry force must be kept together, and that the bulk of it could be best employed as a body at the Conference, keeping our material alive, and giving it improvements it needs.[10]

Although Lansing's words do not display overt hostility toward the Inquiry, Mezes' inference might have resulted from the Secretary's tone or manner. Faithful to his promise, Lansing took up the whole matter with the President, and on October 29 President Wilson set forth his views in a brief note on the question of personnel:

> As I said to you orally yesterday, I think that the enclosed [plan of organization] is much too ambitious a programme, and I would be obliged if you would have a simpler one worked out, in the meantime telling Dr. Mezes that it is so unlikely that anything but the main territorial, political, and racial questions at issue will be settled at the peace conference and practically so certain that all detailed discussions of financial and commercial and other similar arrangements will be delegated by the conference to special

10. Mezes to House, Oct. 26, 1918 (handwritten), House Inquiry MSS, file 33-157, Yale.

conferences or commissions that I think he ought to plan only to carry the men and materials with him which will be serviceable in settling the main questions, together of course with the necessary clerical aid.

The Department [of State] itself in the meantime can work out the necessary minimum personnel and organization.[11]

Additional conferences were held between Mezes and Lansing during the ensuing weeks in which the size of the Inquiry's force at the peace conference was constantly reduced. From House's proposed 75- or 80-member force, Mezes agreed to take 10 members plus 7 assistants, forming a total of 17.[12] The 10 were to be: Haskins (for Belgium); Lunt (Italy); Lord (Russia); Young (Turkey); Seymour (Austria-Hungary); Day (Balkans); Beer (colonies); Jefferson and Lobeck (cartographers) and Shotwell (Library). In addition, there was David Hunter Miller, who had earlier accompanied House to Europe. Again, Bowman's name did not appear. Unless the Inquiry were allowed extra personnel, there seemed little likelihood of Bowman being included except possibly in the role of assistant, but this arrangement seemed hardly politic. So, before D-Day, Mezes interceded with Secretary Lansing with the result that Bowman and several assistants were added to the Inquiry staff, bringing the total of Inquiry personnel authorized to accompany the American commission to 23.[13]

The handling of these arrangements by the State Department did not represent any departure in policy by the President. There was simply no other government agency in a position to cope with the organizational and personnel arrangements. The Inquiry could hardly make any claim, for its function was, strictly speaking, confined to preparation of the American program. It was not equipped to handle the administrative responsibilities involved in managing an entire delegation at an international gathering. But

11. *Foreign Relations of the United States, Paris Peace Conference 1919, 1,* 113. The exact plan of organization to which the President referred is not made clear.

12. Telegram from Mezes to Lansing, Nov. 9, 1918, Lansing MSS, Library of Congress.

13. Letter, Mezes to Lansing, Nov. 9, 1918, Shotwell MSS, Columbia. Another relevant description of the personnel problem is in Mezes to House, Nov. 15, 1918, House MSS, file 10-30, Yale. For a complete list of Inquiry personnel, see infra, p. 337.

Inquiry leaders did resent the manner in which Lansing's department started to arrogate authority unto itself while seeming to subordinate the Inquiry.[14] The reduction in size of the Inquiry force to be used at the peace conference was but the most obvious result of State Department control over the arrangements.

Perhaps all or most members of the Inquiry had assumed that the entire organization would be sent to the peace conference. Late in November, several members wrote angry letters to Inquiry officers expressing intense disappointment and even resentment because their names were not included on the roster. A. A. Young replied to one such letter with these words:

> We did everything that we could to get together a fairly large force for Paris, but the organization of the Conference is in the hands of the State Department and we have been cut down to the bone. Even [A. P.] Winston will have to be left behind. Hornbeck will go but officially merely as a general assistant. I am exceedingly sorry.[15]

Another spirited exchange of letters occurred between F. A. Golder and Isaiah Bowman. Golder complained that he had made continuous sacrifices to remain with the Inquiry, and, unlike other members, would not witness the outcome of his labors at the peace conference. More to the point, Golder said that he had received an attractive offer for work in France early in 1918, but had turned it down after an Inquiry "committee" termed his services "indispensable." Had he negotiated at that time (as did Robert Kerner, who had received a commitment for work at the peace conference as his price for staying with the Inquiry) Golder insisted, he would have received a commitment to attend the peace conference. Instead, "I had trusted your committee to do the right thing and as a result I have before me the humiliating position . . . The Inquiry has used me and now it has thrown me aside indifferent as to the position its conduct places me [in]." [16] Attempting to smooth Golder's ruffled feelings, Bowman placed responsibility with the Department of State, while at the same time informing

14. James T. Shotwell, *At the Paris Peace Conference* (New York: 1937), pp. 14–19.
15. A. A. Young to J. F. Abbott, Nov. 23, 1918, Inquiry Archives.
16. Golder to Bowman, Nov. 24, 1918, Inquiry Archives.

him that fewer than 20 per cent of the Inquiry personnel were being taken to the conference.[17] One other Inquiry member, William S. Ferguson, failed to qualify for a place on the peace commission for a more specific reason. In Bowman's words, "We had placed your name on the original list for recommendation for the peace conference and it was only recently that I learned that you are a British subject. Of course that means that your name had to be taken off again." [18] And so it went, as the Inquiry group was further weeded.

At Paris, Colonel House was growing anxious for the Inquiry contingent to arrive in the French capital and set up shop at the earliest moment, by December 1 if possible.[19] Clerical assistance, House notified Secretary Lansing, could be obtained in Europe from the ranks of American army personnel. Nevertheless, the State Department thought it improper to dispatch the Inquiry in advance of other American commission personnel. On November 13, Lansing wired House:

> It does not seem to me advisable that the Bureau of Inquiry should leave before the rest of the force as they will not be fully equipped with stenographers and others. The President feels that we must economize in the matter of clerical force and expects to draw largely from the army supply in Paris.[20]

The contradiction apparent in this wire did not pass unnoticed. Gordon Auchincloss remarked in his diary how curious it was for the State Department to hold up the Inquiry because clerical support was lacking and at the same time announce that secretarial support would be supplied by the army in Paris.[21] A more likely explanation was the State Department's reluctance to allow the

17. Bowman to Golder, Nov. 27, 1918, Inquiry Archives.

18. Bowman to Ferguson, Nov. 26, 1918, Inquiry Archives. Bowman's letter to Norman D. Harris of November 25, 1918: "In particular we are not permitted to take over anyone as regional expert on the Far East. Your reports will be taken along, the maps having been redrawn and I trust that they may prove to be of real service." Inquiry Archives.

19. Telegram, House to Lansing, Nov. 11, 1918, Wilson MSS, Series II, Library of Congress.

20. Telegram, Nov. 13, 1918, quoted in full in Gordon Auchincloss MSS Diary, Nov. 14, 1918, Yale.

21. Ibid.

Inquiry—House's organization—to obtain a headstart, before the State Department itself could begin functioning in Paris.

Without much fanfare, the American Commission to Negotiate Peace was coming into being. On November 14, Secretary Lansing appointed Joseph C. Grew, chief of the Western European section of the State Department, to be secretary general of the commission.[22] For Grew's assistants, the Department selected Assistant Secretary Leland Harrison and Phillip Patchin. If House's son-in-law, Gordon Auchincloss, entertained designs on the job now filled by Grew, he did not reveal it in his diary:

> This is, of course, the best selection [Grew]. It would be immensely improper for me to do this work and I do not want to do it anyway. I do not want to stay over here as long as the Peace Conference is going to last, and if it ever became known, as it would of course, that Colonel House was one of the Commission, that his son-in-law was the Secretary of the Commission, and his brother-in-law was the chief man in the Inquiry, there would be an investigation and a bitter attack on the part of the Republican members of Congress that we would never get over. My job is going to be to act as private secretary to the Colonel and to help him look after the President when he comes.[23]

Other departments of government, too, were laying plans for sending representatives to the proceedings at Paris. Admiral William S. Benson, Chief of Naval Operations, informed Secretary of the Navy Josephus Daniels on November 10 of plans to have naval officers at the conference to advise on questions of freedom of the seas and maritime law, which Benson viewed as the "main ones to engage the peace conference." The two naval officers whom Benson had in mind for the advisory role were Admiral Harry S. Knapp and Admiral Austin M. Knight, the latter "an able international student." [24] Meanwhile, Benson would remain in Paris. Like the State Department, the Navy Department, and the Inquiry, officers of the Treasury Department, the War Shipping

22. Lansing Telegram to Joseph Grew, Nov. 14, 1918, quoted in full in Gordon Auchincloss MSS Diary, Nov. 14, 1918, Yale. Grew at the time was assisting House on the Supreme War Council in Paris; see Joseph C. Grew, *Turbulent Era* (Boston, 1952), *1*, 331–35.

23. Auchincloss MSS Diary, Nov. 14, 1918, Yale.

24. Admiral Benson to Secretary Josephus Daniels, Nov. 10, 1918, Daniels MSS, Library of Congress.

Board, and the War Industries Board were seriously considering the feasibility of sending their own men as advisers to the conference.

Echoes of the armistice had not yet faded when new economic questions presented by the return to peace pressed rapidly upon the Wilson administration. Wartime measures like the blockade and the flow of commerce and credit across the ocean had to be greatly modified. Policy-makers in the several relevant government departments found themselves without any agreement on American economic measures. American representatives in Europe, observed Gordon Auchincloss, were entirely in a quandary regarding the essentials of economic policy.[25] Aware of this lack of a concrete economic program, Colonel House on November 23 informed the President about the sorry state of the nation's policy on international finance, commerce, and the use of raw materials. Whether the United States government took an interest in these matters or not, America's European associates entertained greater interest in them than in any other questions. Then, without mentioning the Inquiry, House wrote:

> I suggest the advisability of your taking steps to secure a small body of advisers on these subjects either to come with you or to be ready to come over on short notice.[26]

Less than a week following the arrival of House's suggestion, President Wilson signed a lengthy memorandum which most probably had been written by Edwin Gay, director of the Central Bureau of Research and Statistics and former dean of the Harvard Business School. The memorandum explained that the Bureau

25. Gordon Auchincloss to Frank Polk (Counselor of the State Department), Nov. 15, 1918, Polk MSS, Yale. In January the American Commission asked the Treasury Department to send financial advisers. AMMISSION to Secretary of Treasury, Jan. 2, 1919, Wilson MSS, Series VIII-A, Library of Congress.

26. Telegram, House to Lansing, Nov. 23, 1918, Wilson MSS, Series II. Another observer who recognized the importance of economic questions at the peace conference was Jerome D. Green in a letter to Ellery Sedgwick, Nov. 21, 1918, Edwin Gay MSS, Huntington Library. House cabled the President on November 10: "In view of the enormous claims which the French will make on Germany, I think we should get our engineers to make an approximate estimate for our guidance." Wilson MSS, Series II.

of Research operated as an independent agency under direct authority of the President—not unlike the Inquiry. Gay's staff was composed of 1,011 employees "which include . . . many of the most eminent students of economic affairs and experts on research and statistical devices for promptly compiling statistical information." For many months, the memorandum continued, Gay's staff had been collecting a raft of economic information pertaining to the wartime blockade policy, trade agreements, rationing policy, merchant shipping, the allocation of restricted materials, etc. These problems had been dealt with exhaustively and the data compiled in a most thorough and reliable fashion, exploring all aspects of economic activities at home and abroad. In view of the proven ability of the Central Bureau to gather and analyze economic data, the memorandum over the President's signature recommended:

> that the Central Bureau be designated . . . as the official source through which shall be obtained economic data required by the American delegates at the Peace Conference.
> It is believed that there [should] be one authoritative and exclusive source for the supplying of information of this character. If information is sought through more than one source, there is a very considerable probability that conflicting advices will be received which will tend to discredit the whole . . . Cables from Paris already indicate great confusion in estimates of economic conditions which are being made by American representatives gathering there . . . There is no organization at the command of our Government other than the Central Bureau and four allied statistical divisions which is qualified to render this service. The "Inquiry" has been making certain studies of an economic character, but they themselves frankly recognize that these are inadequate.[27]

Just how the President would have learned about "inadequate" Inquiry studies is not clear. There is no doubt, however, that in transferring from the Inquiry to the Central Bureau of Statistics

27. Memorandum Letter from Wilson to Gay, Dec. 2, 1918, Gay MSS, Huntington Library. The President's signature appears on the original. Another informant in Europe who reported to the President on the importance of economic factors in the coming settlement was Edward P. Costigan, member of the United States Tariff Commission. Letter to the President, Dec. 6, 1918, Wilson MSS, Series VIII-A, Library of Congress.

all responsibilities for supplying economic advice and information the President had made a direct attack on the Inquiry.[28]

On December 4, 1918, the *George Washington* carrying the President and his party to the peace conference departed from Hoboken harbor. By this time the Inquiry was but one of several organizations furnishing advisers to the American plenipotentiaries at the Paris Peace Conference. Besides the Inquiry, there would be technical advisers from the armed services, a secretariat recruited from the Department of State to include keepers of minutes, expert draftsmen, keepers of files, registry, indexers, coding clerks. Other advisers drawn from the Department of State would provide technical information on matters of international law and organization. There would likewise be a publicity and printing division, a political and economic intelligence division, a counterespionage division, a financial section, a protocol section, and a general liaison division.[29] In charge of this vast organization would be the youthful Joseph Grew of the State Department.

Among the accumulation of President Wilson's papers at the Library of Congress is a passenger list which enumerates the entire roster of persons accompanying the President aboard the *George Washington*.[30] This list bears the names of 113 passengers. Of this number, only 23 had been associated with the Inquiry. The following Inquiry members made the memorable voyage:

Beer, George L.	Day, Clive	Gray, Louis H.
Blank, W. L.	Dixon, Roland B.	Haskins, Charles H.
Bowman, Isaiah	Frary, D. P.	Hornbeck, Stanley K.

28. A. A. Young, in charge of economic matters for the Inquiry, wrote Edwin Gay on December 3: "I cordially approve of your plan to send men with the materials that you have prepared for us and am very glad that you have been able to arrange it. In order to assist your men in getting the right orientation and contacts, it may be well to ask them to report to me personally in Paris. I shall have a great many irons in the fire, and am not sure how much time I shall be able to give to these matters myself. In any case I shall be glad to turn over as much as I can to more competent hands." Inquiry Archives.

29. Joseph Grew to Secretary Lansing, Dec. 10, 1918, Wilson MSS, Series VIII-A, Library of Congress.

30. Passenger List, U.S.S. *George Washington*, Wilson MSS, Series VIII-A, Library of Congress. Cf. the passage in Thomas A. Bailey, *Wilson and the Lost Peace* (New York, 1944), p. 108: "Accompanying [Wilson] on the *George Washington*, were scores of specialists in history, geography, ethnography, economics, finance . . ."

Jefferson, Mark	Lybyer, Albert	Slosson, Preston
Kerner, Robert J.	Mezes, Sidney E.	Stratton, O. G.
Lobeck, A. K.	Moon, Parker T.	Westermann, W. L.
Lord, Robert H.	Seymour, Charles	Young, A. A.
Lunt, William E.	Shotwell, James T.	

The importance of this voyage escaped few passengers. No fewer than seven diaries endeavored to capture for posterity the atmosphere of excitement and the tremendous ground swell of idealism which pervaded everything.[31] Whatever the President or some individual of authority said, one diarist or another was likely to hear the remark and jot it down.

Once safely aboard the *George Washington,* more than one member of the Inquiry discovered that his idealistic vision of the new world order was already being blurred. State Department assistants who took charge of cabin assignments could find only the dingiest accommodations for Inquiry members. These were located inevitably in the most cramped portion of the ship. It was the rule rather than the exception for four Inquiry men to share a tiny cabin. William Westermann expressed a typical reaction: "Our dreams of the great state in which we were to travel were readily shattered. There were four of us in a small room with five bunks. It is very crowded." [32] But there were even more disagreeable aspects of the passage. William Bullitt, State Department attaché, dryly summed up the chief annoyances that particularly rankled members of the Inquiry:

31. James T. Shotwell, *At the Paris Peace Conference,* pp. 67–84; Robert Lansing MSS Diary, Library of Congress; George L. Beer MSS Diary, Columbia; William L. Westermann MSS Diary, Columbia; Isaiah Bowman MSS Diary (only a small portion now available to scholars), Johns Hopkins; William Bullitt MSS Diary, Yale.

32. Westermann MSS Diary, Dec. 4, 1918, Columbia. In a letter to the author, Charles Seymour, who shared this cabin, contradicted Westermann's claim that it was "small" and disputed the recollections of his colleagues that Inquiry members were disgruntled at shipboard arrangements. Harold Laski, then lecturer at Harvard, commented upon the experts attending the peace conference: "The President is going to have an extraordinary time. I meet almost no one who does not resent his secrecy. The very experts who are going from here are not told what they are to attack and what to defend. House and the State Department quarrel, so he lets House take one set of experts and Lansing another. And now it looks as though the Senate will send a third." Laski to Oliver Wendell Holmes, Dec. 1, 1918, in Mark de Wolfe Howe, ed., *Holmes-Laski Letters, 1916–1935* (Cambridge, 1953), *1,* 175.

169

The arrangement of the ship is hierarchal. The President and Mrs. Wilson live and dine alone in their private apartments. Then there is the President's Dining Room so-called apparently because the President never dines in it—which is devoted to the Peace Commissioners and the guests of the President—mostly female. Then the hoi polloi eats in the large forward ex-lounge. In addition there is a bar downstairs at which only those who eat in the President's Dining Room can obtain drinks. And the occupants of various decks are ordered to smoke in various smoking rooms carefully segregated. Inasmuch as some of the brainiest men on the ship like Professor Haskins and Prof. Beer are four in a room on D. Deck and therefore barred from the upper excellent room, it is rather comic.[33]

Yet, interspersed with caustic complaints over the regulations were occasional discussions relating to the coming work of the conference.

Each diarist preserved definite impressions and conversations which serve to enhance the appreciation of this interlude before the mass convergence upon the French capital. William Bullitt noted that the first two days aboard were terribly dull. The President's cold seemed to dampen everyone's spirits. Shreds and bits of gossip made the rounds of the decks. Bullitt learned, for example, from French Ambassador Jusserand (both the French and Italian ambassadors to the United States were guests of the President) that Wilson's concept of the League of Nations meant nothing more than an agreement by all the nations accepting the peace treaty to "join in coercing any nation which violated [the terms of the peace treaty]."[34] Incredible as this must have sounded, Bullitt accepted Jusserand's version of the President's views as gospel, for there was still very little known of Wilson's ideas. Even

33. Bullitt MSS Diary, Dec. 4, 1918, Yale. Another source of dissension was the inability of Inquiry members to take their wives with them to the peace conference. The State Department provided authorization only for Sidney E. Mezes to take his wife along. See Mezes to Lansing, Nov. 15, 1918, and Lansing to Mezes, Nov. 18, 1918, Lansing MSS, Library of Congress. Some wives followed their husbands at a later time. Other corroborative evidence regarding the conditions aboard ship can be found in Gordon Auchincloss to Frank Polk, Dec. 15, 1918, Polk MSS, Yale; Lieutenant Ralph A. Hayes (liaison officer between the War Department and General Pershing in Paris) to Newton D. Baker, Dec. 18, 1918, Baker MSS, Library of Congress; Joseph C. Grew, *Turbulent Era, 1*, 365–66.

34. Bullitt MSS Diary, Dec. 7, 1918, Yale.

the specialists from the Inquiry, observed Bullitt, did not have the slightest idea what the President expected of them. "Altogether the prospects for a unified, powerful, liberal action seem very slight." [35]

On the night of December 9, just before the evening movie began, William Bullitt was seated next to the President. Bullitt made the most of this opportunity to bring certain matters to the attention of the Chief Executive. He revealed that the general mood aboard ship was one of skepticism and cynicism.[36] As a point of emphasis Bullitt characterized "the brains" on board as being treated "like immigrants . . . [who] felt entirely left out of the game." Bullitt then, speaking candidly, urged the President to meet with the American advisers and discuss his views of the coming peace settlement.[37] The next day, at noon, leading advisers were summoned to meet with Wilson in his office. When the President commenced his remarks, there were ten members of the Inquiry present.

Seated in a semi-circle in front of the President's desk, they listened intently to his frank, off-the-record prognosis of the coming peace conference. Two diaries have left extensive records of this first Presidential interview with the Inquiry force.[38] Isaiah Bowman's and William Bullitt's diaries contain very similar accounts except that Bullitt included certain subjects not alluded to in Bowman's version. Both diaries treat the President's views of the League of Nations in a similar fashion. Wilson admitted that his views on the international organization were still very vague. He did not think any hard and fast constitution for the League could be established for the present. Bullitt's version described the President as advocating a League council composed of ministers accredited to some neutral state such as Switzerland. The council could meet periodically and consider international tensions which

35. Ibid.

36. The late Robert J. Kerner told the author on December 27, 1954, that it was he who had first suggested to Bullitt the desirability of using Bullitt's influence to bring the President to talk with members of the Inquiry.

37. Bullitt MSS Diary, Dec. 9, 1918, Yale.

38. Isaiah Bowman's minutes are available in Charles Seymour, ed., *Intimate Papers of Colonel House, 4,* 280–83, and also in Shotwell, *At the Paris Peace Conference,* pp. 75–78. See also William C. Bullitt MSS Diary, Yale. The brief account in the George L. Beer MSS Diary is quoted in Shotwell, op. cit., p. 74.

contained the potential for war. "War," in the President's quoted words, "must no longer be considered an exclusive business."

> Any war must be considered as affecting the whole world. If any nation refuses to listen to the powers composing the League it is my idea that they should be boycotted absolutely by the other powers, cut off not only from goods, but all train, telephone, mail and other forms of communication—cut off absolutely. Their frontiers would be hermetically sealed.[39]

The President did not believe the plan espoused by the League to Enforce Peace could be adopted. The League's prime function would be to arbitrate disputes; it could readjust boundaries and solve other problems brought before it by the nations and peoples concerned.

Turning to other pressing subjects, the President was somewhat more explicit. The German colonies should become the common property of the League of Nations to be administered by one (or more) of the smaller nations, allowing commercial trading privileges on an equal basis for all League members. It would be of fundamental importance, President Wilson emphasized, for the colonies to be governed primarily in the interest of their native inhabitants. Constantinople too, would be a part of this arrangement, i.e., administered by some small state as mandatory for the League.[40] Bullitt went on to mention the President's discussion of the subject of indemnities. Here the President took the opportunity to assert his opposition to any indemnity except for damage actually done by the German armies. Damage must be assessed and determined by scientific study and then an attempt must be made to have the claims honored. Under no circumstances would Wilson consent to indemnities imposed beyond the actual damage suffered in the war.[41]

Throughout his discussion, the President emphasized the general spirit in which the United States would approach the problems of the settlement. Alone among the victorious nations, the United States was absolutely disinterested. Allied leaders were not fully representative of their peoples. There was much dissen-

39. Bullitt MSS Diary, Dec. 10, 1918, Yale.
40. Constantinople was mentioned only in the Bullitt account.
41. Indemnities were mentioned only in the Bullitt account.

sion between and among the Allies and the United States over peace objectives. For the United States, justice would guide the settlement. The President was nevertheless under no illusions that a peace based upon justice would encounter no opposition. Germany, he considered, would eventually be allowed membership in the League of Nations, but must first pass through a probationary period. This was necessary in order to prove the readiness of the German people for responsible government. Though Russia was not mentioned by name, the President did say:

> The only way I can explain the susceptibility of the people of Europe to the poisons of Bolshevism is that their Governments have been run for wrong purposes, and I am convinced that if this peace is not made on the highest principles of justice, it will be swept away by the peoples of the world in less than a generation. If it is any other sort of a peace then I shall want to run away and hide on the Island of Guam or somewhere else remote, for there will follow not mere conflict but cataclysm.[42]

George Louis Beer's diary corroborates many of Bullitt's recollections. Beer also emphasized the undemocratic, unsociable atmosphere aboard ship. Between December 4 and December 9, Beer mentions, he had significant conversations only with Hornbeck, Bullitt, and Colonel Leonard Ayers, the Army statistican. Beer was also present at the meeting with the President, but his account was far briefer than either the Bowman or Bullitt versions. It does, however, add a few things. When discussing the League of Nations, Beer recalled, the President emphasized the covenants as constituting greater importance than the organization itself. It was necessary to go slowly in working out the League organization. "Woodrow Wilson is heartily sick of the balance of power." The League would be held together by its common property, the former German colonies. Summing up his impressions of the conference with the President, Beer concluded:

> Whole talk frank, witty and full of charm. Wilson convinced that Allies were beaten and that America turned tide and at Chateau Thierry saved the world. Talk demonstrated that he had not gone into details—he frankly said so—and that he had not

42. Bullitt MSS Diary, Dec. 10, 1918, Yale. In a letter to the author, Charles Seymour has recalled Wilson's exact phrase as "the curious policy of Bolshevism."

173

thought out everything. Firm on broad general principles, but flexible as to their precise application. His mind in that respect evidently open, and he said that he depended on us for the facts. While he is in a fighting mood and is prepared to fight for a just peace he virtually said that absolute justice in any specific instance was not attainable . . . I advised Bullitt to suggest to President not to commit himself further until he reaches Paris and sees how ground lies. In all probability the harm, if any has already been done as President has spoken freely—so Bullitt was informed by Jusserand—to Jusserand who has probably already informed his government.[43]

William L. Westermann was not present at the conference until the last fifteen minutes, for he had not been summoned with the others. Nevertheless, his impression both first- and second-hand does not alter or augment the longer accounts. Westermann observed that the President's tone was not grave, but had about it a genial air, and that Wilson never lost his sense of humor even amidst discussion of the most serious problems. Westermann does mention that this was the first occasion when the President outlined his ideas concerning the functions of the League. The President's attitude toward his advisers must have sunk deeply into the consciousness of his listeners, for it has been quoted often:

> You are, in truth, my advisers, for when I ask information, I will have no way of checking it, and must act on it unquestionably. We shall be deluged with claims plausibly presented, and it will be your job to establish the justice or injustice of these claims, so that my position may be taken intelligently . . . Tell me what's right and I'll fight for it; give me a guaranteed position.[44]

These were inspiring words, but their effect did little to remove the disheartened spirits of Inquiry men who felt that the President had been much too indefinite. Beer, Haskins, Young, Hornbeck, and Westermann all considered the President's program

---

43. George L. Beer MSS Diary, Dec. 9, Dec. 10, 1918, Columbia.
44. George Creel, *Rebel at Large, Recollections of Fifty Crowded Years* (New York, 1947), p. 254; David Hunter Miller (uses Bowman's account), *My Diary at the Conference at Paris* (Washington, 1928), *1*, 370–73; Westermann MSS Diary, Dec. 10, 1918, Columbia.

too vague and inadequate.[45] For these men groping about on the deck of the *George Washington,* President Wilson might easily establish himself as the greatest failure in history. A. A. Young even considered the desirability of warning British liberals that they could expect no constructive propositions to emanate from the President, that the burden must be borne by them.[46]

Talks with other plenipotentiaries did not appreciably raise faltering spirits. Lansing and White also appeared before an Inquiry group on December 9.[47] Lansing spoke emphatically about the Anglo-Japanese Treaty of 1916 which he claimed disposed of German islands in the Pacific between the two countries. The Secretary also called attention to population pressure in Japan as constituting a positive motivation for expansion. This expansion should by all means be directed westward toward the Asiatic continent rather than eastward in the Pacific path of American interests. Lansing went so far as to favor Manchuria and Mongolia as proper fields for Japanese colonialism.[48] Later, after the plenipotentiaries had departed, Lansing's assertions were hotly contested by Stanley Hornbeck, the Inquiry Far Eastern specialist, who disagreed with Lansing's analogy between American expansion into the Caribbean area and Japan's position in eastern Asia.[49]

The arrival of the President at Brest on December 14 was greeted with a tumultuous tribute by the French people, an ovation which followed him to his headquarters in Paris. To many in the President's party, including Inquiry members, conditions among the American high command seemed in utter confusion.[50] The President made statements and decisions without consulting

45. Bullitt MSS Diary, Dec. 11, 1918, Yale. Bullitt shared this attitude with all the persons named.

46. Ibid.

47. Conversation with Secretary Lansing, Dec. 10, 1918, no author listed, Shotwell MSS, Columbia; Westermann MSS Diary, Dec. 10, 1918, Columbia.

48. Conversation with Secretary Lansing, Dec. 10, 1918, Shotwell MSS, Columbia. Cf. Lansing's idea expressed here with the very similar proposition introduced by an unnamed American naval adviser at the peace conference later: Document 17, in David Hunter Miller, *My Diary at the Conference at Paris, 2,* 104–07.

49. Conversation with Lansing, Dec. 10, 1918, Shotwell MSS, Columbia.

50. Regarding the triumphal entry of the President's party at Brest, see Lansing to Frank Polk, Dec. 15, 1918, Polk MSS, Yale.

members of his staff. Except for Colonel House, the other American plenipotentiaries were in an utter quandary regarding the duties they were expected to perform.[51] As late as January 1, 1919, General Bliss was heard to remark that he did not know whether or not the commissioners were to have anything to do, for the President appeared to be running the show himself. Since he had not the slightest idea what policy was being favored by the President, Bliss decided the mark of wisdom would be to maintain an intelligent silence.[52] Ignorance of the President's intentions prompted Henry White to request a conference of all American plenipotentiaries "to find out what was going on." [53] According to William Bullitt, White thought this high-handed operation by the President would be fatal for the American delegation when the American commissioners, with no agreed-upon policy, started conferring with French and British delegates whose programs would surely be entirely developed.[54] Lansing had written the President in November asking how far the United States would recognize treaties signed by the Allied governments during the war and how much these treaties should be considered in reaching a final settlement of boundaries. He was especially anxious to learn the President's view of the secret treaties.[55] President Wilson seemed unwilling to take the other plenipotentiaries into his confidence.

Once settled in its headquarters at the Hotel Crillon, the Inquiry found itself in even worse confusion. No central clearing house possessing sufficient authority to make administrative decisions had been arranged in advance. Members of the American commission had little idea of what was expected of them. The abundant correspondence and diary records relating to these first weeks all focus sharply on the chaotic situation. Upon arrival in Paris, the Inquiry leaders discovered to their dismay that the Army's military intelligence section was already established in position as if it intended to function as the chief American ad-

51. William Bullitt MSS Diary, Jan. 1, 1919, Yale.
52. Ibid.
53. Ibid.
54. Ibid.
55. Robert Lansing to Wilson, Nov. 18, 1918, Wilson MSS, Series II, Library of Congress.

visory group.[56] Then, to complicate matters, Colonel Leonard Ayres of the Army's statistical office set up what approximated a rival military advisory center.[57] In their midst, other military staff officers who had been assigned to the peace commission seemed to float about with no apparent ties or authority. In fact, no well-defined channels of responsibility were apparent to knot the amorphous military units. Early in January, the economic hierarchy started arriving from the United States: Hoover; Vance McCormick, chairman of the War Trade Board; Edward N. Hurley, chairman of the United States Shipping Board; and Bernard M. Baruch, chairman of the War Industries Board, all brought with them extensive staffs.

Into this scene of rampant confusion there now appeared John Foster Dulles armed with the President's memorandum assigning authority to Edwin Gay's Central Bureau of Statistics. Dulles and his co-workers expected to assume immediate charge of providing all economic information for the American commission.[58] Upon his arrival in early January, Dulles proceeded to seek out his uncle, Robert Lansing, trying through Lansing to establish himself at the conference. According to one of Edwin Gay's trusted deputies, Lansing was inclined to give Dulles supreme statistical authority, against violent protests from the Inquiry. A controversy developed between Dulles and the Inquiry leadership resulting finally in the intervention of President Wilson in order to achieve some semblance of tranquility. Before a calm descended, the President confessed to A. A. Young of the Inquiry that he had not "to his knowledge ever authorized the arrangement by which Dulles was to be the exclusive channel of statistical communication from Washington to the Peace Conference." [59]

56. John Foster Dulles to Edwin Gay, Jan. 24, 1919 (confidential), Gay MSS, Huntington Library. This letter refers to the situation at the time the Inquiry arrived in France.

57. Report from James A. Field to Edwin Gay, Feb. 8, 1919, "The American Statistical Organization at the Peace Conference," deals in part with the various advisory groups in attendance which served the American commission at the peace conference during December and January, Gay MSS, Huntington Library.

58. Ibid.

59. Dulles to Gay, Jan. 24, 1919, Gay MSS, Huntington Library, "On arriving here I have found a very distinct atmosphere of hostility towards you [Gay] and the plans the carrying out of which you entrusted to me. This was particularly

The upshot found Dulles and the Central Bureau appended to the Inquiry as liaison between the economic and statistical section, on the one hand, and McCormick, Baruch, and Hoover on the other.[60]

These events, including the chaos and controversy, were possibly the inevitable accompaniment to the frustrated beginnings of the quickly formed American commission. James A. Field, a leading official in Gay's Central Bureau of Statistics, in frequent correspondence with his chief in Washington, contributed some insight to an understanding of the members of the American secretariat. Joseph Grew is pictured in these letters as an intelligent fellow endowed with numerous diplomatic charms and graces, "but nobody is aware that Grew has any particular qualifications for organizing a technical staff . . . His personal assistant, Leland Harrison is a sort of exaggerated diminutive of Grew with still less executive qualification." [61] The Inquiry was characterized as an uneven aggregation with some excellent men and others "who impressed me as hardly third rate." [62] Director Mezes was held in low esteem by his subordinates, "but as brother-in-law to House he wields a very strong influence." According to the gossip overheard by Field, Mezes regarded Messrs. Haskins, Coolidge, and Gay together "as constituting what is perhaps the most dangerous gang in American university life and that when Haskins is at Paris and Coolidge is only with difficulty kept in exile in the Near East it would be most hazardous to let the third brigand come to Europe where the conspiracy might be renewed." [63] Through their letters to their chief in Washington, Gay's lieutenants at the peace conference displayed a very low opinion of the Inquiry as a group.

evident on the part of Messrs. Mezes, Bowman and Young. . . . When the cable had come announcing your plans and the prospective arrival of myself and my group, Dr. Mezes endeavored to have us stopped, and presented a formal memorandum shortly after my arrival, which contained insinuations against you which I resented very much and which resentment I expressed plainly. Dr. Mezes stated that he thought you had not acted in good faith in getting the President to sign the memorandum which he did without prior consultation with the Inquiry."

60. James A. Field to Gay, Feb. 8, 1919, Gay MSS, Huntington Library.
61. Ibid.
62. Ibid.
63. Ibid.

When the peace conference at last convened on January 18, the Inquiry was firmly entrenched as adviser to the plenipotentiaries. Although satisfactory evidence that the Inquiry received recognition as the chief advisory body is lacking, logical supposition might presume its status resulted from the weighty influence of Colonel House upon the President. Certainly, by January 18 when the commission was reasonably well organized, the Inquiry provided the chief reservoir for political information, and with the passing weeks members of the Inquiry were assigned positions of power in the many important committees created by the peace conference.[64]

Although Mezes' force continued to be referred to as the Inquiry, it ceased to exist as a separate entity after January 1919. When Mezes and his twenty-two associates boarded the *George Washington,* the Inquiry merged with the American Commission to Negotiate Peace, and assumed a new formal title, "Division of Territorial Economic and Political Intelligence." Henceforth, Inquiry members attached to the peace conference received their salaries through the budgetary appropriation specified for the American peace commission and administered directly by the Department of State. What this meant can be readily gleaned from the financial records of the commission. For most Inquiry advisers, the new status brought an advancement in salary, while

64. Organizational chart of the American Commission to Negotiate Peace, Tasker Bliss MSS, Box 203, Library of Congress. See also Spencer Phoenix (Edwin Gay's chief assistant in Washington) to John Foster Dulles, Jan. 4, 1919 (marked personal and confidential), Gay MSS, Huntington Library, and Memorandum from Lieutenant Ralph A. Hayes to Secretary of War Newton D. Baker, Dec. 26, 1918, in Baker MSS, Library of Congress, and also notation for December 22, 1918, in George L. Beer MSS Diary, Columbia. On January 2, 1919, Sidney Mezes submitted a lengthy brief to the Secretary General of the American Commission, Joseph Grew, asking for an official opinion regarding the conflict between the Inquiry and Gay's organization. The gist of Mezes' remarks was: during the boat crossing, the President had asked A. A. Young, the Inquiry economics chief, to continue to supply economic materials for the American commission. Also on the boat, the President had told Young that he had no recollection of ever speaking to Gay about furnishing economic information for the peace conference. Nevertheless, Mezes asked for a ruling concerning which organization would be the "ONE OFFICIAL SOURCE" for economic information. American Commission to Negotiate Peace Archives, file 184.83/11, National Archives. Evidently the Commission favored the Inquiry in the end, but the author has been unable to discover a record of the decision.

in other cases it substituted a salary for the former dollar-a-year arrangement. Sidney Mezes, for instance, became the highest paid member of the Inquiry contingent, receiving $825 per month.[65] Isaiah Bowman, as second in command and chief territorial specialist, was put on the payroll at $600 per month. There were in all ten members of the twenty-three who in December 1918 received salaries in excess of $400 per month plus living expenses. Non-Inquiry advisers were paid comparable stipends (John Foster Dulles' salary was $500 per month). Meanwhile at Inquiry headquarters in New York, the formal records including account books were closed, the Latin American Inquiry was concluded, and clerical personnel was allotted severance pay.[66]

The Inquiry had moved to Paris, where its fifteen months of preparation and anticipation would be put to the test. The numerous reports and memoranda, the maps, the charts, and the considerable training of more than a score of members would now have a chance to show their worth.

65. 66th Congress, 3d Session, *Senate Document No. 330, Expenditures of the American Commission to Negotiate Peace,* December 8, 1920.

66. Inquiry Account Books, David Hunter Miller MSS, Library of Congress.

Chapter 7

THE INQUIRY AND THE EUROPEAN
SETTLEMENT

FROM THE BEGINNING of its existence, the Inquiry had been organized as a research organization, an independent administrative
agency authorized by President Wilson to produce reports, collect documents, and in other ways prepare the American case for
the peace settlement. In actual practice, most of the Inquiry's
reports which made their way into trunks destined for the peace
conference were written under three quite different conditions.
First, there were the reports compiled by the regular membership of the Inquiry. A second group of reports had been written
by individuals not formally members of the Inquiry but who had
been requested to write on some special subject in which they
presumably had competence. A third category of reports was
written by individuals employed in other government departments and agencies. While writers in category 2 were not under
any discipline or effective supervision by the Inquiry's leadership, writers in category 3 were at least responsible to some government agency whose officers had agreed to coordinate certain
research activities with the Inquiry. This distinction among reports based on the connection of the author with the Inquiry is
not meant to imply that there was any essential difference in the
quality of the reports. It merely points to the fact that only a portion of the Inquiry's productivity resulted from the efforts of staff
members. Furthermore, the remarkable heterogeneity of persons
working on the many problems reduced the possibility for funda-

181

mental agreements in regard to recommendations and conclusions on any important phase of the future peace settlement.

This chapter will attempt an analysis of the Inquiry's reports as they related to the European settlement. It seems neither desirable nor necessary to summarize the contents and consider each report individually. Instead, there will be an attempt to describe a few of the crucial studies, define basic assumptions, and indicate quantitatively, insofar as possible, the scope and distribution of the reports. Although some contain definite recommendations, this practice was never followed universally. Fortunately, a lengthy listing of recommendations was presented to the five American plenipotentiaries at the peace conference under date of January 21, 1919. This report, titled "An Outline of Tentative Recommendations," [1] does not contain the identity of its au-

1. "An Outline of Tentative Recommendations," Jan. 21, 1919 (hereafter cited as OTR), Woodrow Wilson MSS, Series VIII-A, Library of Congress. That this was a product of the Inquiry is claimed in Paul Birdsall, *Versailles Twenty Years After* (New York, 1941), p. 177. Birdsall bases his attribution on David Hunter Miller, *My Diary at the Conference of Paris, 4,* 224–26. James T. Shotwell in his diary, *At the Paris Peace Conference,* pp. 101–02, describes the circumstances under which the Inquiry prepared these recommendations: "[On January 1, 1919, Dr. Mezes] explained that the President wanted our conclusions with reference to every problem. . . . It was decided to prepare a clear statement of the problems and the recommendations which each division of the Inquiry could shape up at the time. Dr. Bowman was to have charge of the preparation of these summaries of the studies and conclusions of the Inquiry. When finished they were assembled in a highly confidential collection consisting of two main parts, the territorial and labor reports on the one hand, and the colonial on the other. The preparation of these documents was the chief work of the days following. It was the foundation work of all our later activity in the special fields to which we had been assigned." On pp. 133–34, Shotwell describes the situation as of January 21, 1919, when the Inquiry completed the first part of the recommendations: "This series of short general statements by the heads of the Divisions of the Inquiry was the answer to President Wilson's request of January first. Each memorandum was kept down to the merest skeleton of an outline so that the whole body of material would not be too long for the Commissioners to have at hand for ready reference. Gathered together by Dr. Bowman, the typewritten pages were bound in a black cardboard cover. . . . The collection was known as the 'Black Book' to those who were aware of its existence. Later an additional companion collection was prepared, with red typed headings and a red binder, to include suggestions not incorporated in the 'Black Book,' especially covering colonial matters. Prior to the actual negotiations, they represented the findings of the American specialists which they recommended to the Commissioners for insertion in the Treaty. In the succeeding weeks there was naturally some modification of these views but the 'Black Book' and the 'Red Book' will remain for the historian the

thor(s). It was a general series of recommendations which sometimes summarized, sometimes synthesized, and in a few instances differed from the findings of individual reports.

At Paris, the Inquiry's contingent was but a skeleton of its former self, a single branch of a sprawling American Commission to Negotiate Peace. As of February 1, 1919, there were hardly 35 members of the Inquiry amongst an organization numbering 1,248 persons.[2] Sidney Mezes and Isaiah Bowman continued to command the unit; yet there were noticeable innovations, as we have seen. No longer was the organization an independent entity responsible only to Colonel House and to the President. Within the Commission's organization, Mezes and his associates found themselves subject to five plenipotentiaries and the Secretariat of the Commission. Even the name "Inquiry" yielded in the official parlance to the more presumptuous title, "Division of Political and Territorial Intelligence," though members continued to refer to themselves informally as the Inquiry.

There is no complete single listing of the reports and documents taken by the Inquiry to the Paris Peace Conference. *An Inventory of Records of the American Commission to Negotiate Peace* published by the National Archives is admittedly incomplete in listing the Inquiry's production.[3] The volume enumerates a total of 1,752 separate substantive reports not including the cartographic materials. A second catalogue located in the Columbia University Library tabulates 1,131 items.[4] The difference in these two totals does not merely reflect the incompleteness of the Columbia catalogue (the Columbia inventory only covers materials submitted prior to November 10, 1918); many items on one listing are not duplicated on the other. A reasonable estimate would place the number of reports and documents produced and collected by the Inquiry before the peace conference somewhere in the neighborhood of 2,000 separate noncartographic items.

---

central statement of the work of the Inquiry and its contribution to the Peace Treaty."

2. Henry White to Tasker Bliss, Feb. 1, 1919, Bliss MSS, Library of Congress.

3. National Archives, "Preliminary Inventories No. 89," Records of the American Commission to Negotiate Peace, compiled by H. Stephen Helton, pp. 1–2.

4. List of Inquiry Reports, Typescript Copy, Columbia Library, Special Collections Division.

These figures by no means represent the productivity of the Inquiry. In a very real sense, the Inquiry collected more than it actually produced. Authors not directly affiliated with the Inquiry (categories 2 and 3) accounted for a majority of the reports, even when reports bearing no evidence of authorship are excluded. Where the evidence for attribution does exist, it is noteworthy that the National Archives inventory shows only 448 of the 1,752 reports and documents to have been the work of *bona fide* Inquiry staff, a bare twenty-five per cent. Similarly, the Columbia listing shows 392 of the 1,131 to be products of Inquiry members, a ratio approximating thirty per cent.

Just as striking is the distribution of reports and documents among the significant geographical divisions. These figures and percentages are taken from the National Archives inventory (as will be all subsequent quantitative figures cited in this chapter), but the percentages do not vary markedly from the Columbia list. European problems accounted for 894 reports (51 per cent); Africa, the Middle East, the Far East, and the Pacific Islands together accounted for 428 reports (28 per cent). Another group of 246 reports (13 per cent) dealt with the Americas, while 184 reports and documents (10 per cent) were concerned with problems of international law, organization, and economics not classified by geographical locality. The Inquiry itself was responsible for between 20 per cent and 35 per cent of the material in each classification except the last where the percentage was much lower. The European materials, for instance, contained 263 titles (29 per cent) whose authors were members of the Inquiry's staff.

More than 50 per cent of the total number of collected reports and documents pertained to European problems. More than 50 per cent of the reports positively attributable to the Inquiry's staff focused upon the European continent. The logic of this emphasis is apparent. To say that Europe accounted for a majority of the Inquiry's materials does little to describe the European problems upon which the Inquiry placed most attention. Of the 894 reports and documents dealing with European affairs listed in the Archives inventory, 174 were devoted to Germany and its territorial frontiers, including Alsace-Lorraine. Austria-Hungary, including the problems of Central Europe, accounted for 140 reports; Balkan problems provided the subjects for 159 items; Russia and the Baltic provinces, including Poland, figured prominently in 203 items. The Western Allied countries—Britain, Belgium, France, and Italy—were considered in 158 reports and documents. Neutral countries of Europe together were treated by 60 reports and documents. The following chart shows how the 263 reports pertaining to Europe, prepared by the Inquiry's staff, were distributed among these categories:

	Reports	Percentage of total
Germany	47	17
Austria-Hungary	52	20
Balkan states	63	24
Russia and Baltic states	82	31
Western Allies	19	07
Neutral states	0	0

Any quantitative classification is only partially successful in conveying an impression of the importance the Inquiry's leaders might have attached to a particular subject or area. Like the financial allocations noted in Chapter 3,[5] where we saw the large proportion of funds allocated to Latin American research, the breakdown of reports according to the number on each major subject can only indicate generalized importance, and this could be illusory. Many of the Inquiry's reports, for example, were only one to five pages long, amounting in reality to brief summaries of statistics or other data. Somewhat more common was the report ranging in length from 15 to 40 pages which attempted some analysis. There were in addition several reports falling into the 60- to 500-page length. A writer might conceivably invest three months or even longer upon a subject and produce a 400-page report. A second writer could in the same time period contribute 20 reports whose total length and relevant value might be minute.

What subjects were encompassed by the Inquiry's reports dealing with Europe? The reports dealing with Germany were rather typical in terms of the variety of subjects covered by the studies, itemized as follows:

5. Supra, Chap. 3, p. 101.

Subject	No. of Reports	Subject	No. of Reports
Documents	4	Alsace-Lorraine	46
History	5	Social welfare	1
Politics and government	10	Cattle and forest resources	2
Boundaries	5	Finance and postwar	
Education	1	economic position	14
Colonies	1	Causes and responsibility	
Pan Germanism	1	for war	1
Public opinion	1	General political and	
Militarism	1	economic situation in	
Commerce and tariffs	30	1918	7
Schleswig	3	Industry	9
Jutland	1	Merchant shipping	5
		Miscellaneous	26

Whatever else might be said about these subjects, it cannot be concluded that economic questions were ignored in the American preparatory work. True, the Inquiry was not responsible for the bulk of the economic studies. A. A. Young, chief of the economics section of the Inquiry, personally prepared a very large number of such studies. It is likewise true that Young was able to obtain numerous studies from many economists already serving in government and industry. The National Archives inventory lists a total of 342 reports dealing with an assortment of European economic problems. Most economic studies in the group bristled with statistical tables of all kinds. As a rule, the economic studies were void of positive recommendations; their authors seemed content to present material evidence and let their facts and figures tell the story. The disposition of Alsace-Lorraine presented a good many questions whose complexity the Inquiry did not minimize. The provinces of Alsace-Lorraine provided the subject for forty-six reports, twenty-seven of which were written by the Inquiry's members. These reports treated the following topics:

Subjects	No. of Reports	Subjects	No. of Reports
History	3	Canals	1
Political problems and		Language and population	2
their solutions	2	Boundaries	1

Subjects	No. of Reports	Subjects	No. of Reports
Plebiscites	5	Private ownership	1
Government	6	Public opinion	3
Who's Who in the		Tariffs and commerce	1
provinces	2	Mineral resources	10
Newspapers	1	Finance	2
Secret societies	1	Bibliography	1
Education	1	Miscellaneous	3

Remote as some of these topics may appear to the immediate settlement facing a peace conference, they were chosen and assigned on the assumption that, should a question arise, American delegates might require all kinds of information.

A majority of the Inquiry's European reports had to do with postwar national boundaries. New political states would in all probability come into existence after the war. The Inquiry's scholars, considering the possibility of new states emerging out of the war, found it necessary to plan desirable, practical boundaries for these states. Hence not only were all the existing German, Austrian, and Turkish frontiers placed under the Inquiry's scrutiny, but the entire network of Balkan frontiers was examined with the assumption that new political entities and federations might later be recognized by the peace conference.

Complications arose at every turn. No one could possibly foresee with absolute certainty the circumstances in which new states would come into existence. It was highly questionable whether the Austro-Hungarian Empire would even survive the war. To what extent would the secret treaty arrangements be recognized and applied by the peace conference? Because of such grave uncertainties, the Inquiry's reports were constantly forced to deal with changing patterns of alternative possibilities. The problem of planning for the peace conference was not simply one which involved assumptions that the status quo in Europe would continue after the war.

Four different approaches were employed in the Inquiry's studies dealing with political and territorial alignments: historical, sociological, economic, and power-strategy considerations. Historically oriented reports, making use of diplomatic treaties

187

and legislative records for the most part, endeavored to justify or oppose any change in a territory's sovereign status on the basis of the historical claims of conflicting groups. While some historical reports did extend in time far back to the Middle Ages, this practice was frowned upon by the organization. The Inquiry's Executive and Research committees prevailed upon writers of historical studies to begin their reports no earlier than 1815 except when earlier events proved vital to the understanding and determination of a given problem.[6] Similarly, historical reports were not to extend into the present beyond the beginning of the war in 1914.

The term sociological embraces a variety of reports all bearing upon population. This approach aimed at classifying a given population inhabiting a particular district to determine its ethnic, religious, and other characteristics. Scholars who used this approach spent much time perusing official census reports and carefully tabulating statistics of the religious, linguistic, or other complexion of the particular society being studied. President Wilson had placed much emphasis upon the concept of "self-determination" as offering the principal means for deciding the ultimate division of land among contesting sovereign states. In his address to Congress of February 11, 1918, the President indicated how important he regarded this principle as a basis for the peace settlement:

> There shall be no annexations, no contributions, no punitive damages. Peoples are not to be handed about from one sovereignty to another by an international conference or an understanding between rivals and antagonists. National aspirations must be respected; peoples may now be dominated and governed only by their own consent. "Self determination" is now an imperative principle of action which statesmen will henceforth ignore at their peril.[7]

The doctrine of "self-determination" proclaimed the right of each people to decide its own political allegiance. Liberals in Europe

6. Instructions to Historical Writers, March 2, 1918, no author, Inquiry Archives.
7. Baker and Dodd, eds., *Public Papers of Woodrow Wilson, War and Peace,* 1, 180. See also Wilson's four principles enumerated in the same address, pp. 182–83.

and America had regarded the principle as offering the fairest means for deciding national frontiers. Nevertheless, even though self-determination might conceivably receive complete support among the delegations at the peace conference, how could it be applied to the potpourri of national strains in Europe? What was to be the criterion by which nationality would be recognized? Many ethnologists believed that language represented the best means of establishing the dominant ethnic affiliation in a mixed population.[8] In any event, the Inquiry's studies included numerous linguistic reports although such other factors as religion, demography, occupational classification, and urban-rural divisions figured prominently. Important as were the sociological reports, the Inquiry's leaders did try to balance the population factor against economic, historical, and political components before arriving at recommendations.

The very large number of economic studies dealt with natural resources, commerce, land tenure, transportation facilities, industrial organization, and agricultural productivity. Detailed studies concerned with mineral production and reserves were conducted especially for those areas being claimed by at least two national states. Both internal and external commerce was examined to determine the extent to which a given area was dependent economically upon other areas. In those instances where the Inquiry's recommendations hinged on economic factors, the availability of crucial mineral resources or a port or some other economic instrument essential to the well-being of a national state provided the decisive condition. Even though the ethnic attachment was not clear, cities and ports were often incorporated in an adjacent state solely on the ground that the city was vital to it.

A smaller proportion of the Inquiry's European reports fell under the classification of political analysis. Under this heading would be included studies of govermental organization, political parties, and power relations of various states. There were studies devoted to the problem of federalism, dualism, and trialism especially where the political organization encompassed a multitude of ethnic groups within the confines of a single national state. Of

8. That the Inquiry used this principle is evidenced in the introduction to the report, "Proposed Boundaries in Austria-Hungary," October 1918, Inquiry Archives.

somewhat greater importance was the problem of national defense, including the creation of frontiers which would follow topographical features favoring defense. Strategic considerations were given more emphasis than questions of power relationships. There were just a few reports concerned with *realpolitik* in the New Europe. Very few of the Inquiry's studies dealt with the large questions of what might be the relationship, say, of Germany toward the small states rising in Eastern and Central Europe. Would Germany be in a position to dominate these new states? This subject was not exactly ignored, but in terms of the Inquiry's total production there was relatively little thought devoted to it.

The Inquiry's organization had been devised along geographical lines. Each section of the European continent was studied by some special committee. The advantages in this arrangement made possible the development of specialists in particular areas. But the procedure did not encourage effective consideration of the large-scale problems which concerned Europe as a whole, or which crossed the confines of a single division. Here lay one of the major defects in the Inquiry's approach to European problems.

Germany, the strongest military and industrial power in opposition to the Allied and American coalition, naturally inspired numerous studies. Several conceptions of the postwar German problem had been discussed in the press prior to the formation of the Inquiry. Secretary of State Robert Lansing's view of the German problem was possibly shared by many informed Americans in October 1917. Just one day after Lansing had conferred with Sidney Mezes and David Hunter Miller, the Secretary wrote a private memorandum in which he declared:

> [Yesterday's discussion with the Inquiry's leaders] has made me wonder whether it is impossible to have a stable peace without rendering the German military power impotent for the future. Is it safe for the world to live with the Beast unless its teeth are drawn?
>
> There are two ways of doing this; one by discrediting Prussianism with the German people; and the other by depriving the German Empire of the means to wage successful war. As to the first of these ways, I am losing the little faith which I had. The German mind seems to be utterly perverted in its conception of right and

honor and humanity. I am coming reluctantly to the opinion that the German people will never change their code of morals or be worthy of trust and confidence. Unless they do, a peace founded on their promises would be worthless and the democratic nations would have to maintain for their own safety a superior physical force to compel compliance. Even then the peace would be unstable. Probably the surer and better way, any means would be justified, would render powerless the physical might of the nation which is responsible for this awful crime against humanity.[9]

Lansing then proceeded to outline several propositions. Along the Danube and the Adriatic, and across the eastern frontiers of Germany, he recommended the creation of strong, populous, independent buffer states even though such states would deprive Russia and Austria of considerable territory. Faced with this barrier to the south and east, German expansion might be checked. To the west, Lansing stood firmly in support of transferring Alsace-Lorraine to France. Once deprived of these mineral-rich provinces, Germany would find itself dependent upon foreign sources for the essential materials to wage war. To the north, Lansing strongly urged the cession of Schleswig-Holstein plus the Kiel Canal district to Denmark. A Germany without the Kiel Canal would find its navy reduced in strength by 50 per cent, for then it would be compelled to divide its fleet to meet the British in the North Sea and the Russian fleet in the Baltic. On the surface at least, Secretary Lansing's terms for Germany were severe. "Her armies must be defeated and her industries ruined." This was not the "peace without victory" once urged by President Wilson; Lansing aimed at rendering the German state impotent.

It cannot rightly be ascertained how many scholars concerned with German questions for the Inquiry were in agreement with the Secretary of State. There is even less evidence to indicate any influence exerted by the Secretary upon Inquiry recommendations. The fact remains, nevertheless, that a very large number of reports directly or indirectly supported a greatly weakened German state as a just price for peace.

The principal Inquiry reports were far from any consensus in favor of returning Alsace-Lorraine to France. E. C. Armstrong's

9. Robert Lansing, Confidential Private Memorandum, Oct. 24, 1917, "Certain Essentials of a Stable Peace," Lansing MSS, Library of Congress.

report on the ethnographic boundary of Alsace-Lorraine amounted to a critical analysis of an official German government report on language divisions made in 1887–88.[10] His conclusion was that despite Germany's efforts to Germanize the provinces, Alsace-Lorraine had not become Germanized in a linguistic sense. Although there had been much governmental pressure exerted upon the local population to use the German language, Armstrong found that the use of French had actually grown, that the French language had gained ground in the prewar years. Similarly, Edward Krehbiel's "Proposal for a Plebiscite in Alsace-Lorraine," completed in March 1918, reasoned, on the basis of Reichstag elections held in the provinces, that the strength of the opposition to the continuation of German control over the provinces was very considerable.[11] Krehbiel concluded his report with the prediction that a plebiscite would favor a status of greater liberty and autonomy for Alsace-Lorraine within the German nation. Charles Haskins, in charge of West European studies for the Inquiry, was not in favor of using any pre-1914 studies for evidence upon which to base recommendations.[12] Conditions had so changed during the war years, Haskins believed, that little could be gained from the earlier materials. Public opinion analyses, consideration of newspaper materials, magazines and books published since 1914 promised a far more effective approach for understanding political trends in Alsace-Lorraine. The maze of historical, economic, and strategic studies of the Alsace question did not point decisively to the justice of returning the provinces to France. They did suggest the desirability of so doing if the objective were to be a greatly weakened Germany.

Once the armistice with Germany was signed, the fate of Alsace-Lorraine seemed sealed. French troops occupied the provinces. France insisted on the basis of the Fourteen Points (which Germany had accepted as the condition for an armistice) that the provinces be returned post haste without benefit of plebiscite or further negotiation. A cumulative Inquiry report bearing the

10. E. C. Armstrong, "Speech Boundary in Alsace-Lorraine," n.d., Inquiry Archives.

11. Edward Krehbiel, "Proposal for a Plebiscite in Alsace-Lorraine," March 8, 1918, Inquiry Archives.

12. Haskins to Isaiah Bowman, March 21, 1918, Inquiry Archives.

title, "Possible Territorial Changes in the German Empire," dated late December 1918, summed up the *fait accompli:* "The loss of Alsace-Lorraine [to Germany] may be considered certain." [13] The Inquiry's Red Book of Peace Preparations, which was probably completed in February 1919, continued in the same vein: "The restoration of Alsace-Lorraine to France with the boundaries of 1870 may be assumed as settled by the acceptance of President Wilson's eighth point and of the terms of the Armistice of November 11, 1918. Discussion is unnecessary." [14] While none of the nations associated with the United States in the war demurred from the principle of restoration, the German delegation, when it submitted its counter-proposals in early June 1919, protested the failure of the Allies to provide for a plebiscite and the application of self-determination for Alsace-Lorraine. Charles Haskins responded to this charge in forthright language:

> In the discussion of territorial questions the German counter-proposals repeat the well known Pan German arguments from history, language, etc., as if we were still living in the age before the war. The modern world can no longer be expected to admit claims based upon the identity of the present German Empire founded in 1870, with the loosely organized medieval empire, which claimed control over Switzerland, the Valley of the Rhone and the larger part of Austria-Hungary and Italy . . . Nor can the assumption for a moment be admitted that German speech is a necessary test of political sympathy with the present German Empire, particularly when it is recalled (1) that in many cases the German language has been forcibly imposed by the German government; (2) that German-speaking peoples, as in Alsace, have long been seeking to escape from the German Empire; and (3) that important German-speaking peoples like German Switzerland have no connection with the German Empire.
>
> Germany, which has never applied the principle of self-determination in annexing any of her territories, now seeks to make a one-sided use of this principle to prevent their loss. In the case of Alsace-Lorraine . . . whose restoration to France . . . has been acknowledged by Germany as a preliminary to the present

13. "Possible Territorial Changes in the German Empire," Wilson MSS, Series VIII-A, Library of Congress.

14. "Red Book of Peace Preparations," n.d., House Inquiry MSS, file 33-105, Yale. Cf. OTR, which declared that the two provinces with their boundaries as of 1870 should be restored to France.

Treaty, an effort is made to introduce a plebiscite for the purpose of delaying the result and confusing the issue.[15]

Haskins' rejoinder illustrates a kind of inconsistency which pervaded the Inquiry. To argue against applying the principle of self-determination to Alsace-Lorraine on the ground that the German government had previously never respected this principle is shadow-boxing. The American President, not the German government, had set forth the doctrine as forming the basis for a peace settlement. The Inquiry's reports show a great many instances where historical claims and the linguistic test, both belittled by Haskins for Alsace-Lorraine, were espoused effectively to justify a proposed settlement in other sectors of Europe. The Inquiry's leaders were sympathetic to the return of Alsace-Lorraine to France because this solution seemed likely to strengthen France at the expense of Germany. Through restoration, France stood to gain valuable mineral resources, especially the iron of Lorraine, which could then be denied to Germany. When they arrived at their recommendations, Haskins and his associates were primarily influenced by the belief that the restoration of the two provinces would contribute to the future peace and security of Europe. Whatever else could be said for historical claims, self-determination, or the inherent justice involved in restoration, these considerations did not materially affect the ultimate Inquiry recommendations.

Far more complicated than Alsace-Lorraine was the question of the disposition of the Saar Valley provinces of Germany. This border area on Germany's northwestern frontier was richly endowed with coal coveted by French industry. Strategic considerations were coupled with France's claim for just compensation for the destruction of French mines during the war in support of the argument for French annexation. At the peace conference, the French government was to claim the Saar on the ground that annexation would provide a requisite component for France's future security. As with his recommendations for Alsace-Lorraine, Charles Haskins had proposed in his pre-armistice reports a settle-

15. Memorandum by Charles H. Haskins regarding the German Counterproposals, June 3, 1919, Wilson MSS, Series VIII-A, Library of Congress.

ment of the Saar favorable to France.[16] Haskins advocated the use of the 1814 frontier as offering the fairest division of the Saar territory between France and Germany. The frontiers of 1815, Haskins insisted, had been imposed after the Battle of Waterloo at least partly with a punitive intent and partly to award the valuable Saar coal fields to Prussia. The line of 1814, which would cede to France most of the Saar territory, with its coal resources and its German population, seemed to Haskins to represent a line of justice. This recommendation rested partly on an historical foundation, but even more firmly upon the principle of France's right to reparation for the "systematic destruction of her coal fields and for other acts of devastation." [17] Nevertheless, both the economic and the political arguments were subject to challenge because of the sizable proportion of the Saar's population whose opposition to union with France was frankly admitted by the Inquiry's scholars. In this situation, however, Haskins was willing to throw the Wilsonian principle of self-determination to the winds. The words of the Inquiry's recommendation for the Saar of January 21, 1919, might well be weighed carefully against President Wilson's concern for ethnic rights and against the Inquiry's recommendations for other European areas, which will be scrutinized below. The recommendation for the Saar stated emphatically:

> The present desires of these [the Saar's] people should not prevent a just disposition of this important coal deposit in favor of a country whose limited coal supplies have been much reduced by unlicensed German exploitations and destruction . . . in the present war.[18]

Moreover, the Inquiry's recommendations made it plain that, deprived of these frontier districts, France's industrial centers in

16. Haskins mentions his pre-armistice reports in a letter to President Wilson, March 30, 1919, Wilson MSS, Series VIII-A, Library of Congress.

17. Ibid.

18. OTR. Bernard Baruch suggested a reciprocal solution for the Saar and for Lorraine, "whereby Germany would be required to furnish the same percentage of the coal output that has heretofore been used in Lorraine; and the French in turn be required to furnish to Germany the same percentage of the iron ore output that had previously been distributed to the territory that still remains in Germany." Baruch to Wilson, April 9, 1919, Wilson MSS, Series VIII-A, Library of Congress.

the north would be highly vulnerable to a sudden attack by Germany. Only basic facts and skeletal recommendations had been incorporated in the Inquiry's pre-armistice reports.

It might be well to carry the Saar question into the actual peace negotiations at Paris as an example of how the Inquiry's recommendations were modified. During March 1919, Haskins maintained steady contact with British experts who were also working on the Saar question. Largely on the basis of these conferences, Haskins was prepared to revise his earlier proposals.[19] In April, Haskins advised President Wilson that the compromise reached by British and French negotiations would provide for the following: (1) all mineral deposits in the Saar belonging to Germany at the time of the armistice would be ceded to France; (2) France would have a perpetual right of working the mines; (3) the German government would indemnify all mine owners for losses attendant to the war; (4) all machinery and equipment would be transferred with the mines, and the value of all property ceded to France discounted from reparations due to France.[20] The Saar would become international territory to be administered under the authority of the League of Nations. All inhabitants could retain their pre-armistice national status, but, Haskins insisted, no obstacle should be placed in the way of anyone changing his national status. Neither fortifications nor any kind of military service would be permitted. At the end of fifteen years a plebiscite supervised by the League of Nations would allow the population an opportunity to decide its national affiliation from three alternatives: union with France, union with Germany, continued political control by the League of Nations. Should the plebiscite favor union with Germany, then the German government would have the option to purchase any economic property which had been trans-

19. Haskins makes this point in a letter to Wilson, April 1, 1919, Wilson MSS, Series VIII-A, Library of Congress. See also Charles Haskins, "The New Boundaries of Germany," in *What Really Happened at Paris* (New York, 1921), ed. House and Seymour, pp. 59–60. Besides discussing the conferences with the British experts, Haskins adds, "President Wilson remained firm against any form of annexation or protectorate . . ."

20. Haskins to Wilson, April 16, 1919, Wilson MSS, Series VIII-A, Library of Congress.

ferred to the French government, at a price determined by a commission of international experts. These recommendations with only minor changes were ultimately accepted and incorporated in the Versailles Treaty. In the end the cause of self-determination triumphed in spite of the Inquiry's earlier opposition to applying that principle to the Saar settlement.

Compared with the thirty studies of Germany's western frontiers actually completed by the Inquiry, the problems of the northern frontiers received scant attention. Two reports considered the problems of Schleswig-Holstein and the Kiel Canal. A third report dealt more generally with Scandinavian problems, touching upon the Schleswig question. Lawrence Steefel's report on Schleswig-Holstein, which surveyed the provinces in a comprehensive, sweeping fashion, provided much essential historical, sociological, economic, and political information.[21] Steefel recommended the holding of a plebiscite in the doubtful central portion, while the southern portion would be conceded to be German without any plebiscite. Edwin Bjorkman, a contributor to the Inquiry and a Scandinavian ethnocentric (to judge by his report), strongly urged that no irredentist feelings be aroused among the Germans of these provinces by allowing the transfer of solidly German sectors to Danish control.[22]

In the Inquiry's Outline of Tentative Recommendations (January 21, 1919), a plebiscite was proposed for the northern zone of Schleswig with appropriate safeguards to prevent any improper German manipulation of the voting.[23] A separate plebiscite was proposed for middle Schleswig where relations with Denmark had not been as close as in the north. Internationalization of the Kiel Canal was recommended.[24] Later, however, Americans participating on the Kiel Canal subcommission at the peace conference were not in favor of changing the status of the canal, and hence did not press for the Inquiry's recommendations. The subcommission's report on April 21 noted, "The American Delegation

21. Lawrence Steefel, "North Schleswig," July 25, 1918, Inquiry Archives.
22. Edwin Bjorkman, "Scandinavian Questions at the Peace Conference," Inquiry Archives.
23. OTR.
24. Ibid.

felt that inasmuch as the Kiel Canal was an artificial waterway entirely within German territory," [25] Germany should be free to exact toll charges and in all other respects control the administration of the canal, but henceforth Germany must agree to settle all disputes arising over the canal's operations through international arbitration. By and large, the sections of the Versailles Treaty relating to the Kiel Canal and Schleswig-Holstein followed the lines advanced by the American advisers on the subcommission, but the Inquiry's reports and recommendations were only partially implemented.

Comparatively slight attention was paid by the Inquiry's staff to the study of Germany's governmental problems. This reticence is particularly noteworthy in view of President Wilson's frequent statements criticizing the German government for its failure to reflect the interests of the German people. A report compiled by Monroe Smith, a political scientist of Columbia University, attempted to indicate the minimal changes required to transform Germany into a Western-type democracy.[26] Reforms in the German states, concluded Smith, were far more necessary than in the central government. All reforms should be instituted toward the end of making government more responsive to the wishes of its citizenry. If the legislative bodies were made responsible to the voters, Smith reasoned, the German emperor's autocratic powers were bound to decline.

A second report, written by Benjamin Ide Wheeler of the University of California, was also concerned with reforming the structure of the German government toward democracy.[27] At the outset Wheeler confessed to an utter lack of the scholarly competency necessary to undertake the study. For his source materials, Wheeler relied upon conversations he had had in the past several years with certain German acquaintances. First among Wheeler's prerequisites for a democratic German state was the basic reform

25. Extract from Report of Subcommission on the Kiel Canal to the Supreme Council of the Allies, April 21, 1919, Wilson MSS, Series VIII-A. See also Henry White to Wilson, April 21, 1919, Wilson MSS, Series VIII-A, Library of Congress.

26. Monroe Smith, "Political Organization of Germany," Oct. 9, 1918, Inquiry Archives.

27. Benjamin Wheeler, "Memorandum on Proposed Democratic Reforms for the German Government," Nov. 14, 1918, Inquiry Archives.

of the Prussian electoral laws: Germany's chancellor must become more responsible to the Reichstag; the monarchy itself must give way to a republican form of government. These two reports, less the product of research than the opinions of their authors, might well be compared with the opinion of Secretary of State Lansing on the subject of German governmental reform.

In October 1918, Lansing was convinced that the Kaiser "will be forced to abdicate." Succeeding the Hohenzollerns, Lansing confidently asserted, would be a republican form of government, "but [a republic] founded on socialism." [28] No sympathizer with socialism, Lansing was nevertheless aware of the possibilities within the dynamics of European politics at a moment when the Bolsheviks in Russia were about to celebrate the first anniversary of their regime. Lansing's memorandum went so far as to suggest the possibility of a Bolshevik Germany. By way of contrast, the two Inquiry reports did not even faintly conceive of possible trends in European politics that could lead Germany toward socialism. The writers' horizon of possibilities was limited to German monarchy and German republicanism.

Its conclusions and recommendations for Germany's western borderlands showed that the Inquiry placed paramount emphasis on economic and political considerations. Such an emphasis, however, did not prevail when the Inquiry arrived at recommendations for Central Europe. Located in the heart of Europe, the Austrio-Hungarian Empire presented a mosaic of intricate, contrasting ethnic population patterns. Superimposed upon the mosaic was a series of complex economic, social, and topographical features, all highly relevant to the settlement of national frontiers. The difficulties confronting the Inquiry's Central European Division were awesome enough. But they were increased by the apparent impossibility of staff agreement even on fundamental assumptions. Would the Austro-Hungarian Empire remain as a functioning entity after the war? Would its component ethnic groups be encouraged to establish independent states? In December 1917 Frank E. Anderson, United States representative in Austria, informed the State Department that there was no possibility or

28. Robert Lansing, Confidential Memorandum on the Future of Germany, Oct. 29, 1918, Lansing MSS, Library of Congress.

chance for revolution within the Austrian Empire.[29] Revolution or no revolution, the Inquiry's staff prepared its reports down to the armistice with several alternative solutions: dismemberment of the empire; federalism; trialism for German, Magyar, and Slavic populations; a reformed dualism.

Robert J. Kerner was one of the most prolific members of the Inquiry's organization. Kerner's numerous reports concerning Central and Eastern Europe were notable for their breadth and also for their dogmatism. Early in March 1918, Kerner submitted a full-scale study which focused upon several fundamentals of the Austrian solution while at the same time it weighed the relations between Central and Eastern Europe—German and Slavic Europe.[30] Both Vladimir Simkhovitch and James T. Shotwell who reviewed this report acclaimed it with such adjectives as "accurate, systematic—This is one of the best studies I have seen." "I have no criticism whatsoever." [31]

Kerner's central thesis was that so far in the war the Central Powers had achieved one major objective, namely the conquest of the Slav. This conquest had been accomplished first by the destruction of the Serbian state; second, by discrediting the Tsar's government through military defeat; third, by the Russian revolution. Kerner's thesis extended somewhat further:

> Undoubtedly, the German war party was satisfied with the latest formula of conquest in the east on the basis of self determination of peoples and if necessary compromise in the West. Self determination for Central Europe and Eastern Europe would mean only one thing; the enslavement or vassalage of the new states to Germany on an economic basis and the prevention of any military danger from the east as Germany faced the west [for one further completion of her mission].[32]

In Kerner's view, the elastic necessary to bind the proposed new states of Eastern and Central Europe closer to Germany would be their agricultural surpluses, for the Russian market was already

29. *Foreign Relations of the United States, The Lansing Papers 1914–1920* (hereafter referred to as *FRLP*), 2, 73–74.

30. Robert J. Kerner, "The German and Austrian Solutions of the Near Eastern Question," March 4, 1918, Inquiry Archives.

31. Quoted in James T. Shotwell to Sidney Mezes, March 19, 1918, Inquiry Archives.

32. Kerner, "The German and Austrian Solution," Inquiry Archives.

overburdened with these very commodities. Germany was also in a position to attract the support of landowners in Eastern Europe who feared a rampant Bolshevism. The large landowners of Eastern and Central Europe, in Kerner's words, had a well-known affinity for the aristocratic-military society found in Prussia, "not the extreme democracy of the Slavs." The price of self-determination, of political independence, for the small states would certainly be economic vassalage to Germany. In place of independence, Kerner proposed the alternative of federalism as representing the one solution capable of preventing the small states from becoming subservient to German power. "If it should happen that the German Austrians can force through the Austrian solution of the Polish Question without federalization, it will be a blow to the cause of the Allies as great as the Russian disasters." An independent Ukranian state also would mark a step in the direction of German domination. "It would do well for the allies to reflect on the influence on them of Germany's domination of the world's greatest grain supply."

Kerner perceived the hidden activities of three groups behind the scenes, pulling strings to strengthen the German position: (1) the Catholic Church; (2) international Jewry; (3) the pacifist movement. Papal interest was directed toward preserving the only large and important Catholic state in Europe. While the shadow of Bolshevism was spreading, the Catholic Church was also having visions of expansion "now that Russia has fallen on Bolshevism." The ominous role of the Jews, in Kerner's view, was more subtle:

> The International Jews, who will now become still more German than they have been, wish to save Austria in order to save their securities and to exploit especially the Jugoslav territories from Vienna, Budapest and Salonika. The Ukraine and Roumania will be forced by the Germans and Austrians to give full privileges to the Jews . . . Thus new avenues are opened up to the Jews who will not use their Austrian securities which would be so much waste paper if Austria were broken up.[33]

Western pacifists were supposedly contributing to a revival of German power by supporting the status quo in Austria. Kerner's paramount concern was to minimize German political influence

33. Ibid.

in east-central Europe. To effect this end, he could not give countenance to the general application of ethnic self-determination. Neither could he support a restoration of the status quo ante in Austria-Hungary, a solution which he believed was being advocated by international Jewry, the Catholic Church, and Western pacifists. American policy, Kerner believed, must encourage federalist elements like the Czechoslovaks, Yugoslavs, Ukrainians, Poles, etc., instead of perpetuating the centralist elements in Austria. "Otherwise we are playing into the hands of the enemy."

The importance of this report by Kerner lay in its provocative, ironclad assertions and predictions. Evidence in support of his assertions was almost totally lacking. Kerner's judgments were set forth in pontifical, prophetic language. Like the ancient soothsayers, Kerner predicted disaster for those who refused to heed his recommendations. He was firmly convinced of the efficacy of federalism in Central Europe.[34] Federalism meant the *autonomous* organization of major ethnic groups operating within the Austro-Hungarian framework. No settlement in the Slavic lands would long stand unless the principal Slavic groups obtained autonomous status. Referring to the Yugoslav nation, he observed, "The scientist may safely conclude that any solution which does not treat the Jugoslavs as one nation is based on unscientific foundations, and hence cannot be considered a permanent solution." Kerner opposed any extreme implementation of the self-determination doctrine in Central Europe on the ground that the creation of tiny nation-states would inevitably invite domination by the great powers.

Whereas Kerner favored federalism, Charles Seymour, who headed the Inquiry's Austrian Division, was working on an alternative solution known as trialism. According to this theory, at least one sizable Slavic group should possess political power equal to that of the German and Magyar groups within the empire. Seymour compared the possibilities for a Yugoslav trialism with factors favoring a Polish trialism. In the event Poland became a full-fledged partner in the empire, Seymour believed, there would be

34. Kerner, "The Minorities and the Solution of the Austro-Hungarian Question," Inquiry Archives; "Résumé of a Brief Sketch of the Political Movements of the Czechoslovaks tending toward the Federalization or Dismemberment of Austria-Hungary, May 17, 1918, Inquiry Archives.

less likelihood of Germany's exerting as strong an influence on Poland's internal affairs as might occur were Poland to become fully independent. And there might be an added advantage in trialism:

> The inclusion of Poland in a partnership with Austria and Hungary might so alter the point of view of the Trialistic State on foreign affairs as to bring about a misunderstanding with Germany.[35]

Seymour, like Kerner, recognized the need for new Slavic states in Central and Eastern Europe.[36] His plan attempted to maintain and even strengthen the Austro-Hungarian Empire for the avowed purpose of creating a major bulwark to German domination.

Fundamental differences continued to separate members working in the Central European Division of the Inquiry right down to the armistice. Economic, linguistic, religious, and historical studies were submitted for virtually every section and population group in Central Europe. The men of the Inquiry were not so favorably inclined toward the disintegration and destruction of the empire as were many officers of the State Department. From at least May 1918, for instance, Secretary of State Lansing advanced the idea that the United States should go on record as favoring the dissolution of the Austro-Hungarian Empire and supporting the national aspirations of ethnic groups desiring independence. He wrote to President Wilson, "In brief, should we not favor the disintegration of the Austro-Hungarian Empire into its component parts and a union of these parts or certain of them based on self determination?"[37] One month later Lansing was even more emphatic. "The United States has no reason to consider maintaining an Austro-Hungarian Empire in the future."[38]

35. Charles Seymour, "Austria-Hungary; Polish Trialism," May 25, 1918, House Inquiry Documents, file 33-108; see also "Jugoslav Trialism," May 25, 1918, House Inquiry Documents, file 33-109, Yale.

36. Seymour, "Slav Aspirations in Austria-Hungary"; "The Corridor Statistical Study," April 1, 1918, House Inquiry MSS, file 33-70, Yale.

37. FRLP, 2, 126–28.

38. Robert Lansing, Confidential Memorandum on American Policy in Relation to the Nationalities Now Within the Austro-Hungarian Empire, delivered to the President on June 25, 1918, Lansing MSS, Library of Congress. Wilson's agreement to the substance of Lansing's proposals is found in Wilson to Lansing, June 26, 1918, Lansing MSS.

Dissolution of the Austro-Hungarian Empire was not willed by the peace conference nor was this solution favored particularly by those responsible for the American preparations for peace. Yet when the peace conference convened at Paris in January 1919, there were few informed persons willing to wager that the empire had any future. Federalism and trialism were indeed quite empty academic terms in January 1919. The war had stirred and intensified national passions in Central Europe to the point that the Dual Empire of the Hapsburgs was in fact passé. By the time the conference began, the major Allies and the United States had already recognized new governments in Czechoslovakia and Poland established by their respective national committees. To that extent the dissolution of the Austro-Hungarian Empire was already agreed upon. The Inquiry's tentative report and recommendations of January 21, 1919, therefore recommended boundaries for an independent German Austria which would include the Crownlands of Upper and Lower Austria, Salzburg, Carinthia, the Viralberg, German Tyrol, and Styria.[39] These suggested boundaries conformed to the historical line except on the Yugoslav and Italian frontiers. A block of Germans, 250,000 in all, was included in the Czechoslovak state, and this arrangement was defended on the dubious ground that the Germans "seem rather to prefer union with the new Czechoslovak state." Wherever practicable, the language line was to serve as the basis for national frontiers. Since the new Austrian state would be landlocked, it was further recommended that it be assured of the use of Trieste and/or Fiume for its commerce.

The Inquiry's recommendations also favored an independent Czechoslovakia and an independent Hungary.[40] By January 1919, the Czech Republic was already a *fait accompli*. Included within its borders as proposed by the Inquiry would be the 250,000 Germans already mentioned, whose economic interests were expected to bind them to the new state. Both the recommended Czech and Hungarian frontiers were essentially based on ethnic considerations, though economic factors did influence the drawing of the lines. As for the sizable group of Ruthenians, the report favored the

39. OTR.
40. Ibid.

severing of the national connection between Hungarians and Ruthenians because the latter had suffered frequently from Hungarian oppression in the past. Any union of Ruthenia and the Ukraine was opposed for fear it might eventually lead to union with Russia. "It is certainly undesirable that Russia should extend across the Carpathians down to the Hungarian plain." Hence, the best alternative—and the one supposedly favored by many Ruthenians—was for Ruthenia to unite with the new Czech state. In general, these proposed recommendations varied only slightly from the final settlement of this area in the peace treaties.

The disposition of Poland could be counted on to provide the peace conference with one of its thorniest problems. Early in the life of the Inquiry, Polish questions were recognized and studied in considerable detail. Forty-two reports were actually completed by members of the Inquiry on the subject of Poland and its fate at the peace settlement. President Wilson's Point XIII in his Message to Congress of January 8, 1918, had declared in favor of an independent Poland. Despite the President's announcement of American policy, the Inquiry's staff found it necessary to consider other alternatives such as Polish trialism within a refurbished Austrian Empire. Should several alternatives arise for discussion at the peace conference, the Inquiry's staff wanted the necessary information on hand with which to handle them. Boundaries had also to be defined, and these were terribly complicated. Large numbers of Germans and Russians inhabited regions claimed by the leaders of Polish nationalism. Was it desirable to sever East Prussia from Germany by creating a Polish corridor? If Poland controlled the Baltic accesses, thousands of Germans might be forced either to cross the corridor or travel by sea between East Prussia and Germany proper. Then there was the problem of Danzig, overwhelmingly German in population but offering the only adequate port facility for the new Polish state.

The usual sources—census reports, voting tabulations, and economic statistics—were used in the preparation of the Inquiry's reports on the new Poland. Two of the most active members of the Polish Division of the Inquiry, Henryk Arctowski and S. J. Zowski, apparently thought there was nothing improper in serving two masters. These two members kept supplying information about the Inquiry's latest instructions to Polish nationalist representatives in the United States. Through Arctowski and Zowski, for instance, Polish nationalist leaders, Roman Dmowski and Ignace Paderewski, learned that the Inquiry had received no instructions to assemble data concerning a Polish corridor. Possessing this knowledge, the two Polish leaders started a campaign in the United States to apply pressure on the President in favor of creating a corridor and establishing Polish sovereignty over the Baltic provinces.[41]

In its Outline of Tentative Recommendations of January 1919, the Inquiry strongly supported the territorial claims of the Polish nationalists.[42] The new Polish state was to include Lithuania, described as being bound to Poland by both historical ties and economic interests. Union, the report declared, was universally favored by Poles and Lithuanians if provisions guaranteeing equality between the two states in a dual government could be agreed upon. Poland, furthermore, was to concede to Lithuania its claims to the administration of Vilna, Grodno, and Minsk. Failing union, the reports noted, there would have to be much more extensive study with respect to boundary arrangements, for the statistics on eastern Poland were by far the most inadequate for any section of European Russia.

Recommendations for other boundary lines of the new Poland also displayed the warmly sympathetic attitude present within the Inquiry's Polish Division toward the aspirations of Polish nationalism. The German-Polish frontier in the west was to conform strictly to the linguistic frontier—an ethnic division. Similarly, for the Duchy of Teschen, later destined to leave an indelible mark on the peace conference, a linguistic line between Czechs and Poles was employed. In the process, Czech claims to the whole of Teschen based on "historical rights" were denied. As for Eastern Galicia, where Ukrainians outnumbered Poles two to one, the report recommended that the region be assigned to Poland "only if the Ukraine is in its present state of chaos," and then only as a fully autonomous region within Poland, an autonomy to be pre-

41. Louis Gerson, *Woodrow Wilson and the Rebirth of Poland* (New Haven, 1953), pp. 96–97.
42. OTR.

served by the League of Nations. At some later date, the population of Galicia would have the opportunity to express its national preference by plebiscite.

Finally, the Inquiry's recommendations reported favorably for Polish claims along the Baltic coastal region, in the area also claimed by Germany. Admittedly there were more Germans than Poles in some sectors of the "corridor" region, especially in the environs of Danzig. Economic considerations were here placed on a higher pedestal than were ethnic factors. The predominance of Germans was deemed less important than the necessity of giving an independent Poland access to the Baltic Sea. East Prussia, though territorially severed from the rest of Germany, "could easily be assured of railroad transit across the Polish Corridor (a simple matter as compared with assuring port facilities to Poland)." With regard to the port of Danzig, a city with a large German majority, the Inquiry recommended that it be included in the new Poland as well.

Wilson's ethnic self-determination was applied wherever the principle could serve to enhance Poland's territorial interests. When economic, political, or historical arguments tended to support the Polish claims, these arguments were advanced. In the course of later negotiations at the peace conference, the Inquiry's leaders held to their position doggedly on the controversial matter of Danzig. Sidney Mezes notified President Wilson on March 31, 1919, that "all our specialists" favored making Danzig a Polish city rather than a free city to be administered under the League.[43] So many Germans (310,000) would at once clamor for union with German East Prussia that the free city would at all times be endangered. The Inquiry's scholars were even more opposed to any compromise which would divide the disputed area between Poland and Germany. On this matter, the Inquiry was repudiated, for a free city status was accorded Danzig in the peace treaty. In other respects, too, the strongly pro-Polish recommendations of the Inquiry were modified in favor of Poland's neighbors. There was, for example, no union of Lithuania with Poland as the Inquiry had recommended.

43. Mezes to Wilson, March 31, 1919, Wilson MSS, Series VIII-A, Library of Congress.

The strong support on behalf of Polish interests among members of the Inquiry often led American negotiators at the Paris Peace Conference to enter special pleas based on contradictory principles. Robert Lord, chief of the Polish Division, for example, supported forcefully the "justice" of holding a plebiscite in the southern districts of East Prussia where there seemed a chance for the new Polish state to pick up additional territory.[44] But applying reverse logic, Lord then opposed a plebiscite in Upper Silesia where Poland might conceivably lose territory containing valuable coal deposits.[45] Contradictions of this kind illustrate beautifully the truth that expert knowledge alone was not an adequate guarantee of objectivity and of freedom from bias even among the so-called disinterested American advisers.

Northern Europe, including Scandinavia and the Baltic provinces of Russia, was considered within the purview of the Inquiry's work. Louis H. Gray, who had been engaged by the Inquiry to study the Middle East, prepared and submitted a report concerned with the disposition of Spitzbergen.[46] This island, located well within the Arctic Circle north of the Scandinavian peninsula, had in 1918 no recognized national status. Gray, after describing the geographical—strategic and mineralogical—value of Spitzbergen, categorically recommended that the island be attached to the British Empire. When the Inquiry's Editorial Committee got hold of the report, it raised strong objections.[47] Too much of the geographical information had been taken directly from the *Encyclopedia Britannica;* the historical part of the report was unsupported by any reference citations. Furthermore, one critic charged that, in his opinion, "the writer's memoranda should ascertain the facts and should explain their significance but should so far as it is possible let these facts then suggest their own conclusions in the light of the general political principles

44. Robert Lord, "Evidences as to the National Sentiment of the Poles in Upper Silesia," June 5, 1919, Wilson MSS, Series VIII-A, Library of Congress.
45. Lord, Comments on Germany's Reply, June 5, 1919, Wilson MSS, Series VIII-A, Library of Congress.
46. Louis Gray, Report on Spitzbergen and Bear Island, Inquiry Archives.
47. Critique on Gray's Report of Spitzbergen and Bear Island, Shotwell MSS, Columbia.

upon which the war is being waged and also of the problem of settlement as a whole which will have to be considered as an entity when the peace conference approaches." [48]

Fortunately not all writers of the Inquiry accepted this extreme view. In any case the American Black Book of February 13, 1919, found amongst the Wilson Papers at the Library of Congress, recommended that government for Spitzbergen be entrusted to Norway as mandatory under the League of Nations.[49] The recommendation recognized the dominance of British economic interests but placed a stronger emphasis on the propinquity of Spitzbergen to Norway. By a separate treaty signed on February 9, 1920, Spitzbergen was placed under Norwegian sovereignty.[50]

Scandinavian studies were not begun by the Inquiry until early in the summer of 1918. Sidney Mezes had suggested during May that the Inquiry make use of the American-Scandinavian Foundation, a private group dedicated to promote closer cultural ties between the Scandinavian countries and the United States.[51] Overriding the objections of Walter Lippmann,[52] several reports were assigned to members of the Foundation. Edwin Bjorkman, a native of Scandinavia, submitted a report on November 29, 1918, dealing with the relations of Scandinavia to the forthcoming peace conference.[53] Though he did not make many specific recommendations, Bjorkman mentioned the Aaland Islands controversy between Sweden and Finland. Sweden had been pressing for the return of these islands since the population consisted largely of "pure Swedes"; economically and culturally the islands were Swedish, as Bjorkman brought out. Yet Bjorkman recognized that

48. Ibid.

49. Black Book No. 2, Wilson MSS, Series VIII-A, Library of Congress. This was the second volume of Inquiry recommendations and was mainly concerned with colonial matters.

50. *Foreign Relations of the United States, Paris Peace Conference 1919, 13,* 35.

51. Mezes to Gordon Auchincloss, May 9, 1918, House Inquiry MSS, file 33-157, Yale.

52. Lippmann to Clive Day, May 27, 1918, House Inquiry MSS, file 33-154, Yale. Lippmann's reason was that Scandinavian studies were not pressing matters.

53. Bjorkman, Memorandum on Scandinavian and Baltic Problems Connected with the Peace Settlement, Nov. 29, 1918, Wilson MSS, Series VIII-A, Library of Congress.

geographically and politically "the islands belong to Finland." The Inquiry's tentative report of January 1919 decided in favor of Sweden:

> The Aaland Islands of Russia should be transferred to Sweden because the population is almost purely Swedish in race and language.[54]

A lengthy report concerning Finland by Samuel Eliot Morison examined historical, economic, ethnic, population, and political problems of this Russian province.[55] There was already in existence a considerable nationalist movement demanding the creation of an independent Finnish state after the war. The Inquiry's recommendations in January 1919 favored an independent Finland because, in the first instance, there was already an active separatist movement in Finland, and secondly because Russia had shown an "intolerance for Finnish national aspirations."[56] Boundaries for the proposed nation were to include an outlet on the Arctic Ocean providing access to the ice-free harbor of Pachenga. In other areas the frontier was to follow topographical and ethnic lines of division. An additional report, undated and in other respects unidentified by authorship, called the "Red Book Number 2" and found among the House Papers, recommended the inclusion in the Finnish state of a number of Finnish-speaking villages then part of the Russian province of Karelia.[57] Strong opposition was here expressed to interference with Russia's control over the Murmansk Railroad and over the Karelian forests. But a Finnish port on the Arctic Sea was nevertheless proposed. At the Paris Peace Conference, an independent Finnish state was finally recognized, although the new state was not granted a port on the Arctic Ocean. The Aaland Islands eventually became the property of Finland rather than of Sweden.

The Baltic provinces of Estonia, Lithuania, and Lettonia (before 1919 historical atlases referred to this area as Livonia) received far skimpier treatment at the hands of the Inquiry than

54. OTR.
55. Samuel Eliot Morison, "Finland," Inquiry Archives.
56. OTR.
57. Red Book No. 2, House Inquiry MSS, file 33-106, n.d., no author cited, Yale.

might have been expected. Lithuania, for instance, was assigned to H. H. Bender for a comprehensive survey. His 218-page report, submitted on October 8, 1918, made use of no Russian source material, but instead was limited to data in Western languages, including German materials of the war years.[58] Lithuanians living in the United States supplied liberal amounts of information for Bender's use. His report concluded with these recommendations: Lithuania deserved "absolute national independence." It should not be united "in any way with Poland," though perhaps a union with the Letts was feasible. In any case, where disputes existed, boundaries should be determined by plebiscite. The entire report bubbles with favorable comment about the "racial virility, ambition, intelligence, and character [of] the Lithuanian stock." Vladimir Simkhovitch's comments summed up the Editorial Committee's reception: "Quite unsatisfactory. It is inadequate both as to sources used and presentation of material." [59]

Reports for Estonia and Lettonia fared somewhat better in the critique of the Inquiry's officers. Independent national status was recommended for these former Russian provinces, and it was specified that ethnic lines of demarcation should govern the settlement of boundaries.[60] Nearly everywhere, the ethnic frontiers coincided with existing administrative districts.

Russian questions did not arouse as strong a sense of immediacy as did the German, Central European, Italian, and Turkish questions confronting the Inquiry. This was partly rationalized by the desertion of Russia from the war early in 1918 and partly by the unstable conditions then existing in Bolshevik Russia. Indeed, the Inquiry reports treated the Bolshevik regime most casually. Just one report in the Inquiry's archives, submitted before April 3, 1918, actually considered the revolutionary situation. The bulk of the Inquiry's studies treated such subjects as "Races of Russia"; "Agricultural Crops in Russia"; "Land Ownership"; "Russian Forest Resources"; and the "Russian Polish Situation." The casual treatment accorded Bolshevism meant in terms of the Inquiry's

58. H. H. Bender, "Conditions and Events in Lithuania since the Beginning of the War," Inquiry Archives.
59. Simkhovitch to Shotwell, n.d., Shotwell MSS, Columbia.
60. OTR.

output that there was not a single report describing systematically the Soviet political or economic program, its program for peace, or its foreign policy. What caused this lack of concern with the current political situation in Russia is a question worthy of speculation. President Wilson was handling the Russian situation personally and with the aid of the State Department. As long as the Department of State was handling American-Russian political negotiations, the Inquiry left these matters alone. Moreover, though not directly involved in Russian questions, the Inquiry's leaders regarded the Soviet regime as quite temporary, from which would gradually evolve a democratic structure. Secretary of State Lansing, however, was under no illusions as to the status and possible threat of Bolshevism to Europe and the Western world. In October 1918 Lansing wrote a private memorandum in which he set forth his ideas:

> There are at work in Europe two implacable enemies of the Individual and its guardians, Political Equality and Justice. These enemies are absolutism and Bolshevism. The former is waning; the latter is increasing.
>
> We have seen Absolutism as the evil genius which plunged the world into the present war. We have fought against it and see its complete defeat drawing very near. The dread of it for the future has passed. A ruling class supported by militarism is no longer a menace.
>
> Meanwhile in Russia disorganized and weakened by revolution appeared Bolshevism, the doctrine of a proletariat despotism. It is opposed to nationality and represents a great international movement of ignorant masses to overthrow government everywhere and destroy the present social order. Its appeal is to the unintelligent and brutish element of mankind to take from the intellectual and successful their rights and possessions and to reduce them to a state of slavery. According to this terrible doctrine, life, property, family ties, personal conduct, all the most sacred rights are subject to the arbitrary will of the leaders of the proletariat.
>
> Bolshevism is the most hideous and monstrous thing that the human mind has ever conceived. It appeals to the basest passions and finds its adherents among the criminal, the depraved, and the mental unfit. . . .
>
> Yet this monster which seeks to devour civilized society and reduce mankind to the state of beasts is certainly spreading westward. Emissaries of the Bolshevists, well supplied with funds, are in Germany and Austria-Hungary preaching their abominable

doctrine to the starving, desperate and ignorant people who have suffered almost beyond endurance. To them any change is better than the present state, so they listen to the call to the social revolution against wealth and government.

The question is as to what will be the result if the proletariat should overthrow orderly governments in Central Europe. A Bolshevik Germany or Austria is too horrible to contemplate. It is worse, far worse, than a Prussianized Germany and would mean an even greater menace to human liberty.

We must not go too far in making Germany and Austria impotent or we may give life to a being more atrocious than the malignant thing created by the science of Frankenstein.[61]

Bolshevism was not simply a Russian problem in 1918, but was threatening the entire European political community. Secretary Lansing had been a bitter foe of Prussian militarism. He had recognized the need for stamping out militarism in Germany, destroying the German potential for war. But, by October of 1918, he had begun to waver; Germany and Austria could not be made impotent, if by so doing the balance of power would favor the new Bolshevik regime in Russia and encourage the spread of Bolshevism throughout Central Europe.

Prior to the peace conference, there was not a single Inquiry report which tried to come to grips with the possible menace of Bolshevism to European society. There had not appeared a single report which dealt systematically with socialism in any area of Europe. Territorial boundaries, ethnic self-determination, commodity and resource studies provided the almost exclusive concern of the membership of the Inquiry. Lansing's statement quoted above should not be viewed as the official attitude of the administration toward the Soviet state. It is cited in order to accentuate the contrasting emptiness, the lack of awareness evidenced by the Inquiry's reports on the situation in Russia. The Outline of Tentative Recommendations of January 21, 1919, reads like a passage from Alice in Wonderland. At some early, auspicious moment, the report glibly stated, the United States should encourage the reunion with Russia of its border regions in the south and west which had seceded—particularly the Baltic provinces and the

61. Lansing, Memorandum on Absolutism and Bolshevism, Oct. 26, 1918, Lansing MSS, Library of Congress.

Ukraine "if reunion can be accomplished within a federalized or genuinely democratic Russia." [62] The economic welfare of these provinces would be improved through such a reunion. The term "democratic" should not be construed to imply a Bolshevik Russia, as the report made clear. If the Bolshevik regime continued in power, then "there seems to be no alternative to accepting the independence and tracing the frontiers of all the non-Russian nationalities under discussion." Whether or not national governments should be recognized in Estonia, Lettonia, and the Ukraine was to be decided by plebiscites.

Bolshevism in Russia was viewed strictly as a temporary, abnormal condition. All of the Inquiry's plans assumed the imminent establishment of a democratic constitutional government in Russia. Independent governments were favored for Finland, Poland, the Armenians of Transcaucasus, and "probably for Lithuania." Were these nationalities to be cast off from Russia, the "Russian economic fabric" would not be jeopardized. At the same time, these peripheral national groups, having experienced prolonged oppression under Russian hegemony, would be enabled to develop "a stronger political and economic life if permitted to separate from the rest of the former Russian Empire."

The formation of an independent Ukrainian state was likewise recommended, "provided Ukrainian nationalism is strong enough to justify that decision." [63] There remained the difficulty of determining whether Russian sympathies in the upper social classes or Bolshevik-anarchist sympathies of the masses would eventually prevail in the Ukraine. Assuming sufficient ardor and enthusiasm among the Ukrainian population and the rise of a separate nation-state, the Inquiry report further suggested the advisability of Eastern Galicia being annexed to the Ukraine. Should Eastern Galicia not be annexed by an independent Ukraine, the alternative would have the new Polish state annex Eastern Galicia providing there were sufficient guarantees for an eventual plebiscite to decide popular preference in the area.

The Crimea too would be included in the proposed Ukrainian state. Here there was no question of ethnic affinity, for the Cri-

62. OTR.
63. Ibid.

means were overwhelmingly Tartar and Great Russian. Neither sociological nor historical facts provided a rationale for this recommendation. Geographic and economic considerations were paramount. An independent Ukraine would otherwise be lodged between the Crimea and Russia proper without any outlet to the sea. The Crimea would provide a Ukrainian state with free accessibility to the Black Sea. The writers of the tentative recommendations were not at all sympathetic toward the formation of an independent Crimean state. The status of "provisional independence" was recommended for Georgia, with the alternative of annexation to the Ukrainian state within some form of federal organization.[64]

As for the Russian Armenians living in the Transcaucasus, the Inquiry's report recommended that they unite with the Turkish Armenians in forming an independent Armenian state.[65] Such a state would bring together contiguous Armenian elements which would provide sufficient strength for the proposed regime. Justification for this Armenian state was based on the principle of "grouping in a common domain people of like religion, political sympathies, and speech."

Prewar Russia, in accordance with the Inquiry's recommendations of January 21, 1919, would be broken up into a number of independent national states. A complete tier would be created extending from the Arctic Ocean to the Black Sea, which would in effect form a buffer separating Russia from Central Europe. These new states would consist of the former western provinces of Russia: Finland, the three Baltic provinces of Estonia, Lettonia, and Lithuania, Poland, the Ukraine, and the Armenian national state. It is not clearly expressed in either the Outline of Tentative Recommendations or in other Inquiry reports and correspondence whether these new independent nations were in fact created in order to act as buffers or whether the Inquiry was simply attempting to apply the doctrine of self-determination to the ethnic groups within the Russian orbit. From the existing evidence the latter seems to provide a more potent motive than the former.

Balkan Europe offered the subject for sixty-three of the Inquiry's

64. Ibid.
65. Ibid.

studies. These studies ran the usual broad gamut, ranging from education, commerce, agriculture, land tenure, linguistic boundaries, religious distribution of population to political parties, diplomatic history, and minority problems. With certain notable exceptions, the typical Inquiry study concerning the Balkan area was weak and cluttered with pronounced biases favoring one or another of the Balkan nationalities. Balkan studies were in yet another sense typical of the Inquiry's output. They lacked any uniform pattern in method, interpretation, or general conclusions upon which recommendations might be based. Partisanship on particular causes was blatant to the extent that it is well-nigh impossible to read any of the Balkan studies without realizing how meaningless the term "disinterestedness" became when the Inquiry's force attempted to deal with Balkan Europe.

The Balkans had not been the subject of much intensive study by American scholars prior to the war. The number of American scholars in the social sciences who possessed sufficient linguistic facility to handle the basic documents from the Balkan area was minute. There was just no corps of scholars familiar with modern Balkan problems from which the Inquiry could draw its staff. As a result, the Inquiry found it necessary to hire students of antiquity whose proficience and mastery of twentieth-century problems could be questioned; or else it was dependent upon the talents of recent immigrants from Balkan countries whose sense of objectivity was often distorted.

Henry White, who was later to be appointed a plenipotentiary on the American commission, wrote to Colonel House in January 1918 deploring the general lack of interest in Balkan questions found in the United States. White asserted:

> In conclusion I should like to register a vigorous protest against the prevailing indifference in this country as to the fate of the Balkans. They are remote, it is true, but this war began in the Balkans, and unless Balkan affairs are properly settled the next War will begin there too.[66]

Lack of interest was not limited to the man-in-the-street; it showed up in the quality of the Inquiry's Balkan reports.

66. White to House, Jan. 15, 1918, Box 3, Henry White MSS, Library of Congress.

One fairly typical example of this utter lack of objectivity and of partisanship was the undated report written by A. Sonnichsen entitled, "The Case for Free Macedonia." Sonnichsen was apparently committed to the cause of Macedonian independence. He wrote:

> There can only be one settlement of the Macedonian Question; that is a settlement which will be permanent. That is the establishment of a free, an independent Macedonia, whose government is based on democratic principles. This is the intense desire of the people themselves. The Macedonians have that same passionate respect for democracy that is now manifesting itself among the Russians [Bolshevism]. I am convinced that their understanding of democratic principles . . . is far more intelligent than that of the Russians for they have been self-conscious longer, and through the revolutionary organization have practiced democracy longer and have become practical through hard experience.[67]

Upon occasion even the critics found these partisan discourses hard on their digestive systems. One such report dealing with Bessarabia provoked Vladimir Simkhovitch to comment:

> This report . . . is wholly without value to the Inquiry. . . . it answers so few of the questions which would occur to anyone interested in the Bessarabian Question . . . None of the geographical problems are here considered . . . The section on economics leaves everything unanswered . . . The bibliography seems to be mostly second hand and uncritical.[68]

Before leaving this matter, it might be well to quote from one other critique. William S. Ferguson, who headed the Balkan Division just before the war's end, found it necessary to castigate a member of his staff for showing extreme partisanship. Ferguson's comments were made in a letter to the writer of the report, Albert Lybyer, accused of pro-Bulgarian bias:

> It seems to me that the section designated "historical" in your report on the Struma front will give umbrage to all who do not accept the Bulgarian point of view in that controversy. It made that impression upon me and what is perhaps more important it

67. Sonnichsen, "The Case for a Free Macedonia," Shotwell MSS, Columbia.
68. Simkhovitch, Critique on Bessarabia, Shotwell MSS, Columbia; see also Shotwell's critique on Balkan Reports, Inquiry Document 40, Inquiry Archives.

seemed objectionable also to Professors Noyes and Coolidge . . .
I think it highly undesirable that in a matter so controversial as this, we should appear to be pro-Bulgarian. Our report, as a whole, would lack weight if it contained so unmistakable an apology for Bulgaria as this section seems to us to contain. Furthermore, it does not seem to me in accordance with the facts to state that Greece and Serbia arranged for a division between themselves of *all* the territory ceded by Turkey, for this implies a disposition on their part to take from Bulgaria Adrianople and the entire region to the Black Sea for a Greco Serbian claim on which, so far as I know, no evidence whatsoever exists.[69]

Lybyer was the scholar who had earlier been investigated by the Justice Department for alleged pro-Bulgarian bias.

Fortunately there were a few reports pertaining to the Balkans in which the authors did attempt to write disinterested papers based on the presentation of reliable evidence. Too often, however, these more creditable reports focused on minor problems; in other instances the authors were content to enumerate a series of material facts without any attempt at analysis, conclusions or generalizations, or recommendations. Ferguson's study of the "Greek Case" possessed these virtues and also these deficiencies.[70] This study was organized in such a way as to bring out the salient facts regarding the Greek government, economic geography, statistics concerned with the various population groups, religious and ethnic factors, and Greek claims for territorial boundaries in the peace settlement. A final section was devoted to the attitude of the major powers toward Greek aspirations. Throughout, there was no special pleading for or against the Greek cause. Ferguson, in other words, attempted to show no personal involvement with his subject matter. This treatment of a Balkan problem was the exception rather than the rule.

Robert J. Kerner contributed several reports considering the possibilities for a Yugoslav national state. As in the case of his studies of Central Europe, his studies of Yugoslavia were written with the stamp of scientific respectability. Yugoslavia was the product of a "natural evolution," which developed despite at-

69. William S. Ferguson to Albert Lybyer, Nov. 23, 1918, House Inquiry MSS, file 33-152, Yale.
70. William S. Ferguson, "The Greek Case," n.d., Shotwell MSS, Columbia.

tempts by the Germans, Austrians, and Magyars to thwart it. "To take any other view is to fall into the hands of German and Magyar historians and scientists whose paid duty it is to discredit this almost miraculous evolution toward a delayed national unity." Kerner showed in his Yugoslav studies the substantial degree of support existing among all groups within the proposed boundaries on behalf of a unified Yugoslav state.

> In other words, Croatia is virtually wholly Jugoslav. Bosnia is awakening. The people of Serbia and Montenegro would regard the creation of an independent Jugoslavia as the fulfillment of their dreams. The opposition which is left within the *ethnic* limits of Jugoslavia is made up of Germans, Italians, and Magyars, in the cities the Jews (who would turn Jugoslav in a decade) and the Mohammedan Agas (who are really Serbs) of Bosnia. . . .
> Whichever way this problem is handled, the scientist may safely conclude that any solution which does not treat the Jugoslavs as one nation is based on unscientific foundations and hence cannot be considered a permanent solution.[71]

In August 1918 Kerner strongly protested the way in which the Inquiry was handling Balkan problems. To a considerable extent his criticisms were applicable and relevant to the Inquiry's entire program. If true, there was need to overhaul the entire Balkan program of studies. Kerner wrote:

> The research on the Balkans is in a chaotic state. Nowhere are the Balkans treated as a whole; nowhere is the external or diplomatic history treated in a scholarly way. Most of the memoranda deal with internal history and over ¾ of these with ethnography or geography, thus putting the bulk of effort on the boundary and nationalistic disputes.[72]

No noticeable change was instituted during the last three months which remained before the armistice.

The tentative report of January 21, 1919, proposed a large number of changes in the national boundaries of Balkan countries. In general, it recommended that boundaries fixed in 1913 after the

---

71. Robert J. Kerner, "A Brief Sketch of the Political Movements Among the Jugoslavs Toward the Federalization or Dismemberment of Austria-Hungary," March 25, 1918, House Inquiry MSS, file 33-60, Yale.

72. Kerner, Memorandum of Suggestions, Aug. 8, 1918, Inquiry Archives.

First Balkan War between Serbia and Rumania, Bulgaria, Greece, and Albania be confirmed as boundaries for the new Yugoslavia.[73] The new South Slav state was to be a federation with autonomous parts for the accommodation of religious, historic, and other differences among the Serbs, Montenegrins, Croats, and Slovenes. On the northwest, Fiume was to be retained "by Jugoslavia [as it] is vital to the interests of the latter." On the south, the report urged that northern Albania be placed under Yugoslavia as mandatory for the League of Nations. Such an arrangement would provide greater economic opportunity for both Albanians and Yugoslavs.

The Inquiry's report recommended an enlarged Rumania to include: (1) the whole of Russian Bessarabia, having a predominately Rumanian population; (2) the Rumanian-populated region of Bukovina; (3) all of Transylvania; (4) about two-thirds of the Banat; (5) the Rumanian-Bulgarian frontier as it existed before the Second Balkan War, with very slight modifications. These recommendations were based upon the principle of self-determination, including in the Rumanian state all areas having a majority of Rumanians. There would be sizable minority groups within the proposed Rumanian boundaries, but the Inquiry was unable to handle these minorities in any alternative fashion which would at the same time give recognition to the Rumanian majorities.

Greek claims for territorial expansion were not, by and large, favored in the Inquiry's recommendations. Boundaries suggested for the north and east were to coincide with Greece's frontiers as established at the end of the Second Balkan War in 1913. There was to be no fundamental change in the northern frontier. Claims by the Greek government to lands located along the northern Aegean coast ran counter to Bulgaria's need for direct access to the Aegean. The Inquiry felt that Bulgaria should not be blocked from the Aegean for the sake of "a shallow fringe of Greeks along the coast." Settlement of the Macedonian claims was to accord with the boundary lines established in 1913 after the First Balkan War:

73. OTR. See also Epitome of Reports on Just and Practical Boundaries Within Austria-Hungary and Epitome of Reports on Just and Practical Boundaries Within the Balkans, no author, n.d., Inquiry Archives. The recommendations coincide generally with those in the OTR.

It is believed that the population of Central Macedonia, which is mixed and still unsettled in nationality, will adapt itself to the rule of Jugoslavia and that that power will be contented with its parts on the upper Adriatic and will resign its former ambitions to hold Salonika.[74]

On the northwest, Greece would extend to include south Albania. Since the Inquiry stood opposed to an independent Albanian state, it favored the union of southern Albania with Greece based on "ethnic affinity and economic advantage." In addition, Rhodes and the Dodecanese Islands, occupied by Italian troops before the war, were recommended for Greek sovereignty on the basis of their overwhelming (80 per cent according to the report) Greek population. Balkan boundaries were therefore to be based upon the principle of self-determination with only slight modifications justified by economic considerations.

Nineteen studies of the Allied countries of Western Europe were completed by the Inquiry's scholars, divided into the following national categories: Belgium, 3; France, 6; Great Britain, 2; Italy, 8. Topics considered in these studies stressed diplomatic history and a consideration of whatever preparations for peace had commenced in the particular country. French and Italian territorial claims were studied from the point of view of these countries' interests. There was no study of British interests in the European settlement, nor any consideration of French interests beyond the scope of Franco-German territorial claims. The Inquiry's reports did take cognizance of the several Allied secret treaties, and before the armistice the texts of most secret treaties were collected and placed in its archives.

Italy's cause at the peace conference was almost responsible for disrupting the American Commission to Negotiate Peace in April 1919, when a crisis arose over Fiume. The American "experts" took positions on *both* sides of the dispute—some were sympathetic and others hostile to Italy's claims. Yet during the months when the Inquiry was laboring over preparations, there had been no serious rupture among William Lunt and his associates who worked on the Italian claims. Lunt, in fact, never completed any report until late November 1918, after the armistice, though he kept his superiors informed of progress. In May, for instance, he

74. Epitomes of Reports and OTR.

reported that he was dividing the Italian subject into five sections: (1) the language boundary and its history; (2) political boundaries and history; (3) Italy's government and the Trentino; (4) public opinion in the Trentino concerning union with Italy; (5) economic development.[75] At the same time, Lunt pleaded for more time in order to examine materials not yet available in the United States.

President Wilson's Fourteen Points Address in January 1918 deeply aroused Italian sensibilities. Telegrams of protest from Italy arrived at the White House and were filed with the State Department.[76] The Italians objected to the President's emphasis upon nationality as the basis for establishing national boundaries. Were the principle of nationality (linguistic frontiers) employed, the Italians insisted, their country would be unable to defend itself against future Austrian aggression. Late in January 1918, at a White House conference with the Italian ambassador, President Wilson related Italy's frontiers to the League of Nations. Mutual defense pacts under the League "would render strategic considerations such as those affecting the Adriatic much less important." And the President continued, "I told him, failing a League of Nations, my mind would be open upon all such matters to new judgments." [77] Apparently, the Italian ambassador did not inject the matter of secret treaties into this discussion with the President, for there is no record of it.

There was nevertheless one Inquiry study of the strategic character of the Austro-Italian frontier written by Ellen Churchill Semple.[78] This report, based upon the examination of the disputed topography, showed the justice in the Italian claims. Any Austrian force invading Italy, Ellen Semple suggested, has only to drop down into Italy; an Italian invasion of Austria would mean literally an "uphill battle." She concluded that the Austro-Italian boundary required correction from the standpoint of nationality and of Italy's defense needs.

75. William Lunt to Dana Munro, May 15, 1918; Lunt to Walter Lippmann, June 26, 1918, Inquiry Archives.

76. Robert Lansing to Wilson, Jan. 25, 1918, *FRLP, 2,* 89.

77. Wilson to Lansing, Jan. 29, 1918, ibid., *2,* 94.

78. Ellen C. Semple, "The Strategic Character of the Austro-Italian Frontier," March 9, 1918, Inquiry Archives.

On December 12, 1918, one day before the *George Washington's* arrival in France, William Lunt, at President Wilson's request, sent him a memorandum with recommendations for the Italian boundaries. Lunt at this time raised strong objections to the granting of Italian claims. His memorandum stated in part:

> The line granted to Italy by the Pact of London, 1915, and coinciding with the line limiting the occupation of Austria according to the Armistice, includes much territory almost purely Jugoslav in character and which is not essential to the interests of Italy either on strategic or commercial grounds. A boundary further to the West, lying between the Pact of London line and the linguistic line, is suggested. (The linguistic boundary is based upon the communal statistics of 1900.)
>
> The main objection to the line of the London Pact is that it would place under Italian rule some 760,000 Jugoslavs who are irreconcilably opposed to separation from their neighbors and kinsmen and whose natural antipathy towards the Italians probably equals that felt toward the Austrian Germans and the Magyars.
>
> In the whole territory claimed by the Italians from the Jugoslavs the Italians form less than one-third of the population, the Jugoslavs form two-thirds. As the claims extend away from the Italian frontier of 1914 the disproportion becomes more marked . . . In particular districts there are practically no Italians, and almost the whole population is Jugoslav.
>
> Italians are not in close commercial relations with the territories concerned. Italian trade focuses around Venice, not Trieste or Fiume which serve almost entirely the countries of the Danube Valley. Italy bases its claims to these provinces on historic claims, and in part upon the fact that in the cities the wealthier educated and business people are chiefly Italians. Strategic and topographic considerations also play important factors in Italian claims.[79]

Lunt recommended a boundary line which the Italian government had been prepared to accept in 1915 from the Austrian government. It promised reasonable strategic defense advantages for Italy in the Alps and also possession of the naval port of Pola. Trieste would pass into Italian control by this arrangement. "In the general interest it is important . . . and desirable, if the Italian consent can be obtained, that Trieste be given international

79. Enclosure in A. A. Young to Wilson, Dec. 13, 1918, Wilson MSS, Series VIII-A, Library of Congress.

status as a free city." [80] Lunt also was firm in his objection to allowing Italy any territory along the Dalmatian coast, since there seemed no just grounds for such a claim.

A military advisory report prepared by Colonel U. S. Grant, Jr., dated December 15, 1918, set forth the view of the United States Military Advisory Mission in Paris on the subject of Italian boundaries for the benefit of General Tasker Bliss.[81] What makes this report significant here is the fact that its recommendations coincided almost to the letter with the proposals of William Lunt. The one major difference was that Grant made no specific provision that Trieste be made a "free city," but on this point even Lunt's proposal had been weak. The Inquiry's tentative report of January 21, 1919, incorporated almost all of these recommendations. Some portions of the statement might well be quoted here:

> It is recommended that Italy be given a northern frontier midway between the linguistic line and the line of the Treaty of London, 1915. This recommendation would give Italy all that part of the Tyrol to which she has any just claim on linguistic, cultural or historical grounds. It would leave no rational basis for irredentist agitation in this direction. . . . The recommended line does not meet those claims of Italy which are based on strategic grounds alone, for the line of 1915 . . . gives incomparably the best strategic frontier. On the other hand, the proposed line does ameliorate the intentionally bad frontier imposed upon Italy by Austria, and some amelioration seems essential if the Italians are to enter a League of Nations with confidence in its ability to render their peaceful existence reasonably secure . . . The task of the League of Nations will be rendered easier and its success made more certain by the adjustment of Italy's northern frontier at least in part along lines which would discourage armed aggression by a powerful German state.[82]

The Italian settlement at the Paris Peace Conference illuminated several prominent weaknesses in the whole European program of the Inquiry. Facts alone were shown to be inadequate in the absence of well-defined principles. Many of the Inquiry's topics had been treated within too narrow a framework and hence there

80. Ibid.
81. Colonel U. S. Grant, Jr., Memorandum for General Bliss, Dec. 15, 1918, Bliss MSS, Library of Congress.
82. OTR.

was no opportunity for the writers to indicate the broad ramifications of their conclusions and recommendations. The basic geographical division of the Inquiry's organization did not give much opportunity for writers to take a broad view in any case. Too many of the persons who were invested with research responsibilities by the Inquiry were hardly qualified in their assigned subjects. Many reports show an extreme bias, a partisanship which flowed from the author's commitment to some special solution at the peace conference. When Woodrow Wilson asked the Inquiry aboard the *George Washington* to give him a "guaranteed position," he was assuming a degree of objectivity which did not exist, perhaps never could exist. Was there such a "guaranteed position" amidst the vagaries of twentieth-century world politics?

Possibly the most astonishing thing was that, despite failings and inadequacies, the European divisions were able to come up with many recommendations, ideas, and facts which facilitated the operations of the peace conference. Before it will be possible to show conclusively that the Inquiry's productivity directly influenced the writing of the peace treaties additional study of the operations of the commissions at work at the peace conference will be necessary. The same recommendations presumably might have been suggested by the British, French, or some other national delegation, so that an idea suggested in an Inquiry report which is found also in a peace treaty cannot be attributed directly or exclusively to the Inquiry. Caution, however, should not minimize the importance of the Inquiry's efforts toward the evolution of the peace settlement.

Chapter 8

AFRICA, ASIA, AND THE PACIFIC

THE PREPONDERANT POSITION occupied by European questions did not submerge or sidetrack the Inquiry's consideration of the weighty African, Asian, and Pacific regional questions. Varied and complicated as were these non-European lands, one common denominator—the dependent relationship of these areas to European states—bound their problems together. Germany's colonial empire before the war consisted of Southwest Africa, German Togoland, and the Cameroons on the west coast of Africa; German East Africa; an array of Pacific islands in the northern Pacific (the Mariana, Pelew, Caroline, and Marshall Islands); a group of islands in the South Pacific (the Bismarck Archipelago, the German Solomon Islands, German New Guinea, and German Samoa); and the German leasehold on the Shantung Peninsula in northeastern China. All of Germany's colonial possessions were certain to be reviewed by the peace conference in the light of the Allied claims and secret treaties. President Wilson had injected the colonial question into his Fourteen Points Address of January 8, 1918, calling for a free, open-minded, and absolutely impartial adjustment of all colonial claims.

In addition to the German colonies, Turkey's weakened empire extending through the Middle East and North Africa provided an appropriate, indeed an anticipated, subject for the peace conference agenda. While the United States was never legally at war with Turkey, President Wilson and the American government

226

fully expected to participate in the Turkish peace settlement. At the same time American interest was directed during the months before the armistice to the problems involving the British, French, Belgian, and Dutch colonies, their administration and future operations.

The Inquiry's studies of African, Asian, and Pacific problems suffered for lack of qualified, trained scholars. With almost no exception, no writer whose services were mobilized by these divisions of the Inquiry could have been described as of "expert" caliber in terms of his assigned subject at the time he started his work. Numerous missionaries, lawyers, and ancient historians took up the cudgels, accepting invitations to submit reports on subjects for which prior knowledge might prove valuable but was not judged prerequisite by the Inquiry's leadership. American higher education had not become alive to African, Asian, and Pacific studies before 1917.

Administratively, the Inquiry maintained separate divisions for Africa, the Middle East, the Far East, and the Pacific Islands. As with the European divisions, persons who worked on one division rarely learned about projects being conducted in the others. At least one leader of the Inquiry, David Hunter Miller, strongly believed "that specialists studying local problems exclusively tend to present solutions that won't fit the whole." [1] But the system prevailed and was continued probably because it involved the fewest organizational complications.

Besides colonial problems per se, the Far Eastern Division of the Inquiry undertook studies of Japanese-Chinese relations. By 1918, China had entered the war. The so-called Twenty-One Demands which Japan had imposed upon the Chinese government were already well publicized in the United States, and the Shantung controversy was brewing. Needless to say, the American Inquiry was not ignorant of these developments. Its resulting reports anticipated definite action on these questions at the peace conference.

The National Archives inventory lists a total of 428 reports and documents pertaining to African, Asian, and Pacific questions, divided as follows: Africa 54 (13 per cent); the Middle East 220

1. James T. Shotwell, *At the Paris Peace Conference* (New York, 1937) p. 153.

(51 per cent); the Far East including India 131 (31 per cent); and the Pacific Islands including Australasia 23 (5 per cent).[2] Inquiry staff members accounted for 145 of these reports, or 34 per cent of the total collection. Reports written by the Inquiry's staff reveal a distribution very similar to that just described for the total collection, as the following chart shows:

	No. of Reports	Percentage
Africa	20	14
Middle East	65	45
Far East	48	33
Pacific Islands	12	8

These reports and documents encompassed a very large number of topics, some of whose relevancy to a peace settlement might appear remote.

African materials collected by the Inquiry illustrate how broadly the American preparatory work canvassed the Dark Continent's problems for the benefit of the American delegation at the peace conference. The following chart shows the number of reports dealing with particular topics:

Topic	No. of Reports	Topic	No. of Reports
General, unclassified	6	Forest resources	1
Colonial questions	5	Physical geography	6
International adminis-		Economic problems	8
tration	1	Sanitation problems	3
Great power interests	2	Education	1
Ethnography	1	Belgian Congo	4
Native government	2	Egypt	2
Native armies	2	South and East Africa	1
Commerce	3	French North Africa	1
Harbors	1	Gold Coast	1
Sierre Leone	1	·Liberia	1

Reports of the Asiatic and Pacific divisions were comparable in scope.

During the first months of the peace conference, the Inquiry's

2. National Archives, "Preliminary Inventories No. 89," Records of the American Commission to Negotiate Peace (hereafter referred to as PI-89), compiled by H. Stephen Helton.

leaders presented to the American plenipotentiaries a concise series of recommendations presumably based on this massive accumulation of reports. Similar in function and format to the Outline of Tentative Recommendations (or Black Book Number 1) covering the several European divisions, this volume, known officially as Black Book Number 2 of February 1919, offered a clear statement of the Inquiry's concepts of a desirable settlement for colonial and Far Eastern areas.[3]

Colonial questions in general and the disposition of enemy colonial possessions in particular had been a topic to which Allied and American diplomatic representatives devoted much thought after the outbreak of war in 1914. Colonel House, even before the dangerous war clouds gathered, had proposed a scheme of economic assistance to underdeveloped areas. Just two days before the Sarajevo crisis broke, House wrote to the President from London:

> I have suggested that America, England, France, Germany . . . [establish] a plan by which investors on the one hand be encouraged to lend money at reasonable rates and to develop under favorable terms the waste places of the earth.[4]

Once the war aroused the belligerents' passions, economic aid appeared terribly academic. The political disposition of the German and Turkish colonial empires assumed paramount importance for Allied and American statesmen. Any plan envisioning economic therapy for "backward . . . waste places of the world" (to use Colonel House's terminology) had to await some decision as to their political status.

Exactly what President Wilson's ideas were regarding colonial questions prior to the armistice cannot be ascertained fully from the few public utterances in which he touched lightly on colonial matters. Point V in the Fourteen Points Address announced the principle of equating the interests of native inhabitants to the interests of the government "whose title is to be determined." [5]

3. Black Book No. 2, Feb. 13, 1919, Woodrow Wilson MSS, Series VIII-A, Library of Congress; Shotwell, *At the Paris Peace Conference*, p. 134.

4. House to Wilson, June 26, 1914, in Seymour, ed., *Intimate Papers of Colonel House* (Boston, 1926), *1*, 264–65.

5. Baker and Dodd, *Public Papers of Woodrow Wilson, War and Peace* (New York, 1927), *1*, 159.

No suggestion was here made advocating international control over colonies; President Wilson was simply adapting the doctrine of self-determination to the colonial peoples. By January of 1918, the restoration of the colonial status quo ante was recognized as impossible. The German colonies had been successfully invaded and occupied by Allied military forces while the Turkish Empire was experiencing continuous Allied military penetration. Wartime propaganda had "exposed" allegedly heinous acts of German barbarism in the African colonies. General native discontent and revulsion toward the German colonial administration were recognized as facts in Allied countries and in the United States. Arab groups in the Middle East were aspiring to throw off Turkish controls and form an independent government. As if these were insufficient reasons for not restoring the German and Turkish empires, there were also the Allied secret treaties involving plans by the British, French, Italian, and Japanese governments for disposition of the spoils of war, meaning in this case German and Turkish colonial territories.

At about this same time, the late months of 1917, interest was mounting in England and the United States in various schemes of international organization. One feature of many of these proposals was internationalization of the enemies' colonies after the war. The American envoy, Walter Hines Page, noted in his London diary the views of British Foreign Secretary Arthur Balfour sometime in 1917:

> Mr. Balfour told me yesterday his personal conviction about the German colonies which he said he had not discussed with his associates in the cabinet. German colonies should not be returned to Germany. Instead, the German colonies especially in Africa should be internationalized. There are great difficulties in such a plan but they are not insuperable if the great powers of the allies will agree upon it, and much more to the same effect, the parts of Asiatic Turkey that the British have taken he thought might be treated in the same way.[6]

Very possibly, President Wilson's mind was also turning over the possibility of an internationalized status for the colonial territories. Annexation of enemy colonies as prizes of war was anathema to

6. Walter Hines Page MSS Diary, undated entry, Harvard Library.

the President's "peace without victory" morality. Some plan was desperately needed which would serve the interests of the colonial inhabitants, provide efficient and honest administration, and at the same time afford commercial opportunities for all nations.

Internationalization and annexation in accordance with Allied secret treaties were the most prominent alternatives for the disposition of the German and Turkish empires at the time when George Louis Beer joined the Inquiry's staff during the fall of 1917. Beer brought to his new assignment a distinguished background as student of British imperial-colonial relations during the seventeenth and eighteenth centuries. Now, focusing his attention upon the colonial questions of the twentieth century, Beer applied his energies with a rare degree of intensity. Though the African questions raised by the Inquiry opened new vistas for him, he endeavored to master the materials as quickly as he could. Impatient with the haste demanded by the Inquiry's leaders, Beer informed his superiors that a hastily conceived and prepared report "would be purely provisional and I am afraid unsatisfactory. I should much prefer to await further material and more exhaustive investigation before reaching any definite conclusions." [7]

His preliminary studies led Beer into a consideration of the several alternatives in Africa. Beer was not disposed to favor international administration for colonies because of the many unsuccessful historical precedents. Condominiums in Samoa, Egypt, and elsewhere "convinced" him that some means other than international administration must be conceived to attain the same goals. His suggestion was a plan which would effect a compromise between a single nation's hegemony and international administration. This plan, suggested by Beer in a letter to Director Sidney Mezes on December 31, 1917, was the mandate system. Since the mandate system ultimately became an integral part of the peace settlement, and inasmuch as this idea was a positive, significant contribution by the Inquiry, the fairly lengthy initial exposition of the concept in its embryonic form should be quoted:

> While I am convinced that the internationalization of Central Africa is neither feasible nor desirable under the existing conditions of nationalism, it seems to me that the chief results desired

7. Beer to Sidney Mezes, Dec. 31, 1917, Mezes MSS, Columbia Library.

from such a course might be effectively secured by other means. In case of any transfer of territory in Central Africa, and possibly even in the existing dependencies, it might, I think be definitely established, *that the state exercising sovereignty in Africa is proceeding under an international mandate and must act as trustee primarily for the nations and secondarily for the outside world as a whole.* There could be elaborated a code of native rights, prohibiting forced labor in all its forms thus assuring to the native his legitimate rights to the soil, and protecting him from the evils of western civilization, such as intoxicants. At the same time, the existing free trade area in Africa could probably be extended and existing provisions for free trade under the Berlin Act of 1885 and specific treaties should be made more definite and more comprehensive so as to secure the open door in the fullest sense possible. In order to make such arrangements effective it seems to me that it would be essential to have a definite agreement to submit all disputes about these matters either to the Hague Tribunal or preferably to some international court especially constituted for this purpose and that the signatories should bind themselves to accept the decisions. There are very considerable obstacles in the way of so moderate a programme, but this appears to me to be the most effective line of advance.[8]

Beer may well have been the first writer to have used the term "mandate" in the sense of commission granted to a single nation on behalf of an international organization to administer the government and affairs of an underdeveloped area.[9] But, as Professor Merle Curti has shown, the principle itself was not new in 1917; it had been "clearly anticipated" at least as early as 1889 in the pages of the *Westminster Review*.[10]

It is worthy of note that although Beer's writings at the end of 1917 and the outset of 1918 had treated the idea of a mandate system, Beer's colleague on the Inquiry, David Hunter Miller, in his authoritative study, *The Drafting of the Covenant*, did not associate Beer in any way with the promotion of the mandate system. Instead, General Smuts of South Africa is credited by Miller with developing its essential features in his paper, *The*

8. Ibid. Italics have been inserted by the author.
9. Ingram Bander, "Sidney E. Mezes and the Inquiry," *Journal of Modern History*, 11 (1939), 199–202; Louis H. Gray, Editor's Preface to *African Questions at the Paris Peace Conference* (New York, 1923), p. xix.
10. Merle Curti, *Peace or War, The American Struggle 1636–1936* (New York, 1936), p. 177.

League of Nations, A Practical Suggestion (London, 1918). According to Smuts, the mandate system would apply only to "territories formerly belonging to Russia, Austria-Hungary, and Turkey"; Germany's colonies were explicitly excluded from the Smuts plan. As the mandate system subsequently evolved at the peace conference, some drastic changes were instituted. What seems clear is that Beer's basic idea, expressed in December 1917, was taken up by Smuts a year later, promoted, discussed, and modified. In a real sense, Smuts complemented Beer's work in the presentation of the idea to the peace conference.[11]

Curiously enough, all of the references to the mandate system in Beer's Inquiry reports are of the most casual nature. James T. Shotwell later explained this casualness in terms of Beer's customary humility, his reluctance to assert his own contributions.[12] Such an explanation is certainly plausible according to those who knew him. On the other hand another explanation may be suggested.

In his first report dated January 1, 1918, Beer dealt with the disposition of Mesopotamia, an area over which Turkey had exercised sovereign control prior to the war. Beer mentioned the economic potential of the area, by irrigation for agriculture and by developing the petroleum deposits. He also cited the possibilities of finding a solution for India's surplus population problem through providing a haven in Mesopotamia for the migration of Moslem Indians. In strong language Beer declared that the chief interests to be considered in the area were first those of the natives and secondly those of British India, "whose real concern in this region outweighs that of the European peoples. British policy in the entire Middle East has largely been dictated by India, not by London." [13] How Beer arrived at this conclusion is not indicated in the report. Yet when it came to the disposition of Mesopotamia, Beer saw only two alternatives. The possibility of a "new

11. David Hunter Miller, *The Drafting of the Covenant* (New York, 1928), *1*, 101–17. J. C. Smuts', "The League of Nations, A Practical Suggestion," can be conveniently found as Document 5 in Volume 2 of this work, pages 23–60. See also League of Nations, *The Mandate System, Origin, Principles, Application* (Geneva, 1945), pp. 13–18, and George Curry, "Woodrow Wilson, Jan Smuts, and the Versailles Settlement," *American Historical Review, 66* (July 1961), 968–86.

12. Quoted in Gray, ed., *African Questions* (New York, 1923), p. xix.

13. Beer, "The Future of Mesopotamia," in ibid., p. 417.

Arabia" he quickly discounted on the grounds that the Arabian peoples were not yet sufficiently mature politically to govern so vast a territory, and moreover an Arab state could easily fall again under the dominance of Turkey. Capital for its economic development might not be forthcoming from Europe and America should an unstable Arab state be established. International administration was also deemed impracticable. Beer held the only way to determine the solution in cases where politically backward peoples required not only political tutelage but also foreign capital was "to entrust the task of government to that state whose interests are most directly involved."

> In the case of Mesopotamia, this state would inevitably be the British Commonwealth on account of, first, the predominant commercial interests of British India and of the United Kingdom in the Persian Gulf and in Lower Mesopotamia; second, the part that British officials have for centuries taken in suppressing piracy in the Persian Gulf; third, the facts that British capital had already before the war been employed in irrigating Mesopotamia and in providing transportation on the Tigris and Euphrates and that since the war very considerable work has been done in draining, in building embankments, and wharfs, and in constructing railroads; fourth, the fact that British India needs an outlet for its swarming millions and has in its surplus Moslem peoples a suitable source of settlers.

Then, immediately in the next sentence Beer introduces his mandate scheme:

> If, however, such backward regions are entrusted by international mandate to one state, there should be embodied in the deed of trust most rigid safeguards both to protect the native population from exploitation and also to ensure that the interests of other foreign states are not injured either positively or negatively. Provision should be made for the full open door, so that not only should all merchandise enter upon the same terms and that railroad rates should be equal, but also that complete opportunity should be given to all nations to participate on an equal basis in the economic development of the country.[14]

Beer nowhere places special emphasis upon the mandate idea. He suggests it almost *en passant* as one possible alternative. The

14. Ibid., pp. 424–25.

implication from the context is that sovereignty under international mandate would reside with the mandatory nation, for Beer had previously rejected international administration and recommended the attachment of the colonial area to the British Commonwealth. Only where commerce and native rights were concerned was the mandatory authority to be subject to international regulation.

His second report, submitted during the latter part of February 1918, dealt with the German colonies in Africa and injected the mandate scheme with the same casualness. Beer discounted any possibility of restoring the African colonies to German sovereignty. All of Beer's colonial reports were characterized by a grave concern for safeguarding the native populations and preventing their exploitation. He was much impressed by the evidence of Germany's maltreatment and persecution of natives in its African possessions. At the same time Beer was convinced that the colonies had been an economic liability to Germany. His proposals in February 1918 called for German Southwest Africa to be placed under the "administration" of the Union of South Africa. But he unfortunately did not define his understanding of the word "administration." Similarly, German East Africa was to become a "colony for India's superabundant millions," although Beer was less sure of the soundness of this proposal. German West Africa would be divided between France and England, whose colonies were contiguous with the German colonies. Only in the last paragraph of this lengthy report did Beer make mention of the mandate system. Here he wrote simply:

> Provided there be effectively established a comprehensive system of international control under which native rights will be fully maintained and the "open door" will always be kept wide open, and provided the mandatory of the Powers be wholly honest in his trusteeship and forego all purely national and imperialistic ends, it matters comparatively little to the world at large which flag flies in the Cameroons.[15]

Nowhere else in Beer's major reports does the mandate principle appear by direct reference.

The Black Book of February 1919 applied the mandate prin-

15. Beer, "The German Colonies in Africa," in ibid., p. 67.

ciple to the disposition of the German and Turkish colonies. It would seem that Beer's reluctance to deal explicitly with the mandate system in his preliminary reports for the Inquiry stemmed not from humility but from uncertainty as to the practicality of the idea. The Black Book asserts the paramount consideration in disposing of all colonies to be the welfare of local peoples. Economic opportunities for their fullest development would be "entrusted to different states acting as mandatories of the League of Nations." Because of the political facts of life—national jealousies and rivalries, the balance of power, etc.—the plums of mandatory administration would be distributed as equitably as possible among the various states. The Black Book also noted how the colonial arrangement might be affected by the willingness of the United States to assume mandatory responsibilities. George Louis Beer, chiefly responsible for the Black Book's recommendations for Africa, was particularly chary about applying the mandate principle indiscriminately to all colonial situations or even to all the former German colonies.

The Black Book did not recommend a mandate over former German Togoland.[16] It simply advocated a division of the area along ethnic lines between France and Great Britain but with a semblance of the Open Door provided for the economic well-being of the area. "The mandatory system in so far as it implies the maintenance of administrative integrity would hamper the development of this small area." [17] The German Cameroons likewise were to be divided between French Equatorial Africa (as a matter of national honor for France) and British Nigeria ("to make the boundary conform in a general way to ethnic and tribal facts").[18] Whatever territory remained after the division was to be transferred to a mandatary, and as mandatary for this section of the Cameroons, Beer recommended the United States. If the United States took on this responsibility in Africa, the pro-

16. Part VI, "The Colonial Questions," of Gray, *African Questions at the Paris Peace Conference* (pp. 431–58) quotes directly those sections pertaining to Africa and the Pacific Islands in the American Black Book of February 13, 1919. Though the published version does not acknowledge the source or date of the original, a comparison of the two shows them to be virtually identical. Because these sections are substantially the same, references will be made when possible to the published version.

17. Ibid., pp. 433–34.

18. Ibid., pp. 435–38.

tection of native rights might be assured. British failure to halt the liquor traffic had provoked considerable criticism in the past from other countries. If the United States refused to take upon itself administrative responsibilities in Africa, and the Inquiry's advisers must have entertained serious doubts, the recommendation named France on one condition, namely that all mandatory regulations pertaining to the equality of economic opportunity be extended to include French Equatorial Africa and West Africa as well, with a single administration over the entire area.

Beer's recommendations for German East Africa, which the Inquiry retained in the Black Book, proposed placing this area under a British mandate which would allow for settlement by British East Indian immigrants. The decision whether an Indian or a British administration would have charge of the area was a domestic matter for the British Commonwealth to decide, Beer held. "The essential thing is that India's need of a country for unrestricted settlement be met." But all the territory formerly included in German East Africa was not specified to be under mandate. The northeastern zone containing several white settlements was to be attached to British East Africa, while a northwestern zone would be similarly excluded from the mandate area and annexed to British Uganda. Racial tensions between predominantly European settlements and Indian communities could be minimized through these proposed divisions of the old German colony.[19]

German Southwest Africa also provided a special instance in which the Inquiry's advisers did not apply the mandate principle. The entire area was recommended for transferral "to the British Empire for incorporation in the self governing Dominion of South Africa." Here the mandate plan was held to be "inadvisable and really inapplicable" and might even hamper the development of the area. No mention was made in the report of the South African government's demands for annexation, but the Inquiry's scholars succumbed completely to South Africa's arguments.[20]

As mentioned above, humility was probably not the compelling reason why George Louis Beer softened the impact of his mandate

19. Ibid., pp. 439–42.
20. Ibid., pp. 443–44.

idea. He was too apt a student of international relations not to realize the various pressures which would be unleashed in pursuit of the German colonies at the peace conference. He undoubtedly realized the obstacles a system of international control might encounter. Anticipating the intense desire in Allied countries for additional territories at the expense of a defeated German Empire, Beer and his associates soft-pedaled the mandate scheme even to the extent of not incorporating the principle throughout their recommendations for the disposition of the German colonies. In support of this contention, the Inquiry's recommendations for North Africa might be brought into focus. Beer's report on Egyptian questions submitted in August 1918, acknowledged and accepted the changes effected by Great Britain in the government of Egypt during the war. At the same time Beer accepted Italy's claims under the Treaty of London of April 26, 1915, for compensation if France and Britain acquired German colonial territory in Africa. Italy had pushed its claims for the extension of its possessions in Eritrea, Somaliland, and Libya. Any alteration of the status quo through annexation of additional territory by Great Britain was likely to bring forth additional claims by Italy. Though Beer held Italy's claims for extending the Libyan hinterland to be sound, he did not sanction the cession of any additional African territories to Italy at the expense of Britain, France, or Abyssinia.[21] All of these considerations weighed heavily upon Beer as is apparent in his several pre-armistice reports.

When it came to the final recommendations for North Africa, failure to apply the mandate principle is especially noteworthy. The Black Book proposed international recognition for the "absolute political separation of Egypt from Turkey" and likewise for the British protectorate over Egypt. The Inquiry, bearing in mind the secret Allied Treaty of April 26, 1915, recommended the extension of Italian Libya "so as to provide access to the Sudan and its trade." But Beer and his fellow authors of the Black Book were opposed to any extension of Libya which would retard French colonial development or British development in the Anglo-Egyptian Sudan. At the same time, the Inquiry recommended that Spanish Morocco be given to France and that the status of Tangier be made more precise by establishing France as the

21. Beer, "Egyptian Problems," ibid., pp. 289–410.

mandatory power responsible for the administration of the city and environs.[22]

While the mandate principle was accepted with certain modifications by the peace conference, the Inquiry's recommendations with regard to Africa were only partially accepted. A modified mandate system was applied far more broadly than Beer had envisioned or recommended. Togoland and the Cameroons became Class "B" mandates; Southwest Africa became a Class "C" mandate; German East Africa was made a British mandate except for a small sector in the northwest which was made a Belgian mandate. It can hardly be argued validly that the Inquiry's recommendations for Africa were followed to the letter.

Though one of the major contributions by the Inquiry to the peace settlement, Beer's mandate idea did not enjoy complete unanimity of support among the American plenipotentiaries. Like Beer himself, Secretary Robert Lansing was not ecstatic over wide application of the idea. But Lansing entertained misgivings about problems which Beer was willing to leave to be worked out in the implementation of the program. Lansing was not satisfied, for example, about the location of sovereignty for mandated territory. Would sovereignty reside with the League of Nations or with the mandatory power? If the answer were the League, would the League carry the attributes of a world state possessing sovereign powers? If the League did not possess sovereign powers, then sovereignty would pass to some national state, or so Lansing believed. In case of misuse, exploitation, or some other cause of grievance, what would be the procedure for redressing the grievance? Although Lansing was not stubbornly opposed to the mandate idea, he felt that these technicalities might "furnish fuel for plenty of controversies unless they are considered and decided. Some men never think of the future workings of a plan but simply say 'there is the plan.' It is a good one. Never mind the details. They are technicalities."[23]

Compared to Africa, the Middle East (defined here as including all of the prewar Turkish territories in Asia) promised to raise

22. Ibid., p. 448.
23. Robert Lansing, "Some Problems of the Mandatory System," Feb. 2, 1919, Lansing Confidential Memorandum Book No. IV, Lansing MSS, Library of Congress.

questions of far greater magnitude and complexity. The Inquiry's studies and recommendations for Africa dealt almost exclusively with colonial matters, the point of view prevailing throughout that Africa was destined at least for the foreseeable future to be under the tutelage of Western civilization. The African peoples were seen as wards in need of protection from the merciless exploitation to which they had been subjected in the past. Beer's mandate plan had been designed for populations not yet ready for self-government. Equal accessibility by Western nations to the markets and natural resources of the African continent were also major concerns emphasized repeatedly in the Inquiry's reports and recommendations.

Many of these problems also existed in the Middle East. Allied governments had made plans for dividing up Arab lands lying within the Turkish Empire. Besides Britain and France, Italy and Greece were pressing territorial claims. Arab leaders, however, were not content to sit back idly and receive the same treatment planned for Africa. Rumblings, faint to be sure, but rumblings nevertheless, of Arab nationalism were sounding through many portions of the Arab world. Then there was the question of a Zionist Jewish state or national homeland to which the British government had become committed by the Balfour Declaration of November 1917. Superimposed upon these nationalistic aspirations and territorial claims was the future of Constantinople and the Straits, the source of much nineteenth-century diplomatic intrigue. Protection for the various denominations of Christians who had developed substantial vested proprietary and missionary interests in the Middle East was still another factor. Last but certainly not least was the complication of abundant oil recently discovered in several regions of the Middle East. How would the oil resources of this area be treated by the peace conference?

In order to illustrate how these disturbing problems were considered by the Inquiry, the following list of topics is provided, showing not only what subjects were considered but also how many reports were completed for each subject. This list covers only the Inquiry's treatment of Turkey proper, not the Turkish Empire: [24]

24. PI-89.

Subject	No. of Reports
General	11
History (including diplomacy)	7
Government	9
Reconstruction	2
Boundaries	4
Population	3
Religious groups	5
Education, hospitals, missions, research	13
Legal rights	1
Economy (including finance, resources, commerce)	38
Status of women	1
Pan Turanian movement	4
Local studies of Turkish communities	17
Reclamation projects	2
American interests	3
European governments' interests	7

These reports rarely drew upon materials in Middle Eastern languages. Most frequently the sources were encyclopedias, missionary materials, handbooks, foreign trade statistics, and information derived through personal conversations and heresay. There is little agreement found among reports submitted by different contributors. The value of these reports can be shown by citing some fairly typical examples culled from the collection.

S. O. Dickerman was assigned the subject of the Independent Sanjak of Karassi (Afyon-Karahisar in the postwar years), an administrative district about 100 miles south and west of Ankara. The report was to deal with the history, geography, peoples, education, economic resources, and important cities in the district. Dickerman indicated that his principal sources were the *Encyclopedia Britannica* and the Historical Introduction to Murray's *Handbook of Asia Minor*. At no point did Dickerman dispute, criticize, or evaluate the reliability of his source materials. His approach was simply to summarize by topic the information found in these reference works. So he writes on page 2:

> The independent Sandjak of Karassi corresponds to the Mysia of antiquity. The ancient Mysians were apparently of kindred stock to the Lydians and Phrygians. We hear of their subjugation first to the Lydian kingdom in the 6th Century B.C. Then to the

241

Phrygian monarchy. On the coast were flourishing Greek Cities: Cyzious, at the north on the sea of Marmora, a colony of Miletus famous for its coinage which was current through the commercial world . . . Mysia was successively a part of Alexander's empire, the Kingdom of Pergamum, the Roman province of Asia, and the Byzantine Empire. . . . Karassi takes its name from one of the Seljuk princes.[25]

No attempt was made to deal with materials that might conceivably arise at the peace conference. In brief, Dickerman seemed completely oblivious of any practical objective for his study.

Another report, prepared by Arthur I. Andrews, illustrates another side of the Inquiry's Middle Eastern studies. Andrews was here dealing with the problem of the Kurds, a non-Turkish ethnic group inhabiting the southeastern corner of Turkey proper. Topics considered by Andrews included a description of the Kurds, Kurdish history, Kurdish literature, Kurdish religion, Kurdish houses, and a consideration of "possibilities of civilized progress." As in so many of the Inquiry's reports dealing with non-Christian peoples, a profound Christian bias is displayed. A few excerpts may provide the best means for assessing the report.

> Yet once more, the term Koord when used in its strict sense applies *too [to?] all the peoples* who are reckoned to [sic] the existing tribes as now recognized Koordish tribes and without references to their origin these tribes have absurbed [?] many Armenians and Syrians. As examples we would mention the Badikan, the Rajdikan, and most of the Koords of Jeboltur . . .
>
> In conversation upon the question, "who are the Koords?", I have found several who like myself have also reached independently the same conclusion with respect to the original Koords . . . By such independent study it has been borne in upon me that the original Koords are descendants of the remnant of the ancient Medes.[26]

On the subject of their literature,

> Still later, in the Eighteenth Century their [there] appeared some poets of note at both Sulermaverya and Kerkovk as well as many inferior ones.

25. S. O. Dickerman, "The Independent Sandjak of Karassi," Inquiry Archives.
26. Arthur I. Andrews, "The Koords," Feb. 20, 1918, Inquiry Archives.

Kurdish religion took Andrews back to the age of Xenophon, from which he brought the story through the Moslem and Turkish periods, being careful to observe how Christian missionaries were not allowed by the Turks to work among the Kurds. Concerning the Kurdish people, Andrews had this to say:

> In some respects the Koords remind one of the North American Indians. They have a tawny skin, high cheek bones, broad mouth, and black straight hair. Their mien too is rather quiet, morose, dull. Their temper is passionate, resentful, revengeful, intriguing, and treacherous. They make good soldiers, but poor leaders. They are avaricious, utterly selfish, shameless beggars, and have a great propensity to steal. They are fond of the chase and of raiding their rivals, are adept in the exercise of frightfulness. Mentally they are slow, though I have met with some notable exceptions.

But there was room for optimism, for in his conclusion Andrews prescribed the basic therapy that would cure the Kurds' ills:

> The men, it is true, are lazy while their women are terribly industrious, another point in which they are like the Indian. But unlike the Indian the Koords are not a decadent race. They have not yet I believe had their chance and they lack cooperation and leadership. Under an upright and sympathetic government they could be led up to become one of the progressive races of Western Asia. Who is to be entrusted with such a noble task and in an atmosphere of religious freedom to guide this Koordish race with the help of Christian missionaries into an acceptance of Christ and Christianity and its attendant Christian civilization?

These were not the ramblings of some luncheon speaker at the club. Andrews was writing a report which was to be used at the peace conference for serious business. How relevant were these loose generalizations to the work at hand? And there were scores of other reports whose value to the peace settlement could best be described as highly dubious. Too few Americans with special knowledge of the Middle East were available.

James Barton, who had been chairman of the Executive Committee for the Conference of Missionary Organizations of North America, was assigned several topics by the Inquiry. Colonel House in his diary made several laudable references to Barton and

243

his ability.[27] In May of 1918, Barton submitted a report suggesting a unified government for the entire Ottoman Empire except for Arabia and Egypt—one government, that is, from Adrianople in Europe to the Caucasus Mountains, Syria, and Palestine. This proposed government, which would take the form of a federation, rested on the assumption that throughout the area the "racial, religious, economic and national questions [were] very similar and capable of uniform solution." How this federation was to be inaugurated, Barton left very much in the air. But he was nevertheless optimistic of eventual success for the proposal. Only the Kurds, among the peoples included, had a reputation for lawlessness, but, as he pointed out, they could be expected to turn into good citizens once an improved government became established. Three courts would administer justice: Christian courts of common law; Moslem courts; and mixed courts. If all litigants were allowed to choose their courts, "there is no doubt that in a brief time the Moslem courts would be deserted." The economy in the federal state could be placed on a sound basis since mineral resources were abundant and agriculture had a mighty bright future. All would run smoothly, especially were the Western powers inclined to extend long-term credits at a reasonable rate of interest. In conclusion, Barton's words painted a rosy version of the future of the Middle East:

> The impression prevails that the people of Turkey would be hard to govern while the reverse is true. Those who are familiar with the different races which make up the population . . . agree that the disorder and oppression of the last century have been so great that there is no race of people within the area who would not welcome any government that would insure safety of life and property and justice in the courts.[28]

Exactly what Barton had in mind when he referred to government in the area was never made explicit by the report. Perhaps

27. On June 15, 1918, House wrote, "Dr. Barton wished my views on Bulgaria and Turkey and whether anything further was necessary to keep this country from declaring war on them. He is very much opposed to it. Our views do not materially differ. I regard him highly." House MSS Diary, Yale. For the similar views of Sidney Mezes, see Mezes to Barton, June 3, 1918, Inquiry Archives.

28. Barton, "Suggested Possible Form of Government for the Area Covered by the Ottoman Empire at the Outbreak of the War," Inquiry Archives.

he considered some international or mandatory authority, for he constantly stressed the need for a strong, stable administration. In any case, the outward glow of optimism which pervades his report was hardly warranted in the absence of substantial evidence.

Another plan for a united, independent Arab state was suggested in a report by Howard Crosby Butler. After a geographical and historical survey of the Arab lands, he proposed that Arabia be united under an Arab caliphate resident at Mecca. The new caliphate would be bound "by friendly relations" to the British Empire while leaving aside "all questions of protectorates." To Butler, Arab society had not been stagnant but had in fact regressed to where it had been 700 years earlier. To be sure, the greatest danger which might follow the establishment of an Arab state "is the danger of rousing once more in the Moslem mind the lust for world dominion." [29] It is noteworthy that Butler fully anticipated the establishment of a Jewish state in Palestine, for the suggested boundaries of the Arab state would touch the Jewish state at the Dead Sea and the Jordan Valley. Lebanon would not be included in the Arab state. The Syrian section would extend along the coast from Lebanon northward to the proposed Cilician borders of the new Armenia. Northern boundaries would be Armenia and Mesopotamia at the Euphrates. Butler emphasized that no effective national consciousness could be perceived among the Arab peoples; that only a narrow particularism existed in the tribe, district, and community.

E. H. Byrne's report on Syria augmented Butler's views on Arab particularism. Only in Syria, he claimed, where the American University at Beirut had exerted much influence, were the nationalistic rumblings clearly audible. Byrne's report is also interesting because it suggested the degree of Arab hostility toward a future Jewish state in Palestine. Although opposed, the Syrian Central Council "will . . . accept a 'national home' for the Jews because they see no way out of it." [30] Discussions conducted in Cairo between Zionist and Syrian leaders during early 1918 were

29. Howard Crosby Butler, "Report on the Proposals for an Independent Arab State," Inquiry Archives.

30. E. H. Byrne, "Report on the Desires of the Syrians," Oct. 7, 1918, Inquiry Archives.

cordial enough and a genuine spirit of compromise was displayed by both sides. These conferences, Byrnes added, concluded on a note sympathetic to the Zionists, who had assured the Syrians that there was no intention of establishing a Jewish state.

By and large the Inquiry reports anticipated the creation of some kind of Jewish commonwealth in Palestine. Yet the very few reports dealing directly with Palestine were of a definite substandard quality. When some of these Middle Eastern reports received criticism from the Inquiry's officers—and most reports were not subjected to full-scale criticism—their sails were trimmed severely. O. J. Campbell's report on Zionism, submitted at the end of 1918, was one such report on which criticism was generously heaped by David Hunter Miller. Some passages from the Miller critique make clear that not all of these reports were received enthusiastically by the Inquiry's high command:

> The report on Zionism is absolutely inadequate from any standpoint and must be regarded as nothing more than material for a future report . . . It has only a paragraph or two of historical resumé and they are both inadequate and wrong . . . It fails to give any idea of the setting of Zionism in Judaism either in the present or in the past.
> A short historical sketch of the movement is absolutely necessary to its understanding. There should be . . . reference to the movements before the Nineteenth Century . . . the new Judaism of the 19th Century . . . anti-Semitism . . . Such an introduction must precede an understanding of the work of Herzl [founder of political Zionism] . . . In form the report is ill organized both in subject arrangement and statement . . . Paragraph 4 goes from Herzl to a Congress; from a Congress to a plateau; and from a plateau to an organization. It reads like a comment on the Mishna . . . The report belongs to a class of material which it is the first duty of the Research Committee to discard . . .[31]

The Inquiry's leaders were not all bamboozled by these reports. Unfortunately, so many of the Middle Eastern reports were submitted in the final weeks of the war that it proved impossible for all to receive critical attention. Some reports contain material which must have seemed hardly credible. Take the report of J. K.

31. David Hunter Miller, "Memorandum on Campbell's 'Report on Zionism,' " enclosed in Isaiah Bowman to O. J. Campbell, Dec. 31, 1918, Inquiry Archives. (Campbell was assistant professor of English at the University of Wisconsin.)

Birge concerning the "Ottoman Turks of Asia Minor." According to Birge, those Turks "who have shown the greatest tendencies to progress have been men whose blood was known to be chiefly Albanian or Jewish, or some other than Mongol kind." Furthermore,

> the Turk is liable to be always inconsistent . . . His lack of executive ability is one of his most conspicuous failings. Inconsistent reasoning is not conducive to justice or to fair and efficient administration of any kind.[32]

Birge described the Turks as "deficient" by comparison with Christians. Though supporting evidence seemed to be lacking ("accurate facts seem to be lacking") the Turkish population appeared to Birge to suffer from "syphilitic diseases." At the same time, the syphilitic Turks were described as "capable of intense loyalty to national ideals." The Turkish race was perhaps "not much behind other races in having a generous sprinkling of good men . . . capable of seeing the faults of their country . . ." Moreover at the International College, observed Birge, "fully 20% of the Turkish boys were so instinctively good that their characters were developing for good at points even where that development had to run counter to national prejudices and tendencies."

As has already been implied, Birge's report was not an unusual example of the Inquiry's Middle Eastern output. Leon Dominian's report on Turkey, dated January 31, 1918, contains very long portions—indeed page after page—of material admittedly "copied" from several official French, English, and American publications.[33] Abraham Yohannon's report on the Assyrians dated February 20, 1918, is so contaminated with the scent of pro-Assyrian and Christian bias that its value at a peace conference would be less than questionable.[34] At the same time the balance must be adjusted slightly, for the Inquiry did produce a minority of creditable re-

32. J. K. Birge, "The Ottoman Turks of Asia Minor," Inquiry Archives. (No biographical information available on Birge.)

33. Leon Dominian, "Report on Turkey" (125 pp.), Jan. 31, 1918, William Yale MSS, Yale.

34. Yohannon (Minister of St. Bartholomew's Church, New York City), "The Assyrians," Feb. 20, 1918, William Yale MSS, Yale.

ports that were informative, accurate, and thoughtfully organized and written.[35]

Without much doubt the most comprehensive of the Inquiry's Middle Eastern studies was the "Report on Just and Practical Boundaries for the Turkish Empire." [36] This report, though undated, was probably produced in October or November 1918. It is important not only for its frank comments and recommendations but because its principal author, William L. Westermann, was the chief Inquiry specialist on the Middle East during the fall of 1918. Later at the Paris Peace Conference he was the chief American territorial specialist for that area. His views on Middle Eastern problems, therefore, would carry more significance than would those of ordinary researchers on the Inquiry Staff. Westermann, ancient historian by profession, saw the Middle East as one amorphous mass of peoples. Nationalism had not yet appeared in the Turkish communities outside of Anatolia and hence had not divided the empire into clearly defined territorial units. Only Arabia could possibly be construed as an exception. Rather than nationalism, Middle Eastern groups had divided along religious cleavages and only secondarily along linguistic lines. Westermann remarked how Turkish oppression over the centuries had kept an uneasy peace among these diverse subject peoples within the empire. Were Turkish overlordship to be removed suddenly by the peace conference, Westermann warned, some substitute would have to be found.

Boundaries in the Middle East could not effectively be based upon ethnic self-determination as the guiding principle. Religious "determination" seemed to offer a preferable criterion. Economic, topographic (including strategic) and linguistic factors had to be weighed heavily in deciding boundary arrangements for all of the seven areas—Armenia, Anatolia, Mesopotamia, Kurdistan, Syria, Palestine, and Arabia—discussed in the Westermann report.

35. Some respectable pieces of scholarship were: Roland B. Dixon, "Eastern Turkestan," Sept. 7, 1918; David Magie, "Report on the Assyrian Christians," Aug. 21, 1918; John M. Vincent, "French Railways in Asiatic Turkey," Inquiry Archives.

36. William L. Westermann, "Just and Practical Boundaries for the Turkish Empire," Inquiry Archives.

A separate Armenian state presupposed the existence of an internationalized status for Constantinople and the Straits as "an absolute requirement for the commercial welfare of the Russians, Transcaucasians as well as the Armenians." An Armenian state would include areas inhabited by Armenian communities, but in the entire proposed state only some 35 per cent of the population would be Armenian. This being true, Westermann did not recommend a completely independent status for Armenia. The Moslems, Kurds, and Arabs, he believed, required protection from the Armenians. The long frontier and shaky economic foundations also lent support for some "strong international control" over Armenia.

An Anatolia deprived of Constantinople and the Straits, Westermann asserted, must not be carved into foreign enclaves or otherwise fragmented. Anatolia was overwhelmingly Turkish. Greek claims to Kavala should not receive American support "unless [the Conference decides] Anatolia is to be broken up." As with Armenia, Anatolia was to be subject to effective international controls for the protection of national minorities.

A Syrian state promised greater economic potential than either an Armenian or Anatolian state largely because of Syria's excellent commercial location. Yet the population had never had any experience in self-government. "Complete independence for them," Westermann insisted, "was out of the question." Moslems, Christians, Druzes, and Bedouins must be brought into greater unity. Westermann and his associates simply felt that this unity must be aided by some stronger agency than merely the "native government." Tutelage then, probably for an extended period, was deemed essential for Syria.

Palestine's boundaries were drawn "to satisfy the aspirations of Zionists for a national state." So began the section concerned with Palestine. Its northern boundary was to be the Kasiniyeh River and Lake Huleh (general outline); its eastern boundary was to be the Jordan River and the Dead Sea; on the south the Sandjak of Jerusalem, including Beersheba and el Andja, would provide the boundary. Zionist claims to the land east of the Jordan could not be accepted, for as of 1918 only one Jewish settlement (Ben Jehuda) had been established in the Transjordanian region. Westermann was quick to point out that, in the proposed Jewish state,

Jews numbered but one-seventh (100,000) of the total population. Aside from the 80,000 Christians, the vast majority of the population was Arab. In a special sense Palestine signified a truly sacred international area for Jews, Christians, and Moslems. Certainly, here would be one area where logic dictated international control. Similarly, because of its reclamation needs, Westermann favored some strong international authority for Mesopotamia instead of a fully independent status. Mesopotamia's desperate need for financial credit would not easily be met without the security and stability which an international authority was more likely to afford.

Only in the case of Arabia did Westermann break from his basic recommendation for international controls over liberated portions of the Turkish Empire. He thought that the best solution for Arabia would be "to allow the independent desert tribes to work out their own destiny along the lines of the patriarchal tribunal government traditional among them." It is interesting to observe that no mandate system was suggested in these recommendations. Apparently Westermann and his staff had not reached any conclusion regarding a specific type of international administration; he was content to emphasize the need for international supervision. Also noteworthy was the absence of any mention of petroleum in the economic sections of the study, though the discovery of oil in the Middle East was not unknown to economists in the United States during the First World War.

Some of these reports appear astounding in retrospect; it is amazing to learn how few were relevant to American interests, plans, or programs for the area.[37] Had there been a willful conspiracy to avoid this subject, the scores of reports produced dealing with the Middle East could not have succeeded more nobly. It was possibly this failure on the part of the Inquiry that prompted the State Department to procure studies on its own. Whatever the reason, Captain Alfred L. P. Dennis, an historian then serving in the army, was requested by the State Department to submit proposals concerning the Middle Eastern settlement for the guidance of the American representatives at the peace conference. His report was brief, to the point, and considered several alternatives

37. The one report which dealt directly with this matter was O. J. Campbell, "American Interests in Turkey," William Yale MSS, Yale.

for American policy.[38] The United States, Dennis began, could justifiably remain aloof from Middle Eastern problems inasmuch as the United States had not become involved in the Turkish military conflict. Abstinence and withdrawal were, however, quickly discarded; if the United States aspired to prevent future international conflict, then it could not maintain an indifferent attitude. The Sykes-Picot Agreement of 1916, which would divide significant portions of Turkey's Syrian provinces between France and Britain, was an ominous portent. The absence of any strong nationalistic tradition in Syria served to encourage the Allied governments in their lust for the spoils of war in this area. Dennis recommended that the United States support a five-point policy. First, there should be a distinct understanding that preservation of order and relief for distressed populations demanded Allied military administration only as a temporary expedient. Second, a high commission should be appointed by the powers and its jurisdiction should extend over three districts—Aleppo, Beirut, and Damascus. But "international administration should be particularly avoided," and the high commission should be recognized only as a temporary necessity and removed as quickly as national unity and stability developed in Syria. Third, boundaries should not separate the interior from coastal portions of the country. These boundaries should extend from the Taurus Mountains in the North "to the Zionist State" on the south. Fourth, a large measure of autonomy should be given to Lebanon within this Syrian union. But under no circumstances should territorial divisions be based on religious determination, that is, dividing Moslems and Christians. Fifth, the creation of a Zionist state in Palestine was assumed.

One additional non-Inquiry report might be mentioned just to indicate that several government departments were considering the American position with regard to the Middle East in advance of the peace conference. In this instance, the undated memorandum concerned oil and was submitted at the behest of Secretary of the Navy Josephus Daniels.

> First at this time [early 1919 on the basis of internal evidence] when with the making of peace, new protectorates and mandatories

38. Alfred L. P. Dennis, "Memorandum on the Syrian Question," prepared at the request of the State Department, Frank Polk MSS, Yale.

are to be established, it is of primary importance that the principles upon which the administration of those territories will be carried out be clearly defined.[39]

At a time when aggressive oil policies were being pursued by the British government, the United States and "its petroleum business" was maintaining a keen interest in the Middle Eastern peace settlement. British control over oil lands had meant the consistent exclusion of foreign interests (Burma and Trinidad were mentioned as examples). The report continued,

> It is now anticipated that Mesopotamia will be brought in some way under British administration. Mesopotamia is regarded as one of the large potential oil fields of the future. Not only is it the desire of Americans to operate in this territory, but having regard to its favored geographical location alone of the world's greatest highways, it is of utmost importance to the United States Government that Americans should be interested there.[40]

American petroleum requirements were increasing yearly, and in 1918 the vast military consumption seemed to threaten domestic resources, or so it seemed to many economists in the United States. The American navy and merchant marine were already almost fully converted to oil burners, and the increased importance of oil for the fleet offered an additional national interest in the outcome of the Middle East settlement. The American government must seek assurance, the report urged, that American petroleum concerns would have at least Open Door access to the Middle East fields. Naturally the American claim could be rationalized as well: "The development of the natural resources of these lands should be directed to the greatest ultimate benefit of the ward [presumably the Arab inhabitants of the oil-drenched lands] rather than to the special interests of the guardian." But one need not be an expert in reading between the lines to comprehend the full intent of the author:

> Unless before Mesopotamia and other territories are actually placed under British Administration there be express provision

39. "Memorandum on Middle Eastern Oil," n.d., Josephus Daniels MSS, folio 365, Library of Congress.
40. Ibid.

made or adequate assurance given to safeguard the free right of entry of the American petroleum industry, its exclusion must be apprehended, to be followed by the exploitation of the oil resources of these lands for the sole benefit of Great Britain and her trade . . .

It is unnecessary to point out the extreme importance to the American nation of maintaining a strong position in the petroleum trade of the world.[41]

These two non-Inquiry-sponsored reports merely serve to underscore the concern which other American government departments felt regarding the outcome of the Middle Eastern settlement.

The Inquiry's recommendations for the Middle East were placed in both the Outline of Tentative Recommendations of January 21, 1919, and the Black Book Number 2 dated February 13, 1919. To a large extent, the recommendations corresponded to the proposals found in the Westermann report, "Just and Practical Boundaries for the Turkish Empire," which apparently served as the initial draft. A few notable additions, however, were made. For Constantinople, the Outline of Tentative Recommendations proposed an international state capable of providing "impartial justice to the various interests of the many states concerned in the commerce that will pass the Straits and to diminish the keen historic jealousies that have obstructed the flow of trade." The international regime would have its governmental organization under a mandatary of the League of Nations or whatever other arrangement was agreed upon by the peace conference. By way of boundaries, the new state would include the "entire littoral of the Straits and of the Sea of Marmora." Any division of this area was deemed likely to cause innumerable legal and commercial difficulties. All adjacent states could have adequate rights of access to waters in the internationalized area. On the European side, the international state's boundaries would extend as far as the Enos-Midia (Inoz-Midye) line; while on the Asiatic side the boundary would "follow in part the line of the Sakaria River, include within its area the towns of Brussa and Panderma," finally emerging on the Aegean Sea at a point just north of Ireh. With such boundaries, the new international state would be able to satisfy its immediate needs

41. Ibid.

for garden and dairy products and for water. Topographically, the boundaries were drawn so as not to separate valley floors from surrounding hill pastures, stream courses, and watersheds. Brussa, a city of 75,000, was specifically included in the new international state "in order to prevent the Turks from making it their capital. As such, it might easily become the center of international intrigues, disturbing the large Turkish population in and about Constantinople, and therefore, the stability and smooth administration of the new independent state." For the Turks, there were good reasons to make Brussa their new capital. It had been the Ottoman capital before Constantinople was captured in 1453, and many Sultans were buried there. As for the Straits themselves, the Inquiry recommended that the Bosphorus, the Sea of Marmora, and the Dardanelles be opened permanently to the commerce and ships of all nations.

An independent Turkish state would occupy the remaining portions of the Anatolian peninsula, according to the Inquiry's recommendations. Smyrna was recognized as possessing a substantial Greek population and the Inquiry "scrutinized with great care" the arguments in favor of assigning the district to Greece, but it decided against this alternative. From all standpoints—political, strategic, and commercial—the Inquiry thought it unwise to allow satisfaction of Greece's claim for territory in Asia Minor. On this point, the recommendation insisted:

> To give her a foothold upon the mainland would invite immediate trouble. Greece would press her claims for more territory; Turkey would feel that her new boundaries were run so as to give her a great handicap at the very start. The harbor at Smyrna has been for centuries an outlet for the products of the Central Anatolian valleys and upland.[42]

For Armenia, the Inquiry recommendations followed closely the Westermann report cited above. Although it was admitted that nowhere in the proposed state would Armenians constitute a majority of the population, the Inquiry justified an Armenian state by such extenuating circumstances as the persecutions and exploitations to which the Armenians had been subjected in the

42. Outline of Tentative Recommendations, Jan. 21, 1919, Wilson MSS, Series, VIII-A, Library of Congress.

past. Non-Armenian elements within the proposed state would receive adequate protection by international guarantee. The new state would be placed under the supervision of a mandatary to be chosen by the League of Nations.

Looking southward, the recommendations of January 21, 1919, favored the establishment of an Arab state in Syria, which would also be subject to the mandate system. While belonging to the Arab world, Syria could claim a sizable European population, close cultural and commercial relations with Europe, a powerful Christian minority, and a more settled society than was common among Arab peoples. No obstacle was to be placed in the way of Syria joining an Arab confederacy, and the Inquiry report observed:

> There is a possibility of the future development of an Arab Confederation which will include all of the Arab-speaking portions of the former Turkish Empire. The present strength of this Arab movement is hard to gauge. It would be the best solution from the standpoint of the welfare and development of the Arab states.

Justification for a separate Palestinian state was claimed on religious and historical grounds. Only in a separate political entity could the aspirations of the Jewish and Christian populations find expression. Although the choice of a mandatary for other proposed states in Asia Minor was left in abeyance pending action by the League of Nations, for Palestine the Inquiry proposed Great Britain. The Inquiry's recommendations sounded strangely prophetic when speculating on the potential for ethnic conflict in Palestine:

> Palestine would obviously need wise and firm guidance. Its population is without political experience, racially composite, and could easily become distracted by fanaticism and bitter religious differences.

The Inquiry apparently held British colonial administration in high esteem for the recommendations justified the selection of Britain as mandatary over Palestine on the basis of Britain's previous experience with "similar situations" in Egypt. Furthermore, the Inquiry warmly supported Zionist aspirations for Palestine recognizing all the while that in 1919 Jews constituted only a small fraction of the total population in the proposed state. The mandate arrangement would continue until such time as the Jewish population reached a majority of the total population and hence could justify the formation of a Jewish state. This section of the report is worth quoting:

> It is recommended that the Jews be invited to return to Palestine and settle there, being assured by the [Peace] Conference of all proper assistance in so doing that which may be consistent with the protection of the personal (especially the religious) and the property rights of the non-Jewish population, and being further assured that it will be the policy of the League of Nations to recognize Palestine as a Jewish state as soon as it is a Jewish state in fact.
>
> It is right that Palestine should become a Jewish state, if the Jews being given the full opportunity, make it such. It was the cradle and home of their vital race, which has made large spiritual contributions to mankind, and is the only land in which they can hope to find a home of their own; they being in this last respect unique among significant peoples . . . England, as mandatary, can be relied on to give the Jews the privileged position they should have without sacrificing the rights of non-Jews.[43]

Again, as with Armenia, historical claims and extenuating circumstances combined to influence the Inquiry's proposals.

No specific recommendation was set forth for the desert regions of the Arabian peninsula. As for the twenty or more tribal groups then inhabiting the peninsula no direct interference was considered advisable. But in the more fertile Tigris-Euphrates Valley northward and eastward from Arabia, the Inquiry thought it desirable to found a separate Mesopotamian state subject, like the other political units in the Middle East, to a mandatory power appointed by the League of Nations. Such a state might very well become a central member of any Arab confederacy, which was an arrangement the Inquiry would not hinder. In any case, the boundaries for the new Mesopotamia (or Iraq) would include all headwater areas of the Tigris-Euphrates drainage basin. Any separation of the headwaters from the irrigated valley floors and lowlands downstream could conceivably create endless disputes

43. Ibid.

which the Inquiry desired to prevent. Once again Britain's colonial administration came in for high praise:

> It is recommended that the policing of the Red Sea, Indian Ocean, and Persian Gulf coasts of Arabia, and the border lands behind these be left to the British Empire.
>
> The Power which understands best how to handle the Arabs is the British Empire. By controlling the coastal areas and the markets along the edge of the desert at which the desert tribes must trade, the British Indian Office has been about to exercise some influence over the inland tribes.

Recommendations contained in the Black Book of February 1919 were in the nature of additions to the earlier proposals in the Outline of Tentative Recommendations. No important changes or modifications were introduced. The island of Cyprus, having been severed from Turkish control by Britain during the war, was claimed by Greece on the basis of an overwhelming Greek population. Yet the Inquiry chose to assume a "hands-off" attitude on this question, asserting instead, "This question is entirely a British-Greek affair and should not come before the Peace Conference." [44] Persia, later to be called Iran, had not figured in the earlier Inquiry recommendations. In February the Inquiry urged that Persia be treated by the peace conference "as an independent and sovereign state and recognized formally as such if that be her desire." No mandate principle would be invoked in the absence of popular demands by the Iranians. Existing boundaries were not to be altered; no obstacles should discourage union of the Tartars in Azerbaijan with the Tartars under Persian sovereignty. Eventually, the Inquiry leaders anticipated, the Tartars in Persia, Azerbaijan, and Russia—all having a common language and religion—might form a single, united government. Meanwhile, the only substantial contribution which the peace conference might make to Persia would be the termination of the Anglo-Russian Convention of 1907, which had divided Persia into spheres of influence.

The Inquiry would have the Middle East resemble Africa with its mosaic of mandates. Governing arrangements were to be tailored to fit local conditions, flexibly rather than rigidly imposed by

44. Black Book No. 2, Feb. 13, 1919, Wilson MSS, Series VIII-A, Library of Congress.

the peace conference. At all times, the primary rights of the local inhabitants were to be safeguarded and enhanced by an Open Door guarantee. If the mandate system were to succeed in providing effective government, then economic as well as political exploitation of the native population must be avoided. Less comprehensive than the African recommendations, the Middle Eastern recommendations in a sense reflected the weakness of the Inquiry's efforts for this area. To a somewhat greater extent than with other areas, the Inquiry's scope of activities was far too ambitious in terms of the limited talent available and the brief time at its disposal.

The reports for Central Asia, India, China, and Japan might well be described together. Economic and political considerations received somewhat more attention in these areas than in the cases of the Middle East and Africa. India and Japan were treated by the following subject divisions as indicated by reports in the Inquiry archives: [45]

India		Japan	
History	1	Politics and government	9
Economy	13	Economy	13
Politics and government	3	Foreign policy	7
		Population	1
		Education	1
		Social unrest	1
		Expansion	2
		Military policy	2
		Korea	1
Total	17	Total	37

That India would be considered at all might cause some amazement, but that so much of the Indian work should have been assigned to one whose qualifications were so terribly meager is even less easily explained. Dorothy Kenyon, responsible for a dozen of the Indian studies, turned them out on a mass production basis. Her output consisted in part of generalities ("Rainfall is a more important factor in India than in Europe though even there it is not universally true that the regions of heavy rainfall always

45. PI-89.

258

coincide with great density of population")[46] or shows little regard for the practical importance of her subject ("Taking the population as a whole, 46% of the males and 48% of the females are married; while 5% and 17% respectively are widowed. In Western Europe only 9% of the total number of females are widowed. A great majority of the unmarried consist of very young children, three quarters of the bachelors being under 15 years of age while a somewhat larger proportion of the spinsters are under 10 years").[47] From the marriage rate she proceeded to a consideration of insanity, deafness, blindness, and leprosy. Conceivably these matters could be relevant to the peace settlement, but the connection was never spelled out. The writer herself seemed unaware of any relevancy. Whatever the shortcomings in her reports, they were less the fault of the author than they were the unfortunate products of the system under which the Inquiry operated.

These features were not entirely overlooked by the Inquiry's critics. One commentary on her report on Indian economics remarked about the logical organization and the exhaustive charts and tables listing statistics, but went on to point out the one glaring weakness, which was the uncritical use of propagandistic literature in order to portray British rule as tantamount to pure and simple exploitation of a helpless country in the interests of British capitalism. The commentary continued:

> Of course it is no part of the business of the Inquiry to act as Attorney for the defense of British administration but there is no reason why the Inquiry should accept a brief for the prosecution. By far the worst report in this respect is the one on "Famines" which lays the responsibility for their recurrence on the economic drain of British rule. Such reports read like an indictment of an enemy country; and even so they should be less obviously unfair. If the aim of these reports is simply the compilation of statistics they are valuable although the Census and the Indian Year Book could almost fill their place; if these reports are intended to give a correct perspective on the problems of India, they are positively misleading.[48]

46. Dorothy Kenyon, "India Population," June 3, 1918, p. 5, Inquiry Archives.
47. Ibid., p. 15.
48. "Critique of 'Report on India Economics' by Dorothy Kenyon," Shotwell MSS, Columbia.

Misleading and nonanalytical are adjectives which could aptly describe Dorothy Kenyon's prolific contributions to the Inquiry. However, India was never regarded as presenting any crucial, burning issues for the peace conference agenda.

With China and Japan, however, the Inquiry's Far Eastern Division was dealing with problems certain to arise prominently at the conference. The considerable length devoted to Far Eastern recommendations in Black Book Number 2—comparable to the attention given to the weighty issues of Central and Eastern Europe in the Outline of Tentative Recommendations—offered ample testimony to the significance of Far Eastern questions.

One group of questions had to deal with the disposition of Germany's and Austria's interests in the Far East. Would the German leasehold in Shantung, in northeastern China, revert to China or would the peace conference honor Japan's claim to the province? How should German economic concessions in China be treated? Should the peace conference admit the validity of the various secret treaties with respect to the Far East? In view of Japan's insistence on special interests, prerogatives, and additional concessions in the Far East, what position might the United States assume concerning the Twenty-One Demands imposed upon China in 1915? Would Japan be allowed to extend its hegemony upon the Asiatic mainland? What principles if any should the American delegation insist upon during discussions of the Far Eastern settlement? Here were questions bound to arise and which no peace conference could afford to ignore, yet only meager financial allocations were provided for the Inquiry's Far Eastern Division (Chapter 3 above). Far more might have been accomplished in preparing the American positions had more money been made available for these studies.

At the time of the Inquiry's inception, September 1917, Colonel House had called to President Wilson's attention the various Japanese desires and national ambitions in eastern Asia. House did not in any respect minimize the dangers confronting the future peace settlement for the Far East. He wrote:

> We cannot meet Japan in her desires as to land and immigration, and unless we make some concessions in regard to her sphere of influence in the East, trouble is sure, sooner or later, to come. Japan is barred from all the underdeveloped places of the earth

260

and if her influence in the East is not recognized as in some degree superior to that of the Western Powers, there will be a reckoning.

A policy can be formulated which will leave the Open Door, rehabilitate China, and satisfy Japan.[49]

House saw clearly the dilemma posed for American policy-makers. Business interests in the United States seemed committed to the Open Door policy; it provided the legal instrument for reaching the Chinese market. At the same time, the United States government was anxiously upholding the territorial props which underlay a politically disunited China. In February 1918, the American minister at Peking was instructed by the State Department to give assurance to the Chinese government that at the future peace conference China would receive the same consideration as other countries then at war with Germany and Austria, "insofar as the American Government was competent" to assure this.[50] This gesture phrased in diplomatic niceties was doubtless intended to ease the grave Chinese fear that at the peace conference the victorious Western powers would grant to Japan the substance of the Twenty-One Demands. The cooling effects rendered by the qualifying phrases hardly afforded any realistic basis for Chinese optimism, nor would such phrases soothe Chinese sensibilities. They merely suggested how complicated and possibly contradictory American interests in the Far East were becoming.

Wolcott Pitkin, lawyer and former political adviser to the Kingdom of Siam, was in charge of the Inquiry's Far Eastern Division from its formation until June of 1918. Pitkin was certainly no expert on Far Eastern matters, as we have already seen. Nevertheless, he was expected to perform the duties of "editor and director of research." [51] Almost immediately after assuming his responsibilities, Pitkin embarked upon the tedious labor of collecting the utterances and statements of all statesmen from belligerent countries with reference to their war aims in the Far East.[52] Very early in the game he learned to his dismay that few Far Eastern maga-

49. House to Wilson, Sept. 18, 1917, Wilson MSS, Series II, Library of Congress.
50. Memorandum from the Department of State to the British Embassy, Feb. 27, 1918, *Papers Relating to the Foreign Relations of the United States, 1918, Supplement 1, The World War* (Washington, 1933), *1*, 635.
51. Walter Lippmann to Sidney Mezes, Dec. 15, 1917, Inquiry Archives.
52. Wolcott Pitkin to E. T. Williams (State Department), Dec. 15, 1917, Inquiry Archives.

zines and newspapers were available in the United States; secondly, that the Chinese and Japanese official utterances were frequently not printed in Western languages; and thirdly, that the difficulty with Chinese pronouncements lay in the reluctance of Chinese statesmen to say anything "for publication." [53] These complications did not deter him. He rounded up American missionaries experienced in the East; he corresponded with American emissaries, including the American minister in Peking, Paul Reinsch, seeking reports and information.[54] By December 1917, Pitkin discovered that he could get nowhere without complete cooperation from the State Department's Far Eastern Division. Such cooperation was provided. Soon, however, the State Department's staff became disgusted because it was performing all the tasks and Pitkin presumably was accepting the credit for the reports. In June, Pitkin was discharged and his place was taken by Norman D. Harris, whose scholarly specialty had previously been colonialism in Africa. Under Harris' direction few reports were assigned or processed, and the Far Eastern Division floundered about helplessly. Not until Stanley K. Hornbeck became affiliated with the Inquiry during the fall of 1918 did the Far Eastern Division begin to assume the importance warranted by its responsibilities.

Many of the Inquiry's reports reflected an unsympathetic attitude toward Japanese expansionistic aspirations. James Abbott, a zoologist at Washington University (St. Louis) who had lived in Japan and had acquired some competency in the Japanese language (judging from his citation of Japanese language sources in his footnotes and bibliographies), submitted several papers. One study on the subject of population and industrial development documented with statistics the tremendous advances in industrialization and urbanization which had caused the Japanese economy to become more dependent upon foreign sources for food supplies.[55] A conspicuous and recent tendency in Japanese industry, Abbott observed, had been its greater commercial dependence upon Chinese markets and sources for raw materials. New indus-

53. Williams to Pitkin, Dec. 18, 1917, Inquiry Archives.
54. Pitkin to Paul Reinsch, Nov. 27, 1917, Inquiry Archives.
55. James Abbott, "Preliminary Report on Population and Industrial Development of Japan," Jan. 15, 1918, Inquiry Archives.

tries, especially iron and steel, could easily lead Japan into "direct conflict" either on account of the opposition of rival European powers or of the Chinese themselves. Similarly, Abbott thought it "inevitable" that, if Japan were to become an important steel producer, it would compete successfully with American producers not only in East Asia but also in South America. Its economic expansion into China meant the likelihood of its coming into conflict with British interests. These were signs which the United States could ill afford to ignore.

A second report, "Social Unrest in Japan," was concerned with the consequences of industrialization and urbanization: [56] high mortality from diseases, the presence of a "floating" male element in the cities; a rampant rise in the cost of living; and a general inflationary spiral. Labor unrest, demonstrations, rice riots, and strikes seemed to parallel wartime prosperity. Huge profits in many businesses did not produce proportionate increases in wages. A troublesome Korean community could also be expected to ignite and feed any class warfare that might get out of control. Japan's government was portrayed as a feudal image anxiously suppressing all possibilities for reform through a tough censorship policy, police action, and an aggressive foreign policy. Its oligarchic leadership might, under certain circumstances, prefer to involve the country in a foreign war rather than grant liberal concessions to the masses. Abbott considered the existence of this predicament a major reason for Japan's intervention in the world war. More significantly he warned that war would be resorted to in the future if there existed a need for an artificially imposed national unity.

War, warned Abbott, would appear to offer fewer liabilities for the oligarchy and the bureaucracy than would concessions granted to the masses. These influential groups, then, might lead Japan toward a policy of industrial imperialism—for markets, raw materials, and national unity.

One suggestive report submitted to the Inquiry's Far Eastern Division was the outline for a government of China written by Samuel G. Blythe. At the time Blythe was considering China's political difficulties, the southern provinces were involved in revolution; Japanese influence was strong in certain localities; the

56. Abbott, "Social Unrest in Japan." Nov. 25, 1918, Inquiry Archives.

financial structure was shaky, outmoded, and ineffective; the outer provinces, lacking any effective political control from Peking, were operating in virtually autonomous status. Three possibilities for renovating the governmental machinery suggested themselves to Blythe: (1) an international commission under great power auspices, but this was doomed to failure because Chinese "customs, religion, inheritances and racial tendencies" were so unique; (2) a protectorate imposed by Japan, also deemed impractical for it would cause greater confusion, tension, and opposition than was present during the war; (3) a China functioning independently, reconstructed with the encouragement of "friendly powers," and this alone would offer China a chance for further progress, relatively free of continuous chaos. Blythe's report contained historical implications, fallacies, distortions, and biases touching many aspects of the Chinese political and economic scene. Only a few excerpts will be necessary to give the flavor of the report:

> The Chinese are naturally a democratic people, but consented to autocratic rule for forty centuries or more because of their philosophy of non-resistance or passivity and their lack of nationalization or national spirit.
>
> Their chiefest concerns are the production of male offspring in order that they, as ancestors, may be worshipped and assured their getting enough to eat. They are ignorant of the meaning of democracy while personally democratic, and indifferent to government as a national function and necessity.[57]

Blythe's panacea for China's ills was the formation of an international holding company which would "teach China how to administer herself." The holding company would in the process allow China to remain independent and sovereign. Membership in the holding company would be limited to those powers having substantial material and sentimental interests in China—i.e., the United States, Britain, Japan, and France. Above and beyond the holding company, Blythe's proposals dealt with suffrage, taxation, provincial governmental organization, and the central government's structure. Suffrage would not be universal for adults or even for males; it would be limited to persons paying at least 100

57. Samuel G. Blythe, "Outline for a Government of China," March 18, 1918, Inquiry Archives.

264

taels in taxes, admittedly a considerable financial qualification. There was need, Blythe reasoned, for some restriction on the suffrage until the Chinese masses became better educated. The provincial governments would require of their officials that they be voters. Provincial legislatures would formulate all provincial laws, but would be regulated in turn by the national government in regard to taxation and certain other particulars. All taxes would be collected by the national government and then funds allocated to the provinces. The odious likin (internal tariffs) would be abolished. Taxes would be collected by presentation of government stamps which would be sold at post offices, banks, and government agencies. This would mean that the currency would be issued and regulated by the national government rather than by provincial or local authorities. The silver standard would be replaced by a gold standard.

China's central government, according to Blythe, should consist of a president serving a single term of six years. A cabinet responsible to the parliament would have charge of administration. All governing bodies would be limited to a small workable size. "Multiplication of Chinese officials means multiplication of administrative and legislative difficulties." The national parliament would have two houses, a senate with one representative from each province and a house of representatives with two representatives from each province. All utilities and national resources would be controlled by the national government. China's financial stability was to be supported by a loan of $50,000,000 from each power represented on the holding company. As a result of these reforms, the Chinese government would be stronger and more responsive to the popular will. In addition, "China by these means can be built up to a great buffer state between a possibly Germanized Russia on the one side and an over-ambitious Japan on the other." These Far Eastern Division studies, needless to say, were not the products of experts.

The Black Book's recommendations showed the same sympathy for Chinese interests expressed in most of the Inquiry's reports. The Shantung recommendations would have canceled the original convention between Germany and China as well as the Chinese-Japanese agreements of May 1915 (the Twenty-One Demands).

By so disposing of prior diplomatic agreements, the Shantung question might then be considered on its own merits. In order to counter Japan's expected demand for Tsingtao (the chief port of Shantung), the Inquiry advised that the port be internationalized. Under no circumstances was Japan to retain control over Tsingtao. Leased territory at Kiaochow was also to be restored to China with compensation allowed to Germany for all improvements.

> There is no sufficient justification for the maintenance of a foreign jurisdiction. The possession of this territory and of the railways by a foreign nation is a menace to China and to the peace of the Far East. China, the sovereign and lessor, wishes repossession.[58]

Railways were to be restored to Chinese control since it would be more efficient for the Chinese government to operate all of the railroads of the country. The Black Book suggested also the desirability of restoring Britain's leased territory at Wei hai wei (on the northern coast of Shantung) to China. This action by Great Britain "would make it easier for Japan to concede the points asked of her," the American report assured. The Inquiry's leaders fully expected Great Britain to comply with this proposal.

All German and Austrian concessions at Tientsin and Hankow were to become international settlements, and Chinese residents would participate in the governmental organization. American policy had since the nineteenth century favored international settlements rather than foreign national concessions in China. Hence this proposal was in no sense novel.

Virtually all privileges which had been extended to Germany and Austria-Hungary in the Boxer Protocol of 1901 were to be terminated. Further payments by China pursuant to that agreement would cease, since the German claims were regarded by the Inquiry's leaders as extravagant when compared to the actual costs incurred by Germany in suppressing the Boxers. Maintenance of separate legation and railway guards permitted to the powers under terms of the Boxer Protocol would likewise be disallowed for Germany and Austria. "Germany and Austria would seem to have forfeited the right to station troops in China for these

---

58. Black Book No. 2, Wilson MSS, Library of Congress.

purposes." The two defeated European powers would also surrender their postal services in China. As the Black Book explained, with such service provided by the Chinese government, there would no longer be a need for foreign governments to operate a duplicate service. The termination of German and Austrian postal service was to be the entering wedge for the elimination of all foreign postal service in China.

In other respects the Inquiry tried to take advantage of the peace settlement to liberalize and otherwise modify the existing treaty structure for China's benefit. Tariff arrangements were to be revised for the purpose of "insuring equality of opportunity" to reach China's markets. It was further recommended that some fixed date be set at which China would receive complete tariff autonomy "if by that time certain conditions [not stipulated] shall have been realized." Meanwhile, some action should be taken to allow China to increase the tariff schedules, thereby increasing revenues. The peace conference was expected to offer the most opportune moment for this action. And, in addition, all members of the peace conference were urged to sign and ratify the Opium Convention of 1912, for the supposed benefit of China.

Although the Inquiry did not recommend complete termination of extraterritorial jurisdiction in China, it did recommend that certain progressive measures be taken in this direction. One suggestion the Inquiry thought worthwhile was for an international court with some Chinese participation. This would replace the foreign consular courts and would provide an excellent opportunity for introducing Western jurisprudence to the Chinese public.

The Inquiry's recommendations tried to relieve China of any commitments under the Twenty-One Demands. These demands stood firmly in the path of a "just settlement" in the Far East. Hence the Black Book recommended that any agreements made between two or more governments

> entered into since the beginning of the war which involve transfers, distribution or allocation of territory or of special rights or privileges or which affect alterations of national jurisdiction and which have arisen out of the war or appertain to the peace settlements, shall be subject to screening for approval, revision, or rejection by the peace conference or by such body or bodies as shall be authorized by the peace conference to deal with them.

The Inquiry's leaders were apparently unsure of so inclusive a provision, for they appended an alternative having the effect of narrowing the meaning to just Japanese aspirations in the Pacific and the Twenty-One Demands. The alternative stipulated that all secret arrangements made since the beginning of the war and pertaining to the Far East be declared subject for review by the peace conference.

Even more specific were the Inquiry's recommendations concerning Manchuria, Eastern Inner Mongolia, and Russian Eastern Siberia. The Convention of May 25, 1915, between China and Japan relating to South Manchuria and Eastern Inner Mongolia, was to be reviewed by the peace conference. The Inquiry deemed it necessary to propose that some international organization, acting under the authority of either the League of Nations or the peace conference, be delegated responsibility for Russian interests in Northern Manchuria until such time as a national government generally recognized by the powers "shall have been established in Russia or at least in Asiatic Russia." This proposal was considered essential in view of "the plan under negotiation . . . placing the trans-Siberian and the Chinese eastern railways under the supervision of an interallied committee." All railroads in Manchuria were then to be placed under international control in order to prevent them from being used in future power struggles among the great powers as they had been used for at least two decades in the conflict between Russia and Japan. Internationalization of railroad operations would likewise make unnecessary the exercise of municipal authority (such as the Russians had enjoyed at Harbin), the collection of taxes by the railroad concessionaires, and the use of foreign soldiers to police the railroads. Should guards be necessary in the future, a Chinese constabulary making use of European or American officers could perform this function.

Moving northward into Siberia, the Inquiry was prepared to offer the Russian maritime provinces as balm to soothe Japanese national sentiments and territorial aspirations in China and the Pacific. Russia was to be asked to sell its provinces east of the "Ussuri and Amur Rivers and north of a line to be drawn parallel to the Railway point north of and near to Vladivostok to a point north of and near to Pogranichnaya (Suifenho) on the eastern frontier of northern Manchuria"; also to sell to Japan the northern half of Sakhalin Island (the purchase price for these territories was to be deducted from the total of Russia's indebtedness to Japan). And finally, the Amur River was to be made accessible to international trade. The Inquiry expected that as a result of these transactions Japan would benefit in increased national security, in the goodwill of the world (how this would result was never made clear), in the rounding out of its "natural" geographic position on the shores of the Japan Sea, in the addition of vast mineral and forest reserves, and in the securing of an outlet for its increasing population.

Apparently a good deal of Allied and American planning had been expended on the disposition of Siberia as the proper area for future Japanese expansion. British Prime Minister David Lloyd George allegedly remarked to French Premier Clemenceau in 1919 that he "did not see what objection could be raised, from a purely European point of view, to Japan remaining in Siberia." [59] From a purely American standpoint it might be equally plausible to appease Japanese aspirations through territorial concessions in Siberia. Both the British and American delegations favored this concession to Japan.

American naval advisers at the Paris Peace Conference were certainly thinking along these lines when they submitted recommendations to their chief, Admiral Benson:

> Owing to the crowded condition of Japan and her increase of population, a situation confronts the world of a nation that is compelled to expand or starve . . . Will it not be better to provide for the future expansion of Japan at the peace conference rather than exclude it and thereby leave in existence an immediate cause of future wars in which Japan might attempt to expand in a direction opposed to the interests of the United States . . . It must be borne in mind that it is of vital interest to the United States to turn Japan toward the Continent of Asia.
>
> Hence from our own interests and future plans, the solution of the Eastern Question would be . . . Japan to be given Eastern Siberia.[60]

59. Quoted in Russell H. Fifield, *Woodrow Wilson and the Far East* (New York, 1952), p. 138.

60. United States Planning Committee, undated memorandum, in David Hunter Miller, *My Diary at the Conference at Paris* (Washington, 1928), 2, 104–07, Document No. 17. Apparently Robert Lansing shared this view. Lansing reportedly

Notice should be taken not just of the conclusion but of the rationale, which was much the same as that behind the Inquiry's recommendations.

The fact that at least two American advisory organizations arrived at the same recommendations, apparently independently of each other, shows how plausible this reasoning was for Americans. It was in this context that the Inquiry approached the problems of the Pacific, more specifically those problems affecting the disposition of Germany's colonies there. Japan claimed all the German colonies north of the equator by virtue of the Anglo-Japanese treaty signed on February 16, 1917. But as George Blakeslee, chief of the Inquiry's Pacific Division, was quick to perceive "the greatest value of these islands to Japan from a naval and strategic view would be in potential or actual conflict with the United States."

The Inquiry's Pacific area studies were very limited. George Blakeslee mobilized the services of his seminar students at Clark University during 1917–18 for the purpose of carrying on the research in the absence of any full-time professional assistants.[61] And, maybe not so surprisingly, Blakeslee was highly enthusiastic about the results achieved.[62] Besides drawing upon his students, Blakeslee made use of materials belonging to the Navy Department and to the State Department. He also made use of missionary reports from the "field"—the Pacific islands with which he was concerned.[63]

Take, for example, a typical Blakeslee Pacific island study delivered to the Inquiry on November 18, 1918. It was labeled "Marshall, Caroline and Mariana Islands in Relation to Japan and the United States." [64] A few of Blakeslee's findings and conclusions

---

told James Shotwell in late 1918 that "he wished Japan to expand not eastward but westward, and thought her possession of the Marshall and Gilbert Islands a source of danger. He thought Manchuria and Mongolia a proper field of expansion . . . in view of the crowded condition of the Japanese islands." Report of Conversation with Secretary Lansing, Dec. 9, 1918, in Shotwell MSS, Columbia.

61. Blakeslee to Mezes, Dec. 6, 1917, Mezes MSS, Columbia.
62. Blakeslee to Mezes, Jan. 10, 1918, Inquiry Archives.
63. Mezes to Robert Simpson Woodward (president of the Carnegie Institution of Washington, D.C.), n.d., Mezes MSS, Columbia; Blakeslee Memorandum on his Progress, January 1918, Shotwell MSS, Columbia; A. A. Young to William Churchill (staff member, Carnegie Institution), Sept. 21, 1918, Inquiry Archives.
64. Blakeslee, "Marshall, Caroline and Mariana Islands in Relation to Japan and the United States," Inquiry Archives.

follows: Japan controlled the commerce of the Marianas before the war to the extent of 82 per cent of the imports and 90 per cent of the exports. In the Caroline and Marshall Islands, however, Japan ranked behind Australia and Germany. Japan had made headway in setting up trading stations on even the smallest islands. Next to the Germans, more settlers in these Pacific outposts had come from Japan than from any other country. Writing in November 1918, Blakeslee did not believe the reports of an Anglo-Japanese understanding regarding the division of Germany's island possessions in the Pacific. Japanese newspapers had been making frequent reference to such an arrangement but Blakeslee discounted the "rumors" for lack of evidence. Even so, he wrote that all classes in the Japanese population agreed on the retention of the islands by Japan. "Japan feels that ownership of the islands will insure peace in the Pacific."

As Blakeslee and others saw the Pacific power struggle taking form, they wondered about this peace insurance. The former German colonies flanked the line of American communications between Hawaii and the Philippines. In Japanese hands they would place Japanese submarine bases at least 1,500 miles closer to Hawaii and the American mainland. Blakeslee's solution was to submit the question to the islanders themselves in a plebiscite, for he observed: "If the natives of the Marshalls and the Eastern Carolines could determine their destiny they would choose to be under American rule. Their reason for deciding in favor of the United States stems from their belief that 'Civilization' had been brought to their islands by the missionaries of the American Board [Protestant] to whom they feel indebted."

In its Black Book, the Inquiry went on record firmly in opposition to the acquisition by the United States of the former German colonies.

> The United States has absolutely no legitimate right to these islands and to advance such a claim would not only be considered a gratuitous affront by Japan but would undermine the moral influence of the United States in the settlement of other questions.[65]

65. George Louis Beer, *African Questions at the Paris Peace Conference* (New York, 1923) ed. Louis H. Gray, p. 455. The section dealing with the Pacific Islands recommendations in Beer's volume is only a brief excerpt from the Inquiry's Black Book No. 2, which deals with the Pacific settlement.

But the Inquiry was just as vehement in its opposition to their annexation by Japan.[66] For this situation, the mandate principle provided an ideal solution. The islands would be completely unfortified and the Open Door policy applied to all commercial arrangements. Native rights would be safeguarded, while forced labor (except for necessary public works) would be specifically prohibited by law. There was never any serious thought given to the alternative of allowing these islands to become independent, nor was there any suggestion of restoring the colonies to Germany. Hence, without violating the spirit of the Secret Treaty of London providing for the division of Germany's island possessions between Britain and Japan, the American advisers recommended the mandate compromise: Japan was to obtain the mandate to all German islands north of the equator, while Britain and its dominions were to receive the mandate to all German possessions south of the equator.

Less specific and of less importance to American interests certainly were the Inquiry's recommendations for inner Asia,[67] perhaps a natural reflection of the very inadequate coverage of this area provided in the preparatory studies. Tibet and Mongolia were relegated to a single paragraph. Should questions pertaining to this area arise, the United States should favor the establishment of a separate commission to deal with them. Should the existing "anarchy and disorganization" persist in Russia, the peace conference should establish several new "independent Moslem states" in inner Asia under the protection of the League of Nations acting through some mandatory power. Where unsure, the course of wisdom was to postpone decision, and this was the course suggested by the Inquiry for inner Asia.

The Inquiry was clearly less well prepared on the problems of Africa, Asia, and the Pacific than on the problems of Europe.

66. Black Book No. 2.
67. Ibid.

Chapter 9

CARTOGRAPHY AND LATIN AMERICA

ALONG WITH THE hundreds of reports and written documents that were produced and collected during the Inquiry's fifteen months of existence prior to the peace conference, maps were recognized as highly essential products of its work. Few reports describing proposed boundary lines, distribution of minerals or populations, military topography, or for that matter any feature capable of geographical representation could be considered complete without illustrative maps. Just as the Inquiry attempted global coverage with its written reports, so also were its cartographic materials worldwide in scope. The inventory of cartographic records produced by the Inquiry in the National Archives, which contains only a portion of the total output, numbers 1,150 maps, and the complete collection may easily have exceeded 3,000 maps. Of the 1,150 maps, 509 are unclassified; 463 deal with the continent of Europe; 78 relate to Africa; 77 describe Asia and the Pacific Islands; and 23 pertain to the Americas.[1] The need for cartographic facilities might have exercised a decisive influence upon the selection of the American Geographical Society as the headquarters for the Inquiry's operations.

One year before the outbreak of war, a conference of cartographers representing thirty-five countries convened in Paris. Among the resolutions adopted at the conference was one favor-

1. National Archives, "Preliminary Inventories Number 68," Cartographic Records of the American Commission to Negotiate Peace, compiled by James B. Rhoads.

ing the production of maps of the world on a scale of 1:1,000,000. Each nation represented was to assume responsibility for sheets depicting its physiography. The United States, however, being the one country in the Western Hemisphere possessing complete cartographic facilities, was urged to assume responsibility for Latin America as well.[2] When war came in 1914, only eight European sheets had been completed: two for Britain, two for France, and one each for Italy, Hungary, Spain, and Turkey. During the war the Allied governments felt the need for an accurate general map of Europe corresponding to the International Millionth Map (as the map 1:1,000,000 came to be called), and the Royal Geographical Society started compiling information under the direction of the General Staff of the British Army for a series of European sheets, "the best equivalent that could be made on short notice of what the International Map would have been if it had been made."[3] In less than a year, a block of seventy-nine sheets had been completed for Europe, excepting Spain and Portugal, north to the 60th parallel and east to the 60th meridian, a block diagram for southwestern Asia, and several sheets for Africa. Although these sheets did not always conform precisely to the Millionth Map's specifications, they did provide a base map for postwar deliberations on a standard scale and format.

Isaiah Bowman, who ultimately supervised the cartographic operations of the Inquiry,[4] had since 1915 been director of the American Geographical Society, the center for cartographic work in the United States. Bowman's training, experience, and central interest had led him toward cartography and toward Latin American studies in particular. He had already expressed dissatisfaction in 1917 with "the disorderly state of even the best collections in the field of Latin American cartography,"[5] and in 1917–18 was considering the production of International Millionth Map sheets for Latin America.

2. John K. Wright, *Geography in the Making: The American Geographical Society 1851–1951* (New York, 1952), pp. 301–02.

3. "The Map of Hispanic America on the Scale of 1:1,000,000," *Geographical Review*, 36 (1946), 1–28.

4. Report on the Inquiry, May 10, 1918, *Foreign Relations of the United States, Paris Peace Conference 1919* (hereafter referred to as *FRPPC*), 1, 94.

5. Wright, op. cit., pp. 301–02.

No American geographer had shown greater enthusiasm for the Millionth Map idea than had Isaiah Bowman. Both as director of the American Geographical Society and as supervisor of cartographic work for the Inquiry, Bowman worked hard to push the idea in the United States. Insofar as the Inquiry was concerned, its Progress Report dated May 10, 1918, listed several maps then in process of completion with scales varying from 1:250,000 for Alsace-Lorraine to 1:26,000,000 for Africa. There were six areas to be represented on the so-called Millionth Map sheets: Poland, Western Russia, Egypt, Rumania, Macedonia, and the Baltic provinces. In addition, the report expressed an intent to reproduce twenty-five sets of the Millionth Map sheets already completed by the British and French governments. With these sheets, the Inquiry planned "to put all data which might be used as evidence at the [Peace] Conference upon Millionth Maps." Using the same scale, the American, British, and French maps could then be used interchangeably for the introduction of proposed boundaries or indeed for any other data as well.[6]

The map needs were discussed in mid-August 1918 by the Research Committee of the Inquiry. It was decided then that the serious shortage of "source maps" be filled from the collection of the American Geographical Society. One hundred sets of the International Millionth Map sheets were to be ordered. At the same time, a general map of Europe on the scale of 1:2,000,000 was to be prepared for the purposes of current research and, possibly, later use at the peace conference. The Committee recognized two distinct phases in the map program's development: (1) reliance on base maps for the recording of many kinds of data; (2) the atlas stage, at which time maps could be prepared in quantity for the conference itself.[7] Although maps of various scales were produced for specific needs, the Inquiry's base maps capable of showing a variety of data proved to be the most popular. There were base maps prepared or collected for every major area of the world, showing mineral deposits, forestation, agricultural use, population density, and even literacy rates, employment data, in-

6. Report on the Inquiry, May 10, 1918, *FRPPC*, *1*, 95.

7. Minutes of the Meeting of the Research Committee, Aug. 13–14, 1918, House Inquiry MSS, file 33-118, Yale.

dustrial development, communication lines, as well as the more conventional political data.[8] At all times the Inquiry strove to purchase or otherwise obtain suitable maps rather than draft maps itself.

Though cartographic records were fast approaching a global coverage during 1918, the Inquiry's expenditure of energies on maps for Latin America lent an unusual note to the preparations for peace. The cartographic project and Latin American studies were rather intimately associated in the Inquiry's organization. Both projects drew their staffs to a large extent from the American Geographical Society; both were collecting materials for use on the Millionth Map. Sidney Mezes explained in 1921 the reasons why the Inquiry started a program of Latin American studies during the final seven months of the war:

> Would South American questions be dealt with by the [Peace] Conference? It seemed improbable, but was not impossible, and if they should be included in the Settlement, the United States would be expected to take a leading part in their consideration. A careful study was therefore made of all South American boundary disputes, of South American history, and of the land, the people and the economic resources and organization of South America. None of this material was used at the Peace Conference though it has been and will be of value to the Department of State.[9]

The possibility always existed of South American questions being raised at the conference, and the United States would naturally assume an influential role in deciding their solution. But Mezes did not give any reason for the thoroughgoing fashion with which the Inquiry attempted to deal with Latin America. He did not make comprehensible the reason behind the disproportionately high budget allowed for Latin American research in comparison to funds made available for the Inquiry's studies of Europe, Asia, and Africa. Nor did he explain satisfactorily why the Inquiry should have been interested in a study entitled, "Preliminary Re-

8. National Archives, "Preliminary Inventories No. 68," Cartographic Records, compiled by J. B. Rhoads.

9. Sidney E. Mezes, "The Inquiry," in *What Really Happened at Paris*, ed. Edward M. House and Charles Seymour (New York, 1921), pp. 3–4.

sults of Geographic Positions and Magnetic Observations in South America," or a study entitled, "The Distribution of Rainfall along the Honduras-Guatemala Boundary Line and its Immediate Vicinity," or another on "The Gold Regions of the Strait of Magellan and Tierra del Fuego." [10]

Certainly the liberal allocation of Inquiry funds and personnel for Latin American projects during wartime by an organization ostensibly responsible for studying the prospects and bases for peace, at a time when other pressing studies were still not completed, requires explanation. The Inquiry's excursion into Latin American studies was not hastily begun, or at least was as well (or poorly) planned as any other phase of the preparations for peace. There is evidence to support the view that the Latin American project received the benefit of more extensive planning than did any other area considered by the Inquiry. Perhaps no other section of the Inquiry was as closely coordinated with the State Department and with other government bureaus as was the Latin American Division.

During Bowman's tenure at the American Geographical Society from 1915–35, approximately 60 per cent of all money made available for research, publication, and salaries went into Latin American projects.[11] His associate, Gladys Wrigley, recalled in 1951, "The inspiration for many of these publications came from Mr. Bowman himself, for example the contributions in the Latin American field." She then proceeded to enumerate several studies executed by Mark Jefferson in 1918 pertaining to climate and human settlement in Chile and Argentina, and those by George McBride of land use in Bolivia, Chile, and Mexico.[12] Both Mark Jefferson and George McBride were working in the Latin American Division of the Inquiry during 1918.

Bowman himself identified the Inquiry's work so completely

10. Listed in National Archives, "Preliminary Inventories No. 89," Records of the American Commission to Negotiate Peace, compiled by H. Stephen Helton, pp. 66–71. For a consideration of the Inquiry's budget for Latin American studies, see supra, p. 102; for its allocation of personnel for Latin American studies, see supra, p. 66.

11. Wright, op. cit., p. 242.

12. Gladys Wrigley, "Isaiah Bowman," Geographical Review, 41 (1951), 7–65.

with that of the Geographical Society that he tended to think of the former as a subordinate auxiliary of the latter. In a leaflet distributed by the Society in 1918, reference was made to the unprecedented amount of energy poured into the preparation of maps by the Society, "augmented by government aid during the war." [13] In the preface to his book, *The New World,* published in 1921, Bowman mentioned the Inquiry in these terms:

> I wish also to record my great obligation to former members of the Commission of Inquiry, an exceptionally able group of scholars, who cooperated with the American Geographical Society in forming an organization which had for its object the systematic collection of data for the use of the American government . . . [14]

The Annual Report of the American Geographical Society for 1920 announced the purpose of the Society's Hispanic-American program. The resemblance between the Geographical Society's tasks and those of the Latin American Division of the Inquiry is too strong for coincidence. The Annual Report said, in part:

> The first step in the development of the program aims at the review and classification of all available scientific data of a geographical nature that pertain to Hispanic America. Topographical data of all kinds, climatic facts and population statistics are of first importance. Account is taken of everything in man's physical environment that affects his distribution, his activities and his economic welfare . . . The work will involve the compilation of maps—topographical and distributional—on various scales; but always including sheets on the scale of 1:1,000,000 which will conform to the scheme of the International Map. It further includes the production of complete distributional maps of Hispanic America dealing with soil, vegetation and land classification. [15]

The Inquiry's plans and entire project for Latin America so closely corresponded to the American Geographical Society's program that it is difficult to dismiss lightly Bowman's possible interest in exploiting the Inquiry's funds and organization for the purpose of furthering his special interest in Latin American research.

13. Ibid., p. 200.
14. Isaiah Bowman, *The New World: Problems in Political Geography* (New York, 1921), p. vi.
15. John Greenough, "Report of January 20, 1921," *Geographical Review, 11* (1921), 292–93.

In November 1917, the earliest portent of Latin American studies for the Inquiry was indicated. James T. Shotwell expressed the hope that David Kinley (then Dean of the Graduate School, University of Illinois) would be kept in mind for "some work connected with Latin America." "He is very keen to do something and I think he would work in very well if the field were delineated so that he might work to advantage." [16] Less than a month later, Shotwell strongly recommended Clarence H. Haring of Yale who "would be a valuable researcher in our work especially in the field of recent colonial and commercial developments bearing upon South America. He reads Spanish, French and German sources freely. He is a young and energetic worker and I think would offer very valuable assistance." [17] But at the time Haring would not accept a part-time job, and there was as yet no regular full-time berth in which he could fit.[18] David Kinley was somewhat more disposed to join the Inquiry task force. At the end of December 1917, he even proposed for study by the Inquiry some ominous international questions which were threatening the peace in Latin America. These were:

1. The controversy between Argentina and Uruguay over the control of the River Platte.
2. The quarrel between Bolivia and Chile over the province of Autofagaster.
3. The controversy between Argentina and Great Britain over the ownership of the Falkland Islands.
4. The quarrel between Chile and Peru over the future of the Tacna-Arica provinces.

In Kinley's view, what was needed most was a study of possible causes of conflict in Latin America, presumably so that the eventual peace treaty could eliminate them. German economic penetration in Latin America was yet another problem which the Inquiry might study profitably. Yet, Kinley cautioned, nothing of great practical consequence could be produced unless special agents were sent to the regions specified for the purpose of procuring accurate information.[19] Already, the Carnegie Endowment for

16. Shotwell to A. A. Young, Nov. 22, 1917, Inquiry Archives.
17. Shotwell to Mezes, Dec. 17, 1917, Inquiry Archives.
18. C. H. Haring to Shotwell, Dec. 19, 1917, Inquiry Archives.
19. David Kinley to A. A. Young, Dec. 31, 1917, Shotwell MSS, Columbia.

International Peace was studying some of the Latin American questions. There were good prospects of Kinley being sent to Latin America under the auspices of the Carnegie Endowment, in which case he could act for the Inquiry as well.[20]

In spite of the correspondence during December 1917, Kinley was still left in the dark about the organization which had requested his services. At the end of January 1918 he wrote to A. A. Young of the Inquiry:

> I have given considerable thought to your suggestion about a South American trip. . . . [It] will be rather difficult because of the multitude of duties I have gotten into here. However, before reaching a decision, I would like very much to know something more about what you want done. Is it your idea that I should make a study of some of the questions . . . [or] is it your idea that I make an effort in South America to get representatives of the various governments together in an informal way. . . .
>
> Finally, simply because I feel the need of getting the right point of view . . . may I without seeming impertinent, ask who are the "members of the group" with whom you are associated, and who are charged with the general oversight of this highly important matter?[21]

Young promptly turned the matter over to Mezes, and no further action was taken for the next four months. At last, on April 12, Mezes informed Young that there was really no point in Kinley going to Latin America on behalf of the Inquiry. Between the Inquiry and the State Department, Mezes announced, there were already sufficient materials pertaining to Latin America.[22] Meanwhile, Young had begun in March to survey the extent to which Britain or some other belligerent was controlling important raw materials in Latin America. This work was actually intended to be performed by the Bureau of Foreign and Domestic Commerce. As Young wrote to Julius Klein, chief of that Bureau:

> We are not interested in the whole range of commodities but merely in the most important raw materials. For Latin America these would be wool, sisal, nitrates, copper, tin, manganese and

20. Young to Mezes, Jan. 4, 1918; Mezes to Young, Jan. 7, 1918, Inquiry Archives.

21. Kinley to A. A. Young, Jan. 30, 1918, Inquiry Archives.

22. Mezes to Young, April 12, 1918, Inquiry Archives.

other ferre alloys, hides and skins, and rubber. Any memoranda that you can send me with respect to the extent and degree of any national control that may have been created with regard to any of these will be greatly appreciated. Do not make this an exhaustive research, but send me what you can within a few days.[23]

In their preliminary planning up to April 1918, the officers of the Inquiry had suggested only Latin American topics whose immediacy for the coming peace settlement could legitimately be established. As to personnel, Charles Haskins, Archibald Cary Coolidge, and Julius Klein (of the Department of Commerce) agreed in April 1918 that W. S. Robertson of the University of Illinois was best qualified for the work. Other names were also mentioned: Percy Martin of Stanford, G. B. Roorback of the University of Pennsylvania, Dana G. Munro of Princeton, and Herman Jones of the University of Texas.[24] In the end, the chief of the Latin American Division was selected by Isaiah Bowman. Instead of choosing a scholar experienced in Latin American politics or history or economic problems, Bowman chose Bailey Willis, a geologist on the staff of Stanford University.[25]

Bowman not only exerted the dominant influence on the selection of personnel to work on the Latin American Inquiry; it can likewise be presumed that by the beginning of May his influence on planning the work was also dominant. But Bowman's voice was never solo. When Latin American studies were started in earnest during May 1918, the program was submitted to the State Department for clearance. So dependent was the Latin American work upon the State Department's support that Walter Lippmann told Jordan H. Stabler, chief of the Latin American Division of the State Department, "It is of fundamental importance that we should have your criticisms, suggestions, and directions at the outset." [26] Throughout the remainder of 1918, the Latin American

---

23. Young to Julius Klein, March 28, 1918, Inquiry Archives.

24. Mentioned in Lester Rowe, Assistant Secretary of the Treasury, to Walter Lippmann, April 23, 1918, Inquiry Archives.

25. Bowman to Bailey Willis, May 8, 1918, Inquiry Archives.

26. Walter Lippmann to Jordan H. Stabler, April 24, 1918, Inquiry Archives. The intimate relationship between the Inquiry's Latin American project and the Department of State can also be documented in Lansing to Mezes, April 17,

projects were intimately associated with the work of the State Department. At the end of May, Stabler returned to Washington from a visit with the Inquiry's officers in New York and wrote to Lippmann lauding the Inquiry's plans and adding certain suggestions: "I cannot express strongly enough my admiration of the way you have planned your campaign and I have been dreaming of the maps ever since I got back." [27] And to Isaiah Bowman, Stabler wrote with equal enthusiasm, "I think you have a most extraordinary organization, and of course your maps have made me think of nothing else." [28] By way of response, Bowman expressed satisfaction "that we can do something useful for the Department of State . . . and . . . we hope that out of the work we are doing there will grow results of permanent value to your Department." [29]

At frequent intervals, Stabler consulted with Bowman regarding the choice of personnel for work on specific Latin American topics.[30] Upon occasion the State Department's approval was necessary in order for the prospective staff member to obtain a leave of absence from his particular institution.[31] At other times the State Department turned over to Bowman or to Bailey Willis documents relevant to the Latin American research or even planned the specific reports desired as was the case with materials bearing on the boundary dispute between Honduras and Nicaragua.[32] When the Inquiry's reports were completed, they were frequently submitted for approval to Stabler's Division.[33] Leaders of the Inquiry often referred to the Latin American

1918; Mezes to Lansing, April 22, 1918; Lansing to President Wilson, April 24, 1918, all in *FRPPC, 1,* 76–82. These documents show clearly that the plans for Latin American studies were approved by the State Department before May 1, 1918.

27. Stabler to Lippmann, May 25, 1918, Inquiry Archives.

28. Stabler to Bowman, May 25, 1918, Inquiry Archives.

29. Bowman to Stabler, May 28, 1918, Inquiry Archives.

30. Bowman to Stabler, June 3, 1918, and June 24, 1918; Mezes to Stabler, July 24, 1918, Inquiry Archives.

31. Bowman to Mezes, June 17, 1918, Inquiry Archives.

32. Bowman to Stabler, June 25, 1918; Bailey Willis to Glenn Stewart, chief of Central American Affairs, Latin American Division, State Department, Aug. 15, 1918; Ferdinand Maye, State Department aide, to Mezes, June 13, 1918, Inquiry Archives.

33. Bailey Willis to Stabler, Aug. 8, 1918, Inquiry Archives.

studies as being directed by the State Department. This connection was customarily made in order to obtain the cooperation of a private organization which might not be familiar with the name, "the Inquiry." Or the affiliation was exploited in order to obtain a recommendation for some prospective staff member or a leave of absence from some institution for a desired staff member.[34] But in a letter written in October 1918 Bailey Willis expressed in somewhat stronger terms the connection between the Inquiry's Latin American work and the State Department. The letter in question was written to Ray Lyman Wilbur, president of Stanford University:

> The Latin American Division is regarded by the Directors of the Inquiry and also by those officials of the State Department who are familiar with its work as an essential research auxiliary of the State Department. Its value in the settlement of boundary disputes now submitted to our government for mediation has been conclusively demonstrated. It is hoped, therefore, that even after the peace conference, the Division may go on in some form under the auspices of the State Department as a research organization.[35]

Although the State Department was more intimately connected with the Inquiry's Latin American Division than were other agencies of government, a large number of government bureaus did cooperate in the work. Topics dealing with petroleum resources were turned over to the United States Geological Survey.[36] In answer to a question from its chief, George Smith, on the scope of the report desired by the Inquiry, Bowman informed the Geological Survey that, for the Inquiry's purposes, Latin America meant all of the area "from the Rio Grande to Patagonia including the West Indies. This will doubtless prolong the work past the time which you had set, but that seems the wisest course to pursue, and we shall therefore hope that you can undertake the entire program." [37]

34. Bailey Willis to P. A. Martin, professor at the University of California, July 29, 1918; Bailey Willis to Ralph Arnold, May 27, 1918, Inquiry Archives.

35. Bailey Willis to Ray Lyman Wilbur, Oct. 15, 1918, Inquiry Archives.

36. Bowman to George Smith, chief of the Geological Survey, May 28, 1918; Smith to Bowman, June 4, 1918, Inquiry Archives.

37. Bowman to Smith, June 6, 1918; Smith to Bowman, June 8, 1918, Inquiry Archives.

The Inquiry also received the benefit of agricultural studies performed by the Office of Farm Management of the Department of Agriculture. These studies had to do with the geographical distribution of crops and livestock in South America, systems of land tenure plus whatever else the Inquiry desired in the way of agricultural studies.[38] Julius Klein of the Bureau of Foreign and Domestic Commerce likewise made available to the Inquiry the services of his staff for studies of Latin American trade.[39] Meteorological data were processed and reported directly by the United States Weather Bureau.[40] By the summer of 1918 so much of the Inquiry's Latin American work was being delegated to appropriate agencies in Washington that it was thought proper and necessary to appoint a special liaison man to be on hand in the capital to coordinate the work. It was finally decided that Lincoln Hutchinson, professor of economics at the University of California, be appointed special agent of the State Department *and* of the Commerce Department to coordinate Latin American research for the Inquiry.[41] Before the end of June 1918, seven government bureaus had agreed to cooperate in this endeavor:

1. Division of Latin American Affairs, Department of State
2. Latin American Division, Department of Commerce
3. Bureau of Soils
4. Bureau of Plant Industry
5. Office of Farm Management
6. United States Forest Service
7. United States Geological Survey.[42]

In New York, the headquarters of the Latin American Division was located in the School of Architecture (Avery Hall), Columbia University. Here advantage was taken of the drafting rooms and equipment for the construction of the many maps.[43] It was in

38. O. E. Baker to Bailey Willis, June 6, 1918, Inquiry Archives.

39. Klein to Bowman, June 27, 1918, Inquiry Archives.

40. C. F. Marvin, chief of the United States Weather Bureau, to Bailey Willis, Aug. 3, 1918, Inquiry Archives.

41. Julius Klein to Bowman, June 27, 1918; Bowman to Klein, July 5, 1918, Inquiry Archives. Anderson advised Hutchinson to accept the position: Chandler Anderson MSS Diary, June 28, 1918, Library of Congress.

42. Bowman to House, June 22, 1918, House Inquiry MSS, file, 33-137, Yale.

43. Bailey Willis to W. H. Carpenter, acting director of the School of Architecture, Columbia University, Sept. 20, 1918, Inquiry Archives.

New York that the officers of the Inquiry developed their plans for the Latin American research. The first master plan had taken shape in April 1918 and divided the proposed work into nineteen categories as follows:

1. Natural resources of all kinds
2. Foreign concessions and investments
3. Foreign loans
4. Export trade
5. Import trade
6. European colonies and settlements
7. Areas colonizable by Europeans, by Asiatics
8. Territorial disputes
9. Domestic political groups
10. Budget analyses and tax systems
11. Commercial possibilities in relation to European needs
12. American assets and liabilities in each state
13. Exact account of participation by each state in the war, including any damages suffered
14. Government organization in each country
15. Electoral processes
16. Islands of the Americas
17. Ethnography, population distribution, and demography
18. History
19. International law and lawyers.[44]

What relationship most of these topics had to the eventual peace settlement is not quite clear.

By June, Bowman had made various modifications. All of Latin America was to be projected on maps with the scale 1:2,000,000, twenty-six sheets in all. Additional maps would show hypsometric data, rainfall, vegetation and forests, grazing industries, population, and ethnography. Detailed research would concentrate on the land problems of Latin America and upon international boundary disputes.[45] Two weeks later, on June 22, 1918, Bowman revealed to Colonel House his intention to concentrate on the Guatemalan-Honduras boundary controversy. But insofar as the other projects were concerned, Bowman must have felt that some more elaborate explanation was called for. He informed House

44. Outline for South American Studies, n.d., Mezes MSS, Columbia. Enclosure in Letter, Mezes to Secretary Lansing, April 22, 1918 in *FRPPC, 1,* 77–81.
45. Bowman to House, June 6, 1918, House Inquiry MSS, file 33-127, Yale.

that research on soils was being carried forward by the Inquiry and its auxiliaries "in order that the soil assets of any country may be known at the Peace Conference just as we propose to know forests and minerals." And he continued in a didactic tone:

> We take soil as a matter of course. In reality it is the real basis of human life and the most nearly permanent resource known. In the case of ceded territory the soil value is in the long run more important to the people than forests and minerals.[46]

But land, soils, weather, minerals, vegetation, and agriculture did not exhaust the Inquiry's plans for Latin American studies. Historical research was designed to trace a wide number of social questions to the very beginnings of colonization. Bailey Willis spelled out the Inquiry's intentions in this way:

> In general, our historical studies will be directed to the development of the colonial possessions of Spain, especially insofar as they determine the dominions of different countries at the time of Independence. South American boundary disputes, which we are called upon to consider, surely go back to the boundaries of the Intendancies and back of that to the Audiencias and it is important that we should be able to follow these out in detail. In so doing, a study of church records is often a matter of material interest.
>
> Another line of historical investigation is the origin of the European peoples who have gone into the different parts of South America and the evolution of the human race that we know as Latin American. This involves tracing the lines of immigration, studying the background of European history and developing an understanding of the peoples in South America. I feel sure that your knowledge of the psychology of the Spanish peoples will be particularly valuable in this connection.[47]

Again, it seems almost preposterous that such historical questions as the evolution of the Latin American "race" could be considered fitting material for an organization seeking to gather studies in preparation for the peace settlement.

If Isaiah Bowman had been instrumental in supporting so elaborate a program of Latin American studies, the program must also have been approved at various stages by Colonel House and by

46. Bowman to House, June 22, 1918, House Inquiry MSS, file 33-137, Yale.
47. Bailey Willis to A. M. Espinosa, professor at Stanford University, Aug. 22, 1918, Inquiry Archives.

Jordan Stabler of the State Department. It is most surprising that no real opposition developed within the Inquiry itself toward the extensive treatment of Latin American subjects when the primary responsibilities for which the Inquiry had been established had not yet been discharged. But the abundant correspondence in the Inquiry archives fails to show that even a mild protest was raised. Only at one point was there any likelihood of serious danger to the elaborate program of Latin American studies. In late July 1918, when the crisis between Bowman and Mezes had erupted, Mezes announced that henceforth Latin American studies were to have the lowest priority on the Inquiry's schedule; "that the work in Europe, Asia, and Africa should take precedence over that in Latin America . . ." [48] Yet there is no reason to believe that this directive resulted in the reorganization of the Inquiry. Had this issue been a major cause for disagreement between Mezes and Bowman, surely the matter would have been reflected in correspondence and in the volumes of memoirs subsequently published. Neither the correspondence nor the memoirs gives any hint of controversy over the validity of the Latin American Division's work. Once Bowman gathered the organization's reins tightly in his hands during August 1918, there was no slackening of effort among the Inquiry's Latin American staff. In fact, the work actually proceeded with a decided spurt.

Of the almost 300 reports and documents pertaining to Latin America which found their way into the National Archives after the peace conference, many dealt with international boundaries and quite a few related Latin America to the war. But what provides as much interest is the number of reports concerned with trade, mineral production, navigation, climate, agriculture, and industry. The emphasis placed on economic matters reflected in the Argentine materials might be described as typical of this emphasis, as shown in the following table:

No. of Reports	The Argentine—Subjects
4	The Territorial Waters of the Estuary of La Plata.
3	Boundaries of the Argentine Confederation.
2	Boundaries between Argentina and Uruguay.
7	Argentine commerce.

48. Bailey Willis to E. O. Baker, July 26, 1918, Inquiry Archives.

287

No. of Reports	The Argentine—Subjects
1	General Argentine economic conditions.
1	Argentina and the War.
5	Documents (mostly treaties).
4	The Argentine merchant marine.
3	Argentine wool production and processing.
1	The Island of Martin Garcia.
1	Minerals.
2	Agricultural commodities.
1	Cattle grazing.
1	Argentine steel production.[49]

Few of these reports related directly or for that matter indirectly to the peace settlement. The reports may have proven useful to the State Department in later years; the copies which remained with the American Geographical Society may have been used in the production of maps, such as the Millionth Map, which was brought to completion in the postwar years.[50]

After the armistice, during November and December 1918, the question arose of what should be done about that part of the Latin American program which was still in progress. None of the workers intimately associated with this project (except Bowman, of course) was taken to the peace conference. Bailey Willis, who remained in New York, was quite sure that the Inquiry's program of Latin American studies would be encouraged and allowed to continue in Washington.[51] Harriet Church, assistant to David Hunter Miller who had charge of the financial records, appealed to Miller, then in Paris, for a decision as to whether the Latin American Division could continue after the account books were

49. National Archives, "Preliminary Inventories No. 89," Records of the American Commission to Negotiate Peace, compiled by H. Stephen Helton, pp. 68, 171–74.

50. When the author visited the American Geographical Society in the summer of 1951, he found a vast collection of Inquiry reports being stored in the basement of the building. Whether these reports were used or not has as yet not been determined. John K. Wright, historian of the American Geographical Society, informed the author in the fall of 1955 that W. A. Briesemeister, who as a young man had been a cartographer with the Inquiry, later expressed the opinion that the Inquiry's studies of Latin America actually marked the beginnings of the Society's Millionth Map program.

51. Harriet Church to David Hunter Miller, Dec. 21, 1918, House Inquiry MSS, file 33-144, Yale. Mark Jefferson directed cartographic work at Paris.

closed for other divisions of the Inquiry on January 31, 1919. Apparently Miller consulted with other leaders of the American Commission, for he notified Harriet Church that the Latin American Inquiry would have to drop the curtain and close its books as of January 31.[52]

Thus came to an end the strange excursion of the Inquiry into Latin American studies. After all the effort and appropriations used by the division, no recommendations or proposed policies emerged as had been the case with the European, African, Asian, and Pacific Island divisions. At least with the benefit of hindsight it would appear that the considerable attention devoted to Latin American affairs was not warranted in an organization dedicated to the task of preparing American policy at the peace conference. Perhaps when the Isaiah Bowman Papers, presently locked up at the Johns Hopkins University Library, are made available to students in 1975, many of the puzzling questions and motives concerning the Latin American project, about which speculation still continues, will fit snugly into place.

52. Inquiry Account Books, David Hunter Miller MSS, Library of Congress. Some $1600 was authorized for the use of Bailey Willis after January 31, 1919, when the Inquiry Account Books closed. Authorization was provided in Telegram AMMISSION to Frank Polk, Acting Secretary of State, Jan. 28, 1919: "The expenditure of sixteen hundred dollars referred to by Dr. Bailey Willis for purposes stated is authorized and approved by the President." Archives of the American Commission to Negotiate Peace, file 184.83/17, National Archives.

Chapter 10

ECONOMIC PROBLEMS AND
INTERNATIONAL LAW

CONTRARY TO A VIEW given credence by John Maynard Keynes in his *Economic Consequences of the Peace*, Woodrow Wilson *did*, when he arrived at the peace conference, have "plans . . . schemes . . . [and] constructive ideas . . . for clothing with the flesh of life the commandments which he had thundered from the White House." [1] Not always distinguished or even scholarly, the Inquiry's reports dealt with a multifarious assortment of problems. Plans, schemes, and ideas there were in all sizes, shapes, and forms. Even Keynes' special bailiwick, economics, was not ignored in the shuffle of planning for the peace settlement. Similarly, some elaborate studies had been undertaken on the problems of international law which seemed likely to arise, and any review of the Inquiry's labors would not be complete without calling attention to its concern for international organization, the crowning panacea of the Fourteen Points.

Economic studies ranged over a broad front. Slightly more than 700 reports and documents falling within some category of economics were produced or collected. These reports, including both economic studies of a given area or country and studies unclassified by region, represented almost 40 per cent of the total mate-

1. John Maynard Keynes, *Economic Consequences of the Peace* (New York, 1920), pp. 42–45.

290

rials prepared in advance of the peace conference.[2] It is difficult to convey an adequate impression of the many topics considered in this aggregation of reports, but perhaps the magnitude of the whole can be indicated through one of the important parts. The economic studies of Germany were divided among the following topics: [3]

Subject	No. of Reports	Subject	No. of Reports
Trade and tariffs	18	Nonmineral resources and	
Economic and financial		commodities	6
conditions	16	Industry	8
Money and banking	5	Technological	
German plans for		development	1
reconstruction	3	Shipping	6
Mineral resources	9	Cattle and livestock	1
		Miscellaneous	7

Although the subjects considered for other areas did not always correspond precisely with those selected for the German projects, the latter could be regarded as generally representative. Included within the 700 economic studies, however, were 153 reports having to do with economic conditions within the United States.

To obtain the materials for the reports, the Inquiry relied for the most part on technical specialists employed in other government bureaus. A. A. Young, chief economist for the Inquiry, endeavored to coordinate and direct these reports, but no one individual could be responsible for such a vast array of economic studies. Almost every wartime agency, in addition to the regular departments of government, contributed to the files. Extensive subcontracting was the rule rather than the exception; in fact, only about 6 per cent of the total number of reports were produced by Inquiry members. Young once attempted to justify the

2. National Archives, "Preliminary Inventories No. 89," ed. H. Stephen Helton. Appendix X infra contains a list of the reports in economics, showing the various subjects treated and the number of reports per subject. These 700 reports include economic studies of specific countries and regions in addition to the reports unclassifiable by specific geographic region.

3. Ibid.

practice of assigning reports to other government bureaus. In a letter to H. Parker Willis of the Federal Reserve Board, he wrote:

> In general I may explain that the Inquiry is working on the assumption that its function is merely to see that the right sort of researches are made, and that it realizes that the researches themselves have to be undertaken in most cases by the organizations which have these matters in hand, and which, it is reasonable to expect, will be called upon to furnish advisers to the American conferees on the problems in their respective fields.[4]

Perhaps because of this practice, the economic reports reflected a great variety of viewpoints, interpretations, and conclusions.

Studies considering mineral production were made by geologists attached to the United States Geological Survey. Beginning in February 1918, the Geological Survey designated certain specialists to begin systematic work compiling mineral data for use at the peace conference. Joseph B. Umpleby, assistant chief of the Section of Metalliferous Deposits and also chief of the Section of Foreign Mineral Deposits, was placed in charge of this operation. All together, Umpleby's staff consisted of twelve specialists in addition to the usual drafting, clerical, and stenographic assistants. This staff divided its work into seven principal categories: (1) the distribution and extent of mineral deposits throughout the world; (2) the sources of mining districts for current and prewar mineral production; (3) the location of mineral resources in areas of proximity to national boundaries; (4) the contribution of mineral resources in disputed areas to the ability of the enemy countries to pay indemnities; (5) the probable future smelting and related industries of Germany in view of the loss of Alsace-Lorraine and Upper Silesia; (6) the relation of French iron ore supplies to French coal resources and consequent requirements of coal from Germany; (7) questions involving the mineral consumption of industrial and maritime countries and changes brought about by the war.[5] This geological work proceeded without pause even after the cessation of military hostilities. Umpleby himself was transferred to Paris in April 1919, taking with him copies of the geological studies.[6]

4. A. A. Young to H. Parker Willis, Oct. 26, 1918, Inquiry Archives.
5. Joseph Umpleby MSS, file II, University of Washington.
6. Ibid.

One example taken from the research on minerals might suggest how the investigations were conducted. Eleanora F. Bliss had been assigned to report on the consumption of the most important mineral commodities in the seven largest countries of Europe and in the United States. These countries, she wrote, consumed 80 per cent of the world's output of coal and 94 per cent of the iron ore. For all the commodities discussed (antimony, chrome ore, coal, copper, iron ore, lead, manganese ore, nickel, phosphate rock, platinum, pyrites, sulphur, tin, tungsten ore, and zinc), except for pyrite, manganese, and tungsten, the United States was the largest consuming nation. As each mineral was considered, statistics recording the consumption of each nation in proportion to the world's production were collected, with 1913 being used as the base year. A clear attempt was made to show the various sources of each mineral on which the respective consuming nations depended. Smelting capacity, industrial consumption, and the relative importance of countries as producers were items covered in the supporting statistical tables.[7] The studies rarely included any practical proposals or recommendations. They did pretend to be authoritative and accurate guides to the pertinent facts.

A. A. Young turned over numerous financial assignments to the Treasury Department and to the Federal Reserve Board. The latter's responsibilities were to include a consideration of the financial reserves and credit conditions for Belgium, Poland, the Balkans, and Turkey with reference to German Treasury obligations. As one possibility, Young urged that the assets of the Reichsbank or of the German Treasury be placed under international trusteeship until international credit arrangements were clarified. There were also problems arising from the many wartime restrictions on the international movement of gold. When these restrictions were later lifted, "will it be necessary to safeguard our [United States] interests . . . in this particular?" Gold reserves and their redistribution after the war posed a disturbing problem which Young invited the Federal Reserve Board to study. By the end of October 1918, H. Parker Willis could report that all such prob-

7. Eleanora F. Bliss, "A Study of the Consumption of the Most Important Mineral Commodities in Europe and the United States," Umpleby MSS, file I, University of Washington.

lems were receiving attention and were in the process of being studied by staff members on the Board.[8]

Only eighteen of the eighty economic reports for Germany were concerned with international trade. Early in the Inquiry's existence, Sidney Mezes and David Hunter Miller circulated certain proposals on the subject of economic penetration, a subject important enough to be classed as the "chief cause of international friction in the last two generations." [9] The term "economic penetration" was defined to mean domination of the "great powers" over alien populations, the development of spheres of influence in Asia, Africa, and even the Americas with the accompanying imperialistic competition for the spoils. To correct these abuses, the two Inquiry officers urged the establishment of stable, efficient governments in the "penetrable areas." More practical and realistic was their suggestion for the universal application of the Open Door policy, and some greater measure of protection against the dumping practices followed by various trading companies. As long as some governments adhered to the practice of supporting their merchants in foreign lands, the memorandum advised, unilateral action to reverse this trend would be utterly worthless. The peace conference was expected to correct the most serious abuses in international commercial activity, for aggressive or at least unrestrained commercial policies could undermine the future peace.

Regulation of international trading policies was the most important single recommendation of the preparatory studies on postwar trade. Frank Taussig of the Tariff Commission contributed a memorandum dealing with the commercial aspects of the settlement in which he opposed any retaliatory or punitive measures by the victorious governments. Under no circumstances should the United States favor or oppose any particular trading policy, whether free trade or protectionist. Instead, American policy must lean heavily on the principle that every sovereign nation possessed the right to decide its own commercial policies free from external interference, with the sovereign authority extending to include its colonies as well. The United States should strive to attain most-

8. H. Parker Willis to A. A. Young, Oct. 30, 1918, Inquiry Archives.
9. Miller-Mezes Memorandum on Economic Penetration, Dec. 27, 1917, Miller MSS, Library of Congress.

favored-nation status in its commercial relations with all countries. Taussig, like Mezes and Miller in their memorandum, suggested an international Open Door providing "the same terms for all" even though occasional minor exceptions (e.g., reciprocal arrangements between the United States and Cuba) must necessarily be continued.[10] Bernard Baruch, chairman of the War Industries Board, favored the placing of responsibilities for the enforcement of the Open Door with the League of Nations.[11]

Consideration of minerals, trade and finance did not preclude study of the general economic conditions in European countries after the war. Although the Inquiry and its several auxiliaries could have pursued the subject far more extensively, Germany's economic potential was not neglected entirely. Allied claims for restoration, compensation, and indemnity were being pressed. President Wilson in his Points VII and VIII had endorsed the principle of compensation and restoration for Belgium and the invaded portions of France. But there remained the difficult questions of what would constitute just compensation, on what basis would compensation be determined, and what burden would be imposed upon Germany?

David Hunter Miller's paper on the "Financial Position of Germany" looked ahead to conditions after the war for the purpose of analyzing what part Germany could undertake in reconstruction. Miller took issue with the rather widespread contention that Germany would emerge from the war in nearly bankrupt condition. He examined six indices of economic health: (1) material resources wholly undeveloped; (2) material resources in process of development; (3) internal improvements; (4) commodities available, including gold; (5) shipping; (6) foreign investments. With these measurable yardsticks, Miller went on to consider Germany's internal war indebtedness of $25,000,000,000 as well as the depletion of various resources caused by the war. The debt in itself, Miller suggested, was not indicative of economic weakness. Since labor provided "the chief ultimate . . . expense in

10. Frank L. Taussig, "Memorandum on the Policy to be Followed by the United States in International Negotiations on Commercial Policy," n.d., House Inquiry MSS, file 33-24, Yale.

11. Bernard Baruch to Woodrow Wilson, Oct. 23, 1918, Wilson MSS, Series II, Library of Congress.

war," Germany had exploited the huge reserves of prisoner-labor, forced labor in occupied Belgium, and only incidentally had it imported labor from neutral countries. But when imported labor was employed, the cost had always managed to be balanced by German exports to the same neutral countries. Finally, Miller drew a sharp distinction between the destruction of wealth per se and the prevention of the expansion of wealth. He contended that German losses in the latter category were actually slight as compared to the destruction of economic capacity in Allied countries.[12]

President Wilson's attitude toward the principle of indemnity evolved and broadened considerably during the last year of the war. In his Address to Congress of February 11, 1918, the President placed himself firmly in opposition to "annexations . . . contributions . . . [and] punitive damages" as principles to be applied in the formulation of peace.[13] This did not rule out, however, compensation to be paid "for manifest wrongs done." [14] At least in the Fourteen Points Address of January 8, 1918, and in certain subsequent statements, Wilson had made allowances for the collection of indemnities. His distinction between punitive damages and payments for manifest wrongs committed by the enemy formed the essential features of David Hunter Miller's consideration of the "American Program and International Law" completed in July 1918. In Miller's view only those losses which reflected violations of international law would justify the exaction of indemnities. Belgium would thus be entitled to full reparation because of the illegal violation of its neutrality by German

12. David Hunter Miller, "The Financial Position of Germany," n.d., no author listed on copy in the David Hunter Miller MSS, Library of Congress. According to a note in the memorandum, copies were sent to Shotwell, Lippmann, and Mezes. Attribution to Miller and the approximate date (November 1917) are based on a letter from Mezes to Miller, Nov. 27, 1917, Mezes MSS, Columbia, in which acknowledgment for the memorandum on the Financial Position of Germany is expressed.

13. Baker and Dodd, *Public Papers of Woodrow Wilson, War and Peace* (New York, 1927), *1*, 180.

14. David Hunter Miller, "The American Program and International Law," July 31, 1918, Document 13, in *Reparations at the Paris Peace Conference*, ed. Philip M. Burnett (New York, 1940), *1*, 371. The quotation is taken from President Wilson's communication to Russia, June 9, 1917, which Miller uses in his memorandum.

military forces; France, Rumania, Serbia, and Montenegro could present claims for damages by illegal action of the enemy. The sole yardstick for awarding compensation was to be the legality of the act for which compensation was asked. Miller likewise suggested that reparations-indemnities-compensation questions should not be considered by the peace conference but should instead be reserved for consideration at a special conference convened for this particular purpose.[15]

It is not known for certain which members of the Inquiry or of the State Department, if any, concurred with Miller in his analysis and recommendation. The American Commission to Negotiate Peace was to embrace a great many diverse opinions on the subject of compensations. A. A. Young in late December 1918 circulated a memorandum which suggested an "American Policy with Respect to Indemnities." [16] Young believed that indemnities should be compensatory rather than punitive. Whatever payments were to be exacted from the defeated nations should be based upon actual losses. He was amenable to having governments present and support the claims of their nationals. Personal claims would be measurable. The loss of a family's breadwinner, for instance, was to be estimated financially as far as possible, and an adequate insurance and pension system instituted. Young's principle that "actual personal compensation is the purpose as well as the measure of the indemnity" was really punitive to a degree. Germany and its allies were not to be permitted to present similar claims. At least, Young implied that only the victors would receive compensation.

In contrast with Young's emphasis on the compensatory principle as forming the desirable basis for indemnities, Secretary of State Lansing recognized in indemnities a just means for punishing those countries responsible for the outbreak of the war. Those countries "guilty of bringing on the ravages of war must compensate the victims of war." [17] Even before the armistice, Lansing favored such a course, though at the same time he recognized

15. Ibid., 363–78.

16. A. A. Young, "A Suggestion for American Policy with Respect to Indemnities," Dec. 28, 1918, Document No. 69 in ibid., 474–75.

17. Robert Lansing, Memorandum on the Subject of War Indemnities, Oct. 30, 1918, Confidential Memoranda, Lansing MSS, Library of Congress.

that Germany could not afford to pay heavy indemnities. Interest payments alone would tax all its resources, he declared. One solution to which the Secretary devoted considerable thought called for the Central Powers to repudiate their internal war debts and to devote their national incomes—or some substantial portion thereof—to indemnities. Lansing compared the defeated Central Powers to defeated revolutionaries; in neither case would financiers stand to recover loans. Furthermore, a precedent could well be recognized by which creditors investing in governments starting wars would not be paid. If no financiers could be found to place money at the disposal of aggressor states, then perhaps this precedent could contribute toward lasting peace, or in the words of Secretary Lansing, "Would not persons in the future scan closely the character of a war before investing their wealth in war securities?" In a sense Lansing was being pulled by opposing magnets: he was convinced of German war guilt and sought punitive damages; he was not certain of Germany's ability to pay substantial compensation. Possibly in the back of his mind there still lurked the specter of an economically weakened Germany falling under the heel of an even more ominous foe, Bolshevism.[18]

These were matters which had not engaged the serious attention of the Inquiry except for Miller in the months before the armistice. Questions concerning indemnities and reparations somehow remained outside the purview of the Inquiry's activities except as these matters were incidental to the consideration of other problems. With the coming of peace, various branches of government started assuming responsibilities for determining the principles of compensation and the means for their application. The Inquiry's Outline of Tentative Recommendations of January 21, 1919, devoted an entire section to economic matters, but there was no mention of indemnities, reparations, or other forms of compensation. The Inquiry's recommendations were concerned solely with problems of international trade and international labor. With respect to the former, they opposed any interference with the right of each national government to levy its own tariff schedules, thus following the proposal of Frank Taussig. At the same time, however, the Inquiry sought nondiscriminatory tariff policies

18. Supra, pp. 212–13.

which in effect would grant to all nations a most-favored-nation treatment. Tariffs would not be used as a lever for disposing of or acquiring special favors in the international community. Furthermore, the Open Door arrangement for colonies was pushed. Even with equalization of tariff treatment, a nation would still be able to discriminate, but at least this would provide "a large and definite accomplishment." [19]

A second commercial recommendation called for the abolition of preferences given by a government to the shipping of its own nationals through harbor charges and certain other discriminations. Surtaxes imposed to benefit domestic ports at the expense of foreign ports were also clearly opposed. Specifically cited as one example of this abuse was the additional duty of 10 per cent *ad valorem* levied on foreign goods imported into the United States via Canada or Mexico. An exception might be British imperial preference arrangements, toward which the Inquiry looked with benevolence. Imperial preference was "so clearly bound up with the prevailing trend of opinion in the Dominions respecting the political unity of the British Empire that the abrogation of the system is hardly a matter open for discussion." Other discriminatory trade pacts between contiguous states (Spain and Portugal, Norway and Sweden) were likewise condoned. Finally, the Inquiry went on record as favoring the establishment of an international trade commission whose responsibility it would be "to compile world trade statistics; to investigate and report upon the facts in cases of alleged violations of the agreement stabilizing equality of trade conditions."

With regard to international labor legislation, the Inquiry recognized as a logical point of departure those general agreements which were already in existence among European states. The Inquiry proposed the inclusion in the treaty of peace of the following three provisions drawn from existing agreements:

1. The prohibition of the employment in industrial labor of children less than fourteen years of age.
2. The imposition of proper restrictions upon the night labor of women and youths less than sixteen years of age.

19. Outline of Tentative Recommendations, Jan. 21, 1919, Wilson MSS, Series VIII-A, Library of Congress.

3. The application of domestic protective labor legislation to resident and migratory aliens.[20]

The Inquiry looked forward to periodic conferences in the future which could consider international aspects of labor problems. It suggested the establishment of a bureau of labor which could carry on continuous studies and could compile statistics and report periodically on trends and other pertinent matters.

It is worth underscoring the fact that the Inquiry's recommendations on economic matters rested on the assumption that some international organization would exist. Although the blueprint was not yet precisely drawn, the Inquiry was proposing a network of specialized international agencies to report on conditions and also to regulate and enforce the decisions agreed upon by the member states. There was thus some need for studies concerned with international law and international organization.

International law had a peculiar status in the totality of American preparations for peace. As of November 1917 there was a division in the Inquiry, directed by Joseph P. Chamberlain, handling these problems. At the same time, Secretary of State Lansing was considering the formation of a group within the Department of State to study questions of international law. Chamberlain, in November 1917, described the function of the international law section of the Inquiry as analogous to that of a legal counselor to a client. Laws, decrees, and diplomatic correspondence would be studied to determine the rights and contentions of the several belligerent states in regard to the international law in existence prior to the war. Chamberlain's division was also charged with studying any "grounds for claims for damages which will be made as a result of seizures and destruction of property during the war." Naval warfare provided another kind of legal problem. Submarine use and the doctrine of continuous voyage constituted questions of international law as well as of economic warfare. Even Chamberlain regarded a portion of this work as falling properly within the province of the State Department. At least such problems as the interoceanic canals and the legal status of

20. Ibid.

Persia and the Congo would be appropriate responsibilities for the State Department.[21] Early in December, Chamberlain went so far as to suggest a single staff from the ranks of the Inquiry and the State Department which would bring together the work on international law. This idea of a single, integrated staff, however, never did materialize. Instead, the responsibilities were divided. Essentially, the State Department was to have charge of those problems arising directly out of the war: relations between neutrals and belligerents; financial claims of one country against another for damages; reparations and indemnities.[22] The Inquiry, on the other hand, would emphasize studies of more fundamental, long-range questions. At the end of January 1918, Chamberlain resigned as director of the international law section of the Inquiry, and this post was assumed by David Hunter Miller.[23]

By February 1918, Miller was working for the Inquiry and for the State Department, and was therefore able to coordinate the work in international law of the two organizations. Both groups operated with apparently little friction. Even as early as December 1917, Lester H. Woolsey of the State Department had sent a list of proposed subjects for study to the Inquiry's officers. On his list, Woolsey included the following: "The rights and obligations of African tribes, the native states of India (compare the North American Indians)"; "A classification of the States of the World according to the canons of international law." [24] In January 1918, when Secretary Lansing was in the process of forming the International Law Division within the State Department, Colonel House recorded a conversation with the Secretary:

> I feel now that I can work very much more freely with Lansing in regard to the gathering of the data for the peace conference. I therefore arranged for David Hunter Miller, who has charge of the international law section, to come to Washington and confer with Lansing, James Brown Scott, and Woolsey of the State De-

21. J. P. Chamberlain to Shotwell, Nov. 21, 1917, Inquiry Archives; Chamberlain to Mezes, Dec. 18, 1917, Inquiry Archives.

22. Chamberlain to Mezes, Dec. 4, 1917, Inquiry Archives.

23. Mezes to Lester Woolsey, Solicitor of the State Department, Feb. 11, 1918, Inquiry Archives.

24. Woolsey to Mezes, Dec. 15, 1917, Inquiry Archives.

partment. I left Lansing a happy man because, as he said to me before, he would rather go to the peace conference than do any other thing in life.[25]

House evidently had felt that he could not work freely on the preparatory work without receiving full cooperation from the Secretary of State. Lansing, on the other hand, perhaps believed that his chances of participating in the peace negotiations would be strengthened if the State Department had a share in at least some phase of the preparatory work. Consequently, during February 1918, a committee of three men—James Brown Scott, Lester H., Woolsey, and David Hunter Miller—was formed at the State Department to study certain questions of international law.[26] As has already been suggested, Miller provided the liaison between the two organizations.

At least twenty-one reports, prepared by the State Department and the Inquiry, concerned questions of international law. These reports were later included in the files of the American Commission to Negotiate Peace at Paris. These reports, preliminary to the peace conference, could be grouped under the following subject headings: [27]

Subject	No. of Reports
American program for international law	1
Freedom of the seas and merchant shipping	6
Sanctions	2
Neutral rights	1
War on land	1
Aeronautics	2
Protection of minorities	1
Treaties	2
International labor legislation	1
Miscellaneous	4

Greatest emphasis was thus devoted to questions of commerce and the use of the seas. One such report, written by Manley O.

25. House MSS Diary, Jan. 28, 1918, Yale.

26. David Hunter Miller to Mezes and Lippmann, Feb. 14, 1918, Inquiry Archives; David Hunter Miller, *The Drafting of the Covenant* (New York, 1928), 1, 18; Carnegie Endowment for International Peace, *Yearbook of 1918* (Washington, 1918), p. 22.

27. National Archives, "Preliminary Inventories No. 89," pp. 17–18.

Hudson in March 1918, was entitled, "The American Program for Freedom of the Seas." Hudson here viewed President Wilson's pronouncement of "absolute freedom of navigation upon the seas alike in war and peace" as a wholly new doctrine of maritime law. If accepted by the peace conference, it would cause the abandonment of such restrictive devices as the blockade, contraband, visit and search, and continuous voyage, which had previously been considered legal instruments of warfare. Hudson then proceeded to apply an extreme interpretation to President Wilson's Point II:

> This program involves much more than the success of the century old American contention for immunity of private property (not contraband) at sea. It constitutes a larger emasculation of sea power. It would exempt government owned ships and goods from capture; it would abolish the extension of contraband which was always made in the agitation for the immunity of private property; it would restrict the use of naval forces to actual naval combat, to transporting troops and munitions, and to bombarding coast defenses. All of this too is to be achieved at the end of a war in which the use of sea power as an instrument for opposing land power has been more clearly demonstrated than ever before in the history of the world.[28]

He connected the control of the seas to the League of Nations. The League would become the effective regulatory authority over the high seas, or to use Hudson's language:

> What then is to be the law of the sea of the future? Simply this —in behalf of the League of Nations, all or any part of the sea may be closed completely or partially. The League itself must be in a position to make free use of the effective weapons of sea power. Against the commerce of a recalcitrant nation, the ports of all other nations may be closed, seas may be mined, naval power may be used without restriction. The President's program involves nothing short of the complete internationalization of the high seas. In the past there has been no imperium of the seas. Attempts to establish it by various nations failed three centuries ago, with the result that the seas have been left a "no man's land" in which maritime anarchy prevailed, except as national law intervened. In the future, the high seas are to be an international

28. Manley O. Hudson, "The American Program for Freedom of the Seas," March 18, 1918, David Hunter Miller MSS, Box 83, Library of Congress.

domain, subject to international regulation. As international territory they will be more readily policed in time of peace and in time of war. An International Convention for the Safety of Travel at Sea, for instance, must be adopted.[29]

Interesting as Hudson's ideas are, for all practical purposes they proved to be outmoded by the pre-armistice agreement of 1918. Freedom of the seas, as Wilson and his associates regarded it, became a purely academic matter during the peace negotiations in 1919. The subject never really emerged for discussion in the official sessions of the peace conference.

By the end of June 1918, the international law division of the State Department reported on its progress to Secretary Lansing. Its program called for the collection of texts and documents, treaties, conventions, and agreements made by the belligerents, diplomatic correspondence and utterances of the war period, and a series of special monographs. In short, "including as far as can be foreseen, every authority which may be called for at the Conference."[30]

While members of the International Law divisions expended their energies on preparatory studies, David Hunter Miller was instrumental in drafting two memoranda which would have practical significance prior to the peace conference. In late June of 1918, Miller sent to House a memorandum on a peace protocol. A preliminary agreement in the form of a protocol, Miller contended, should be approved by the belligerents some time before the armistice. The protocol would provide, in effect, the fundamental rules of the conference. It would not require ratification because of its preliminary nature, but would seek to find agreement on the principles for peace and in this sense facilitate the actual operations of the conference. Attention was called to the need for precise language in the protocol. Among the items which Miller suggested for inclusion in this document were the following:

> (1) A specific and definite, though not detailed, agreement as to certain questions:
>> a. Belgium;
>> b. Evacuation of France;

29. Ibid.

30. David Hunter Miller to Secretary Robert Lansing, July 1, 1918, House MSS, Yale.

    c. Alsace-Lorraine;

    d. The Austro-Italian frontier;

    e. The annulment of all treaties, agreements and con-
tracts made between or among any of the Central Powers
since 27 July 1914, and also the annulment of all existing
treaties, agreements or contracts which are secret in whole
or in part, to which any one of the Central Powers is a
party, and a consent to the publication of all the said
writings.

    (2) For such questions as were not specifically determined in
the Protocol itself it would provide substantially, in the terms of
the Program laid down by the President on January 8, 1918, a
modus procedendi for arriving at a state specifically that every
agreement was to conform in substance to the four principles of
the President of February 11, 1918.

    (3) It would deal summarily with compensatory (and puni-
tive) indemnities, the details being left to the Conference.

    (4) It would certainly provide [the procedural arrangements]
for the later Conference . . .

    (5) It might contain provisions for an Armistice.

    (6) It might contain provisions for a simultaneous congress of
all the powers including the neutrals either with or without the
Program for the consideration of the simultaneous congress.[31]

Although the international protocol never materialized, the suggestion was more than interesting; it contained an astounding proposal. It was to be signed (but not ratified) by "all the belligerents" in the war, not merely by members of the victorious coalition.
And just so there would be no question about his intended meaning, Miller included the following paragraph:

    The Protocol would probably be signed in the capital of one
of the belligerents, for example, in Washington. . . . and in such
a case an ambassador or ambassadors of a neutral power or powers would probably be authorized to sign on behalf of the Central
Powers, and would necessarily be provided with a formal "power"
giving him such authority.[32]

Miller's second memorandum dealt with the legality of an American President's attendance at a peace conference on foreign soil.
The date of this memorandum was October 7, 1918, more than a
month before the armistice was signed. Two questions were in-

31. Miller to House, June 28, 1918, House Inquiry MSS, file 33-112, Yale.
32. Ibid.

volved: First, did the American Constitution permit the President to attend a peace conference in Europe; second, in the President's absence would his powers and duties devolve upon the Vice President? Miller held that if the President determined that his presence at the peace conference as Executive and Commander in Chief of American forces was advisable, "such presence is not only within his functions under the Constitution, but is also a solemn duty imposed upon him." Since the attendance of the President would be pursuant to his powers and duties under the Constitution, then to have the Vice President assume Presidential responsibilities because of the Chief Executive's "inability to discharge the powers and duties of the said office" would amount to a "contradiction in terms, in fact, and in law." The powers of the Presidency, Miller indicated, were indivisible. Under the American Constitution, the President alone could decide the time, manner, method, and place for the performance of his duties. Hence there was no constitutional restriction on the President's participating in the peace conference if it were held on foreign soil.[33]

A host of other questions ranging from disarmament proposals to immigration questions received the attention of the international law divisions in the Inquiry and the State Department. While the brunt of the disarmament studies was borne by the War Department,[34] David Hunter Miller proposed a means for controlling armaments through the regulation of the world's nickel production. Nickel, an important ingredient in industrial and armaments production, was mined in only three important places— Canada, New Caledonia, and Finland. These relatively few sources would be controlled and operated by the League of Nations or some other constituted international agency. The indispensable value of nickel to modern military requirements coupled with the few sources of the mineral resulted, he felt, in an ideal arrangement for the limitation of armaments.[35]

33. Miller to House, Oct. 7, 1918, Frank Polk MSS, Yale.

34. Walter Lippmann to Secretary of War Newton D. Baker, Oct. 27, 1917; Baker to Lippmann, Nov. 1, 1917, both in *Foreign Relations of the United States, Paris Peace Conference 1919* (Washington, 1942–47), *1*, 12–14. See also Colonel Embrick, Notes on Reduction in Armaments, Feb. 3, 1918, Tasker Bliss MSS, Library of Congress.

35. David Hunter Miller, "The International Control of Nickel as a Factor in Peace Negotiations," n.d., Shotwell MSS, Columbia.

The Inquiry's Black Book Number 2 (February 1919) included a section devoted to immigration policy. Often considered as falling exclusively within the province of domestic legislation, immigration policies were being injected into the proceedings at Paris in 1919 by the Japanese government. Members of the Inquiry were not without sympathy with the charge that Occidental countries were applying policies based on racial discrimination against Orientals. The need for some international action by the peace conference to establish more equitable immigration procedures was explained by the Inquiry's staff at Paris as follows:

> It is generally admitted that something must soon be done—the increasing sense of dissatisfaction on the part of peoples of Oriental countries with what they consider the unjust discrimination of Occidental countries against them must be reckoned with. Neglected, the question is a constant source of embarrassment in international relations and it may lead to conflict in some region or other.[36]

To correct what appeared to be a potential cause for future conflict, the Inquiry recommended that the peace conference adopt the rule which would accord reciprocity as the principle governing immigration, naturalization, ownership and use of land, opportunity to trade, and related problems involving aliens and immigration. Furthermore, the Inquiry favored the establishment of a special international commission "whose duty it shall be" to formulate rules and to attempt the settlement of international disputes over immigration matters. On the issue of equality and reciprocity as applied to immigration and naturalization, the United States delegation at the peace conference did not adhere to this point of view when the question of racial equality was ultimately raised by the Japanese.

In the months before the armistice, the Inquiry's Division of International Law devoted much attention to the proposed League of Nations. It will be recalled that there had been included in the Inquiry's memoranda of December 1917 and January 1918 a section on the League of Nations which was presumably considered

36. "General International Action with Regard to the Right (Privilege) of Immigration, of Naturalization, and of Opportunity in Respect to Residence and Trade in Foreign Countries," Black Book No. 2, Wilson MSS, Series VIII-A, Library of Congress.

by the President in the writing of the Fourteen Points Address of January 8, 1918.[37] Later reports which dealt with the League of Nations were written by Manley O. Hudson, and they delved deeply into various aspects of the proposed international organization, with some emphasis being placed on the relationship of the League to the member countries, including the United States. Following the President's idea, Hudson's reports made the League a central prop in the peace settlement, around which all other sections would be arranged. The League would develop out of the many international precedents established during the war period. Blockade arrangements, Hudson hoped, would become the basis for effective economic sanctions to be invoked against future aggressor states. Similarly, Hudson anticipated that the League would be in a constant state of evolution. It could not rise full-blown, but must adapt to changing circumstances. Advantages provided by League membership must be so obvious that no state could afford to remain outside. The League's machinery would be simple at first, but would expand as required. The purpose of the League would not be merely the prevention of international conflict; the League must advance positively toward correcting conditions which could conceivably lead to conflagrations. Only to a degree would the League rely upon public opinion, for Hudson squarely recognized that the authority of the League must "be backed by the united force of all nations." A successful League, Hudson declared, must not stifle peaceful changes in the status quo; it must add a new dimension to the concept of sovereignty so that no nation could disregard the "general will" of the community of nations; it must meet the needs for foods and raw materials and transportation by assuming constructive measures which would cope with economic scarcities. Yet at no time would the League bind any nation in advance to a course of action "except to join in international action in the interests of the common order." [38]

37. Supra, pp. 149–50.
38. Manley O. Hudson, "A League of Nations," n.d., David Hunter Miller MSS, Box 83, Library of Congress. Many of the same points are reiterated in M. O. Hudson, "Memorandum on International Organization," n.d. (on the basis of internal evidence, after July 4, 1918), David Hunter Miller MSS, Box 83, Library of Congress.

This outline, though at times suggestive and definite, left many details hanging loosely. In another memorandum, Hudson advised that the League, being the central feature of the peace settlement, could not be effected at any later international congress. There could be no postponement; the League must be established by the peace conference. All questions confronting the peace conference must be integrated in the League organization. Presumably the peace conference would be dominated by the great powers, a situation far more conducive to the planning of an international organization than a general international conference at which small nations could easily hinder the proceedings—as Hudson believed to have happened at the two Hague conferences. Other states not participating directly in the peace settlement could be assured of consideration and even of consultation in the formulation of the international organization. And to drive his point home, Hudson suggested that inclusion of the League on the agenda of the peace conference would allow some additional latitude for bargaining with reference to other terms in the settlement. His phrasing of this point was especially interesting:

> Some of the belligerents whose inclusion is desired may be induced to enter the League if they feel that by so doing they can influence other features of the Settlement.[39]

Inasmuch as the League must function in a world of intensified nationalism, Hudson believed, it should be international in form rather than supernational. This arrangement would allow the League to rely on national military and naval establishments rather than attempt to form a supernational military force. As the representative of the organized world, the League must strive to become sufficiently inclusive to discourage the formation of rival leagues. Alliances within the League would not necessarily disrupt it as long as such arrangements were held distinctly subordinate to the League itself. League covenants, according to Hudson, must provide adequate guarantees for the political independence of member states. The territorial integrity of member states must likewise be guaranteed except when invasion of a member state

---

39. M. O. Hudson, "Tentative Suggestions for a General Association of Nations," n.d., David Hunter Miller MSS, Box 83, Library of Congress.

was authorized by the League. Racial and ethnic minority groups living within member states as well as populations residing in areas lacking self-government would receive protection should it be required. International treaties, in order to be binding, would have to be submitted to the League and thus made public. Secret treaties and treaties in which the parties refused to submit disputes to the "Court or Council" would be considered invalid.[40]

Hudson's proposals regarding the League's machinery did not advocate any tampering with existing international organizations. The League itself would have two instruments, a council composed of all member states, and a court. Whatever the basis for representation in the council, the League's work would be expedited if the great powers were to have more representation than other states. The council itself was to meet periodically for purposes of discussing and/or deciding questions affecting the world community. More frequently, however, the members would meet in more specialized subcouncils or committees to consider problems of more limited interest. There could conceivably be a council of the great powers; a council of European nations; a council of American nations. But the real authority in the League would remain with the plenary body, whose duties would include some legislative powers (not specified), the appointment of some executive ministry, and the power to codify international law. Legislation to be binding upon members would have to receive a vote of three-fourths of the members.

Any consideration of American participation in the League of Nations might logically anticipate the attitude of the United States Senate which would have to consent to ratification of the peace treaties. Manley Hudson was fully aware of the potential obstruction to American participation in international organizations—and thus to their activities—which the Senate could offer. He wrote an undated memorandum entitled "The Senate and International Organization," [41] in which he called attention to previous experience of the United States in various international organizations, especially American participation in the work of the Universal

40. Ibid.
41. M. O. Hudson, "The Senate and International Organization," n.d., David Hunter Miller MSS, Box 83, Library of Congress.

Postal Union. Once the United States joined the Postal Union, Hudson declared, Executive Agreements were used to fulfill American obligations in the Union rather than treaties requiring the consent of the Senate. The substitution of the Executive Agreement for the treaty had greatly facilitated the work. Hudson therefore proposed a similar arrangement for the League. In other words, after the United States became a member, Congress could pass a general act authorizing an administrative official (representing the United States) to conclude "international arrangements of an administrative character," thus forestalling any objection that a part of the treatymaking power was being circumvented. Hudson did not even consider the possibility that the Senate might fail to ratify the peace treaties and thus prevent American membership in the League in the first instance. He seems to have assumed that the United States would become a member. It was after the United States had become a member that he feared the Senate might thwart American participation. Three alternatives were suggested by Hudson with which to meet this supposed threat from the Senate: (1) Changes in public opinion on American participation in world affairs might make possible a constitutional amendment which would give the President greater authority in handling America's obligations to the League and free him from having to submit certain kinds of international agreements to the Senate for ratification; (2) In a more optimistic vein, there might be a possibility that the changed attitude of the American public regarding United States participation in world affairs might likewise produce a change in the Senate which would allow for the participation of the United States in carrying out the obligations of the League; (3) On the whole, Hudson regarded the best course as being the following: "so far as possible, the participation of the United States should be accomplished through administrative cooperation." In the end, Hudson had to admit that the United States Senate was a force which had to be reckoned with if the United States were to join and become active in the League. He concluded on an almost prophetic note:

> There seems to be no way in which these objections to the Senate's delegation of its power can be wholly avoided, and it must

311

be kept in mind in framing any schemes for United States participation in world government.[42]

Throughout the Inquiry's papers dealing with trade, finance, and international law, the theme of international organization could be distinguished. World peace involved not solely the construction of just boundaries. A lasting peace in 1917–19 seemed possible only when such matters as commercial competition among nations, labor conditions, financial arrangements among nations, and the availability of raw materials to all nations were regulated for the benefit of the world community. The Inquiry members working on these topics were hopeful that a method for accomplishing these ends would be provided in the establishment of an international organization.

42. Ibid.

Chapter 11

THE BALANCE

Whenever there must be a meeting of the minds in the preparation of any agreement, there is one apparently universal rule which always has its influence; that rule is this: any definite, detailed draft prepared in advance by one of the parties will to some extent appear in the final text, not only in principle but even in language. No matter how many differences of opinion, no matter how much the various papers may be recast and amended, something of the beginning is left at the end.[1]

Woodrow wilson's absorbing interest in a righteous peace may well have provided the moral justification for his advocacy of American intervention in World War I.[2] His public addresses during 1916–17 displayed that intense concern with which he later approached the many questions involved in the peace negotiations. With the advent of the Inquiry in September 1917, the President's idealism was tempered by a realistic awareness of the serious obstructions in the path of a just and lasting settlement. There was in evidence his explicit recognition that American objectives were sometimes at variance with the national objectives pursued by America's partners in the war. The President hoped and even expected that, with the instrument of the Inquiry, sys-

1. David Hunter Miller, *The Drafting of the Covenant* (New York, 1928) *1*, 3.
2. Arthur S. Link, *Wilson the Diplomatist* (Baltimore, 1957), p. 89.

tematic planning might result in the attainment of the kind of peace he sought. A more emphatic statement in defense of the national interests could hardly have been expressed than the one written by Wilson when he initiated American preparations for peace. Colonel House was asked to undertake the study of those objectives which America's cobelligerents would be "inclined to insist upon as part of the final peace arrangements . . ." He and his staff should then (in the President's words):

> formulate our own position either for or against them and begin to gather the influences we can use; in brief, prepare our case with a full knowledge of the position of all the litigants. . . .[3]

It is clear that in starting the machinery for the construction of a durable peace, President Wilson had his feet solidly on the ground; his action was prompted by a deep-seated concern for safeguarding the national interests of the United States. Unfortunately, the Inquiry was not able to satisfy the President's high expectations. During fifteen months of operation, it poured forth a steady stream of reports, but these contained few well-conceived, systematic plans for peace.

By the end of October 1917, the Inquiry bore a decided academic stamp. Historians, economists, political scientists, and geographers had been appointed to its staff. This reliance upon academicians, however, did not, as we have seen, imply that the staff was composed of experts. Few members of the Inquiry could, by reason of qualifications for their assigned work in the peace preparations, be rightly regarded as experts in 1917–18. On this subject of "expertness" and the selection of Inquiry personnel, Charles Seymour's observation, written almost thirty-five years after the armistice of 1918, is especially appropriate. Seymour recalled:

> My appointment to the Inquiry came about, I suppose, through my friendship with Isaiah Bowman . . .
> House was not concerned with the hiring of members of the Inquiry. Mezes was responsible in a titular sense, although the choice was almost invariably Bowman's. . . .
> The selection was generally made on the basis of general capac-

3. Wilson to House, Sept. 2, 1917, in R. S. Baker, *Woodrow Wilson, Life and Letters* (Garden City, 1927–39), 7, 254.

ity and scholarship. Very few regional experts were available. Lord was a specialist in [on] Poland. Beer had broad knowledge of contemporary as well as historical colonial conditions. Haskins knew his French history and politics. But Day, and Lunt, and I, myself, had not special knowledge of the regions to which we were assigned. Westermann as a classical historian was supposed to know about the Near East, but he found a difference between Syrian politics and papyri. We were kept on because Bowman liked our reports. Of course Hornbeck knew something about the Far East but he learned most of it from 1919 on. Subordinate positions were sometimes given to more specialized students as in the case of Kerner . . .[4]

This absence of qualified talent compelled the Inquiry's leaders to bring into the organization an aggregation of ancient historians, archeologists, medievalists, scholars concerned with early American history and other subjects not immediately related to recent world problems.

Plans for the Inquiry's organization, as they evolved during the pre-armistice period, were much too ambitious, failing to take into consideration the limited qualifications of the staff, the unavailability of good, current source materials, the sharply limited budget, and the extreme haste which characterized much of the operation. Every portion of the world became fair game for the Inquiry. As the organization mushroomed in size, and the scope of the work increased, the result was less supervision, less criticism, and less coordination, with more quantity but poorer quality of product. It became more and more difficult for the staff of one division to know what was being done in a related division. Then, too, the distribution of a large portion of the preparatory chores among various government agencies, private agencies, and persons outside the organization tended to lower overall standards. The resultant products featured a great many methods and an almost endless variety of conclusions. Too few of the reports made any attempt to indicate their relevancy to the anticipated peace settlement. In a vast number of instances, because of the particular subjects assigned, the authors would really have been hard pressed to show direct relevancy. The reader of the almost 2,000 Inquiry reports now housed in the National Archives might easily

4. Charles Seymour to the author, Oct. 7, 1953.

315

draw the conclusion that the officers of the Inquiry were only interested in the collection of facts, and were, at the same time, not particular as to the form the finished research took. But this judgment would be both harsh and unfair. Inquiry leaders did strive to obtain reports of high quality, but apparently the snowball rolled too far too fast and eventually got out of control.

Nominally, at least, the Inquiry was an autonomous, administrative bureau responsible only to the President. Having taken no part in forming the Inquiry, Congress barely took note of its existence prior to the armistice. It has been asserted that the State Department, not receiving the assignment of preparing for the peace conference, remained aloof from the Inquiry's operations.[5] There is, however, abundant evidence that, as autonomous as the Inquiry appeared from the outset, it was bound by strong ties to the State Department. Plans governing the Inquiry's organization were submitted for the approval or criticism of Secretary of State Lansing. Personnel attached to the State Department contributed a substantial number of reports; certainly no fewer than 30 per cent of all reports were written by persons employed by the Department at home or abroad.[6] Source materials were generally made available to the Inquiry's scholars by Lansing and his staff. Most of the completed reports were submitted to the State Department, whose senior staff officers regularly visited the headquarters of the Inquiry and consulted with the Inquiry's personnel. Ordinarily the State Department did not interfere in the selection of the Inquiry's staff, but at least two members of the Inquiry, Albert Lybyer and Edward Krehbiel, were subjected to loyalty investigations at the insistence of the State Department. Furthermore, several prospective members were effectively disqualified when the Department objected. On those few occasions when the Inquiry dispatched agents overseas to procure desired information, arrangements were always cleared through the State Department. Plans for Latin American research were submitted to, and approved by, the State Department during April and May

5. Graham H. Stuart, *The Department of State* (New York, 1949), pp. 246–47.
6. An estimate based on the listing of the Inquiry's reports in the National Archives, "Preliminary Inventory Number 89," Records of the American Commission to Negotiate Peace, ed. H. Stephen Helton.

316

1918, and funds for this venture were allocated directly to the Inquiry by Secretary Lansing. With regard to international law, preparations were carried on jointly by both organizations although two staffs were maintained. Thus almost from the moment when Colonel House contacted William Buckler in London, during April 1917, until the armistice period, the State Department exercised a truly active and decisive influence over the arrangements for the peace settlement generally, and over the Inquiry's operations in particular. The Inquiry began its life as an independent governmental organization. Yet its dependence on the State Department steadily increased, due partly to the Inquiry's need for current information possessed by the State Department but also, in large measure, to the inadequately qualified staff assembled for the Inquiry itself. With the approach of peace, more and more of the American preparations came to be delegated by the Inquiry to numerous government agencies, principally the State Department.

The secrecy which pervaded much of the Inquiry's activities did not, as we have seen, preclude the maintenance of cordial relations or cooperation with the official preparatory commissions then functioning in England and France. Reports and maps were freely exchanged. Early in 1918, Douglas Johnson of the Inquiry was sent to Europe in order to study at first hand the operations of the Allied commissions. Sir William Wiseman, chief of British Intelligence in the United States, as well as representatives from other Allied governments and groups aspiring for nationhood, kept a very close watch over the operations of the Inquiry. Upon occasion, they even endeavored to influence reports which involved their special interests in the settlement. As a consequence of the Inquiry's relations with the Allied governments, information about the American preparations was usually as available to the governments at London and Paris as it was at Washington. Elsewhere in America, the activities of the Inquiry were successfully hidden from public view.

When at last the peace conference was ready to begin its arduous chores in January 1919, the United States delegation was equipped with approximately 2,000 separate reports and documents covering about every subject likely to arise for discussion and many that were not. For more than fifteen months, the Inquiry had been preparing for the conference. A significant nucleus of the American advisers who converged upon Paris in December 1918 and January 1919 had therefore been gaining some mastery over the materials. Moreover, the Americans at Paris had at their disposal, by the end of January 1919, a series of definite recommendations for the solution of many thorny questions. These reports and documents, the experience afforded to certain advisers, and the definite program were all positive consequences derived from the Inquiry's labors.

No effective yardstick can possibly measure the influence exerted by the massive accumulation of reports and, in addition, by the 1,150 or more maps produced and collected. There were actually so many reports that it cannot be properly determined just how many were read and systematically used at Paris and how many remained sealed in their original shipping crates. Only a bare handful has ever been published,[7] in sharp contrast with the practice followed by the British and French governments which began publishing the work of their preparatory commissions in 1920.[8]

The role of the Inquiry's staff at Paris can be assessed more readily. When the *George Washington* dropped anchor at Brest, there were only 23 members of the Inquiry abroad. Of about 150 persons who had participated in the work of the Inquiry, not more than 35 participated in the work of the peace conference. In this respect, the American Commission to Negotiate Peace made limited use of the Inquiry. Numbers alone, however, are not an adequate index; the functions performed by this crew of veterans can reveal much about the Inquiry's contribution to the peace settlement.

With the commencement of the conference, the rather unob-

7. The only body of Inquiry reports which have been published consists of certain papers by George Louis Beer in *African Questions at the Paris Peace Conference* (New York, 1923), ed. Louis H. Gray.

8. British reports are published in 157 volumes under the general title, *Handbooks Prepared under the Direction of the Historical Section of the Foreign Office* (London, H. M. Stationery Office, 1920). Six volumes in this series have never been published. French reports are published in two large volumes. See Comité d'études, *Travaux du Comité d'études* (Paris, Imprimerie nationale, 1918–19).

trusive title, "the Inquiry," yielded to the more pretentious title, "Division of Territorial Economic and Political Intelligence." Mezes' staff at Paris, besides using some of the Inquiry's old-timers, drew additional members from the military and naval establishments and from the special wartime administrative agencies in Washington. As of March 27, 1919, for instance, the Division numbered 113 persons, of whom 42 were civilians and 71 were military or naval personnel.[9] The following distribution chart, while not indicating the number of personnel having had Inquiry experience, shows military or civilian affiliation of the membership in terms of assignment:

Administrative			Geography	
Civilians	6		Civilians	5
Army	12		Army	15
Austria-Hungary			Germany	
Civilians	1		Civilians	1
Army	2		Navy	1
Balkans			History	
Civilians	3		Civilians	3
Army	2		Army	1
Colonial			Inner Asia	
Civilians	1		Civilians	1
Army	1		Army and Navy	0
Economics and statistics			Italy	
Civilians	5		Civilians	1
Army	8		Army and Navy	0
Ethnography			Russia and Poland	
Civilians	1		Civilians	4
Army	1		Army	6
Western Asia			International law	
Civilians	4		Civilians	2
Army	2		Army and Navy	0
Western Europe			Library staff	
Civilians	1		Civilians	3
Army	2		Army	18

As important as were certain Inquiry members in the work of the peace conference, it would be a grievous mistake to think of the Inquiry as the dominant organ in the proceedings of the American

9. Memorandum on the Organization of the American Commission to Negotiate Peace, March 27, 1919, *Foreign Relations of the United States, Paris Peace Conference, 1919* (hereafter referred to as *FRPPC*), *11*, 543–45.

Commission. The small force was at all times outnumbered by personnel drawn from the State Department and from other civil departments at Washington, not to mention the military staff representatives who served as technical advisers. As of May 1, 1919, of the 62 members of the American Commission who were formally known as delegates and technical advisers, 19 had had some experience with the Inquiry during the pre-armistice period; 13 were officers of the Army and Navy; and another 13 were members of the State Department contingent. The remaining 17 came from the many specialized bureaus and departments which had dispatched representatives.[10]

Several of the Inquiry's members were given the opportunity to apply their knowledge and participate in the actual work of negotiating the peace settlement. Archibald Cary Coolidge and Robert J. Kerner were sent to Central Europe to observe and report on conditions there during early 1919.[11] Several other members of the Inquiry received appointments as American representatives on various international commissions or subcommissions to which much of the conference's work fell. Director Sidney Mezes and later Archibald Cary Coolidge were appointed American representatives to the Central Territorial Committee, while another Inquiry veteran, Parker T. Moon, served as American Secretary for the same commission. David Hunter Miller of the Inquiry's Division of International Law was assigned to the Commission on International Regime of Ports, Waterways, and Railways, and Manley O. Hudson, from the same division, was named alternate on this commission. A. A. Young, who had been in charge of the Inquiry's economic studies, was selected to be American representative (and was actually chairman) on the subcommission which considered customs regulations, duties, and restrictions. Young also served as American delegate on the subcommission concerned with economic treaties. On the subcommission handling Czechoslovakian affairs was Charles Seymour, who had led the Inquiry's division on Austro-Hungarian questions. Two other men,

10. Composition and Organization of the Preliminary Peace Conference, May 1, 1919, *FRPPC*, *11*, 552–57.
11. Lansing to Coolidge, Dec. 26, 1918; Joseph C. Grew to Coolidge, Dec. 26, 1918; Coolidge to Grew, Dec. 27, 1918, all in *FRPPC*, *2*, 218–19. The reports of the Coolidge Mission are found in *FRPPC*, *12*, 240–371.

Isaiah Bowman and Robert H. Lord, acted as American representatives on all subcommissions considering Polish questions, including a commission that formulated the East German frontiers. Clive Day, Charles Seymour, Archibald Cary Coolidge, and Douglas Johnson were at times the American representatives responsible for deciding on provisions for Rumania and Yugoslavia. Day and William L. Westermann served as American members on the subcommission deciding Greek and Albanian questions. Charles H. Haskins was one of the American representatives working on Belgian and Danish problems. Samuel E. Morison served on the Baltic commission. George Louis Beer sat for the United States on the commission considering Moroccan affairs and also on the commission formulating the provisions governing the German colonies. Beer and Louis H. Gray were alternates for Colonel House on the commission working on colonial mandates. Stanley Hornbeck represented the United States on the commission studying the disposition of Tientsin. James T. Shotwell was a member of the commission for international labor legislation. The Inquiry members who sat on these international commissions did not have to improvise their policies entirely: [12] they had at their disposal a series of concrete recommendations formulated at the request of the American Commission to Negotiate Peace.

Secretary of State Lansing claimed in his reminiscences that the Commission functioned without benefit of any definite program or even of policies conceived in advance.[13] Despite this assertion, the Commission did have a draft program which encompassed nearly all of the territorial questions pressing for the attention of the peace conference. It is quite true that the Inquiry's recommendations were never endorsed by the American commissioners and therefore never constituted an American program in any official sense. It is also true that at times the American plenipotentiaries chose to disregard or to modify these recommendations sharply when negotiating at the conference, as President Wilson did when considering the disposition of the Saar. Nevertheless, these proposals constituted the collective judgments of

12. Composition and Organization of the Preliminary Peace Conference, April 1, 1919, and Oct. 1, 1919, in *FRPPC*, 3, 63–153.

13. Robert Lansing, *The Peace Negotiations* (Boston, 1921), pp. 190–92.

the Inquiry's leaders at the peace conference and might well be regarded as the climax to the fifteen months of preparations.

The recommendations provided by the Division of Territorial Economic and Political Intelligence were completed during the first month of the conference. They were in no sense random proposals culled from the numerous reports. Just as the Inquiry's Executive Committee had in December 1917 drafted a memorandum which the President used in formulating some portions of his Fourteen Points, so in January and February 1919 the Inquiry's forces at Paris produced the several American "colored" books.[14] Any consideration of the Inquiry's influence upon the peace settlement must proceed cautiously, however. A casual influence cannot be proven simply through the existence of parallels between propositions found in the colored books and corresponding provisions in the peace treaties. It is clear that as the peace negotiations progressed, a variety of fresh complications made it increasingly difficult, if not impossible, for the American plenipotentiaries to embrace the entire program submitted by Inquiry members even if it were to be admitted that the recommendations were sound at the time they were composed. The tempo of international politics was moving rapidly forward in 1919; a proposal which might appear perfectly valid in January would not necessarily be so by April or May. Consequently, some of the Inquiry's proposals were to become academic and inexpedient by the time the peace conference acted upon the questions with which they were concerned. In one sense, then, a comparison between the Inquiry's recommendations and the ultimate provisions in the treaties of peace cannot do much more than round out the historical record. Yet an appraisal of the American effort in preparing for the peace settlement should indicate which parts of the Inquiry's program won a place in the treaties, which were only partially realized, and which were disregarded.[15] This should make it pos-

14. The Inquiry's colored books were "The Outline of Tentative Reports and Recommendations Prepared by the Intelligence Section, In Accordance with Instructions, for the President and the Plenipotentiaries," Jan. 21, 1919 (sometimes known as Black Book No. 1) and Black Book No. 2, Feb. 13, 1919, both documents being located in the Wilson MSS, Series VIII-A, Library of Congress.

15. The text of the Treaty of Versailles (with Germany) including annotations can be found in *FRPPC, 13,* 3–754. Texts of the Treaty of St. Germain-en-Laye

sible to discern, with some greater precision than has been possible heretofore, the origins of the multitude of provisions in the various peace treaties, with special reference to American interests and contributions.

Since Woodrow Wilson's Fourteen Points served as the basis on which the Central Powers sued for an armistice, it could be expected that the specific territorial provisions demanded by the President in his Address of January 8, 1918, would find satisfaction in the peace settlement. Thus the restoration of Belgian territory (Point VII), the restoration of Alsace-Lorraine to France (Point VIII), and the establishment of an independent Polish state (Point XIII), in some respects the most practical of Wilson's Points to implement, were not dependent solely upon Inquiry support. On questions with which the Wilsonian Points had not specifically dealt, a comparison between the Inquiry's proposals in the colored books and the relevant articles of the treaties indicates that the Inquiry's recommendations prevailed, at least partially, in numerous instances. The disposition of Schleswig-Holstein closely followed the lines suggested by the Inquiry. Its advocacy of a tier of independent states which would, in effect, separate Russia from Central Europe received recognition through the establishment of the independent states of Finland, Estonia, Latvia, Lithuania, Poland, Czechoslovakia, Hungary, and Yugoslavia. In the negotiations over the Saar Basin, the Inquiry's original proposals calling for transfer of the Saar to France were compromised in the Versailles Treaty; the treaty provided for an interim period of fifteen years during which the Saar would be administered under the auspices of the League of Nations after which a plebiscite would decide the region's future status. While it is true that the Inquiry had suggested that Danzig be placed under Polish sovereignty, the peace conference did not entirely disregard other

---

(with Austria) and of the Treaty of Trianon (with Hungary) and of the Treaty of Neuilly-sur-Seine (with Bulgaria) can be found in H. W. V. Temperley, ed., *A History of the Conference at Paris*, 5, 170–365. Political clauses of the Treaty of Sèvres (with Turkey) are conveniently set forth in J. C. Hurewitz, ed., *Diplomacy in the Near and Middle East, A Documentary Record 1535–1956* (Princeton, 1956), 2, 81–87. All of the peace treaties are conveniently found in Carnegie Endowment for International Peace, *The Treaties of Peace, 1919–1923*, 2 vols. (New York, 1924).

solutions for Poland when it made Danzig a free city. The establishment of the Polish Corridor separating East Prussia from Germany proper was one part of the Inquiry's program which was accepted. Spitzbergen, for which the Inquiry had favored mandate status under Norway, was placed under Norwegian sovereignty. The Aaland Islands, which the Inquiry proposed should be placed under Swedish control, were transferred to Finland. The plan for an independent Ukrainian state to include Russian Crimea, which was supported by the Inquiry, never materialized in the final peace treaties. The Inquiry had not advocated the breakup of the Austro-Hungarian Empire, but the Empire's liquidation was virtually a fait accompli when the peace conference convened. Contrary to the Inquiry's hopes, Austria was compelled to cede to Italy the South Tyrol, the Trentino, Trieste, Istria, and several islands off the Dalmatian coast. The Inquiry opposed Italian annexation of Dalmatian coastal lands, and these lands were effectively denied to Italy. On the other hand, the Inquiry's position favoring international status for Trieste was disregarded when the former Austrian port was transferred to Italian sovereignty.

Annexation by Rumania of Transylvania, a large portion of the Banat of Temesvár, of the Bukovina, and of Bessarabia was successfully favored by the Inquiry. When it came to the Greco-Bulgarian controversy over Eastern Thrace, the Inquiry's recommendations in support of Bulgarian claims were shelved by the peace conference. Greek interests prevailed, and Bulgaria was therefore denied direct access to the Aegean Sea. Likewise, the Inquiry's proposal favoring the division of Albania between Yugoslavia and Greece was turned down as was also the idea of awarding the Dodecanese Islands and the Island of Rhodes to Greece rather than Italy. Thus the Inquiry's program with regard to Europe was partially realized.

Turning now to the settlement for Africa, Asia, and the Pacific Islands, some of the Inquiry's recommendations also prevailed here. The mandate system, promoted by George Louis Beer, was generally accepted for the former German colonies in Africa and the Pacific. In actual practice, the peace conference went far beyond the Inquiry's expectations, as we have seen.

With regard to the Middle East, the Inquiry had hoped to restrict Turkish sovereignty to a portion of Anatolia. The Straits and Constantinople would form a separate international zone. Under the Treaty of Sèvres (August 20, 1920), Turkey renounced all rights over its far-flung empire in North Africa and Asia Minor. The Straits were internationalized although Constantinople remained a part of Turkey. Armenia was declared a free and independent state, conforming to the Inquiry's solution. Then the mandate principle was applied to the former Turkish provinces in Asia, also as favored by the Inquiry.

The Inquiry's recommendations for the Far East included the canceling of all secret agreements pertaining to Shantung and proposed the internationalization of the port of Tsingtao. In no case was Japan to be allowed to retain control over Tsingtao. All leased territory around Kiachow was to be returned to Chinese control as well as the railroad rights formerly possessed by Germany. German and Austrian concessions at Tientsin and Hankow were to be converted into international settlements. Furthermore, the Inquiry desired the liberalization of tariff arrangements in China for the benefit of that country. The Inquiry favored placing Russian interests in China and also all railroad operations in Manchuria under some international management. In order to satisfy the current Japanese drive toward expansion, the Inquiry proposed allowing Japan to exercise a free hand in the Russian provinces east of the Ussuri and Amur rivers and at the same time to purchase from Russia the northern half of Sakhalin Island. All of Germany's colonies in the Pacific were to be made mandates under the League of Nations. Except for the provisions pertaining to mandates for the former German colonies in the Pacific, almost none of the Inquiry's recommendations for the Far East was inserted into the peace treaties.

Those territorial arrangements advocated by the Inquiry which prevailed in the peace treaties were largely limited to Western Europe, Poland, parts of the Balkans, and the Middle East. Recommendations with regard to Russian provinces, Italy, and the Far East in particular proved least successful. Beer's mandate system for the German colonies in Africa was effectively championed at the conference. If the Inquiry's colored books represented the one comprehensive program of the American delegation for the rearrangement of territorial boundaries, in terms of the final peace treaties their recommendations can hardly be considered as failing to achieve fruition. Since the Inquiry's personnel at Paris functioned in the capacity of territorial experts, and since the American Commission had within its fold additional sections (or divisions) handling economic and legal questions, it is not surprising to find that very little attention was paid to the Inquiry's economic and legal studies.

There were, however, certain economic problems which were touched upon in the Inquiry's recommendations. Though no proposals were made regarding indemnities, reparations, financial problems, enemy property, national indebtedness, contracts, prescriptions, and judgments (subjects treated at some length by the peace treaties), the Inquiry's recommendations did embrace such topics as international trade and international labor. The Open Door and equality of commercial opportunity on a nondiscriminatory basis were proposals warmly endorsed by the Inquiry. Discrimination in national shipping practices was opposed, though specific exceptions were to be allowed. In the field of labor, the Inquiry favored the establishment of legal safeguards for the protection of women, children, and aliens. Insofar as these general principles found their way into the peace settlement, they were directed solely at the enemy nations. With regard to international labor, however, Article XIII of the Versailles Treaty, which sets forth the Constitution of the International Labour Organisation, offered comprehensive provisions for the protection of many categories of labor.

Once the peace conference got under way, old Inquiry hands realized, often to their dismay, that the rugged, academic individualism which had characterized their labors in the pre-armistice period might have to yield to cooperation and compromise. They were not accustomed to team work, to the rough and tumble of diplomatic negotiation with the almost inevitable necessity for the compromising of differences. Members who had served the Inquiry were inclined to think of their recommended formulas as constituting the sole, "scientific" solutions for given, complicated questions. Hence they were at times outraged when their advice was not accepted in toto by the leaders of the American Commission.

In February 1919, for example, William L. Westermann learned from Isaiah Bowman that a report which Westermann had sent to the American plenipotentiaries concerning a settlement for western Asia had been substantially altered by Sidney Mezes. A statement entirely unfavorable to the "proposition of a 'Jewish state'" (although favoring an independent Palestine) had been changed entirely, becoming instead a recommendation for a "Jewish state." Westermann's report, revised in this way, had then been shown to several British delegates with whom a joint report was to be prepared later. As Westermann confided to his diary:

> I must therefore reject the report when it comes up for consideration and then have a talk with Dr. Mezes because this sort of thing is impossible. Many of the ideas are not mine at all, and [it] reads like a valedictorian high school address.

Again, Westermann was understandably bitter on March 25, when he heard that the "higher ups" had decided that American delegates "must conform" to British and French opinion in regard to granting territory in Asia Minor to the Greeks. "I had held out in the Committee on Greek claims against the British and French decision to give a large chunk about Smyrna to the Greek kingdom." Consequently Westermann filed a vigorous protest with Mezes, sending a copy to Colonel House, "because I think that he [Mezes] may have lied about the orders from the "higher ups.'" [16]

Not only did certain specialists like Westermann lose confidence in, and respect for, their superiors, but on occasion the academicians in the American Commission could not agree among themselves on the proper recommendations to lay before the American plenipotentiaries. Outbursts of disagreement arose over the disposition of Shantung, the proper boundaries of the new Polish state, and most particularly the settlement of Italy's frontiers.

On the surface, the Fiume controversy involved the clash of Wilsonian principle with the power realities of the new order in

16. Westermann MSS Diary, March 25, 1919, Columbia.

Europe. Disinterested studies produced by the academicians who served the Inquiry seemed to point conclusively to the justice of Yugoslavia's claims to Fiume. William Lunt, the chief Italian specialist on the Inquiry, joined by Charles Seymour, Isaiah Bowman, Douglas Johnson, Clive Day, and A. A. Young during March and April 1919, pressed for making Fiume part of Yugoslav territory on the basis of ethnography, self-determination, historical ties, and economic need. The six American advisers stressed that the slight Italian plurality in Fiume was of recent origin (since about 1880–90) and resulted from "artificial encouragement by the Hungarian government which held a comprehensive interest in developing an alien rather than a Slav majority in the city." [17] They reminded the President that en route to France in December he had directed the men of the Inquiry: "Tell me what's right and I'll fight for it. Give me a guaranteed position." For more than a year the Inquiry's "experts" had been busily gathering data, and the conclusions they reached on the basis of the facts now seemed clear: Italy should not receive Fiume. But it must be recalled that the academicians on the Inquiry had, in their reports, never emphasized the power realities in the postwar world. The Inquiry staff at Paris clung tenaciously and inflexibly to Wilsonian principles in the face of the new power structure rising out of the war. Wilson was compelled to take continuous cognizance of the new power alignment, but his critics were highly reluctant to do so.[18] Two weeks later, on April 17, the "six" again filed their protests against the ceding of Fiume to Italy. This time they argued that Italy had entered the war simply to acquire "loot." Yugoslavia, a small, relatively weak nation must be accorded the justice of its claim. The issue was joined as follows:

> Italy entered the war with a demand for loot. France and England surrendered to her demand. Of all the world's statesmen the President alone repudiated a war for spoils and proclaimed the

17. Memorandum concerning the Disposition of Fiume by the chiefs of the Italian Division, the Balkan Division, the Austro-Hungarian Division, the Division of Boundary Geography, and the Division of Economics to Wilson, April 4, 1919, Wilson MSS, Series VIII-A, Library of Congress.

18. On Wilson's effectiveness as a negotiator, see letter from E. T. Williams to Assistant Secretary of State Breckenridge Long, Feb. 21, 1919, in Long MSS, Library of Congress.

just principles of an enduring peace. The belligerent nations including Italy, agreed to make peace on the President's principles. Italy now insists that she must carry home an ample bag of spoils or the government will fall.

If Italy gets even nominal sovereignty over Fiume as the price of supporting the League of Nations, she has brought the League down to her level. . . . The world will see that a big Power has profited by the old methods: secret treaties, shameless demands, selfish oppression. . . .

If Jugoslavia loses Fiume, war will follow. When it comes, the League will be fighting on the wrong side.[19]

On the opposing side in this controversy, amongst the advisers serving the American Commission, were former Inquiry stalwarts —Sidney Mezes, George Louis Beer, David Hunter Miller, and James Shotwell. Beer, for instance, believed that the Italians were "infinitely" more advanced culturally than were the Yugoslavs. Hence, as he phrased his position: "It is far preferable to have . . . Jugoslavs under Italians than the contrary, if there is no other good alternative." [20] And on another occasion he confided, critically: "Geographers have had too much influence in these commissions." In view of the several thorny dilemmas, Beer found himself "absolutely pessimistic as to the future of Europe and am inclined to believe that the League of Nations is doomed if it is ever started." [21] After all, Italy was an existing national power in southern Europe; Yugoslavia could expect to become little more than a second-class influence in world politics and civilization.

The upshot of the debate among the technical advisers was that although the Fiume question was never actually settled by the peace conference the American delegation was torn with dissension. There was suspicion, as well as allegations of intrigue, dishonesty, and coercion. Though some of the technical advisers became disgruntled, even cynical, at the proceedings, there were not extensive resignations from the ranks. Most of the former Inquiry hands remained in Paris until May and June when the Versailles Treaty reached its final drafts and was signed. A few mem-

19. Letter from Bowman, Lunt, Day, Johnson, Seymour, and Lunt to Wilson, dated April 17, 1919, Wilson MSS, Series VIII-A, Library of Congress.
20. Beer MSS Diary, March 15, 1919, Columbia.
21. Beer MSS Diary, March 21, 1919, Columbia.

bers continued to remain into the summer and fall of 1919, participating in the negotiation of peace treaties with Germany's allies.[22]

Most of the omissions, mistakes, and inadequacies which marked the Inquiry's operations over its span of fifteen months before the peace conference would perhaps have occurred had the State Department fully dominated the American preparations for peace. The Inquiry, like any institution of its time, reflected the assumptions and values of the early twentieth century. Its virtues and failings stand firmly against the backdrop of its times. Progressive ideals had placed a heavy premium on social planning. Experts, specialists of all kinds, were often credited with possessing both the particular skills and personal disinterestedness considered desired requisites for social planning. Reform of the world's society to prevent future international warfare became the assignment for the Inquiry's engineers. There was, then, the assumption that the expert could, given the tools, provide a "guaranteed position," as the President put it.

The generation which assumed that the "guaranteed position" could be taken in international affairs was also partially blinded by the aura of science. According to plan, the Wilsonian peace was to be a scientifically arranged settlement, to be based precisely on the existing evidence and on the Wilsonian principles. This credo implied that international policies functioned in a truly rational universe. The many Inquiry reports heavily charged with statistical tables and "facts," often with no interpretation, no recommendation, and no obvious frame of reference, bear ample testimony to the "scientific" spirit which permeated much of the Inquiry's work. All of the presumptions—expertness, disinterested-

22. Preston Slosson, "Just What Wilson Did at Paris," *The Independent,* Jan. 21, 1920. There were letters expressing the intention of members to resign or expressing extreme criticism of American policy at the conference, as follows: Samuel E. Morison to Joseph Grew, May 13, 1919, Lansing MSS, Library of Congress; A. A. Berle, Jr., to Grew, May 15, 1919; Joseph Fuller to Grew, May 15, 1919; George B. Noble to Grew, May 15, 1919; John Storck to Grew, May 14, 1919, copies in the Tasker Bliss MSS, Box 69, Library of Congress. See also report of William Bullitt's conversation with Secretary Lansing, May 19, 1919, Bullitt MSS, 51–20, Yale. For the best brief discussion of these controversies among the American advisers at Paris, see Paul Birdsall, *Versailles Twenty Years After* (New York, 1941), pp. 266–88.

ness, and scientific objectivity—which characterized the Inquiry's efforts should not be construed, however, to imply that the reports and recommendations were concerned exclusively with facts and figures. Inquiry members were often predisposed to favor French and Polish causes or other interests and were at times willing to compromise or even flout the Wilsonian principles. Disinterestedness is not a special trait of scholars; it was never a universal attribute possessed by Inquiry members.

In retrospect, after nearly four decades, members of the Inquiry can still recall the hectic, frenzied atmosphere pervading Paris during the peace conference. Idealists and realists, nationalists and internationalists were all in evidence. Revolution, counterrevolution, Bolshevism, and a revived German menace were all real or imaginary specters always present in the background to intimidate the delegates. Allied secret treaties, the special interests of the Japanese, the French, the Italian, and the British governments were always projected into the foreground as stern deterrents to the righteous, lasting peace settlement sought by President Wilson. Yet the American program at Paris did not suffer tragic defeat. The American delegation, when its labors at the peace conference were concluded, could honestly reflect that, considering the obstacles, it had run a good race. A substantial portion of the American program, including the League of Nations, had come through unscathed. Despite numerous crises and obstacles, it would seem that the drama of American preparations for peace, in which the Inquiry had performed the starring role, had proved its value. William Lunt, who had guided the Italian studies for the Inquiry, later appraised the role of the American "expert":

> The so-called experts had available for the information of the commissioners a large amount of pertinent information on many of the questions involved in the negotiations. The commissioners did not have time to make detailed investigations and I think that they relied on much of the information supplied by the experts. In some instances the experts had a direct influence on the results.[23]

Another Inquiry veteran, Samuel Eliot Morison, observed, in a similar vein:

23. William Lunt to the author, Oct. 3, 1953.

The Inquiry was an intelligent and rational means of gathering data in advance of the peace conference. The activities of the Department of State up to that time did not permit of any such studies; there was no conflict, but everyone realized that the Department was not equipped to do it. . . . It was not even faintly suggested that President Wilson or Secretary Lansing would read these reports, but that they would form a basis of reference material which the Peace Commission could use.

It is true that former members of the Inquiry who attended the peace conference left Paris in a somewhat baffled state of mind because they felt that their expert knowledge had not been used. I was one of such people. Looking back, however, I realize that there were considerations of international politics, strategy and common courtesy to our allies which in many, perhaps the majority of cases, prevented President Wilson from following his experts' advice.

On the whole, however, the peace treaties followed expert advice about boundaries, etc. much more closely than they did the advice of economists on preparations . . .[24]

Sidney B. Fay, who worked on the preparations but did not attend the peace conference, has testified further on the importance of the Inquiry:

I think the importance of American experts in writing the treaty was very great (and sometimes unfortunate, e.g., in regard to the Polish settlement).

On the whole I think the Inquiry did a fine job and was of great help in moderating the political hatreds and ambitions of the delegates of the different countries at the Peace Conference. Our experts were sometimes doctrinaire, but generally were on the side of fairness, common-sense, and sound long-run solutions. I have always been sorry that my own recommendations in regard to Latvia and Estonia were not followed. I argued that they be joined with Russia in a federal union of some kind with large autonomy; that from every point of view—political, economic, historic—they were a part of Russia; that if given complete independence they would certainly come into conflict with Russia because they formed Russia's natural outlet to the Baltic; and that in such a conflict they were too small and weak to maintain their independence. Events of 1939 seemed to show that I was right. But my advice was not taken.[25]

24. Samuel E. Morison to the author, Sept. 23, 1953.
25. Sidney B. Fay to the author, Sept. 23, 1953.

Preston Slosson expressed the opinion "that in some cases, the experts were of decisive importance in fixing American policy." [26] Perhaps the most appropriate comment on the Inquiry's role has been made by David Hunter Miller:

> Your question on "The Importance of the American Expert or Professional Scholar" appears to me to require something like the formulation of an imaginary Treaty of Versailles, as it would have been written without participation in its preparation by American experts, and perhaps with (perhaps without) the aid of British, French and other technical advisers; and then a comparison of this theoretical version with the Treaty text . . .[27]

It is virtually inconceivable to think of the peace treaties of 1919 assuming the form they did without benefit of the enormous preparatory effort exerted by the Allied governments and the United States. Britain, France, Italy, and Japan all had clearly defined objectives in the peace settlement. The governments in London and Paris had formed commissions whose function it was to get "their cases ready and their pipes laid" well in advance of the peace conference. Lacking the Inquiry, however inadequate it seemed at times, the Wilsonian cause at Paris might easily have suffered to a greater extent than was actually the case. At least the American plenipotentiaries were able to compete successfully with the weapons of facts, figures, and previously assembled recommendations of other national delegations when the peace negotiations began in earnest. Wilson's program for peace could easily have floundered had the United States delegation been handicapped upon its arrival in Paris by the absence of a comprehensive corpus of reports and recommendations to clothe the President's principles with the necessary justification for their practical application. Both Wilson and House recognized that should the conference fail to provide for a stable international comity American security would be endangered. Any threat to the peace, wherever it occurred, would affect American interests directly or indirectly. Hence the scope of the Inquiry and the American program for peace reached global proportions. Perhaps there is no better measure than the work of the Inquiry to indicate that the United States by 1917 had reached the status of a great world power.

26. Preston Slosson to the author, Oct. 3, 1953.
27. David Hunter Miller to the author, Oct. 27, 1953.

APPENDIXES

APPENDIX I

JANUARY 1918

Cyrus C. Adams	$275.00	Walter Lippmann	$500.00
Henryk Arctowski	200.00	Robert Littel	65.00
J. C. Bonbright	150.00	Armin Lobeck	183.33
William Briesemeister	58.14	J. W. McGuire	275.00
Leon Dominian	175.00	Margaret G. Marsh	140.00
Arthur Eckhardt	72.50	William S. Monroe	50.00
F. R. Flournoy	74.00	Parker T. Moon	150.00
F. A. Golder	245.00	F. K. Morris	75.00
L. H. Gray	120.00	Wallace Notestein	250.00
W. H. Hobbs	150.00	W. H. Pitkin	416.66
Lazarovitch		Ellen C. Semple	150.00
Hrebelianovitch	50.00	Charles Seymour	300.00
Manley O. Hudson	200.00	James T. Shotwell	541.66
Abraham Johannsen	30.00	Albert Sonnichsen	50.00
F. W. Jones	150.00	A. P. Usher	100.00
Robert J. Kerner	200.00	M. F. Wilson	125.00
Edward Krehbiel	200.00	A. P. Winston	200.00
Charles Krisch	150.00	Allyn A. Young	250.00

ADDITIONS IN FEBRUARY 1918

Robert Lord $166.66

ADDITIONS IN MARCH 1918

W. H. Hatts	$150.00	William F. Mathews	$100.00
Dorothy Kenyon	108.33	F. H. Newell	232.90
Robert Lord (sharp salary increase)	500.00		

ADDITIONS IN APRIL 1918

Clive Day	$300.00	W. E. Johnson	$150.00

* Personnel Records, David Hunter Miller MSS, Library of Congress.

ADDITIONS IN MAY 1918

H. F. Monroe $100.00

ADDITIONS IN JUNE 1918

Osgood Hardy	$ 90.00	F. B. Norris	$175.00
Norman D. Harris	200.00	Eugene Van Cleef	216.66
George McBride	90.00		

ADDITIONS IN JULY 1918

Bertha H. Ehlers	$100.00	I. M. Rubinow	$400.00
Nevin M. Fenneman	73.00	William L. Westermann	200.00
Frederick Merk	50.00		

ADDITIONS IN AUGUST 1918

W. J. Haye	$ 86.66	L. Jezioranski	$127.05
Charles Horney	120.80	David Magie	1.00
Nora Horney	96.66	(honorarium)	
Margaret Howe	83.33	Mason Tyler	100.00

ADDITIONS IN SEPTEMBER 1918

Frank M. Anderson	$400.00	William E. Lunt *	$ 1.00
Sibyl Baker	112.50	(honorarium)	
Richard B. Barrett	66.66	Albert H. Lybyer	300.00
William J. Blank	105.78	B. L. Miller	125.00
A. Briesemeister	135.00	Doska Minical	125.00
Thomas Burk	135.00	Max Roesler	200.00
Glenn Coleman	108.33	W. L. Schurz	173.00
Stuart Davis	100.00	Vladimir Simkhovitch *	333.33
Theodore de Booy	200.00	John Smallwood	125.67
Donald P. Frary	136.15	A. Solowy	108.33
N. M. Goldenweiser	100.00	J. B. Stubbs	175.00
Bertha Henderson	166.66	Charles R. Sweeney	87.50
		V. V. Tchikoff	150.00
		Bailey Willis *	130.00

* These men had been working for the Inquiry prior to this month, but their names appeared on the account books for the first time in September 1918.

PERSONS DRAWING NO SALARY

George L. Beer
George H. Blakeslee
Isaiah Bowman
Archibald Cary Coolidge
Edwin D. Dickinson
William E. Dodd
D. W. Johnson
Andrew Keogh

William E. Lingelbach
C. C. Maxey
Sidney E. Mezes
David Hunter Miller
Dana C. Munro
Pauline Stearns
Mary E. Townsend
Raphael Zon

APPENDIX II

INQUIRY PERSONNEL AS OF OCTOBER 30, 1918
CLASSIFIED BY FUNCTION °

DIRECTOR   Sidney E. Mezes

AFRICA

G. F. Andrews
George L. Beer

Nevin M. Fenneman
Alice Ryan

AUSTRIA-HUNGARY

Richard B. Barrett
Thomas Burk (half-time)
Clive Day

Florence A. Hague
Robert J. Kerner
Charles Seymour
Charles Sweeney

BALKANS

H. W. Bell
Thomas Burk (half-time)
William S. Ferguson

W. S. Monroe
G. R. Noyes

DIPLOMATIC HISTORY

Frank M. Anderson
Donald Beddoe
Joseph P. Chamberlain
Ellen S. Davison
William A. Dunning
William Jaffe
L. M. Larsen

Albert A. Lybyer
Charles H. McIlwaine
H. L. Munro
Florence Poast
James T. Shotwell
Preston Slosson
Mary Wingebach

ECONOMICS

John B. Andrews
J. C. Bonbright
F. R. Fairchild

F. W. Jones
Marjorie Lappan
A. A. Young

° Personnel Records, David Hunter Miller MSS, Library of Congress.

FAR EAST

Katherine E. Butchelder

Norman D. Harris

A. P. Winston

GENERAL RESEARCH

W. C. Abbott

Isaiah Bowman

Austin P. Evans

L. H. Gray

Max Handman

Bertha Henderson

A. F. Keene

Parker T. Moon

Thuesdda Schaeffer

V. V. Tchikoff

INTERNATIONAL LAW

Ruth Bache-Wig

Glenn Coleman

F. C. Hicks

Manley O. Hudson

David Hunter Miller

Charles G. Stratton

Laura Turnbull

Frank L. Warrin, Jr.

ITALY

William E. Lunt

LATIN AMERICA

Sibyl Baker

Theodore de Booy

Leon Dominian

Marie Lobeltern

George McBride

Doska Minical

F. B. Morris

Max Roesler

W. L. Schurz

Helen Treckel

Eugene Van Cleef

Bailey Willis

MAPS—CARTOGRAPHY

Charles Besswerger

W. J. Blank

John W. Braback

W. Briesemeister

Mary Carwood

Stuart Davis

Mark Jefferson

Douglas Johnson

Charles Kirsch

A. K. Lobeck

W. F. Mathews

Herman Nagel

341

MAPS—CARTOGRAPHY (*cont.*)

H. D. Ralphs
Ellen Semple
Everett K. Taidor

Russell L. Wiget
C. Witenberg

PACIFIC ISLANDS

George H. Blakeslee

REFERENCE AND ARCHIVES

William Amos
Gladys Beddoe
Mary E. Bigger
W. L. Deenklee
Donald P. Frary
Annie Hamay

Albert E. Levy
E. C. Richardson
Vladimir Simkhovitch
Florence Storck
Albert Suglio

RUSSIA

Arthur I. Andrews
Henryk Arctowski
Roland B. Dixon
Sidney B. Fay
N. M. Goldenweiser
F. A. Golder
Charles Horvey
L. Jezioranski

Robert Lord
William H. Reed
I. M. Rubinow
A. Solovy
Ethel Towers
Dorothy Trinkle
S. J. Zowski

WESTERN ASIA

O. J. Campbell
David Magie
F. H. Newell

John M. Vincent
William L. Westermann

WESTERN EUROPE

Hetty Goldman
Charles H. Haskins
Frederick Merk

Wallace Notestein
Lawrence Steefel

APPENDIX III

MEMORANDUM REGARDING THE ORGANIZATION OF THE INQUIRY, NOVEMBER 13, 1917 *

1. Give each man engaged written instructions in memorandum form.
2. Appoint an executive manager and centralize correspondence.
3. Suggest that central committee lunch together twice a week.
4. Classification of Material Declarations Relating to the Settlement.

DIVISION I

Assemble at once for:

Belgium	Bulgaria	Lithuania
Alsace-Lorraine	Greece	Ukraine
Trentino, Trieste	Roumania	Courland
Dalmatia	Poland	Finland
Jugoslavia	Bohemia	Turkey

the following information:

1. Official Statements by governments.
2. Semi official statements in newspapers.
3. Speeches of authorized spokesmen of significant organized propaganda.
4. Articles by leading specialists.

DIVISION II—Bibliography

Prepare card index of official source material upon which claims can be based. Government statistics, private surveys likely to be quoted. This is a bibliographical task, should contain explanations of how to use material; where it is to be found—in this country—and abroad. In conjunction with it, and arranged for convenient reference, there should be a critique of this source material showing probable bias and estimated inaccuracy. This should be assembled from learned journals.

* Shotwell MSS, Columbia.

Standard reference works, carefully sifted, on all the powers . . .
Should be completed January 1, 1918. Inspect material December 10, 1917.

DIVISION III—Maps

1. Series of maps, of uniform or adjustable scale, on a transparent medium, showing all boundary claims made by governments, subject peoples, and important political groups.
2. A series of maps showing racial and religious composition of the areas based on official statistics; where disputes exist, based on claims.
3. A series of maps showing existing resources covering zones of dispute in detail; interior areas may be summarized; engineering projects uncompleted and probable, such as railroads, canals, tunnels, dams, etc.
4. A series of maps, adjustable to the foregoing, showing international trade routes.
5. A series of maps showing spheres of influence, special concessions, protectorates, disguised and avowed: for each power, for each backward territory (Remarks: Prof. Bowman in charge) (1, 4, 5 to be completed by December 10, 1917; 2 to be completed by January 1, and 3 to be completed by February 1, 1918).

DIVISION IV—Social and Economic Problems of Disputed European Areas

1. Special economic problems of disputed European Areas.
   a. Data especially assembled for transferable areas showing
      (1) estimated share of public debt borne by area under old sovereignty.
      (2) estimated contribution of revenue under old sovereignty.
      (3) ownership, capital value, probable condition of fixed plan in area.
      (4) system of land tenure, prevailing in the area.
   b. Data on estimated cost of restoring physical damages incurred during the war by destruction, by deterioration, by obsolescence.

2. Sociology of Disputed European Areas.
   a. Existing school facilities.
   b. Existing religious regulations.

344

c. Existing legal and political inequalities.
d. Form of government.
e. Political parties.

(Remarks: 1-a . . . to be completed by February 1, 1918;
   1-b . . . to be concluded by March 1, 1918;
   2 . . . to be completed by January 15, 1918.)

Division V—Scarcity and Monopoly

1. Analysis and survey of those materials which are essential, their distribution, the possibility of substitutes with special references to:
   a. Military preparations.
   b. National key industries.

(Remarks . . . to be completed by February 1, 1918.)

Division VI—International Trade

1. Material assembled in accordance with memorandum of Mr. David Hunter Miller. Supplementary arrangements of material to show political significance of international interdependence.
   a. Each nation's essential needs, the source from which they can be drawn, the nature of the control exercised over those supplies by the controlling nation or nations.
   b. The machinery of international priority.
   c. Steps taken by each of the Powers, established by its own sovereignty.
      (1) internal preference.
      (2) preference to allies and friendly neutrals.
      (3) storage of materials.

(Remarks . . . to be completed at latest March 1, 1918.)

Division VII—International Law

1. Assemble all important texts.
2. Digest experience on reduction of sovereignty.
   a. Communications.
   b. Protectorates.
   c. Joint administrations.
   d. Interferences, interventions and guarantees.

(Remarks . . . to be completed by February 1, 1918.)

345

DIVISION VIII—Political Conditions of Great Powers

1. Strength of parties.
2. Origin in population.
3. Demands.
4. Who's Who among leaders.
5. Constitutional arrangements.
6. Political view of important economic groups.

(Remarks . . . to be completed February 1, 1918.)

DIVISION IX—Neutrals

1. Their dynastic, economic, military and political dependence upon:
   a. Central Powers
   b. Russia
   c. Japan
   d. Great Britain
   e. United States

The purpose of this division is to show the probable position of the neutrals especially those adjoining Germany at the Peace Conference, so as to estimate the political significance of German concessions and the nature of desirable counter concessions on the part of the Allies.

(Remarks: This cannot be done without the assistance of State Department and can await return of Colonel House.)

DIVISION X—Proposals

1. Suggestive plans.
2. Critique of plans.
3. Technique of Peace Conferences.

(Remarks: 1 to be completed by December 15, 1917; 2 is to be a continuous task; 3 to be completed March 1, 1918.)

DIVISION XI—Editing and Epitome of all Material

(Remarks: Mezes, general supervision; Shotwell, Archives; and Lippmann, summary and report.)

APPENDIX IV

ACTIVITIES OF THE INQUIRY
NOVEMBER 27, 1917 °

ACTIVITIES OF THE INQUIRY

Activities   I. Planning and Procedure.
Activities II. Collecting Data.
Activities III. Digesting Data.
Activities IV. Editing Data.

AGENTS OF INQUIRY

Agent   I. In Politics and Government—Chief W. Lippmann.
Agent   II. In Geography—Chief I. Bowman.
Agent III. In Social Science and History—Chief J. T. Shotwell.
Agent   IV. In Economics and Business—Chiefs D. H. Miller and
              A. A. Young.
Agent   V. In International Law—Chief J. F. Chamberlain.
Agent   VI. In Strategy—Chief to be named.
Agent VII. In Bibliography—Chief to be named.

FIELDS OF INQUIRY

Field   I. The Powers.
              (1) The Friends—The United States, British Empire, etc.
              (2) The Enemies.
              (3) The Neutrals—Denmark, Holland, etc.

Field   II. Debatable areas and unfortunate peoples.
          (1) Alsace-Lorraine   (5) Jews
          (2) Schleswig   (6) Pacific Islands
          (3) Trentino   (7) Nationalities of Eastern Europe
          (4) Baltic Littoral   (8) China, Turkey, Middle East

Field III. International Business.

Field   IV. International Law.

Field   V. International Cooperation.

° Mezes MSS, Columbia.

347

APPENDIX V

REPORT ON THE INQUIRY, MAY 10, 1918 *

PART I

The work of the Inquiry consists of the following sections:

1. The western front—Belgium, Luxemburg, Alsace-Lorraine, from the left bank of the Rhine to the occupied part of France.

2. The head of the Adriatic—the Trentino, the Isonzo, Istria and Trieste, the Dalmatian coast.

3. Austria-Hungary—including the Czecho-Slovak and Jugo-Slav movements.

4. The Balkans—Montenegro, Serbia, Albania, Bulgaria, Greece, the Greek islands, and the Greek fringe on the coast of Asia Minor.

5. The Ottoman Empire—Thrace, Constantinople, the Straits, Anatolia, the Armenian vilayets, Syria and Palestine, Mesopotamia, the Arab states.

6. Persia, Afghanistan, and Beluchistan.

7. The former Russian Empire—the Polish area, including Galicia, Teschen, East and West Prussia, Posen, Silesia; Lithuania, Courland, Estonia; White Russia; Ukraine; Finland, Great Russia; Siberia; the Caucasus; Mohammedan Russia; Russian Central Asia.

8. Roumania and Bessarabia.

9. Africa—Northern Africa, Tropical Africa, Southern Africa.

10. The Far East—Japan, China, French Indo China, Siam.

11. The Pacific Ocean—the Dutch colonies, the German colonies, Australian claims, the American naval position.

12. South and Central America.

In addition to these analytical territorial studies, the following synthetic research is in progress:

* Inquiry Document No. 882, *Foreign Relations of the United States 1919, The Paris Peace Conference*, 1, 82–83.

348

13. The commercial relations of Central Europe in the east, west, and overseas.

14. Political and commercial developments and plans of the British Empire.

15. The world situation as to minerals, agricultural products, manufactures, shipping, commercially strategic lines of transportation, British, German, French, Italian firms doing foreign business, timber resources of the world, raw material possibilities, tariffs, credit.

16. The needs and political affiliations of the European neutrals.

17. Projects for educational, sanitary, and fiscal reform in backward areas, especially Turkey, the Balkans, and Africa.

18. A special diplomatic policy history of the world in its bearing upon problems of the settlement.

19. The diplomatic policy of each of the Great Powers.

20. A current collation, summary, and analysis of public commitments in all countries, affecting the settlement, together with an examination of sources upon which claims are based.

21. The collection and analysis of plans proposed for settling questions likely to arise at the peace conference.

22. International Law—the collection of treaties and precedents, statements of legal questions involved in the President's program, with particular reference to the League of Nations, the equality of trade, and equality upon the high seas.

23. The production of a series of maps and graphs embodying the results of research.

24. The collection of detailed primary reference maps on all parts of the world which may come under discussion.

25. The selection and planning of a library to be assembled at short notice, for use at the conference itself.

26. The revision and current use of all material in the Archives, and the training of a corps of expert advisors and assistants competent to use this material.

27. The framing of plans for transforming the present staff of the Inquiry into a secretariat for the use of the peace commissioners.

28. Detailed critiques of reports and other material.

29. The central direction of the research and administration of the staff and equipment.

APPENDIX VI

NOTES ON THE INQUIRY
NOVEMBER 30, 1918 *

(Extracts)

.   .   .

Of organization on the part of the Inquiry it is necessary to say there was none whatever when the organization began work in this building [Geographical Society]. The Society donated the time of its draftsmen for nearly a month and demonstrated the necessity for having a thoroughgoing map program worked out. The use of the maps became so general and the demands for them so imperative that plans and arguments had to be framed from time to time for the consideration of the Executive Committee composed of Miller, Mezes and Lippmann. These plans were always thrown back in such a manner as to imply that they should be done by the Geographical Society which of course had no funds for such work . . .

On May first I submitted a program to the Executive Committee which was disregarded and it developed later, that is about August first, that a very much modified program had been framed by Lippmann and put into the hands of Storck [an administrative assistant] for execution.

In the meantime one experiment followed another under the direction of Lippmann until both the map program and the drafting staff became entirely disorganized and demoralized. This situation was not remedied until July and August as related hereafter.

During the months of May and June the state of disorganization of the Inquiry had become so extreme that about half of the principal men on it had told me that they were going to resign. In preparation for my own action in the matter I decided to take 3 weeks vacation so as to allow things to come to a head. This decision was made in May. I determined to stay on very friendly relations with both Mezes and

* No author, but attributed to Isaiah Bowman. Shotwell MSS, Columbia.

Lippmann until I went away for vacation. Between the time that the decision was made and the latter part of June, Mr. Lippmann had found himself in an extremely uncomfortable position being unable on the one hand, to guide the work of the Inquiry successfully and, on the other hand, finding himself more and more restricted by Dr. Mezes. I had several conversations with Lippmann about Mezes. I told Lippmann that I would not plot against [someone] whom I characterized as a very stupid director. Lippmann said he could do nothing because he had been so closely connected with Mezes and he agreed with me as to his stupidity and added that he was also lazy and that it took him (Lippmann) several hours each day to get him to do things such as to write letters, arrange for necessary interviews and in general keep his desk in order, and that lately it had become so disorderly that he could do nothing with him. Directly after his leaving, Mezes sent out a memorandum regarding relations with government bureaus which was extremely distasteful and ill-advised, and just before Lippmann left, he and Mezes ordered the stopping of work on the base map of Europe 1:3,000,000. When I heard of these facts I wrote Dr. Mezes a letter, copy of which is attached, saying that the Inquiry was in a bad state of disorganization and suggesting considerable changes. I returned to the office on July 16 and at Dr. Mezes' suggestion took up with him on several occasions the problems of the Inquiry. I told him that he was a weak director and that we needed a strong one, and I also told him that both Lippmann and myself had in conferences criticized his administration. When he prepared a Balkan memorandum with the assistance of [Parker] Moon only and sent it to the State Department without consulting with others on the staff I told him what I thought of Moon and his own way of managing the affairs of the Inquiry and offered my resignation. This he asked me to postpone for two days until he had time to think it over and consult Colonel House. He changed his mind and consulted [David] Miller instead. Mr. Miller over his private line from his downtown office to Magnolia had a forty minute conversation with the Colonel giving him in detail his opinion of both Mezes and myself as well as Lippmann. The result of this was that Colonel House asked me to become executive officer of the Inquiry and Dr. Mezes asked me to be responsible for men, money and plans of the Inquiry from that time.

I had a long conference with Mr. Miller on the question of both Mezes and Lippmann and he was outspoken in his comments on both and especially Lippmann. He said that he never knew of anyone who worked with Lippmann who did not "hate" him. Some time after this

351

I wrote a letter to Colonel House, . . . and this was followed by a visit to Colonel House on August 27 or 28. During this visit he asked me what the trouble was with Lippmann and not wishing to bother him with all the details I told him that Lippmann was a bad influence on the Inquiry chiefly through his tendency to disorganize whatever work was started by anyone else, taking men off work for his own special purposes.

Colonel House thereupon told me precisely why he had Lippmann on the Inquiry and asked me to keep secret both the comments that he made and the fact that he made them. His comments were as follows: He said that the Administration had to cooperate with the extreme liberals of the country and that he could think of none who had so much influence and was at the same time so easy to get along with as Lippmann, and he had therefore selected him to represent the Liberals. He asked me further if I could think of anyone who was so agreeable as Lippmann, and he added, "Don't you think that he is the least vocal of that crowd?" He then stated that should Lippmann return he would plan with me just what work he should do and that probably the best plan was to have Lippmann do some specific things directly for him (Colonel House). During the following months Lippmann got into trouble with the military authorities. The first reports from Paris said that the propaganda work organized under Lippmann was proceeding well and this brought forth a storm of criticism within the Military Intelligence Branch. . . .

THE WORK OF THE RESEARCH COMMITTEE

Returning now to the organization of the Inquiry as I planned in my capacity as executive officer the day on which Dr. Mezes made me responsible for "men, money and plans," and without consulting either him or Mr. Miller, I prepared a memorandum to be sent to all the division chiefs . . . I knew I had Miller's support and I wished to put Dr. Mezes' oral directions to me on record and to test out the sincerity of his statement that the administrative work of the Inquiry was in my hands. I appointed a Research Committee . . . and after the memorandum had been sent out, sent a copy to Mezes' desk the following morning. Whereupon he called a meeting of the Executive Committee and tried to make modifications in the plan and to suggest the manner in which it should be carried out. Though I had not previously consulted Mr. Miller or solicited his support he came to my support voluntarily and blocked every suggestion Dr. Mezes made with the result that from that time on Dr. Mezes did not interfere

352

at all with the administration of the work and for the first time in the history of the Inquiry the work became orderly and effective and constructive. The Research Committee continued its meeting and its work through August and September and was terminated about October 20 by order of Colonel House who had left for Europe about that time. At least Dr. Mezes said that he had ordered the changes. All the committees were disbanded and the Inquiry was ordered to be placed on a peace conference basis. Dr. Mezes was more and more uncomfortable under these arrangements because, though I kept him informed of the actions of the committees and he received copies of all minutes, he saw his own influence and power slipping away and he did not attend the last three meetings of the Executive Committee. The last meeting he attended was a stormy one in which we discussed the organization chart for the peace conference. He lost his temper and told me that I was trying to get rid of the Executive Committee. He presented a dissenting opinion and an alternative chart and both these were very roughly handled by Mr. Miller who told Dr. Mezes that his chart and his plans would not take care of *any* of the items of discussion at the peace conference. Dr. Mezes saw himself without any influence and interviewed Colonel House in the matter with the result that Colonel House asked Mr. Miller to undertake some additional work in Washington which would keep him there. Then Colonel House made preparations for sailing and left the organization of the Inquiry on a peace conference basis in Dr. Mezes' hands.

APPENDIX VII

STATEMENT MADE BY DR. ISAIAH BOWMAN CONCERNING THE REORGANIZATION OF THE INQUIRY, NOTES TAKEN MARCH 14, 1932 *

(Extracts)

In the first week in July, 1918, Lippmann received a Commission in the Army and went to Europe as a member of the Intelligence section. In June, Dr. Bowman went off on his holidays and did not return to New York until late in July. Most of the members of the Inquiry had been threatening to leave during the preceding months as they became more and more annoyed at Lippmann, but when he left, and they had to deal directly with Mezes they found him so much worse that they told Dr. Bowman they had decided to quit. Dr. Bowman did nothing except to urge them not to, and to get them to wait a little longer, reminding the group that it was the Peace Conference that mattered, and that as soon as they actually got to Paris they would be able to deal directly with Commissioners, since all would ignore Mezes in Paris.

[The accuracy of this first paragraph is open to some question, for the decision to hold the peace conference in Paris was not made until several months later.]

Then one day towards the end of July or beginning of August Dr. Bowman had a call from Mr. Miller, who came up to see him and explained that he had been talking over long distance to House, at Magnolia [House's summer home in Massachusetts], and that House wanted Dr. Bowman to come up and discuss the problem with him. Dr. Bowman went up to Magnolia during the first week of August. House asked him just what had been the trouble with Lippmann and Mezes, and then asked Dr. Bowman if he would take over the running of the Inquiry, if Colonel House gave him complete charge of men, money and plans. As Dr. Bowman could not think of anything this did not include, he accepted.

Dr. Bowman then returned to New York and sent for Professor Haskins, Professor Shotwell and Professor Young. The four met and Dr. Bowman proposed that they form themselves into a "research committee" to take over all the power turned over by House. They agreed,

* Shotwell MSS, Columbia.

354

and Dr. Bowman then wrote a memorandum outlining the decision and future plans and put it on Mezes' desk at the Inquiry, and asked him to attend the meetings of the Research Committee. This was the first intimation that Mezes had of what had been happening. Mezes came to the first meeting of the Committee but he never came to another. The work went on and nothing further was said until House sailed for Europe (October 16, 1918). A day or two after he sailed, House sent Mezes a radiogram from the ship saying substantially this: Please take charge of Inquiry and organize it with respect to the problems that will come up at the Peace Conference. This was his way of taking back what he had given to Dr. Bowman in his interview in August at Magnolia, but he had not had the nerve to tell this to Dr. Bowman but had waited until he was at sea and wired Mezes. Mezes then showed the radiogram to Bowman and announced that he would then take charge of the Inquiry. (The sequel later however was his request that Bowman go to Washinton to see Lansing.)

Therefore, on October 18 or 19, Dr. Mezes took over the Inquiry. Apparently during the next two weeks he worked out a plan of the people that he wanted to go to the Peace Conference, and this plan did not meet Secretary Lansing's approval. When he had drawn up this plan he asked Dr. Bowman to come up and see it, and he showed Dr. Bowman the list without Dr. Bowman's name and said he didn't see how he could take Dr. Bowman along. (Dr. Bowman had been the buffer between Mezes and the rest of the Inquiry, but Mezes, being unable to play fair himself, assumed that Bowman had not been playing fair with him. Actually when the Research Committee saw the radiogram from House they wanted to leave at once, but Dr. Bowman convinced them to stay on and wait till they got to Paris.) Dr. Mezes, after showing Dr. Bowman the list, suggested that he might go along as Clerk. Dr. Bowman refused with thanks, and the next day Dr. Mezes called him in again, having obviously had a terrific emotional struggle with himself, and told Bowman that he might scratch off the list the name of any man he wished and take his place—he would be especially pleased to have him take Professor Haskins' place. After Dr. Bowman refused, Dr. Mezes, on his own initiative, went down to Washington to talk the matter over with Lansing. (Whenever he did anything on his own responsibility, he got into trouble.) Lansing probably said plenty and Mezes came back a very unhappy man.

Secretary Lansing went to a cabinet meeting on October 28 and showed the President Mezes' list. The conversation probably went about like this: The Secretary to the President, "Mezes is House's brother-in-law. The case is difficult to handle. Will you give me a letter that I may show him, to enable me to select my own personnel for the peace conference." As a result of this talk the President on the 29th of October wrote to Secretary Lansing: "As I said to you orally yesterday, I think the enclosed is much too ambitious a programme, and I would be obliged if you would have a simpler one worked out, in the meantime telling Dr. Mezes that it is so unlikely that anything but the main territorial, political and racial questions at issue will be settled at the peace conference, and practically so certain that all detailed discussions of financial and commercial and other similar arrangements will be delegated by the Conference to special conferences or commissions, that I think he ought to plan only to carry the men and materials with him which will be serviceable in settling the main questions, together of course with the necessary clerical aid. The Department itself in the meantime can work out the necessary minimum personnel and organization."

Secretary Lansing sent this letter (Dr. Bowman remembers that he sent the original of the letter) to Mezes along with the following letter, dated October 31, 1918:

"I submitted your diagram of the proposed personnel for the peace conference to the President after Cabinet meeting on Tuesday, the 29th. After a brief discussion of it I left it with him for his consideration. This morning he returned the diagram to me with a letter, a copy of which I enclose.

I think it would be very well, therefore, after you have thought the matter over, to arrange to come here and see me. Possibly you could do so early next week. Meanwhile I will endeavor to work out the organization in accordance with the President's suggestion, from the Department's standpoint."

At the same time as Dr. Mezes received this from Secretary Lansing he received a cable from House dated November 1, 1918 asking him to send by cable advice as to program and difficulties of Inquiry since his (House's) departure, and asking to be informed fully by cable regarding this work. Obviously House, knowing that there would be difficulties as a result of his earlier radiogram to Mezes, wished to check up on what Mezes was doing. But Mezes could not send the above letters to Colonel House and admit his own failure, and a further trip to Washington on his part was likely to lead to further difficulties. So he had to look around for some other method, and, as Dr. Bowman was the only man on the Inquiry that he had at least been talking to, he called Dr. Bowman in and showed him the letter from the President to Lansing (although he did not show Bowman the wire from House) and asked him to go down to Washington and try to straighten matters out. Bowman went down to Washington and saw Leland Harrison and others and talked matters out, especially in regard to organization, had a chat with Lansing, and then returned and reported to Mezes.

. . .

After Dr. Bowman came back and reported on his trip to Washington, Mezes drew up another final list, again leaving Bowman's name off. Secretary Lansing, however, saw the omission and called Dr. Mezes' attention to it. Therefore Mezes, being completely caught, had to do the generous thing, and since Bowman was going anyway, Mezes suggested that Bowman be Chief Territorial Specialist. Lansing promptly accepted this title, and it remained.

Dr. Bowman, before going to Paris, had asked not to have an administrative position, as he was tired out from the work in New York. But when they got over to Paris, they found no organization there at all, and in a very short time the Commission asked Bowman to resume the job that he had taken from House in August, and shortly after, early in January, the Intelligence Section was organized, and Bowman was appointed Executive Officer of it. He divided this into a certain number of Divisions, with different men as Chief of Division, etc. . . .

APPENDIX VIII

TOTAL EXPENDITURES OF THE INQUIRY ITEMIZED *

Total Expenditures	$241,200.00 †
Regional Research	28,724.68
Topical Research	13,874.36
General Research	6,524.21
Map Program	16,116.40
Administration	5,856.50
Reference and Archives	7,291.82
Incidentals	23,541.90
Latin America	35,000.00
International Law	11,000.00
Research Salaries	139,895.08
Clerical Salaries	28,533.59
Clerical Temporary Service	8,135.77
Personal and Traveling Expenses	19,178.59
Library	2,936.55
Printing and Stationery	16,925.81
Equipment	9,885.57
Telephone and Telegrams	1,499.42
Postage	5,807.73
Petty Cash	217.43
Refund to Secretary of State	8,401.89

* Inquiry Account Book, David Hunter Miller MSS, Library of Congress.

† The first column of figures below totals $147,829.87; the second column totals $233,015.54 (when the refund to the Secretary of State is deducted), neither figure corresponding precisely to the figure of total expenditures indicated in the document.

APPENDIX IX

I. PRACTICAL TASKS OF THE CONFERENCE IN WHICH THE INQUIRY CAN HELP [*]

1. Establish or provide for the establishment of boundaries.
2. Set up or provide for the setting up of governments.
3. Estimate strength and weakness of doubtful states, and make a study of the status each might be given affecting particular states.
4. Draw up or provide for the drawing up of economic arrangements.
5. Provide for the safeguarding of minorities or of weak peoples.
6. Provide for "equality of economic opportunity" (most favored nation clause, etc.).
7. Rewrite or provide for the rewriting of international law in general and as applied to specific problems.
8. Bear in mind diplomatic history—ditto.
9. Study various forms of international or joint control.
10. In certain cases, make a study of plebiscites and similar devices for ascertaining the desires and interests of the populations concerned.

II. REGIONS CLASSIFIED BY TASKS

1. The establishment of provision for the establishment of boundaries will have to be undertaken for Poland, Alsace-Lorraine, Trentino, Trieste, Austria-Hungary, the Balkans, and Turkey. The establishment or provision for the establishment of boundaries may have to be undertaken for fragments of Russia, the nucleus of Russia, Slesvig, Belgium, Luxembourg, North Africa, Tropical and South Africa, Latin America.

2. The setting up of [sic] provision for the setting up of governments will have to be undertaken for Poland and Austria-Hungary. The setting up of [sic] provision for the setting up of governments may have to be undertaken for the fragments of Russia, the nucleus of Russia, the Balkans and Turkey.

3. Estimates of the strength and weakness of *doubtful states will have* to be undertaken for the fragments of Russia, the nucleus of Russia, the Balkans and Turkey.

4. The drawing up or [sic] provision for the drawing up of economic

[*] House Inquiry Report, Drawer 33-10, House MSS, Yale.

359

arrangements may have to be undertaken for the fragments of Russia, the nucleus of Russia, Poland, Belgium, Luxembourg, Alsace-Lorraine, Austria-Hungary, the Balkans, Turkey, North Africa, Tropical and South Africa, the Far East and Latin America.

5. Provision for the safeguarding of minorities or of weak peoples will have to be undertaken for Turkey and Tropical and South Africa. Provision for the safeguarding of minorities or of weak peoples may have to be undertaken for the fragments of Russia, the nucleus of Russia, Poland, Austria-Hungary, the Balkans, North Africa, and the Pacific Islands.

III. CONFERENCE

How Inquiry can help with regard to each major task of Conference: ethnic-racial boundaries determined, stability or instability of racial distribution as affected by change of political boundaries and governmental action, by economic forces, by religious forces, by other cultural forces, etc., but all with stability or instability in mind.

Historic facts and national or racial aspirations as indicating boundaries.

Economic facts and needs as indicating boundaries—as a *well balanced* economic unit, access to ports, and markets, i.e., minor units that should not be disrupted, etc.

Defensive needs as indicating boundaries.

International commitments and obligations as affecting proposed boundaries.

Government: Inquiry can give some account of political, economic and military strength and weakness of "states" and what participation in government peoples have had, and an estimate of their capacity for self government.

Inquiry can give some account of provisional governments that have claimed to represent them.

APPENDIX X

DISTRIBUTION OF THE SUBJECTS REPORTED
BY THE ECONOMICS DIVISION *

Subject	Number of Reports	Subject	Number of Reports
Agriculture	18	Finland	1
Copyright	1	France	31
Finance	15	Germany	80
Hides and skins	2	Great Britain	17
Interallied organization	5	Greece	2
International organization	2	Hungary	6
Minerals	18	India	9
Nitrogen	1	Ireland	4
Reconstruction and		Italy	12
natural resources	4	Japan	14
Rubber and gutta percha	3	Latin America	5
Shipping	10	Mexico	1
Tariffs	14	Netherlands	5
Wool	3	New Zealand	2
		Norway	1
Africa	13	Portugal	4
Alsace-Lorraine	7	Rumania	13
Austria	16	Russia	50
Austria-Hungary	13	St. Pierre and Miquelon	1
Balkans	2	Samoa	1
Baltic provinces	2	Scotland	7
Belgium	3	Serbia	4
Bulgaria	8	Spain	20
Brazil	2	Sweden	2
Chile	4	Switzerland	9
China	23	Turkey	26
Denmark	1	Ukraine	7
England	15	United States	153
Far East	4	Wales	2

* National Archives, "Preliminary Inventories No. 89," compiled by H. Stephen Helton.

BIBLIOGRAPHY

MANUSCRIPT COLLECTIONS

Chandler P. Anderson Papers, Library of Congress.
The Archives of the Department of State for 1917–18, National Archives.
The Archives of the Inquiry, National Archives.
Gordon Auchincloss Papers, Yale University Library.
Ray Stannard Baker Papers, Library of Congress.
George Louis Beer Diary, Columbia University Library.
Tasker Bliss Papers, Library of Congress.
William H. Buckler Papers, Yale University Library.
William C. Bullitt Papers, Yale University Library.
Josephus Daniels Papers, Library of Congress.
William E. Dodd Papers, Library of Congress.
Edwin F. Gay Papers, Huntington Library, San Marino, California.
Thomas W. Gregory Papers, Library of Congress.
Leland Harrison Papers, Library of Congress.
Edward M. House Papers, Yale University Library.
Robert Lansing Papers, Library of Congress.
Breckinridge Long Papers, Library of Congress.
Sidney E. Mezes Papers, Columbia University Library.
David Hunter Miller Papers, Library of Congress.
Walter Hines Page Papers, Harvard University Library.
Frank Polk Papers, Yale University Library.
James T. Shotwell Papers, Columbia University Library.
Joseph B. Umpleby Papers, The University of Washington Library.
William L. Westermann Diary, Columbia University Library.
Henry White Papers, Library of Congress.
Woodrow Wilson Papers, Library of Congress.
William Wiseman Papers, Yale University Library.
William Yale Papers, Yale University Library.

PRINTED AND PUBLISHED GOVERNMENT DOCUMENTS

France, Comité d'études, *Travaux du Comité d'études*, 2 vols. Paris, Imprimerie Nationale, 1918–19.

United States Congress, *Congressional Record*, 52–57 (December 7, 1914, to February 24, 1919).

———— 65th Congress, 2d Session, *House Report No. 212, Report on Deficiency Appropriation Bill, Fiscal Year 1918.*

———— 66th Congress, 1st Session, *Senate Document No. 76, Report of Conference between Members of the Senate Committee on Foreign Relations and the President of the United States, August 19, 1919,* Washington, Government Printing Office, 1919.

———— 66th Congress, 1st Session, *Senate Document No. 106, Hearings Before the Committee on Foreign Relations, United States Senate on the Treaty of Peace with Germany Signed at Versailles on June 28, 1919 and Submitted to the Senate on July 10, 1919 by the President of the United States,* Washington, Government Printing Office, 1919.

———— 66th Congress, 3d Session, *Senate Document No. 330, Expenditures of the American Commission to Negotiate Peace,* Washington, Government Printing Office, December 8, 1920.

United States Department of the Army, Historical Division, *The United States Army in the World War 1917–1919: The Armistice Agreements and Related Documents,* Washington, Government Printing Office, 1948.

United States Department of Justice, *Annual Report of the Attorney General of the United States for the Year 1917,* Washington, Government Printing Office, 1917.

———— *Annual Report of the Attorney General of the United States for the Year 1918,* Washington, Government Printing Office, 1918.

United States Department of State, *Papers Relating to the Foreign Relations of the United States, the Lansing Papers 1914–1920,* 2 vols. Washington, Government Printing Office, 1939.

———— *Papers Relating to the Foreign Relations of the United States, Paris Peace Conference 1919,* 13 vols. Washington, Government Printing Office, 1942–47.

———— *Papers Relating to the Foreign Relations of the United States, 1917, The World War, Supplement 1,* Washington, Government Printing Office, 1931.

———— *Papers Relating to the Foreign Relations of the United States, 1917, The World War, Supplement 2,* 2 vols. Washington, Government Printing Office, 1932.

———— *Papers Relating to the Foreign Relations of the United States, 1918, The World War, Supplement 1,* 2 vols. Washington, Government Printing Office, 1933.

—— *Papers Relating to the Foreign Relations of the United States, 1918, The World War, Supplement 2,* Washington, Government Printing Office, 1933.

—— *Peace Conference Records and Other State Department Publication Projects,* Washington, Government Printing Office, 1939.

—— *Postwar Foreign Policy Preparation 1939–1945.* Department of State Publication 3580, Washington, Government Printing Office, 1949.

United States National Archives, *Handbook of Federal World War Agencies and Their Records 1917–1921,* Washington, Government Printing Office, 1943.

—— "Preliminary Inventories Number 68" (mimeographed), Cartographic Records of the American Commission to Negotiate Peace, compiled by J. B. Rhoads, Washington, National Archives, 1954.

—— "Preliminary Inventories Number 89" (mimeographed), Records of the American Commission to Negotiate Peace, compiled by H. Stephen Helton, Washington, National Archives, 1955.

EDITED COLLECTIONS OF DOCUMENTS AND PAPERS

American Historical Association, *Annual Report of the American Historical Association for 1918, 1,* Washington, Government Printing Office, 1921.

Baker, Ray Stannard, *Woodrow Wilson, Life and Letters,* 8 vols. Garden City, Doubleday, Page and Co., 1927–39.

—— *Woodrow Wilson and World Settlement,* 3 vols. Garden City, Doubleday, Page and Co., 1922–23.

—— and Dodd, William E., eds., *Public Papers of Woodrow Wilson,* 6 vols. New York, Harper and Brothers, 1925–27.

Beer, George L., *African Questions at the Paris Peace Conference,* ed. Louis H. Gray, New York, Macmillan Co., 1923.

Burnett, Philip M., *Reparation at the Paris Peace Conference,* 2 vols. New York, Columbia University Press, 1940.

Carnegie Endowment for International Peace, *Official Communications and Speeches Relating to Peace Proposals 1916–1917,* Washington, The Endowment, 1917.

—— *Official Statements of War Aims and Peace Proposals, December, 1916–to November, 1918,* prepared under the supervision of James Brown Scott, Washington, The Endowment, 1921.

—— *The Treaties of Peace 1919–1923,* 2 vols. New York, The Endowment, 1924.

Lake Mohonk Conferences on International Arbitration, *Report of the First to the Twenty-Second Annual Lake Mohonk Conference on International Arbitration 1895–1916*, 22 vols. Mohonk Lake, 1895–1916.

Miller, David Hunter, *The Drafting of the Covenant*, 2 vols. New York, G. P. Putnam's Sons, 1928.

—— *My Diary at the Conference at Paris*, 21 vols. Washington, privately printed, 1928.

Moore, John Bassett, *Collected Papers of John Bassett Moore*, 7 vols. New Haven, Yale University Press, 1945.

Porter, Kirk H., *National Party Platforms*, New York, Macmillan Co., 1924.

Snell, John, ed., "Wilson on Germany and the Fourteen Points," *Journal of Modern History*, *26* (December 1954), 364–69.

AUTOBIOGRAPHIES, DIARIES, LETTERS, MEMOIRS

Angell, Norman, *After All*, New York, Farrar, Strauss and Cudahy, 1952.

Baruch, Bernard M., *The Making of the Reparation and Economic Sections of the Treaty*, New York, Harper and Brothers, 1920.

Bonsal, Stephen, *Unfinished Business*, Garden City, Doubleday, Doran and Co., 1944.

Creel, George, *Rebel At Large, Recollections of Fifty Crowded Years*, New York, G. P. Putnam's Sons, 1947.

—— *The World, the War and Wilson*, New York, Harper and Brothers, 1920.

Daniels, Josephus, *The Wilson Era*, 2 vols. Chapel Hill, University of North Carolina Press, 1944–46.

Duggan, Stephen, *A Professor at Large*, New York, Macmillan Co., 1943.

Grew, Joseph C., *Turbulent Era: A Diplomatic Record of Forty Years 1904–1945*, ed. Walter Johnson, 2 vols. Boston, Houghton Mifflin Co., 1952.

Haskins, Charles H., and Lord, Robert, *Some Problems of the Peace Conference*, Cambridge, Harvard University Press, 1920.

Hoover, Herbert, *The Ordeal of Woodrow Wilson*, New York, McGraw-Hill, 1958.

House, Edward M., and Seymour, Charles, ed., *What Really Happened at Paris*, New York, Charles Scribner's Sons, 1921.

Lane, A. W., and Wall, L. H., eds., *The Letters of Franklin K. Lane*, Boston, Houghton Mifflin Co., 1922.

Lansing, Robert, *The Peace Negotiations: A Personal Narrative*, Boston, Houghton Mifflin Co., 1921.

―――― *War Memoirs of Robert Lansing*, Indianapolis, Bobbs-Merrill Co., 1935.

Lloyd George, David, *The Truth About the Peace Treaties*, 2 vols. London, Victor Gollancz, 1938.

Masaryk, Thomas, *The Making of a State: Memoirs and Observations 1914–1918*, London, G. Allen and Unwin, 1927.

McAdoo, Eleanor W., *The Woodrow Wilsons*, New York, Macmillan Co., 1937.

McAdoo, William Gibbs, *Crowded Years: The Reminiscences of William G. McAdoo*, Boston, Houghton Mifflin Co., 1931.

Nicolson, Harold, *Peacemaking 1919*, Boston, Houghton Mifflin Co., 1933.

Phillips, William, *Ventures in Diplomacy*, Boston, Beacon Press, 1952.

Seymour, Charles, ed., *Intimate Papers of Colonel House*, 4 vols. Boston, Houghton Mifflin Co., 1926–28.

Shotwell, James T., *At the Paris Peace Conference*, New York, Macmillan Co., 1937.

Tardieu, André, *The Truth About the Treaty*, Indianapolis, Bobbs-Merrill Co., 1921.

Villard, Oswald G., *The Fighting Years: Memoirs of a Liberal Editor*, New York, Harcourt, Brace and Co., 1939.

Willert, Arthur, *The Road to Safety: A Study of Anglo-American Relations*, London, D. Verschoyle, 1952.

NEWSPAPERS

Chicago Evening American, 1917.
Chicago Examiner, 1917.
Chicago Tribune, 1917.
Los Angeles Evening Express, 1917.
New York American, 1917.
New York Times, 1914–19.
Philadelphia Public Ledger, 1917.
The Times (London), 1917.

SECONDARY SOURCES: HISTORIES, TREATISES, SPECIAL STUDIES, AND BIOGRAPHIES

Albrecht-Carrié, René, *Italy at the Paris Peace Conference*, New York, Columbia University Press, 1938.

Bailey, Thomas A., *Woodrow Wilson and the Lost Peace*, New York, Macmillan Co., 1944.

Bander, Ingram, "Sidney Edward Mezes and 'The Inquiry,'" *Journal of Modern History*, 11 (1939), 199–202.

Bartlett, Ruhl J., *The League to Enforce Peace*, Chapel Hill, University of North Carolina Press, 1944.

Beer, George L., *The English Speaking Peoples*, New York, Macmillan Co., 1917.

Bell, H. C. F., *Woodrow Wilson and the People*, Garden City, Doubleday, Doran and Co., 1945.

Bernhardt, Joshua, *The Tariff Commission: Its History, Activities and Organization*, Institute for Government Research, Service Monographs of the United States Government Number 5, New York, D. Appleton and Co., 1922.

Binkley, Robert C., "New Light on the Paris Peace Conference," *Political Science Quarterly*, 46 (1931), 335–61, 509–47.

——— "Ten Years of Peace Conference History," *Journal of Modern History*, 1 (1929), 607–29.

Birdsall, Paul, "The Second Decade of Peace Conference History," *Journal of Modern History*, 11 (1939), 362–78.

——— *Versailles Twenty Years After*, New York, Reynal and Hitchcock, 1941.

Bowman, Isaiah, *The New World: Problems in Political Geography*, New York, World Book Co., 1921.

Butler, Nicholas M., *The Rise of a University: The University in Action from the Annual Reports 1902–1935*, New York, Columbia University Press, 1937.

Carstensen, Vernon R., and Curti, Merle E., *The University of Wisconsin: A History 1848–1925*, 2 vols. Madison, University of Wisconsin Press, 1949.

Curry, Roy, *Woodrow Wilson and Far Eastern Policy 1913–1921*, New York, Bookman Associates, 1957.

Curti, Merle E., *Peace or War, The American Struggle 1636–1936*, New York, W. W. Norton, 1936.

Déak, Francis, *Hungary at the Paris Peace Conference: The Diplomatic*

368

History of the Treaty of Trianon, New York, Columbia University Press, 1942.

Dominian, Leon, *The Frontiers of Language and Nationality in Europe*, New York, Henry Holt, 1917.

Dugdale, Blanche E. C., *Arthur James Balfour*, New York, G. P. Putnam's Sons, 1937.

Fifield, Russell, *Woodrow Wilson and the Far East*, New York, Thomas Y. Crowell, 1952.

Gabriel, Ralph H., *The Course of American Democratic Thought*, New York, Ronald Press, 1940.

Gerson, Louis L., *Woodrow Wilson and the Rebirth of Poland 1914–1920*, New Haven, Yale University Press, 1953.

Heaton, Herbert, *Scholar in Action, Edwin F. Gay*, Cambridge, Harvard University Press, 1952.

Hill, Norman, *The Public International Conference*, Stanford, Stanford University Press, 1929.

Holt, W. Stull, "Historical Scholarship," in *American Scholarship in the Twentieth Century*, ed. Merle E. Curti, Cambridge, Harvard University Press, 1953.

Howe, Mark A. de Wolfe, *Portrait of an Independent, Moorfield Storey 1845–1929*, Boston, Houghton Mifflin Co., 1932.

Hoxie, R. Gordon, et al., ed., *The Faculty of Political Science, Columbia University*, New York, Columbia University Press, 1955.

Humphrey, Richard, "The 'Official' Scholar: A Survey of Certain Research in American Foreign Policy," in *Essays in Honor of Conyers Read*, ed. Norton Downs, Chicago, University of Chicago Press, 1953.

Jessup, Philip C., *Elihu Root*, 2 vols., New York, Dodd, Mead and Co., 1938.

Keynes, John M., *The Economic Consequences of the Peace*, New York, Harcourt, Brace and Howe, 1920.

La Follette, Belle, and La Follette, Fola, *Robert M. La Follette*, 2 vols. New York, Macmillan Co., 1953.

Landau, Rom, *Ignace Paderewski, Musician and Statesman*, New York, Thomas Y. Crowell, 1934.

Leopold, Richard W., *Elihu Root and the Conservative Tradition*, Boston, Little, Brown, and Co., 1954.

Link, Arthur S., *Wilson the Diplomatist*, Baltimore, Johns Hopkins Press, 1957.

—— *Woodrow Wilson and the Progressive Era 1910–1917*, New York, Harper and Brothers, 1954.

369

Livezey, William E., *Mahan on Sea Power*, Norman, University of Oklahoma Press, 1947.

Luckau, Alma, *The German Delegation at the Paris Peace Conference*, New York, Columbia University Press, 1941.

Lybyer, Albert H., *Macedonia at the Paris Peace Conference*, Indianapolis, Central Committee of the Macedonian Political Organization, 1944.

Mamatey, Victor, *The United States and East Central Europe 1917–1918*, Princeton, Princeton University Press, 1957.

Mantoux, Étienne, *The Carthaginian Peace: or the Economic Consequences of Mr. Keynes*, New York, Charles Scribner's Sons, 1952.

"The Map of Hispanic America on the Scale of 1:1,000,000," *Geographical Review*, 36 (1946), 1–28.

Marston, F. S., *The Peace Conference of 1919, Organization and Procedure*, New York, Oxford University Press, 1944.

Martin, Laurence W., *Peace Without Victory: Woodrow Wilson and the British Liberals*, New Haven, Yale University Press, 1958.

Mayer, Arno J., *Political Origins of the New Diplomacy*, New Haven, Yale University Press, 1959.

Morison, Samuel E., *Three Centuries of Harvard 1636–1936*, Cambridge, Harvard University Press, 1936.

Nevins, Allan, *Henry White: Thirty Years of American Diplomacy*, New York, Harper and Brothers, 1930.

Noble, G. Bernard, *Policies and Opinions at Paris 1919: Wilsonian Diplomacy, the Versailles Peace, and French Public Opinion*, New York, Macmillan Co., 1935.

Notter, Harley, *The Origins of the Foreign Policy of Woodrow Wilson*, Baltimore, Johns Hopkins Press, 1937.

Osgood, Robert E., *Ideals and Self-Interest in America's Foreign Relations*, Chicago, University of Chicago Press, 1953.

Palmer, Frederick, *Bliss Peacemaker: The Life and Letters of General Tasker Howard Bliss*, New York, Dodd, Mead and Co., 1934.

Pierson, George W., *Yale College and University 1871–1937*, 2 vols. New Haven, Yale University Press, 1952–53.

Platig, E. Raymond, "The Inquiry at the Paris Peace Conference," Unpublished Master's Thesis, Emory University Library, 1949.

Rogers, Walter P., *Andrew Dixon White and the Modern University*, Ithaca, Cornell University Press, 1942.

Rudin, Harry, *Armistice 1918*, New Haven, Yale University Press, 1944.

Schmitt, Bernadotte E., "The Peace Conference of 1919," *Journal of Modern History*, 16 (1944), 49–59.

Seymour, Charles, *American Diplomacy during the World War*, Baltimore, Johns Hopkins Press, 1934.

—— *Geography, Justice, and Politics at the Paris Peace Conference of 1919*, New York, American Geographical Society, 1951.

Smith, Arthur D. H. *Mr. House of Texas*, New York, Funk and Wagnalls Co., 1940.

Stuart, Graham H., *The Department of State: A History of Its Organization, Procedure, and Personnel*, New York, Macmillan Co., 1949.

Symons, Farrell, *Courses on International Affairs in American Colleges 1930–1931*, Boston, World Peace Foundation, 1931.

Temperley, H. W. V., ed., *A History of the Peace Conference at Paris*, 6 vols. London, Institute of International Affairs, 1920–24.

Tillman, Seth P., *Anglo-American Relations at the Paris Peace Conference of 1919*, Princeton, Princeton University Press, 1961.

Tozer, Nancy, "The American Response to the Allied Secret Treaties Negotiated During World War I," Unpublished Master's Thesis, University of Wyoming, 1961.

Trask, David F., *The United States in the Supreme War Council: American War Aims and Interallied Strategy 1917–1918*, Middletown, Wesleyan University Press, 1961.

Walworth, Arthur, *Woodrow Wilson*, 2 vols. New York, Longman's Green, 1958.

Ware, Edith E., *The Study of International Relations in the United States*, New York, Columbia University Press, 1934.

Wright, John K., *Geography in the Making: The American Geographical Society 1851–1951*, New York, American Geographical Society, 1952.

Wright, Quincy, *Mandates under the League of Nations*, Chicago, University of Chicago Press, 1930.

Wrigley, Gladys, "Isaiah Bowman," *Geographical Review*, 41 (1951), 7–65.

Wriston, Henry M., *Executive Agents in American Foreign Relations*, Baltimore, Johns Hopkins Press, 1929.

INDEX